THE WORl

Tapan Raychaudhuri was educated at Barisal Zilla School, Scottish Church College, Presidency College and Balliol College, Oxford. During his college days he was imprisoned for his participation in the Quit India movement. After obtaining his postgraduate degree in history from Calcutta University, he went on to do a DPhil (Calcutta and Oxford) and a DLitt (Oxford).

In the course of a long and distinguished career as a historian and academician, he has been lecturer in Calcutta University, professor of economic history at the Delhi School of Economics, professor and chair of history at the University of Delhi, reader in modern South Asian history, Oxford University, and professorial fellow, St Antony's College, Oxford. He was promoted to an ad hominem chair at Oxford from which post he retired in 1993 as professor of Indian history and civilization. He is now emeritus fellow, St Antony's College, Oxford.

Professor Raychaudhuri has been deputy director, National Archives of India (1957–59); acting director, National Archives of India (1957); director, Delhi School of Economics (1965–67); visiting professor/fellow at Pennsylvania, Duke, Berkeley, Harvard, El Collegio de Mexico, Australian National University, Ecole Pratique des hautes etudes, Paris; Wissenschaft kolleg, Berlin; and Woodrow Wilson Center, Washington.

He is the author of *Bengal under Akbar and Jahangir: An Introductory Study in Social History*; *Jan Company in Coromandel, 1605-1690*; *The Cambridge Economic History of India* (general editor, with Dharma Kumar; editor, vol. I with Irfan Habib); *The Indian Economy in the Nineteenth Century* (with D. Morris et al.); *Europe Reconsidered: Perception of the West in Nineteenth Century Bengal*; *Perceptions, Emotions, Sensibilities: Essays on India's Colonial and Post-colonial Experiences*; *Memoirs of Haimavati Sen* (translated from Bengali; edited with Geraldine Forbes). His books in Bengali include *Romanthan*, *Bangal-nama* and *Prabandha-samgraha*.

He received the Padma Bhushan in 2007 and has been made National Research Professor in 2011.

The World in Our Time

A Memoir

TAPAN RAYCHAUDHURI

HarperCollins *Publishers* India
a joint venture with

New Delhi

First published in India in 2011 by
HarperCollins *Publishers* India
a joint venture with
The India Today Group

Copyright © Tapan Raychaudhuri 2011

ISBN: 978-93-5029-132-0

2 4 6 8 10 9 7 5 3 1

Tapan Raychaudhuri asserts the moral right to be identified
as the author of this work.

The views and opinions expressed in this book are the author's own and the facts are as
reported by him, and the publishers are not in any way liable for the same.

All rights reserved. No part of this publication may be reproduced,
stored in a retrieval system, or transmitted, in any form or by any means,
electronic, mechanical, photocopying, recording or otherwise,
without the prior permission of the publishers.

HarperCollins *Publishers*
A-53, Sector 57, Noida, Uttar Pradesh 201301, India
77-85 Fulham Palace Road, London W6 8JB, United Kingdom
Hazelton Lanes, 55 Avenue Road, Suite 2900, Toronto, Ontario M5R 3L2
and 1995 Markham Road, Scarborough, Ontario M1B 5M8, Canada
25 Ryde Road, Pymble, Sydney, NSW 2073, Australia
31 View Road, Glenfield, Auckland 10, New Zealand
10 East 53rd Street, New York NY 10022, USA

Typeset in Adobe Caslon 11/13.9
InoSoft Systems Noida

Printed and bound at
Thomson Press (India) Ltd.

*For Leela, Bhunu and Hashi,
guardians of my little world*

Contents

Preface ix
Foreword: Amartya Sen xi

PART I

1. Beginnings: Comilla, Where I Was Born—Also My Mother's Home — 3
2. Nabalok Babu's Lodge: Dawn of Consciousness — 14
3. Those Who Were Near and Dear — 30
4. Lords of the Land — 55
5. A Taste of the Sea: Cox's Bazaar — 73
6. Pains of Exile — 81
7. Nest of the Gentry — 96
8. College Days: 'Quit India' and a Taste of Prison Life — 132
9. Presidency College: The Great Famine, Hindu–Muslim Riots and the Partition, 1943–47 — 152
10. Homeless in Calcutta: Early Years in an Academic Career — 184

PART II

11. Oxford, 1953–57 — 205
12. The Journey Home — 237
13. Unemployed in Calcutta — 259
14. A Bureaucrat in Delhi: Sharing the Joys of Freedom — 265
15. Return to Academics: DSE and Delhi University — 276
16. Back at Oxford — 312

Preface

In 2006, I published a volume of memoirs in Bengali under the title *Bangal-nama*. In Bengali, the word 'Bangal' is often used in a derogatory sense to mean a yokel from East Bengal. So *Bangal-nama* would mean the life story of a yokel from East Bengal. It had been serialized in a Bengali literary journal, *Desh*, over a period of months, and proved to be very popular when published as a book. It described, inter alia, the lifestyle of an extinct social group, the Bengali zamindars, who dominated the rural, and to some extent the urban society as well in that part of the world for more than a century. It disappeared almost overnight in 1947-48. The account of my childhood has the history of that extinct subspecies of mankind for its background. As such it may be of interest to a wider readership beyond the boundaries of the two Bengals.

This volume is not a translation of my Bengali memoirs, but an entirely new work meant for a different audience unfamiliar with Bengal, its society and culture.

I have spent more than forty years of my adult life outside India, most of it in Oxford. The story of my encounter with the West also might interest people who provide the readership for studies of the Indian diaspora, fictional and non-fictional, especially because I come from a family of Indian nationalists, followers of Gandhi. I was brought up to oppose the Raj, participate in the struggle for freedom and, at the same time, admire deeply Europe's civilization as represented by England. The traumatic events in the last decade of the Raj, the Quit India movement in which I took part, spending a short period in prison for my pains, the 1943 famine in Bengal which took three million lives, the Calcutta riots of 1946 (remembered as the 'Great Calcutta Killing'), and the final trauma of the Partition are all parts of the narrative which follows. I was witness to these events in my youth. With an eye to the likely readership, I have devoted more space to things unfamiliar to a Western readership and less to more familiar themes like Oxford now and fifty years ago, when I had my first experience of the place. I have been generally reticent about myself because I lack the courage to write honestly about my follies and foibles, which are plentiful. I see no point in presenting half-truths. I publish this book in the honest, though perhaps mistaken, belief that it contains material which might be meaningful to a varied readership in the English-speaking world.

Tapan Raychaudhuri
Oxford, October 2011

Foreword

This is a wonderful account, by one the leading historians of India, of the story of his life and of the class of landlords of Bengal to which his family belonged. That class, once extremely powerful, but increasingly beleaguered by self-doubt, disappeared almost overnight with the political changes that went with the independence and partition of India in 1947. In the hands of Tapan Raychaudhuri—a captivating writer—the lives, thoughts, concerns and contradictions of this doomed social group have come vividly to life. This is a superb book, demonstrating that seriously enlightening history can also be great fun to read.

Amartya Sen
October 2011

Part I

1

Beginnings: Comilla, Where I Was Born—Also My Mother's Home

I was born in 1926 in the town of Comilla in the south-eastern part of Bengal. The date of my birth in the Bengali calendar coincided with that of Rabindranath Tagore: 25 Baishakh. As the poet was and still is the most revered iconic figure of modern Bengal, our relations and friends and of course I myself were never allowed to forget this burdensome coincidence and the totally irrational expectations roused by it in my parents' mind. This had generally unfortunate consequences for me.

Comilla is now the locus of some interesting developmental experiments in Bangladesh and hence prosperous. It was also fairly prosperous, by Bengali middle-class standards, around the time I was born. By this I mean that food was cheap and plentiful, a large proportion of the inhabitants lived in brick-built houses, the streets were clean and the town was famous for its 'banks and tanks'. The banks were witness to the Bengali economic enterprise of the early twentieth century. The tanks, known as sagars, the Bengali word for sea, belonged to a bygone age and were the gift of local rajas. Unlike most other infrastructural developments of the pre-colonial era, these had profited from the 'benign neglect' of the alien rulers and hence survived undamaged.

The house I was born in belonged to my mother's uncle who brought her up as well as her six siblings. My grandfather died at the age of thirty-nine leaving his younger brother the responsibility to look after his young family—a widow aged twenty-six and her six children plus one still in her mother's womb. There was a story current in my mother's family concerning my grandfather's death which I find entirely credible. Some astrologer had predicted that he would die at the age of thirty-nine and this prediction was duly fulfilled. My grandfather died on his thirty-ninth birthday. Since he had been expecting to do so for some two decades and had ordered his life on the basis of a silly prophecy, there was nothing miraculous about it proving to be true. He had virtually programmed himself to die on a specified day. He left some seventy thousand rupees in 'Company papers'—that is, government promissory notes—a considerable sum at that time. It was whispered that his brother got a thumb impression on a document from his sister-in-law who was unconscious from shock at the time and used it to acquire those notes. If this allegation is true, one should add that he spent the amount several times over in bringing up the seven children and marrying off the girls into decent middle-class families.

The terms for family relationships in Bengali have a focus totally different from that of their English counterparts. Generic terms like grandparent or uncle/aunt do not exist. Instead, you have very precise terms denoting specific relationships: father's father and mother are Thakurda and Thakuma; mother's father and mother are Dadamashay and Didima, respectively; father's sister is pishima; mother's sister is mashima and so on. But these distinctions collapse at another level. The word Dadamashay applies to mother's uncles as much as to her father. And Dadu is what one calls parents' fathers, uncles and, often, men of their generation with whom one is not related in any way. As I did not remember my father's father who died when I was not yet three and my mother's father who died before I was born, the only Dadu I ever knew was her uncle, Rai Bahadur Bhudhar Das. Unlimited indulgence to children is generally considered the prerogative of grandparents in our part of the world

Beginnings

and I received it in abundance from two persons, my grandmother whom I called Ajima and, in a curiously indirect way, from the formidable Rai Bahadur Bhudhar Das, her brother-in-law. As my father's mother also died when my father was a boy of ten, my sole experience of indulgent affection or 'spoiling' was from the said two sources.

Bhudhar Das, to repeat, was a formidable person, probably the most successful lawyer of eastern Bengal in his days. He was incapable of demonstrative affection and children treated him with awe. I did not. The reason was simple. His practice often brought him to our home in the district town of Barisal and in the afternoon he used to rest on an old sofa, the upper part of his body bare. This habit exposed his very sizeable belly which bore some resemblance to a dhak, the huge drums beaten on all auspicious occasions, especially the worship of Durga, the Mother-goddess. Denied access to real drums, I used this human substitute with great glee. The famous lawyer never interfered with this musical enterprise. Looking back, I think he was a very lonely man and suffered from the solitude which is often the price for great success. He was incapable of showing affection. Allowing his sizeable belly to be beaten like a drum was the farthest he could go in expressing emotional affects. This was enough to communicate responses very satisfying to a child: it was my first experience of intense, uninhibited affection.

In his youth Bhudhar Das was involved in revolutionary activities (what would have been described as 'terrorism' today) and once escaped a trap laid by the police to arrest him by dressing as a woman. Since he was nearly seven feet tall, the incident does not speak highly of police efficiency in those days because women of that height were an unknown species in Bengali society. However, Bhudhar Babu eventually lived down his revolutionary credentials and was appointed public prosecutor by the colonial government. This change in fortune probably fostered a hitherto unknown loyalty to the Raj. The government also conferred on him, as a reward for that loyalty, the title of Rai Bahadur, an honour only a step below knighthood.

I have a distinct impression that the Rai Bahadur was not a happy man. He hardly had any communication with the members of his family or, for that matter, anyone else. As I grew up, my contact with him was restricted to invitations on Sunday to share his English breakfast during our visits to my mamabari—literally, the home of my maternal uncles. It was whispered that he was in love with the wife of a colleague. But to the best of my knowledge the 'affair' did not go beyond spending an hour with the lady on his way home after the day's work at court. I doubt if he ever declared his love, but the object of his affection probably guessed by virtue of the famous feminine intuition.

Though I was born in Comilla, our visits to my mother's home were infrequent. My uncles and their mother had moved to a sizeable bungalow next to Bhudhar Das's palatial house. On my father's side, we came from an old zamindar family. Loosely translated as 'landholders', the term zamindar had complex meanings which I shall explain later. Briefly, it meant that for several generations we had derived our livelihood from rental income from agricultural land leased out to peasant farmers. Till the twenties and thirties of the last century, the social status of zamindars was high in Bengal. And it was not customary for a son-in-law enjoying a high status to make frequent sojourns in his in-laws' house. In our case, I do not recall a single occasion when my father visited his in-laws. We—that is, two brothers and our sister—accompanied our mother when she went to stay for a few days with her mother and brothers every two to three years. These were pleasant as well as unpleasant occasions.

The pleasure derived from the continuous and abundant supply of delicious food. What we had at home could not compare, despite our social status. This superiority derived mainly from three circumstances: My grandmother, who lived with her youngest son, owned two milch cows. In season they yielded about thirty litres of milk per head each day. After satisfying all the needs of the family, inflated to some fifteen to twenty persons through the influx of married daughters and their children—and these 'needs' included consumption of milk, butter, ghee and milk sweets loved by all Bengalis—some twenty litres of milk remained as surplus. The surplus was placed in a sizeable brass cauldron and then left to simmer on a clay oven fired by wood for some two to three hours. The end product was something very thick, creamy and indescribably tasty. As children we were told tales from the Hindu mythology. Amrita, Bengali for ambrosia, the food of the gods and the very virtuous who made it to paradise, featured prominently in these improving stories. It was my firm belief that the thickened milk or kshir produced from the milk of grandma's cows was a variant of amrita. It must have been vouchsafed to us in this terrestrial life for our exceptionally good karma in several previous incarnations. Good works in merely one previous life could not possibly explain access to such unearthly pleasure.

The second source of unbounded pleasure was the many fruit trees in grandma's kitchen garden which was, in effect, a sizeable orchard. Despite the multiple miseries of her long widowhood (she survived her husband by more than sixty years) the lady was an incurable optimist. She planted a variety of fruit trees, likely as well as unlikely to grow in the deltaic soil of south eastern Bengal. These included grapevines which produced bunches of luscious but inedible sour grapes. Undaunted, grandma transformed them into jam or jelly: their sugar content had to be considerably higher than the weight of the fruits. The garden also produced less sour fruits. Unlike at home, in Comilla, the land of freedom, we were allowed to climb these trees and gather fruit at our pleasure. This too, we ascribed to our exemplary good behaviour in previous lives. We were optimistic about what Paradise held for us in the future. But mamabari, the home of one's maternal uncle, was an acceptable anticipation of those future pleasures. True, there were no houris or heavenly damsels for our delectation in Comilla. But then, we had not yet reached the age when one properly appreciates such joys.

My youngest uncle was a contractor. His business included a bus which ran on the local transport route and a truck working for a dealer in fish. The returns from the latter had a component in kind: a couple of river fish every day, each weighing a few kilograms, plus the spare 'small' fish recovered from the truck when it was washed at the end of its trip. The latter too weighed several kilograms. The inverted commas are meant to convey that the fish were not really small. And this vast quantity of fishy matter was cooked daily for the delectation of family members, domestics and the workers who manned the truck and the bus. The story did not end there. The truck usually came back after lunchtime. Grandma was insistent that the children must not starve. Well, there was little danger of that. When we returned home after our stay in her place we resembled the very sizeable castrated goats dedicated by devout Muslims to the service of Allah, which meant that they were eventually slaughtered in His name but for the gratification of the faithful. This similarity was not missed by fellow students at school and they had an enjoyable time calling us khodar khashi, castrated goats dedicated to Allah. However, to return to my fishy tale, large river fish was cheap and plentiful in Comilla. To prevent the dear grandchildren from starving, a couple of these were bought from the market for our lunch. Fish might be a cheap or partly free commodity, but the oil and fuel needed to cook them were not. My uncle had a very sizeable income. He was also a man free from the usual 'bad habits', gambling and whoremongering, yet he never had any savings and died in abject poverty after the partition of the country. It is my belief that our consumption of inordinate quantities of fish contributed to this unhappy end result.

I have thus far described the pleasures of mamabari. The pains derived from an unfortunate social-cum-personal situation. Being zamindar meant being treated as royalty by the poor peasant farmers who were our tenants; the relevant English/Hindi word is ryot, but in Bengali these hapless people were called praja which means subjects. When we encountered the ryots, they did treat us as their lords and masters. Only a child who had attained sambodhi or enlightenment at an unlikely age could remain impervious to being the lord of several thousand human beings, however miserable. The self-esteem thus generated was fostered by the social attitudes common in the small towns of eastern Bengal. As members of a zamindar family, we were treated by our schoolteachers with an unmistakeable degree of deference. Only the attitude of our fellow students acted as a healthy corrective. They took great delight in calling us children of jamadars, or sweepers: the two words, jamadar and jamidar (i.e., zamindar) differ only in a vowel sign. I remain deeply grateful to those robust youths but for whom our vanity could have touched totally unacceptable and ludicrous levels.

My brother, Arun, older than me by nearly three years, had been badly infected by the virus of snobbery. The vice could not be indulged freely in our home town, thanks to the ribald resistance from our fellow students. But in far away Comilla, there was no harm in giving it a try in our dealings with our cousins. Needless to say, this was not appreciated, especially the references to the elements of westernized lifestyle adopted since my grandfather's days. Sitting at table for our meals, instead of on flat wooden seats on the floor and eating off chinaware in place of round bell metal thalis, was at the centre of the transformation, even though we continued to use our fingers instead of knives and forks. Furthermore, our diet included Western dishes like soups, roasts and pudding unknown to the average Bengali home. Casual reference to such exotic food did not endear us to our cousins. In fact, they provoked sardonic comments. Arun, disappointed and hurt, would express his resentment at not being treated as a social superior in a strange admonition to me which was way beyond my comprehension. He would instruct me to sever all relations with these cousins, inadequately respectful to the zamindar's children, 'if I had the blood of Rohini Sen or Ashwini Datta in my veins'. Being unfamiliar with the mysteries of procreation and physiology, I had no idea as to how someone else's blood could flow in my veins or, if it did, how did that make it obligatory for me to boycott my cousins. Later, when the mysterious phrase acquired some meaning for me, I realized that Arun was sadly mistaken. No way could the blood of either Rohini Sen or Ashwini Datta flow in my veins, at least through any legitimate channel. Rohini Sen, amateur scholar, novelist and historian, was my grandfather's eldest brother and the most famous member of the family. We grew up to take an inordinate pride in this connection. The custom of levirate, honoured in the great epic, Mahabharata, might have rendered the transmission of blood implied in my brother's admonition possible, but it had ceased to be respectable since that more virtuous age when dharma, or righteousness, in the form of a cow, still had the use of two legs. In our dark and profoundly sinful Kali Age, when she was reduced to the use of a single leg on which she barely managed to stand in extreme discomfort, these happy practices had become anathema. As to Ashwini Datta, the great moralist and leader of the agitation against the Partition of Bengal in 1905, and thereby the glory of Barisal district, he was only a friend of the family, not entitled to the rights of levirate even in the more righteous Dwapara or the Age of the Epic. Arun introduced his name in the discourse on family honour simply to enhance our status, even though this implied a solecism. Well, to return to my story, the duty to boycott our cousins he imposed made our sojourn in mamabari utterly miserable for me. Even the sweets, fish and half-ripe fruits were no compensation for my unnatural state of isolation. The weekly invitation to Bhudhar Das's breakfast table was the only ray of light.

There were a few other compensations. Chief among these were visits to the man-made lakes (one of which, Dharmasagar, was only a few minutes' walk from our uncles' home) and less frequent ones to Maynamati, a low mound under which were buried some thousand-year-old archaeological remains. Growing up in a riverine area flatter than the brim of a hat, the Maynamati 'hills' were an incredibly challenging natural feature—the highest such feature I was familiar with was the Chandmari 'hill' of Barisal, a thirty-foot high artificial mound where the local police had their rifle practice. Familiar with tales of assaults on Kanchenjunga and Mount Everest, I identified with the heroes lost on those Himalayan slopes when climbing breathlessly the heights of Maynamati. Hopes of excavating its mysterious past at some future date fired my ambition to become an archaeologist/historian at some future date.

As to the sagars, we were not unfamiliar with man-made lakes in Barisal, but the Comilla lakes were truly the products of royal patronage and princely glory and this was reflected in their very

Beginnings

impressive size. My experience limited to more modest man-made lakes, I found the term sagar or sea quite appropriate for these royal enterprises. The extensive banks of Dharmasagar were also the site of camps for the visiting circus troupes. Gawking at the circus animals was a pleasure without any price tag. Once when we returned from Dharmasagar having seen the camp of Rammurti, the famous wrestler and circuswalla, we were invited to report what we had seen. My four-year-old cousin Pratima, stood forth as the foreman of the jury and described Rammurti: 'Oh yes. We did see Rammurti. He was tied to a tree, had a very long snout and kept swinging from side to side.'

The modest pleasures vouchsafed to me in Comilla included the regular visits from a fakir dressed in a loose gown or alkhalla made of bits and pieces of fabric collected from the discarded garments of other people. This multicoloured dress was a source of wonder to me and I felt a spontaneous regard for its wearer who entertained us with songs and dances based on his not very easy life story. One song-and-dance sequence summed up that experience. Loosely translated, it went as follows:

> I am the brother of Rahimchand, Fakirchand and Karimchand
> I visit the market from time to time
> And there for my pains I am thrashed black and blue
> And my backside has lost its cover of skin.

This sad song was no exercise in self-pity; it was presented with great gusto and a very vigorous dance number. I joined in the dance, encouraged by the fakir. One day, for reasons unknown, he stopped coming. My career as a dancer was thus ended and I lost the chance of having a great future as a protagonist of eastern dances so highly regarded in the West today. This is especially to be regretted because the fakir's style was unique.

The one consistently happy thing I remember from those days of carnal pleasure and mental agony was Ajima's affection and unlimited indulgence. The lady was entirely tireless. When she was not cooking or making sweets, she would work hard at gardening or making woollen jumpers for her seven children and twenty grandchildren—each of us was presented with a deftly woven new jumper each winter. Besides, there were the thirteen bratas or ritual celebrations in the twelve months of the year in honour of multiple local deities who were not members of the official Hindu pantheon. Each brata implied elaborate preparation. These included the modelling of various clay images such as a very lifelike crocodile for one of the bratas. Ajima crafted the dolls herself and they had a professional quality. But the high point of the bratas for us kids, and, I suspect, for the adults as well, was the special food cooked for each of them. These sacred delicacies associated with particular bratas, like seven fried and thirteen boiled vegetables, were cooked only once a year—it was sacrilege to cook them at any other time. At the end of each brata, Ajima would read out the improving tale associated with it in a sing-song voice. These tales or panchalis sang the glory of the deity in question and the merits which one derived from observing the brata. The panchali also listed the simple ethical tasks, mainly domestic duties, enjoined on the humble householders of rural Bengal, especially the women. The tales all had happy endings, but I know not why they brought tears to my eyes and I would end up crying inconsolably. Perhaps the heroes' multiple sufferings before they arrived at the happy denouement were the cause of my tears. They were probably tears of joy as well as sorrow. My favourite was the brata in honour of Satyanarayan, a composite deity amalgamating the god Narayan with a Muslim holy man, Satya pir. The myth in question expressed the very old Indian belief that all religions were essentially the same. My father and grandfather were confirmed atheists, but their relaxed liberal outlook did not impose any ban on participation in these folk rituals. The bratas were not celebrated in our home. I suppose this was partly because they involved too much work. But they were the focal points of my visit to our mamabari and I hankered for them throughout the year.

Ajima's long life of total dependence on others was in no sense a happy one. But the fact was in no way obvious. She was always full

Beginnings

of fun and had a very large stock of ribald jokes strictly unsuitable for minors. Some of these could bring blushes to adult cheeks as well. Despite the very heavy load of self-imposed chores, she even found time to read serious literature in Bengali and write elaborate letters to all her progeny and their children. Living to a very great age, inevitably she had to endure bereavements. She outlived two of her sons and two sons-in-law. From a senseless belief that she would be unable to stand the shock of these bereavements, everybody tried to keep the news of the deaths from her. She was staying with us in our rented Calcutta flat when the news came of her second son's death. She was of course not told. But she guessed what had happened and said, very quietly: 'Kalu is gone, no?' Receiving no reply, she sat down on the floor and cried piteously for a while, then got up and went back to do whatever she was doing.

When she was eighty, she fell out with her youngest son with whose family she had lived for many years. This uncle remarried after the death of his first wife. Ajima felt that the children were being mistreated by their stepmother and decided to leave her son's home with the children. Her hope was that her other two sons and the sons-in-law would look after them. But this was after the Partition of the country; her sons and daughters were now refugees in West Bengal and no one was enthusiastic about taking on the burden of three young children. Ajima went and saw the chief minister of the state, Dr Bidhan Chandra Roy, who gave her one of the two-room houses built for the refugees in a not very salubrious suburb of Calcutta. She sent her sons and daughters a long list of various things she needed for her new home. The list included a grape vine and, in the unfavourable climate of Howrah on the outskirts of Calcutta, the creeper duly flourished and produced bunches of fruits, no doubt exquisitely sour. Ajima died of cancer when she was eighty-six. She was then staying with her eldest grandson. When we called on her, there was an unbearable stench of rotting flesh in the room—the cancer had gone very far indeed. She made only one request—that we should go to the Kali temple and pray for the end of her suffering. That is the last time I saw her.

2

Nabalok Babu's Lodge: Dawn of Consciousness

My early years were spent for the most part in Barisal, a riverside town (population then, 100,000; 500,000 in 1974) which was the headquarters of Backergunj district in eastern Bengal. Our house stood on the banks of the river Kirtankhola. The peculiar name, Nabalok Babu's Lodge or Nabalok Lodge for short, by which it was known to the local people, requires some explanation. The word 'nabalok' means minor. The original owner of the house, my great-grandfather, Prasanna Kumar Sen (Raychaudhuri was a secondary and acquired surname, an assertion of the fact that we were zamindars) came to live in it when he was still a minor. His father, Rajkumar, was poisoned by his Brahmin guru and a co-conspirator, the diwan or chief financial officer of his estate, one Mr Mahalanabish (no relation of the famous statistician and progenitor of Indian planning). The crime was facilitated by the devout Rajkumar's practice of drinking a glass of sherbet every morning, sanctified by the touch of his guru's toes. The event was commemorated in a local ballad still current in that area, probably by virtue of its bawdy overtones. A loose translation is given below.

> In the village of Kirtipasha lived a famous Babu,
> Rajkumar by name.

Nabalok Babu's Lodge

What can I say of his noble deeds
Wonderful to recall.
His Diwan, Mahalanabish,
A black sheep born of decent parents
Conspired with the guru
And put poison in his sherbet.
Oh, the bastard, the bastard whose sister must be screwed!
As for the sun-dried rice-eating Brahmin?
Cut open his arse
And take out the sugar, butter and ghee
The scoundrel had eaten all these years
Oh the bastards, the bastards whose sisters we must screw.

This noble verdict of the people was not carried out in practice. However, the English district magistrate, one Mr Bayly, rescued the five-year-old Prasanna whose life too was at risk. It is said that the Englishman looked after him as a member of his family for several years. Aware of the prejudices in chaste Hindu society against commensality with impure aliens, he got Prasanna married to a six-year-old and then set him up in the bungalow on the river which came to bear the under-age owner's name. Prasanna Sen was a sub-teenager at the time and hence the odd name—the house belonging to a gentleman who is a minor. Family lore has it that the six-year-old Shashthipriya, revolted by her husband's outlandish ways, made him learn Bengali and taught him to eat with his fingers, off a bell metal thali and seated on a flat wooden pidi very painfully. This was the Bengali way of eating. No wonder Prasanna emerged from this baptismal of fire a strong, taciturn and highly energetic man.

It is not clear whether the bungalow by the river was bought from some European or constructed specially for the Babu who happened to be a minor. It was very much like the colonial houses favoured by the English in Bengal and the furniture, which probably came with the house, was mostly Regency with some later additions from the Victorian era.

My earliest memory of physical sensations involved one of these pieces of furniture. It was an old couch, covered with black leather, which could be folded up to look like the letter V. Only a person of my size—I was four years of age—was privileged to lie on it when it was thus folded, a fact which gave me a sense of distinct superiority over other members of the family. This was my throne and no sibling could challenge my claim to it. I had heard that the great king Asoka had to fight and kill ninety-nine brothers to secure his accession. My accession had gone entirely unchallenged. If I close my eyes I can still recall the cool and somewhat rough touch of that black leather which was torn in places, the result of extreme old age. The memory brings an exquisite sensation of pleasure and warm comfort which is unique in my experience. Soon, the leather covering had outlived its utility and had to be replaced. I roared in protest like a rampant bull, but to no purpose. As consolation, the discarded leather was used to cover a wooden club, the favourite weapon of Bhima, the second of the Pandava brothers in the epic tale, Mahabharata. That mindless brute had become my role model and hence the gift of a club by way of compensation. But the weapon was not shaped like the ones I saw in the illustrations to Mahabharata and I soon lost interest.

As the area was swampy and the level of underground water very high, the house was constructed on a row of arches called 'caleps' (I failed to find any English word to describe the feature) to keep the floor at a safe distance from the often soggy ground. The dark space under the caleps was the seat of infinite mystery, of terror and gothic romance. Rakshasas or ogres with especially long canines and faces, which were highly distorted versions of their human counterparts, hid there during the daylight hours. They came out in the darkness of the night to forage. A miserable fate awaited children who ventured to step out of the house after nightfall. One peeped under the arches at lonely noontime hoping to catch a glimpse of the feared creatures believed to be relatively ineffective by daytime. One heard strange whispers and giggles. Their source was the extremely daring kids from neighbouring homes who half disbelieved the stories about the rakshasas. But there were other non-human denizens of the calep—monitor lizards of impressive size and highly repellent gait, snakes, both venomous and less threatening varieties and, as occasional

Nabalok Babu's Lodge

visitors, skunks and ferret-like creatures locally known as bham (for reasons unknown, in Bengali the word is also a pejorative describing awful old men). The last two species came mostly at night to try and catch the poultry that was reared for their eggs as well as meat. This caused great commotion and our father went out with a shot gun to scare away the intruders. The skunks held their ground using a weapon peculiarly their own—an awful stench which would keep the air unbreathable for days after these episodes. I know of no other creature that uses farts as a weapon of mass repulsion. Incidentally, for the sake of scientific accuracy, one should record that the source of that stench was not the bowels, but a highly specialized gland. Since the product smelt too much like especially obnoxious farts to make any significant difference, this scientific fact was of limited interest to non-specialists like us.

Snakes, especially the poisonous varieties, being plentiful and ubiquitous, were the objects of obsessive tales in Barisal. Some of these were true, but the majority were a compliment to the lively imagination of the local people. Every home had a 'poison stone', a shining white object which was credited with the ability to suck out any poison, turning blue in the process. The white stone, turned blue, was thrown into a bowl full of milk whereupon the stone slowly regained its white colour imparting its blueness to the milk. I have no idea how this happened or if the stone actually had the efficacy attributed to it. On many occasions I have seen ojhas, i.e., shamans who had specialized in curing snake bites, attending to some unfortunate, allegedly bitten by a snake. Some of the persons so treated did recover. Probably they had been bitten by non-poisonous snakes or some other non-lethal creature or the victim had simply sought temporary glory in high drama.

The legends about snakes which flourished in Barisal would have enriched the tradition of gothic horror stories if translated into European languages. The locals took great pride in their machismo (shared by the fair sex who were not to be trifled with) and the tales were informed by that pride. It was generally believed that the common Barisal way of taking revenge was to catch a cobra, tickle its tail and then throw the raging beast into the enemy's bedroom at night. Not a very ethically correct act, but certainly effective. The snakes were attributed superhuman intelligence and fixity of purpose. One of the tales I heard about was how one unfortunate had made the mistake of killing a baby snake. The mother followed him around for a month and then, one moonless night, at the auspicious midnight hour poured all her venom into the miscreant's veins. Some of the tales attracted the supernatural and age-old Hindu beliefs. There was, for instance, the moral tale about a cruel mother-in-law who had driven her daughter-in-law to suicide. When the son brought home his new bride and the mother-in-law removed the veil to see her face, out came a hissing cobra and struck her beyond any hope of recovery. It was not necessary to explain to any true son or daughter of Barisal that the said cobra was an incarnation of the unfortunate first wife. At last the scores were settled.

The obsession with snakes meant that creatures reputed to be their enemies were encouraged. These included the monitor lizard of repulsive gait and a bird with frightening red eyes known paradoxically as 'the queen of snakes'. Probably, the fact that traditionally royalty consumes their subjects explains the paradox. One member of the anti-snake brigade, mongoose, was reared in many a Barisal home as a pet. These creatures were cuddly, frisky and covered in soft hair. I longed for a pet mongoose, but could not convince the adults to get me one, on the ground that the beast habitually bit the hand which fed it. This was a mistake because the experience of being so bitten would have prepared me for similar misfortunes which crowded my adult life.

Later, I have often wondered as to why hairy animals like the mongoose are acceptable to humans but not hairless creatures like monitor lizards. This is of course not true of all cultures. In England, for instance, where animals are generally preferred to humans as objects of demonstrative affection, tarantulas and bats have made the list of dearly beloved pets and Harrods had a line in green lizards. But I am talking of the less enlightened generality of mankind and they surely prefer the hairy to the hairless. It is my submission that this preference is an atavistic throwback to the early and hairy days in the history of our species when our ancestors were happy to embrace exceedingly hirsute partners. Probably for similar reasons, Islam insists that women must cover their hair very carefully. The medieval Arabs were a virile race: the slightest sight of feminine hair reminded them, disturbingly, of more exciting things. But such scientific-sociological ideas did not occur to me in childhood when I preferred mongoose to lizard quite mindlessly.

I write of these things because in childhood all sorts of birds and animals crowded my consciousness. It took me a long time to realize that there is any reason to distinguish between humans and other living beings as objects of affection and wonder. Perhaps my decision to settle in England was partly determined by this psychological failure to discriminate. I suffered from an inconsistency in this respect. I longed to touch the wild birds and animals (only of the hairy varieties) like the yellow mynah bird locally known as gubre shalik (cow dung–eating mynah), the green parrots, the wild turtles and the porpoises (only whose smooth backs were visible when they briefly came up for air in the river), but when I did touch the poultry reared in our backyard, I felt extremely uncomfortable. Their impatient wriggles enhanced my acute sense of discomfort. Like quite a few bhadralok homes in the town, we also had a couple of milch cows whom I admired from a distance, but was too scared of their horns and hooves to get very close. When they gave birth to calves, I felt courageous enough to touch and feed the latter, but the rough touch of their tongues put me off.

In the 1930s, automobiles were a rarity in Barisal—so far as I remember, there were only two, one a Studebaker belonging to the Muslim zamindar, Khan Ismail Chaudhuri (which, in its old age, was sold to us) and the other a baby Austin. The latter's owner was Captain Harabilas, a doctor who had served in Mesopotamia during the First World War. Horse-drawn carriages were the common mode of transport and were to be seen in many bhadralok homes. We had a brougham and a hackney carriage and a couple of horses to draw them. One of these had, in fact, suffered a decline in status.

A Waler, it was originally bought for my father to ride when he was a young man and addicted to such pastimes. It was later reduced to the ignominious task of drawing carriages. My elder brother, Arun inherited my father's love of horseflesh and a Manipur pony arrived to satisfy his aspirations. I was a cautious person from the very beginning. The ancient sage, Chanakya, had advised that a sensible human should maintain a distance of at least one hundred cubits between self and all things with hooves and horns. I have never found any good reason to ignore this sane advice. Arun was inspired by the epic tales of Asvamedha sacrifice; a horse with an attendant was sent forth to all neighbouring and faraway kingdoms as a symbol of overlordship. Anyone detaining the horse had to fight it out with the ambitious monarch who owned it. When the victorious horse returned home, he was sacrificed in style by strangulation which gave him an impressive erection. The chief queen had simulated sex with the sacrificed horse, so virile in death, in the hope of producing heroic as well as very fecund sons. These interesting later bits of the tale were not known to us in childhood. Arun merely sought glory. He failed to perform any Asvamedha sacrifice in his later life which was, in fact, rather sad. But childhood ambitions are not a bad thing and deserve to be encouraged. So Arun marched forth on the strand with a placard stuck to his pony's forehead: *Arun Babu's horse for the Asvamedha sacrifice—stop him if you dare*. Since no one dared, I suppose my brother became the legitimate overlord of all he surveyed, i.e., full one mile of the Barisal strand uninhabited by any human. Fortunately for his future queen, she was not yet on the scene.

As a child, I felt an irresistible attraction towards things which scared me. The river flowing by our bungalow was the ultimate source of such scary attraction. The lady who brought me up, Joti, used to take me to the river to bathe. I held on firmly to her hand, my heart seared by a hundred apprehensions. The sandy banks of the river contained, among other things, turtle and tortoise eggs; containing little albumen, they could be turned into delicious omelettes and Joti never failed to collect them. Sometimes we met their progenitors, fairly harmless creatures with delicious meat. But they could bite.

Though the sage Chanakya had no specific recommendations regarding how to deal with non-poisonous reptiles, I imaginatively stretched the intention of his cautionary words and maintained a safe distance. The river itself was a source of endless thrills. First, there was the fear of drowning. I held firmly on to Joti's hand to avoid this threatened calamity and thus never learned to swim properly. The porpoises, fortunately, had also read Chanakya and kept a fair distance between themselves and unreliable humans. But what were those dark things floating too close to one for comfort? Crocodiles or pieces of dry wood? Every year some people were taken away by crocodiles and I am still not sure whether I wished the unidentified objects to belong to that species. But the sense of fear despite the security afforded by Joti's firm hold was delicious. Then there were the Kangats, small river sharks. I have never seen one but heard from Joti fearsome tales of their preternaturally sharp teeth. There was the famous case of the man who had lost a leg to a Kangat but felt nothing until he had come out of the water. How did he manage on his one leg without a crutch? Such scepticism was not popular with Joti and I too implicitly preferred the tale to be true.

One striking fact about my childhood memories is that everything seemed much larger and brighter than what I remember as an adult. I went to Barisal after an absence of many years in 1974. Our bungalow, then inhabited by a Muslim family, appeared literally to have shrunk in size. As a child, my day began with collecting flowers for Joti who worshipped little images of Radha and Krishna to the accompaniment of devotional songs sung in a broken and highly non-musical voice. I remember that the multicoloured flowers I collected seemed to shine with some inner illumination and the fragrant ones overpowered me with their sweet odour. Under the big fruit and flowering trees, decorative bushes had grown luxuriantly. My favourite were the taro leaves dotted with red and white marks which looked like drops of sandal paste. Rain- or dewdrops floating precariously on those leaves, shone like pearls. It was my ambition to carry these jewels to my room and keep them for an indefinite period. It never worked; the drops of water fell off the leaves as soon as I picked them up.

The brightness of the flowers and leaves I saw lingered in my memory. When I was a graduate student at Balliol, Aldous Huxley had recently published his two accounts of the mescalin experience. Some doctors had decided to experiment with the substance and one of them was a Parsee neurologist who was doing some post-doctoral work at Oxford. I volunteered to be a guinea pig for his experiments. After I was given a dose of mescalin, the doctor first played some classical music on his gramophone and then took me to the Christ Church cathedral. The brightness of the painted glass suddenly brought back vivid memories of the shining colours I used to see in childhood and the Beethoven symphonies sounded exquisite in a way with which nothing in my experience before or after could compare. Maybe, our sense perceptions have a kind of sharpness in childhood which we lose with age. The mescalin temporarily revived that intensity of perception. Unfortunately, I was very sick afterwards. Still, I felt grateful for that brief return to an intensity of sensations I had not known since childhood.

To repeat, there was something almost Anglo-Saxon in the depth of my interest in animals, so much so that I really preferred them to humans, my phobias and anxieties regarding them notwithstanding. Juran Babu, an employee in our estate office and a family friend, encouraged my hopes and fantasies in this regard. He used to carry me on his shoulder to the strand with its beautiful row of jhau (fern) trees—the Pakistani military authorities cut these down during the liberation war (leading to the foundation of Bangladesh) and thus turned a most beautiful avenue into a dreary macadamized road. Alongside that avenue was the Bell's Park named after one Mr Bell who, as district collector, had once presided over the destinies of the local natives. Famous for his eccentricities, he noted down in his diary all the choice pejoratives in the Bengali language which he applied to his unworthy subordinates whenever appropriate. On one noteworthy occasion, he summoned back his personal assistant, dressed in hand-spun khadi, a token of nationalist sympathies, to hurl at him a newly acquired word of abuse—he had forgotten to use it during the hour-long diatribe he had just showered on the

Nabalok Babu's Lodge

hapless clerk. 'Tumi haramjada-o achho,' he articulated calmly and distinctly. The words translate into English as 'You also happen to be a bastard.' 'Haramjada', or bastard, was the new word he had learnt but unfortunately forgotten to use it the first time round.

To return to my animal tales, I rode on Juran Babu's shoulder to the park named after this eminent person mainly to see the race horses. On winter mornings, syces massaged their muscular haunches, and in the dense fog one could still see smoke rising from the animals' bodies. Juran Babu, who had promised to buy me a puppy and a lamb during our march to Bell's Park, now had to face a new demand. 'Juran Babu, what about a foal?' Juran pointed out some logistic problems. Foals grew up into mature horses or mares and hence could not fit into my scheme to keep them under my bed. Moreover, horse as a species, including foals, were inclined to kick. That, as I knew, could be painful. I did not press the matter any further.

My dreams of mongooses and lambs as pets were not realized. But Juran Babu kept part of his promise. On one of his trips to Calcutta, he did procure for me a little yellow puppy which, he claimed, was of authentic English origin, a bilayti kutta in other words. For evidence, he drew attention to the bent ears of the animal, widely believed to be a sure sign of aristocratic canine origin like chinlessness in their human counterparts. The noble animal had been bought for ten rupees from the Muslim cook of a white Englishman. Hence there was no room for doubts. My father expressed his reservations claiming that bent ears could be produced by pricking that part of the canine anatomy with fish bones. Such scepticism was brushed aside by the excited members of the household, thrilled by the arrival of a being of English origin. Joti fed the pup with rice and milk. Bawsha, our four-foot-tall domestic, procured good cuts of goat meat for the privileged guest. Still, in due course, the bent ears straitened up and the dog's true native origin became obvious for all to see. Juran Babu claimed that the terriers did have straight unbent ears. The family wag commented that the animal, which had been given the name Fido, was indeed a terrier, but belonged to the subspecies, 'Roadesian', a street or pie dog whose fellow creatures were to be met on the road. It was soon obvious that he was in no way related to the pedigreed dogs whose photos could be seen beside my grandfather's.

With the increasingly clear articulation of Fido's identity, the puppy lost his status and associated privileges. Rice, milk and best cuts of goat meat were replaced by leftovers on our plates. Gradually, that source of nutrition also became scarce. Fido began to haunt the dust bins near the ramshackle eating-house-cum-inn maintained by us for the employees of our estate. At times hunger drove Fido to try and steal food from their kitchen. Tapu (short for Tapan) Babu's bilayti puppy, as he, now the butt of unkind parody was dubbed, had been reduced to unspeakable misery. I looked on helplessly because I had no access to either cash or sources of decent food. One day Fido came back to our courtyard dragging his hind part. Somebody had broken his spine with a blow. My father sent for the vet. He came and administered a lethal injection to end the creature's misery. That night I could not sleep. In the morning, for the first time in my life, I did not get up to collect flowers for Joti's daily worship. My pillow was wet with my tears. This was my first experience of sorrow which knows no consolation.

Between the river and our house were an orchard and a kitchen garden. Mangoes, jamun, lychee, myrobalan, papaya, star fruit and a variety of flowering trees of some age filled the orchard. The mangoes, like their fellow products throughout the district, were not edible. This loss was compensated by the other fruits and the Kurchi flowers, used to produce a deliciously fragrant sherbet. In winter, the kitchen garden was of especial interest to us children, because of an abundant crop of green peas, picked and eaten straight off the vine. The river was visible from our bedroom window and we counted the various steamers belonging to an English company, River Steam Navigation Company (RSN for short) which glided past on their way to or from Dacca, Khulna, Chittagong and other towns of lower Bengal. Some of these steamers were named after birds we had never seen—pelicans, penguins and so on. These had become familiar friends and we knew at what hour of the day we could expect which steamer. An approach road on the other side of the house led to the main street. Beside it was a lantana hedge covered by a golden creeper, alok lata (creeper of light) which had no roots. Next to the hedge was a fish pond which had suffered from long neglect and emitted a poisonous odour. This did not stop us from fishing in it or the locals from having an occasional swim.

On one side of the house, separated by a high wall, was the impressive bungalow of a Eurasian family that rejoiced in the name of Brown. It was rumoured that they were of Portuguese origin or, more likely, low-caste Hindus converted to Catholicism by the Portuguese. There were many such converts in Backergunj, especially in the southern part of the district, whose conversion dated back to the sixteenth century. The Browns became wealthy through trade and then opted for their English surname. After this, no further contact with the natives was permissible, even though their surname described their pigmentation very adequately. Of course, we never met the Browns socially. Our own counter-snobbery was expressed through the term firingi, half-caste, which we used to describe the true social origins of our Anglophile neighbours.

On the other side of the house beyond the wall was the habitation of our less privileged fellow countrymen. Their houses were mud-built with roofs of straw or corrugated iron. In the villages, each caste had its distinct area of habitation. In the district town, this pattern of caste-based habitation had broken down. Where one lived depended more on one's financial standing than on one's caste origin. Our less privileged neighbours belonged to a variety of castes and occupations—barbers, grocers, goldsmiths, gardeners, office employees and so on. All the dwellers of these kutchha (mud-built) houses were not poor. The very wealthy Sahas, traders and moneylenders, owned a large two-storeyed house in this area. They in fact offered to buy up our share of our bungalow and the zamindari estate when we left East Pakistan after the Partition. This offer was of course turned down. Our misfortunes would have been mitigated to some degree had we been less vain about our social standing and accepted the Sahas' offer. Our standing derived partly from our caste, Baidya, considered the second highest in Bengal after the Brahmins. The peculiarities of caste behaviour ordained that we could take food offered by some of the lower castes like the Sahas, so long as it was not boiled. Fried food was, however, OK. I especially enjoyed the fried flower-fritters offered in our barber's home, but unfortunately custom demanded that these had to be offered salt-free. The mysteries of these caste laws have still remained opaque to me. Even more mysterious and highly embarrassing was the custom which ordained that adults of the lower castes should touch the feet of a four-year-old—me, because I was a twice-born and they were not. I would shrink into a corner hoping to escape, but that was never to be. Incidentally, the Baidyas, the physician caste, had been claiming the twice-born status only since the eighteenth century. The validity of that claim is not beyond question.

The children from the said mud-built houses came to play in our courtyard as soon as the heat of the sun had dwindled a little. This crossing of class borders was not very popular with the elders, but the social code of the day precluded total prohibition. They compromised by urging the neighbours' kids to go back home as soon as decency permitted. Their anxiety had its roots in the belief that the children of the poor, like the serpent in the Garden of Eden, were repositories of knowledge, good and evil, especially the latter. In other words, living in close proximity to adults with little chance of privacy and in families who still practised child marriage, they knew all about sex and were likely to pass that unwelcome knowledge on to us, supposedly innocent children. The fact that the supposition in question was misplaced did not matter. Among our little friends were the two Bengis, ogo (theirs) and mogo (ours), who delighted in playing bride and groom with us, the Babu's sons. Mogo (ours) was also an Olympic champion in the game known as 'Crocodile, crocodile'. Ogo (theirs), the grocer's daughter, was especially keen to play the bride and groom game with my handsome brother. Since she would be married off before long, she had a fair knowledge of what that institution was about. Our mother was anxious that this unwelcome knowledge might be passed on to us through precept and practice. Jagadishya, a five-year-old who took upon himself the arduous moral duty of keeping men away from the river ghat where the women bathed was, of course, an authority on such matters. Once the person he was shooing away turned out to be his revered father. Jagadishya spent the next month in bed. That our parents should be worried about such company made sense. But nothing untoward happened. We passed from childhood to adolescence with our morals intact. The knowledge of 'good and evil' had, of course, been acquired long before that transition.

For me that knowledge came in a traumatic way. Chandra Bhuimali's daughter, Shanna, aged nine, was the beauty of our budding grove. Though a member of the subaltern class, Chandra enjoyed a certain social status for a variety of reasons. First, the Bhuimalis, while a lowly caste as gardeners, were free from the stigma of unclean work. Moreover, their profession was considered one of artistic excellence and as flowers were essential for all ritual worship, certain sanctity was attached to their work. And Chandra had enhanced his status by laying skilful claims to supernatural healing powers. These came as a gift from certain deities with whom he was in regular communion. Chief among these were the disease deities, especially those of smallpox, Shitala, and of cholera, Ola Bibi (a Muslim name, presumably because their not always very healthy meat diet rendered the community especially susceptible to the goddess's favours). As a result, Chandra was held in awed respect and during the appropriate season was much in demand. In his role as a healer, he was bedecked in a cheap red shawl, had a wreath of red hibiscus (sacred to Kali) round his neck, held a bunch of broomsticks in one hand, and a bell in the other which he rang in a slow rhythm to the accompaniment of jerky dance steps. It was an impressive sight. And within minutes, Chandra went into a deep trance, rolled his eyes and produced an uncanny voice. Duly impressed, even some members of the higher castes touched his feet on such occasions. This was OK because his human body had become temporarily semi-divine by virtue of possession by the deity. Thus Chandra was really somebody and his official designation, bhandari or storekeeper, was really the cover for a sinecure. Besides, in our town house there were no bhandars, or zamindari stores to keep.

Thus Shanna had a twofold claim to distinction: her undoubted beauty and her father's spiritual prowess which was widely accepted as real. She indeed was the belle of our ball. One unfortunate afternoon, the beautiful Shanna stopped coming to play in our courtyard. For most of us this implied a deprivation, especially so for my brother who was indeed very keen on her. We knew that at a certain age the girls were no longer allowed to come and play in mixed company. But Shanna certainly had not reached that age. My brother and I began to ask our playmates from the mud-built houses if they knew the reasons for Shanna's absence. They looked at one another and said nothing. But it was clear that they were hiding some dark secret. What could that be? One day Bengi (mogo, ours), a straight shooting person, could not hold her tongue any longer and blurted out the truth.

'Her father has sold Shanna to Saha,' she told us in a distant unexcited way. Sold Shanna? Are human beings sold in the marketplace? Like pumpkins and gourds? Do fathers sell their children? I felt utterly confused. Then one day my father summoned Chandra and asked us to leave the room. From the next room we could hear very clearly the conversation which took place.

'I hear you have sold Shanna to Saha?'

After a moment's silence came the reply: 'That is true, sir.'

'How could you do such a thing?'

'I really have no choice. She is a pretty girl. All the rascals in our locality are after her. I do not have the means to marry her off into a suitable family. At Saha Babu's she will live a comfortable life. I have three other daughters. What Saha is paying will enable me to arrange decent marriages for them as well.'

'But she is only a child!' my father exclaimed, 'Are you sure she will not kill herself?'

'No sir, she is no child. She will be ten next summer. Saha Babu is a person with a very kind heart. He will take her home only when she comes of age. Everything will be all right, sir. Not to worry.'

'Kind heart indeed!' said my father. 'Then ask the scoundrel to summon a priest and have a proper marriage.'

Chandra looked shocked. 'How can that be, sir! We are low-caste people.

Saha of the kind heart did not wait till next summer, but took Shanna home soon afterwards. Perhaps she had come of age, according to his calculation. Mr Saha's very kind heart was lodged in a pot-bellied, hairy, repulsive body. Our knowledgeable Jagadishya explained to me the biological purpose behind the deal in question, giggling all the while. That night I had an awful nightmare. A scary and repulsive animal, a cross between a monitor lizard and a crocodile, with a festering hide was tearing Shanna to pieces. The creature had a human head and that head belonged to Saha Babu. That ghastly scene has recurred in my dreams ever since. In a single day, my childhood came to an abrupt end. There was no longer any hope of collecting pearls from taro leaves. The flowers lost their luminescence. I had been banished from the Garden of Eden. A deep sense of loss enveloped my consciousness. I never saw Shanna again.

3

Those Who Were Near and Dear

Once on a journey back from London to Oxford, my only fellow passenger in the train compartment was a maulvi. The sun was about to set and the devout gentleman spread his neat little mat on the floor for his evening prayer. When his prayers were over, I decided to have a conversation with him: I know of no Asian who finds taking such initiatives unseemly. How long had he been in England, I asked. I gathered from his reply that he did not speak any English and had been in the country only one month, on what was his first visit. I switched to my execrable Hindustani Urdu and was relieved to find that the gentleman could follow what I was saying. In course of that brief dialogue (he got off at Reading) he made a remarkable statement which, I thought, was a brilliant summing up of the difference between the two social cultures of Britain and South Asia. 'Yahan insaniyat zyada, muhabbat kam.' To translate, 'Here they are rich in qualities which we consider worthy of human beings, but their capacity for love is less.' It was the other way in our part of the world, he implied. I found myself agreeing with that shrewd judgement. The Bengali society in particular is not famous for its material achievements or for its record of institution building which expresses and facilitates a high quality of civic life. But what makes the consequent inadequacies tolerable and informs our impoverished existence with a measure of happiness is the depth and ease of inter-human relationships. If I may generalize, I have come across this felicity for communication and spontaneous emotional responses in my encounters with people from many parts of Asia, but very rarely in my encounters with Western men and women. No, I am not suggesting a revival of the Orientalist discourse—the question as to whether the twain can ever meet, and this time with the balance tilted in favour of Asians. My generalization is an untested statement based on casual observation covering half a century and should be treated as such. Its superficiality however would not justify casual dismissal.

I have introduced this amateurish sociological observation to explain an important element in my early socialization: our relation with our domestic servants and what I learnt from that source. Poet Tagore in his autobiography has described his childhood as one dominated by domestic servants; he borrowed a phrase from medieval Indian history—Rule of the Slave Dynasty (that is, the first Turko-Afghan dynasty, some of whose rulers began their lives as slaves) as its apt description. In the wealthy, aristocratic and very extended Tagore family, the domestics constituted a 'cordon sanitaire', relieving the parents, especially the mothers, from the trying task of child rearing. The children were, in effect, often motherless in their vie quotidienne. The father was almost always a remote figure. The numerous servants, thus empowered, acted like petty tyrants: hence the analogy of the slave kings. These facts imparted a quality of misery and angst to the experience of childhood.

Though we belonged to the same occupational group as the Tagores—that of the zamindars—the domestic servants were fewer and less powerful in our modest home. This was not true of the servants employed by the estate, especially in the villages. They had flamboyant descriptive titles like bhandari (storekeeper), pujabarir chakar (servants of the chapel) etc., were numerous and whatever their duties had been in earlier times, these had dwindled into non-specific functions or no functions at all. This way, many of these men and women enjoyed sinecures in our days. Their main activity, so far as I could see, consisted in quarrelling at the top of their voices—that is when no poor ryot was available to receive humbly the benefits of their shouted abuse. Near about a hundred in number, they were often not paid in cash but got their livelihood from the land grants they had received in the past. As servants of the zamindari estate, they enjoyed a certain status in the village and exercised a measure of tyranny on the more humble land tenants. The tyranny usually took the form of illegally extracting field products and occasionally petty cash. We regarded these men and women with some awe, because they were used to exercising authority, but fortunately for us, our dealings with these petty tyrants were strictly limited.

While the ejmali (shared) servants whose services were supposed to be shared by all the coparceners of the estate were somewhat remote figures, the domestics who worked for the individual families, which were a cross between the extended and the nuclear type, were not. My great-grandfather had four sons of whom my grandfather was the youngest.

Each of his three brothers had several sons who lived in 'joint families' while the demands of their occupational lives pushed some of these sons towards adopting the nuclear pattern of lifestyle. My father was an only son and so our family structure was nuclear from the very beginning. The older form of family structure which meant cousins sharing the same family home, especially the same food cooked in the undivided kitchen (the Bengali word for this arrangement was 'ekannabarti', that is, people sharing the same food), appears to have broken down in my grandfathers' days. All our property, including the houses in the village and the district town were jointly owned. There had never been a formal partitioning of property, but each 'nuclear' or 'extended' family had their own quarters in the village home. Only the 'reception rooms' were shared by all. The town house where I grew up was inhabited by only our immediate family in my childhood. Later, another branch of the family—first cousins of my father, their wives and children—came to share it.

This lengthy introduction, I felt, was necessary to explain the affective ambience of my childhood. We, that is, our parents, brothers and sister, lived with our servants in that house with a curious name—Nabalok Lodge. The annual visit to the village home during the Puja season in autumn, when the various deities (all female) were worshipped in style, provided the joys of close encounter with our cousins and coparceners. Of that, more later.

As we were relatively modern, by which I mean urbanized in our outlook and life habits (for instance my mother and aunts never observed purdah although they didn't ever join the menfolk at table when we had guests), the habitual distance between parents and children, often the hallmark of more traditional families, was not part of our childhood experience.

Yet it would be true to say that we spent the greater part of our time with our servants rather than with our parents. No, they did not have the extralegal powers over us that those in the Tagore household or in the families of some of our cousins enjoyed. Our childhood experience throws up no memory of the servants' tyranny. This was partly because in our urbanized family, the social distance from the servants was quite clearly spelt out and we were never in any doubt that we were their superiors. The nature of the servant–employer relationship in the homes of our cousins who lived in the village was somewhat different. There the children used kinship terms like Dada (elder brother), Didi (elder sister), Kaka (uncle—literally, father's younger brother), Mashi (aunt, literally, mother's sister) in addressing the servants. The fiction that the servants were members of the family had a certain reality about it in these households. Our urbanization meant that such intimacy in conduct and associated affects were things of the past. Some of our cousins were frequently chastised by their servants. The cook, if a Brahmin, had his feet touched on ritual occasions by members of the family as tokens of obeisance, for one must not forget that Brahmins, regardless of their occupation, were bhudevas, gods on earth. Such crossing of class barriers was unthinkable in our own family.

But the clarity of class distinctions in our family was somewhat muddied through the presence of one person, Joti or Joti Didi, which meant elder sister. Unlike the servants, she was allowed to sit on our beds and chairs and she called my father by his first name. The explanation for this violation of class barriers lay in our family history. My grandmother died when my youngest aunt, Padma (later the wife of Kiran Shankar Roy, a Congress leader and an influential member of the cabinet in West Bengal after the Partition) was one month old. My grandfather, Binod Kumar had advertised for an ablebodied woman to look after her. Joti became the successful applicant for the job. Binod, who had married for love a renowned beauty of fourteen (remember, the same age as Juliet) whom he had first seen bathing in a river, was quite heartbroken at the death of his very beautiful wife. He was only thirty and could have easily remarried without attracting any criticism, but refused to do so mainly because of his great affection for his only son, Amiya. He did not want to risk adding further claimants to the four annas, that is, 25 per cent share of the Barahisya estate which Amiya would inherit. Joti fell victim to this act of renunciation. She became my grandfather's mistress, a fact I became aware of only when I reached adulthood. She was a 'victim', because my grandfather did not provide for her in any way and trusted his son and daughter-in-law to look after her the rest of her life. This worked for many years, but she was thrown out in the last years of her life and died in penury. My father, a Gandhian moralist, looked upon his father as an ideal parent who had sacrificed his happiness for his son's sake. He was entirely blind to the great injustice Binod had done to Joti.

I knew Joti only as the person who had reared aunt Padma in her infancy and looked after me in my childhood. Joti came from a family of reasonably affluent peasant-farmers and belonged to the weaver caste. She had been married off at the age of three to a boy of five who died of smallpox a couple of years later. All she remembered of her marriage was that she had been placed on a large bell metal thali in which she was carried round the child bridegroom on the wedding day; she was too sleepy to do the ritual perambulation by herself. My eldest brother was born handicapped, and my parents' next child, Arun, was only a year younger to him. My mother was fully occupied looking after these two children. The third child, I, was left to Joti's care. In my infancy and early childhood I was virtually motherless. Joti assumed the mother's role and poured on me all the affection she was capable of. Hers was a highly demonstrative affection expressed in the crude language of country folk. This provoked in me an extreme distaste which I expressed with the violent heartlessness only children are capable of. I made fun of her plump body. When I became sufficiently articulate, I would suggest that soon she would be invited to join Rukmabai's circus party whose chief elephant had just died. Joti, unable to cope with such barbs, would appeal piteously: 'Oh my precious, that is not a proper way to talk.' Aware that the barb had hit its mark, I would further embellish my monstrous diatribes. And as Joti shed tears, I felt vastly amused to see an adult cry, because this was an extremely uncommon sight in Barisal, the proud land of machismo. I became aware of the monstrosity of my conduct many years later. By then Joti had left us and was, in fact, dead. To quote her words, often studded with folk wisdom derived from India's high and ancient philosophy, 'she had cut the bonds of Maya (meaning illusion and also attachment) and left', a very optimistic perception of death.

I still remember with some embarrassment and a touch of angst that I never reciprocated Joti's deep and abiding affection towards me. The only feeling her proximity generated in me was one of extreme irritation. But in one area of our domestic life, my sympathies were with her. Our family was too civilized for the vulgarity of open quarrels shouted out at the top of one's voice, a common feature of Bengal's idyllic rural life. Yet I could sense an undercurrent of mutual hostility between my mother and Joti. My mother, Pratibha or Tulu (her pet name), had come into our family as a girl in her early teens. Joti claimed that she had performed the ritual task of welcoming the child bride into her new home, a claim hotly denied by my mother. One fact was, however, clear. Joti had tried to play the mother-in-law—much to my mother's disgust. When her authority was resisted, she complained to my grandfather with false accusations and my mother was duly scolded. On the old man's death, the tables had been turned and Joti was at my mother's mercy. But her mercy, expectedly, was in short supply. Oftentimes, I felt that Joti was being treated unjustly.

This perception was probably unfair if one took a long-term view of the situation, but, I, a virtually motherless child, lacked the maturity to do so.

In a family of beautiful men and women, I was an ugly duckling. The inadequacy of my looks and the relative darkness of my skin were objects of frequent comments from relatives and neighbours. Joti's unstinted admiration for my qualities of head and heart as well as my looks acted as a balm. I was grateful to her at least for these reasons.

Later, when I began to do well at school, my position in my family circle improved considerably. At the first sign of academic abilities, the child is overpowered with insufferable expectations from the elders in a Bengali home. Nowadays, these expectations are simple and uncomplicated. The bright child, it is hoped, will eventually go to an English-medium school, proceed thence to some American university and emerge as a star in the corporate world, earning millions of dollars and providing for the parents an annual trip to the USA and Europe. Since Amartya Sen won the Nobel Prize in economics, the expectations have acquired an additional dimension: ideally, the gifted progeny should someday be a Nobel laureate as well. But this additional expectation is not pressed too seriously. A dollar income counted in hundreds of thousands is return enough for the parental investment in rearing a gifted child. In our childhood, under the benign rule of the Raj, unemployment was rampant and as a result, material expectations were low—close to absolutely nothing. This negative economic truth generated fantasies in the minds of parents for their children, for which the sky was hardly the limit. First, you had to stand first in every examination in your class ('Never stood second' is a common description of the successful man in Bengal). I have heard this said of me often enough. As a matter of fact, I never stood first and most of the time came second. Secondly, in adulthood, the promising child was expected to emerge as a great man, nineteenth-century style, like the great scholar and reformer, Vidyasagar, or the charismatic monk, Swami Vivekananda, who carried the message of Hinduism to modern Europe and America. Since these were remote and somewhat unlikely ideals, parents dreamed that their bright child would at least become an ICS officer. Even in our nationalist family, such expectations were not absent. The contradiction between being a Vivekananda and an ICS officer simultaneously were always slurred over. In my case, the burden of parental expectation was further enhanced by the accident of my date of birth. Besides these expectations—of being a Vidyasagar, a Vivekananda and an ICS officer—I was also expected someday to equal in my achievements the Nobel laureate poet, Rabindranath, the most revered cultural icon of modern Bengal and, undoubtedly, a genius of extraordinary stature. This last expectation had horrendous consequences. I began at one stage to write poems, luckily for a brief period. The world should be grateful that I did not throw that deadly stuff at them.

As for Joti, she of course thought that I was the most marvellous thing that had ever happened under the sun, but her knowledge of the world was too limited for spelling out the possible track of my undoubtedly brilliant future career. Meanwhile, this semi-literate person conferred on me the benefits of her world view and knowledge of the Hindu tradition. The latter, surprisingly, was quite extensive. When lecturing to my students abroad I often emphasize the fact that non-literacy is less of a barrier to understanding one's rights and duties as a citizen than is often imagined. A person like Joti, who knew the intricate details of our very complex myths and had a full understanding of their ethical implications, was surely not less qualified to be the citizen of a modern state than the literate Briton whose knowledge of sociopolitical reality is derived primarily from regular study of the tabloids, especially the third page.

Joti, strictly speaking, was semi-literate. She could read, but not write. As soon as I became literate in both these senses, she appointed me her amanuensis for the exclusive purpose of writing her letters. This was a limited and somewhat repetitive task. The letters were always addressed to her nephew Kalipada who lived in the village of Gayeshpur, post office Eruali in the district of Murshidabad. The queries too were always the same—about the state of cultivation and the harvest and the health of Kalipada and his family. By way of information, there was a general statement concerning Joti's habitual ill health (not true), the satisfactory state of her adopted family (rarely true) and a concluding statement regarding the utter hopelessness of her situation (based on existential truth) in which the only ray of light was I. Then I had to sign off for her as 'hatabhagini Joti', that is, Joti the unfortunate—which she was, but at that point in time I was unable to see how or why.

My day began with collecting flowers, whether fragrant or not, but never any blossom of extra-Indian origin because they were not adequately sacred, being polluted by their mlechchha (impure foreigner) association. These flowers were meant for Joti's daily ritual worship of Radha and her divine partner Krishna: the situation was slightly anomalous, because Radha happened to be the wife of Krishna's maternal uncle. But such things are irrelevant in the world of divinities. Besides, Krishna was God incarnate. No one had the gumption to tell Him what He could or could not do. Of course, the modern Victorianized Hindu interpreted the legend as symbolic: Krishna was the Ultimate reality, Radha, his beloved, the human soul wishing to break away from worldly bonds (like respect for the marriage vow) for union with the Deity. Of course, these higher truths were inaccessible to me in my childhood. I found the Radha–Krishna legend a pretty story and that was enough. As both my father and grandfather were atheists, there was no daily ritual worship of any deity in our family and my only religious education was under Joti's tutelage. She was a Vaishnava, a follower of the sixteenth-century saint Chaitanya. The ideas and practices of the Krishna Consciousness movement derive from the same source. Her prayer usually took the form of kirtana—devotional songs sung in a broken voice to the accompaniment of copious tears. In the West, these songs can be heard now, thanks to the Krishna Consciousness movement. Vaishnavism was a religion of love: the Deity was worshipped as one's child or lover. Joti's Deity, despite the presence of Radha, was the child Krishna: I was encouraged to assume His role and dance to her tuneless kirtanas. She did much more to bring our traditions home to me. As I have already said, she could read and I benefited from the fact. She read out to me all the legends of Krishna, the Ramayana and the Mahabharata as well as many of the mythical tales in Bengali translation. By age seven, I knew a vast amount of religious/mythical lore as a result.

Besides, she taught me a very important lesson for which I have remained forever grateful. She was the person who took me with her to the homes of our subaltern neighbours where, given her own origins, she felt perfectly at home. When chided by my parents for taking me to such unsuitable places she would make a face and whisper to me, 'All human beings are the same. Your parents do not know this.' Vaishnavism is an egalitarian faith which questions the inequities of the caste system. Joti taught me a simple truth. It has informed my life all these years. Chaitanya, the founder of neo-Vaishnavism, was not a socialist. But the faith he preached was rooted in the same affects that inform all egalitarian doctrines, socialism and Christianity included.

Joti was asked to leave the shelter of our family when I was a teenager. She had said something unpardonable. I felt that a grievous wrong was being done, but was powerless to prevent it. While leaving, she gave me a gold necklace, probably a gift from her aristocratic lover. 'Give this to your wife when she comes,' she said. By the time she came, the necklace had been lost.

Three to four domestic servants, including a cook, often from Orissa were the usual adjuncts to middle-class Bengali family in the thirties and forties of the last century. Since their pay ranged from five to ten rupees a month (a pound was equal to thirteen rupees, but these international measures were no real indicators of the purchasing power of those amounts), they slept somehow somewhere spreading their bedroll on the floor and were given minimalist meals which were very different from what the family of their employers ate; the bulk of their wages was sent home by money order. I knew this because I had to fill up the necessary forms. Amazing as it may sound, those measly amounts had some purchasing power. As I enjoyed going to the market to buy vegetables and fish, I was often given half a rupee to buy the day's requirement of those items for our family of nine persons (including the retainers). When, as a treat, I was given one whole rupee to spend, we required at least one porter to carry the stuff home, that is, in addition to the servant who accompanied me. The price revolution is even more sharply felt by the fact that the hilsa—Bengal's favourite delicacy which is beyond the means of most Bengalis at its current price, 350 to 500 rupees per kilogram, (it weighs one to two kilograms on an average)—was then sold eight to sixteen fish per rupee. Price of rice, the staple of Bengali diet, has risen some four hundred times, over the last seventy to seventy-five years.

For such reasons, some Bengalis of my generation look back on the days under the Raj as a blissful time.

I, sadly, am not one of them. The Raj still remains for me an abomination, a memory of humiliation and hence a 'Satanic government' as Gandhi described it, relative cheapness of food notwithstanding. But its evil perhaps derived more from stupidity, a total incapacity to understand how other people felt and reacted, rather than any innate sadism. Perhaps it is difficult to run other people's lives arbitrarily without some blunting of both sense and sensibility. Of course there were great exceptions: but they were exactly that, exceptions to the general rule. The British establishment has created grand myths about the wondrous efficiency of their bureaucracy. Its falsity is very easy to prove. The snobbery which characterized British society also got translated into a faith in racial superiority and writers like James Mill seriously believed in Indians being somehow inferior to 'nobler' animals. Such belief was central to the social outlook of many Britons who served the Raj. Lord Hastings records his faith in it in writing even before he had set foot in India. Besides, imperialists everywhere were famous for considering whatever was to their own advantage as the source of universal welfare. The British, as the most successful imperialists of their time, left all others cold at the door in this particular game of complacent self-deception. Incidentally, that blissful level of food prices, the bliss qualified by low incomes and extensive unemployment, collapsed in 1943 when the rising price of essential foodgrains caused three million deaths by starvation in Bengal. Incidentally, I have met very few people in the UK who have heard of this catastrophe or, if they have, believe that the colonial government had any part in it. I shall return to this theme later, in the appropriate context.

Bawsha, alias Basanta Kumar Shankhabanik, to give his full highsounding name in which he rejoiced, was four feet tall and the selfappointed leader of our three domestics. Now, his two supposed followers, who were of normal height, and Joti whose position was ambiguous, of course, did not accept this claim to a superior status. But this did not bother Bawsha. For had he not been the servant-in-chief to the Honourable Binod Kumar Raychaudhuri, member of the Legislative Council, in whose company he had taken part in the Delhi Durbar of 1911? George V, the King Emperor had looked upon Bawsha with pleasurable amusement or so Bawsha claimed. The Barisal-born prime minister of pre-partition Bengal, Fazlul Huq, indeed never failed to enquire after him when he visited us. Neither Noga, who was an Oriya, nor Dharma, our cook of the same ethnic origin, could lay claims to such exceptional distinction.

In truth, in my grandfather's circle, Bawsha was indeed an object of interest by virtue of his size and highly flamboyant ways. In course of time, he decided that he was a member of the secret service or CID. He 'bengalicized' the name of that department and rechristened it 'si-oi-tee' and thus made it more accessible to the hoi polloi. In accordance with his claim, he got tailored for himself a khaki police uniform bedecked with numerous pockets. In one of these he carried a small note book and a pencil. Their purpose was to record information regarding the nefarious activities of various enemies of the Raj and, generally, about people with criminal propensities. There was only one problem concerning this duty entrusted to Bawsha by the famous si-oi-tee: he could neither read nor write. No matter, Bawsha in his assumed role of a member of the si-oi-tee could still manage to collect the occasional anna (one-sixteenth of a rupee) from the local shopkeepers. This helped sustain his one addiction, a drink at the local toddy shop. When that drink was brandy or whisky stolen from my grandfather's drink cabinet, which lay unused since my father's conversion to Gandhism, the four-foot-tall hero proudly proclaimed, Aij bilayti (today it is of English origin). The phrase passed into our family vocabulary. Aij bilayti, we said, whenever the meal was of Western orientation.

I am not sure that Bawsha's claim to membership of that feared arm of the state was entirely spurious. The police, and in fact many of the higher functionaries of the Raj up to the level of the viceroy, often spoke and acted with such singular stupidity that any improbable action on the part of the Raj now seems possible to me. Lord Hardinge declared that God (no less) had ordained that English should be the major world language; Willingdon thought that Gandhi was a Bolshevik, his successor that the man was the most successful humbug in history and, while I was working for the Indian National Archives, I saw a fat file recording Jawaharlal Nehru's nefarious activities as a communist. I have often wondered how a country as large as ours could be ruled for so long with such phenomenal misperceptions about its people and concluded sadly that we must have been even more stupid than our rulers. And that is saying a very great deal.

The police did take a kindly interest in my father's political activities. He left his postgraduate studies in 1920 to join the Non-cooperation movement and had remained a follower of Gandhi ever since. Since all activities of the leader and his followers were out in the open, the si-oi-tee need not have wasted their resources on keeping a tab on them. Yet a bored-looking individual was always to be seen at the point where the approach road to our house began. It was always the same person, seated on a stool, smoking foul-smelling bidis. He probably spent his time contemplating the cosmos. But perhaps he also had a more immediate task. The political workers who visited my father included revolutionaries who once believed in violence, but had accepted the Gandhian doctrine of non-violence. The police, justifiably, could not be sure about their conversion. Besides, some of the younger cadres of the Indian National Congress, members of the party's local volunteer body, had not really abjured violence. They, to quote a saying that was popular at the time, had accepted non-violence as a policy, not a creed. In other words, if the time seemed propitious, they would again pick up guns and revolvers with alacrity and have no compunction in killing a few servants of the Raj. One of these young men, a teenager who was among our regular visitors, actually stabbed to death in broad daylight a sub-inspector of police: the over-zealous official had walked over the bodies of volunteers, male and female, picketing a liquor shop, going way beyond his call of duty. Incidentally, the police tore out all the hair on the young man's head, yet failed to extract the names of his co-conspirators. Of course, such men required watching. Was Bawsha the right person for that noble task? Well, I have read CID reports of incredible stupidity (an important source material for research on the Raj!). Even in his least enlightened moments, Bawsha could not have competed with the astounding gormlessness of those reports. The truth of this matter—Bawsha's role in saving the Empire—will always remain an unsolved problem of Indo-British history. But it is well to remember that in that noble story of the greatest empire in man's recorded past, hardly anything is impossible.

Bawsha's temper was often on a short fuse. When the occasion arose, he tried to impose his authority on his recalcitrant 'followers' by brute force. To equal their height, an unfair advantage, he would jump on to the nearest table or chair so that he could shower blows on them from a position of relative advantage. Even the most determined enemy would burst into laughter at the sight and hence Bawsha invariably won. The respected member of the si-oi-tee thus remained convinced of his invincibility.

Bawsha, after my grandfather's death, had no specific duties. But he had some exceptional skills like 'curling' a pleat at one end of the dhoti—called the kochano, to produce the style preferred by Bengali gentlemen. And he happened to be an excellent cook, especially in the Anglo-Indian cuisine. His piece de resistance was the 'cutlet', a term applied to meat from various parts of an animal's or a bird's body, basted or minced and then fried in batter as one piece. Bawsha would spend half a day mincing or basting the meat until it was reduced almost to a paste yet, miraculously, somehow holding together as one piece. The end product of this exercise was delicious beyond words. His other unspecified tasks included forcing us children, to take our bath, eat our meals and go to bed when we should. Since his ideas about time were highly original, the performance of this duty took unexpected forms. 'It is past one o'clock, still you are not to be seen anywhere near the bathroom. You are in for a really hard time today, I assure you,' Bawsha would announce with a grim expression on his face. 'Bawsha, it is only 11.'

'So? What am I telling you? Twelve follows quickly on eleven. And when that happens, how far is one o'clock!'

This philosophical view of time (If winter comes, can spring be far behind?) was matched by his other original ideas on the subject, most manifest in his calculation of his own age.

'How old are you, Bawsha?'
'How long ago did the Delhi Durbar take place?'
'Twenty years ago.'
'Hm, the 1883 flood?'
'Forty-eight years.'
'Add the two. What do you get?'
'When did your grandmother die?'
'Some thirty-five years ago.'
'Add that.'

By this method of calculation Bawsha's age soon reached 176. He thought for a while and said, 'I don't think it is that much. But I am certainly over sixty.' When we were very young, he could drag us to the bathroom or our bedroom when necessary. But by age five, we were stronger than the si-oi-tee officer. Then he used his secret and ultimate weapon. He would tickle us into submission with his short and nimble fingers. This was an exquisite torture and we had to submit. His authority thus remained undiminished.

Those Who Were Near and Dear 45

If Bawsha taught us discipline and Joti introduced me to the Hindu tradition, Noga was our mentor in all matters political. He was what would be called today a 'freedom fighter'. The police of the Raj had imprinted the relevant certificate on his skull in the form of a ghastly scar—a memento of the mass agitation against the Simon Commission.

The all-white Parliamentary Commission on constitutional reform in India had been rejected by all political parties in the country and the Indian National Congress had organized a countrywide agitation against it. Wherever the members of the Commission went, they would be greeted with hostile demonstrations. 'Go back, Simon' was their slogan. The members had become so paranoid that once in Delhi, they summoned the police at midnight. After a long and gruelling day they could no longer take the persistent cacophony of slogans. Only, the demonstrators this time proved to be none other than Delhi's jackals. In Cuttack, the capital of Orissa, a pleasant surprise awaited the Commission's members. They were greeted with drums and cymbals and the demonstrators did a very vigorous kirtana to the tune of these musical instruments.

The words of the ditty were music to their ears. 'Go back-ko simono, go back-ko simono', the protesters chanted. This improvement on the English language was of course incomprehensible to the members. Unlike the commissioners, however, the police were not delighted. Hence the scar on Noga's skull. At the slightest provocation, he would re-enact the scene of his martyrdom. To the accompaniment of a drum beaten with great vigour, he would scream out the dreaded slogan which had sounded so sweet to the members of the Commission.

Noga's views on the contemporary political scene were an interesting entry point to subaltern perceptions. He was convinced that the Mahatma was Kalki, the tenth and future incarnation of Vishnu, who would bring to an end the rule of the mlechchhas, i.e., impure foreigners, in one great battle on the banks of the river Narmada as predicted in the Hindu myths. I found it a bit difficult to reconcile the image of this gentle man clad in a very short dhoti with that of the Brahmin warrior resplendent in armour, prophesied in the sacred literature and narrated to me by Joti. But Noga was privy to the secret behind this riddle. At night, the Mahatma discarded his loincloth, dressed as a warrior and riding a white horse (looking somewhat like our Waler, Jack), paraded his troops. After the mlechchhas had been expelled, he would ascend a golden throne studded with jewels and bring back Ramrajya—Rama's rule—as Vishnu's final incarnation, who was the same as Rama, the seventh incarnation. If anyone was under the delusion that Nagendra Parida of village Balikuda in Cuttack district would not take part in the great battle on Narmada's bank, he must be blind despite having eyes. I imagined with awe Noga, the patriotic hero in full armour, fighting the British on the banks of the Narmada, under Gandhi's leadership. My soul was overcome with high regard.

Our cook Dharma's forte was knowledge of the social order as prescribed by Manu and the other authorities in Smriti—the normative texts on correct ritual and social conduct, which the sahibs mistook for law books. It takes a great deal of imagination to confuse the pundits with English lawyers, but there you are. However, Dharma's knowledge of the shastras was congenital, or so he claimed, by virtue of the caste in which he was born. As a Hindu child, I too was not entirely ignorant of the shastras. Das or Dasa was a Sudra surname—that much I knew—so, how could Dharmananda Dasa be a Brahmin? Dasas were indeed Sudras in Bengal, where in fact everybody was a Sudra, members of the lowliest caste just above the Untouchables, the noble Brahmin explained. But in Orissa, where Jagannath, the Lord of the Universe, had decided to settle, preferring the place to all others, the local Brahmins were his preferred servitors; hence Das or Dasa, the servants of Jagannath, specially selected by the Lord himself. To underline his superiority in the caste order, he stated, that if we ever touched him while he was having his meals, he would have to stop eating. This was an experiment too tempting to resist. As Dharma sat down for his midday meal, I would touch him and stop him from bringing his meal to a satisfactory conclusion, until one day my mother discovered my anthropological experiment. I was thrashed within an inch of my life.

Those Who Were Near and Dear 47

Dharma had some school education. At the great Battle of Kalinga, the cause of intense repentance to Emperor Asoka, he told us that Kalinga (read Orissa) and not the emperor had won. The history books were evidently mistaken. How did Dharma know? Well, his ancestor had fought in that great battle of the third century BC! That was a conversation stopper. The Oriya Brahmins, specially selected servants of the Lord, evidently performed multiple functions not authorized by the caste system.

Barisal had a sizeable group of Oriyas working as cooks, domestic servants, coolies at the steamer ghat and independent workers carrying water from the roadside taps to private homes. The community was large and often provided audience for troops of street players from Orissa who presented folk plays based on the two epics and the myths. These folk performances echoed in some ways the great tradition of Sanskrit plays. The dramatis personae were introduced by a sutradhara or impresario; the actors would appear in front of the audience and then be asked to dance and sing—which they did. The sutradhara would announce: Rama auchi, Sita auchi, ebe nacha kuru, nacha kuru (Rama has arrived, Sita too, now be pleased to dance). As the folk plays, Jatras, were presented in a very different style in Bengal and nobody danced, this business of not only Rama and Sita but the demon king Ravana and the monkey god Hanuman as well dancing was a source of amusement to the Bengalis in the audience. The dance sequence in which Ravana, the demon king, and his nephew did a duet appeared singularly inappropriate to me. It violated all the rules of deference on which Bengali social conduct was based. But the victory dance of Hanuman and his monkey army, with Vibhishana, the principled brother of Ravana who had gone over to the enemy, holding on to Hanuman's tail was pure delight. That scene was repeated on our return home from the show with Noga in the role of Hanuman and us bringing up the rear. Dharma did the singing.

Mena or Menajaddi (probably a distortion of the noble name Minhajuddin) looked after our cows. His official designation was ghesera or grass-cutter, but his duties were more extensive. He was diligent in his duties, but not particularly bright. One rainy day, he had taken the cows out to graze by the riverside but came back without them. He was asked, with some alarm, what had gone wrong. He had come back to fetch an umbrella, he explained, for otherwise the cows might get drenched. A bit short on worldly common sense, Mena was however full of folk wisdom. The sparrows slept with their feet pointing skywards, he told us, to prevent getting crushed when the sky collapsed—which was sure to happen someday. This posture had been unnecessary in the days when the sky was located on the earth's surface. But one day a peasant woman got fed up because the sky got in her way when she was sweeping the courtyard. One fell blow from her broom and the sky was thrown up where we now see it. Obviously, it cannot stay there forever. Whatever goes up must come down some day. This entirely logical but ominous prediction caused me considerable concern. Emulating the sparrows, I tried to sleep with my feet pointing skywards for a few days, then gave up because it was too arduous. If the sky must fall, let it.

There was another side to Mena's personality. He was the disciple of some pir, a holy man, in the Sufi tradition. He sang songs attributed to a medieval saint, Manik Pir, a man of the people if he did indeed exist, and danced in tune with them.

> He indeed is Manik Pir,
> the boat to cross this river.
> Jainal renounced the world
> at his behest
> and stopped eating candied sugar.
> Take Allah's name and make the prophet
> the focus of your life, its polestar
> and you will cross this vile abyss
> swinging your hips without care.

So sang Mena swinging his not very ample hips.

I never saw Mena offering namaz or observing fast in the month of Ramadan, perhaps because the Sufi tradition is non-ritualistic, but every evening he would sing a song.

'Oh God, oh my friend, take pity on my state,' he sang and tears would roll down his cheeks. Brought up as a non-believer, in my early youth I sometimes wished I could share the deep and life-enhancing emotion which suffused Mena's being at such moments.

My atheism never stood in the way of my enjoying Tagore's mystical poetry or the sayings of the saint, Ramakrishna. No, in the light of the limitless suffering of living beings, I have never been able to believe in the existence of a benign Father, resident in heaven looking tenderly after our welfare. The shrike snatching pieces of flesh off its live victim stuck on a thorn, part of the Divine order of things, symbolizes for me the Infinite Mercy that allegedly permeates our universe.

But the concept of divinity probably represents the ultimate in human imagination. Like great art or literature, it can enhance one's consciousness without being literally true.

Mena was literate. He introduced me to the folk culture of Bengali Muslims. He read out from punthis or Bengali booklets printed from right to left, emulating Arabic. They contained Islamic lore or tales from the Middle East written in a curious Bengali full of Perso-Arabic vocabulary. Some of the authors' statements were a bit confusing. In a description of a battle scene, we were told, numberless soldiers died in their millions. When counted, the number killed was found to be thirty-five thousand. An outstanding instance of adjusting the margin of error! Then there was the tragic tale of Rustam. The hero got on to the back of his horse 'and walked'. Of course, there has to be space for poetic licence in every literature.

My childhood was sweetened by my ruminations on a land of infinite mystery of which I had only a distant vision. Kauar Char, the Island of Crows, was a village on the other side of the river, directly opposite our house. We could see the cottages, animals and men from our housetop, all reduced in size by distance. I imagined that this might be the land of Lilliputs or at least one of the kingdoms described in our fairy tales. There was no way I could cross the river and find out. Kalu-da, an elder cousin from our village who often visited us, was an expert boatman and would take me as his helping hand when he 'borrowed' one of the dinghis moored near our house and went on brief riverine adventures. 'What about going to Kauar Char?' I sometimes timidly suggested.

Kalu-da responded with supreme lack of interest, 'Why? What is there to see or do?'

I did not have the least idea. How could I explain that that was the precise reason for my interest? Kauar Char thus remained for me forever unvisited.

We had, however, one very tenuous link with that land of mystery. Jayna, who assisted our gardener Hashmatali and performed all the more arduous tasks, came from Kauar Char. He was paid three rupees per month for his pains. He came early in the morning, dressed in a lungi with the upper part of his body usually bare and would be made to work without a stop until evening when it was time for him to leave. His mode of transport was a dangerously dilapidated boat which Kalu-da and I occasionally 'borrowed' at great risk to our lives. The only word I ever heard Jayna utter was 'Ze' or 'Yes, sir,' a semi-mute acknowledgement of Hashmatali's numerous orders, which were screamed out with great violence. He probably had his meagre meal of pantha or fermented rice before he left home and fasted till he returned in the evening. I never saw him eat anything except on the rare occasions when we offered him some food. On these occasions, his face lighted up with joy: for this man, any food, however humble, appeared to be a source of delight. I never saw any other expression on his face, which only seemed to register the fact of his hopeless defeat at the hands of life.

I wish what I have just written were literally true. One day there was a great hullabaloo in our house: some precious metal utensils had got lost, in other words, stolen. Who could be the thief? Suddenly, Hashmatali, a born tyrant, decided that his underling Jayna was the culprit. For did he not come from across the river? Who had a better chance to steal and hide the loot? If you needed further evidence, just consider his meek demeanour. Was it not an obvious camouflage for criminal intent? It was amazing how quickly everybody was convinced that Hashmatali was right. After all, that shrewd character knew his man. Jayna was duly interrogated, administered a couple of slaps by Hashmatali and sacked. The police were not summoned out of pity for the poor man. Throughout these procedures Jayna did not utter a single word: there was no scope for his usual 'Ze'. I saw him when he was leaving. Tears were rolling down his emaciated cheeks. I have never seen greater misery imprinted on a human face.

Several years later, we left Barisal for good, following the Partition of the country. We had to leave everything behind. As we went out of our gate in a horse-drawn carriage, I remembered that expression on Jayna's face. At last we were in the same position as he was on that dreadful afternoon. Only, we had some hope. He had none. He had never had any.

Two families, both under the care of my grandfather, were an important part of our childhood. Shital Jyatha or Uncle Shital, was a medical licentiate who happened to be a self-taught, creative artist. A number of young men were supported by our family in my grandfather's days. They lived in the several outhouses with corrugated iron roofs inside or around our compound wall. Shital, a young Brahmin, was grandfather's favourite and actually lived in one of the rooms in the main building. He sang kirtanas or devotional songs, painted, sculpted, acted and could do a hundred other things, some of which were beguiling to us children. Among these miscellaneous accomplishments was storytelling, occasionally accompanied by shadow play. Uncle Shital cut out figures from newspapers and cast their moving shadows on a screen. As we were still unfamiliar with cinema, this was a cheap substitute, but infinitely more enchanting, thanks to Uncle's skill in storytelling. The stories covered a very wide range, from Bengali fairy tales interspersed with occasional songs to tales of African adventures, Rider Haggard's *She* and Marie Corelli's *Sorrows of Satan*, not entirely suitable for kids. Shital Jyatha drew upon the Ramayana and the legends of Krishna as themes for his pictures painted both in watercolour and oil. Later, he built up a modest business producing oleographs from his paintings, which were quite popular. Recently, there has been a revival of interest in these oleographs and they featured in an exhibition on popular art. What made his company joyous for us children was the whimsicality of his approach to everything, including teasing. He was supremely dismissive of most people's intelligence. Most people were 'idiot's eggs', we being leading members of that species. Joti the Unfortunate was the butt of most of his jokes and numberless songs were composed to serenade the poor woman. Joti used to pick spinach from the kitchen garden. Uncle Shital recorded this noble act in immortal song:

> There is great commotion in the kitchen garden
> Someone is picking greens
> To the swinging of very fat arms
> From East to West and North to South.

He would stop only when Joti's screams reached ear-splitting levels. Every morning, we would wake up to his kirtana—he sang from the goshtha cycle celebrating the child Krishna's morning games with the cowherd boys. But his grand performances of Mathur, the sad story of Krishna departing to Mathura leaving his beloved Radha and the milkmaids in Vrindavana, sung in front of audiences of hundreds, were very moving occasions. Many among the listeners were overcome with emotion. On those nights we went to bed weeping bitterly with pity for Radha's viraha, the heartbreaking separation from her beloved.

The many stories of Uncle Shital's adventures were incredible but true. They were authenticated by the testimony of my father, his constant companion in youth. The least credible among these was the story of Uncle holding on to the tail of a shark so that he could enjoy an effort-free swim; the logic behind the enterprise was that the creature's anatomy prevented it from turning round to devour Shital. Another memorable occasion was when he nearly died, trying to drink up at one go the steamy froth of milk, a famous delicacy of Benares. His fall from a high branch of a magnolia tree could be corroborated by material evidence. The jagged branch of the tree had sunk into my father's arm, who had tried to save him. He carried on his body this memento of a friendship full of danger, for the rest of his life.

My grandfather, impressed by Shital's artistic talents, showed some of his paintings to the English district magistrate, Mr Bell. He sent these on to the principal of the Government Arts School in Calcutta who proposed to send Shital to Italy for advanced training. But this village boy was not willing to go that far. He was certainly no wallflower, as was evident from his public performances of kirtana and his penchant for stellar roles in amateur theatricals. But Europe was much too far and unfamiliar. A door of great opportunity thus closed on Shital Banerji. He remained a folk painter painting in the style of the much more famous Ravi Varma.

In the 1930s, Father decided to settle in Calcutta and rented a house next to one Uncle Shital had bought. The two friends made plans to use Shital's artistic talents for financial gain. They set up a company to manufacture dolls and dummies as a cottage industry using a minimum of machinery. To start with, it was a success. But some misunderstanding developed between the two partners. In any case we had to return to Barisal, leaving it to Uncle to run the company alone. There was one very heavy price to pay for the breach in my father's friendship with Shital, as far as we the children were concerned. It produced a vacuum in our lives nothing could fill. We dearly loved that highly talented man, full of whimsical playfulness.

The other family very close but unrelated to us was headed by Uncle Bhuiya, alias Bisweswar Das, head clerk, Barisal collectorate. He lived in a kutchcha house under a myrobalan tree close to our orchard which stood between the river and our house. Myrobalan is a bitter-tasting fruit but, surprisingly, if you drink water after eating one of these, the water tastes sweet. Uncle Bhuiya's was a one-bedroom cottage. The parents, two daughters, two sons and their spouses all slept on a very wide bed apparently without embarrassment. If Uncle Shital's forte in entertaining us was singing and storytelling, Uncle Bhuiya concentrated on dances. Allegedly, these were of varied ethnic origin—English, French, German, Japanese, and Zulu—though they all looked the same to us. Only, the Zulu dances were performed with a greater degree of vigour and accompanied by blood-curdling shrieks. As an adult I was privileged to see a ballet performed by Nureyev. Without question, Uncle Bhuiya left him cold at the doorpost.

He carried a case for his looking glass out of which he gave us bits of 'sen-sen', a sweet peppermint which we craved. He himself took a little opium out of the same case. One day, he returned from his office limping and screaming with pain. He had put his right foot into a bowl of melted and boiling lac used for sealing documents. The English district surgeon operated to take his foot out of his laced shoe. Though poor, he enjoyed this privilege, owing to his standing as a middle-ranking official. But he never got up from his bed again. He would hold on to our hands when we visited him, tears rolling down his old cheeks. But the supply of 'sen-sen' for us and opium for himself did not stop. Bhuiya died of the trauma he had suffered, closing another chapter in the story of our childhood.

The dearest and nearest person in my childhood was someone of whom I had no memory. This was my grandfather. His photos in which he was accompanied by his family or his pedigreed dogs and horses were all over the place. My parents, Joti, Uncle Shital and Bawsha were all full of stories about him, so that I never felt that I did not really remember him. Apparently, he had dearly wished for a granddaughter when I, his third grandchild was born. He was bitterly disappointed and consoled himself by dressing me up as a girl. If this early experience has produced any deviant tendencies in me, I must say I have not noticed. I was about three when he died and the shock made me very ill for some time. But then a child's sorrow is brief, though intense. It passed as did all my memory of this man.

4

Lords of the Land

As I have said before, we were zamindars, literally, holders or owners of land, whose livelihood depended on the rent paid by the peasant farmers to whom the land had been leased out. But vestiges of medieval practice gave the zamindars in Bengal considerable power over the peasant tenants or ryots, who treated them as their overlords. The usual form of address when the ryots met the zamindars was maharaj—'great king'—applied indiscriminately to all male members of the zamindar family. The great king's income might be as little as fifty rupees (less than four pounds at the exchange rate current till the 1950s) per month, sometime less; still in the eyes of the ryot he remained a figure of grandeur and power, incredibly remote.

Our ancestor, Krishna Kumar Sen, came from a family of Ayurvedic (indigenous medicine) practitioners, members of the Baidya caste, second in caste ranking in Bengal. They had migrated from Vikrampur in Dhaka district and constructed a mud-built house in the village of Kirtipasha sometime in the sixteenth century. Its foundations survived till our days, though the structure must have been repaired and reconstructed many times over the intervening centuries. We considered that mud-built structure to be our true home, though the sizeable brick-built house close by was where we lived. Ayurveda, the ancient system of medicine, was based on

Sanskrit texts and hence there was a tradition of Sanskritic learning in the family. During the interregnum between the Turko-Afghan and Mughal rule in Bengal in the sixteenth century, the legendary twelve bhuiyans or landlords controlled the eastern part of the province. The number twelve denotes simply a conventional figure; the actual number of warlords or petty princes varied from time to time. Krishna Kumar accepted the office of Diwan, chief financial officer, in effect the manager of the estate, under one of them, Raja Satrajit of Bhushana. He was rewarded with a piece of 'property' in the village of Kirtipasha for some act of extraordinary loyalty. The property or taluk was named after Krishna Kumar's two sons, Rajaram and Kashiram. When it was eventually partitioned, the elder branch got the slightly larger share and the younger the smaller. Hence the two branches and their respective properties came to be known as Barahisya, the holders of the larger share and Chhotahisya, those of the smaller. We were the descendants of Rajaram, the elder brother.

There is a great deal of misunderstanding regarding the zamindari system. Originally, the zamindars were revenue collectors and/or people who had seized political power over indeterminate areas during periods when the central authority was weak or virtually absent. They never had proprietary rights over the land they controlled. They collected revenue and were paid in shares of the amount collected, if the political boss was some higher authority, not rent. Under the British, the revenue-collecting zamindars gradually emerged as owners of the soil until under Governor General Lord Cornwallis, an Irish landlord, they were made full proprietors of the land, with revenue payable to the government fixed in perpetuity.

For reasons far from clear, his Irish experience convinced Cornwallis that this would be to everybody's benefit. There could be no greater mistake. The zamindars did nothing to improve productivity as had been expected of them. Left virtually free to increase the rent at will, they had no incentive to invest in improvements and became petty tyrants emerging as a class of idle bloodsuckers. The peasantry was steadily impoverished. Subject to a rising burden of rent, plus numerous illegal extra demands and without any security of tenure, they too had no incentive to improve the land. Over time they became hopelessly indebted to usurious moneylenders and many became landless. The history of agriculture in Bengal became one of sustained misery. But the world demand for jute in the late nineteenth century changed the economic and social situation for a section of the peasantry in Bengal. But more about that later.

Owing to the system of inheritance current in Bengal, the zamindari property was shared between all the male children of the owner or owners. There was rarely any formal partition. Only the income was shared and other assets like houses and moveable property informally distributed for use among the coparceners. My great-grandfather, Prasanna Kumar, an exceptionally energetic person, had substantially enlarged his property which he left to his four sons, of whom my grandfather was the youngest. My father was an only son, but his three uncles had three to four sons each, who received a twelfth or sixteenth part of the property. This meant that their monthly allowance from the property, an appropriate portion of the income net of the expenses of managing the estate and various other charges on the joint property, like the ritual pujas and hospitality, could be a measly amount. The reason why some of us did not actually starve was the fact that a part of the income, legal and illegal, came in the form of foodstuff. Throughout the year, there was a steady flow of grains, vegetables, fruits, fish, meat and milk from the ryots or tenants. Whenever the ryots visited the zamindar's estate office in the village or the district town, they gave the zamindars and family members small gifts in cash or kind. We were forbidden by our elders to accept these, but this admonition was not always respected. Strictly speaking, these gifts were voluntary and not forcibly extracted. But for a poor peasant, such gifts, enforced by custom if not extralegal pressure, must have been a burden. A piece of vegetable was, after all, a day's meal for his family and it is unlikely that it could be given away without strain. The real abwabs, or extra legal extractions, were more painful. For instance, when there was a wedding in the zamindar's family, a shadiana or wedding tax was collected: for a poor peasant the sum involved could be really a burden. Our north Indian counterparts, like the Taluqdars of Oudh, made more imaginative innovations in this practice in keeping with modern times. Inter alia, they collected motorana, automobile tax, when they felt like buying a car. We were not that powerful.

In the 1950s, there was a great deal of discussion among the historians of Bengal about the zamindari crisis in the province during the early decades of the century. As a sufferer from the consequences of the said crisis, let me record my understanding of what happened. My great-grandfather was the sole owner of the property which he had extended several times over. His four sons, men of culture and good taste, did not bother with the dirty work of estate management, but spent their time enjoying the fruits of their father's hard labour. The managers and petty rent collectors took full advantage of their indifference. By my father's time there were twelve coparceners sharing the net income from the property. Had the evil system persisted, by our time the number of coparceners would have been seventeen. Meanwhile, the income from the estate had decreased steadily. This was mainly due to mismanagement. The coparceners could not agree on how to run the estate. The estate officers and rent collectors, quite poor themselves, made hay and oppressed the peasantry as best as they could. Only there was the old problem about drawing blood from stone: the peasantry had reached the limit of their paying capacity. On the other hand, those with bigger holdings had prospered, thanks to the world demand for jute, among other things, laying the foundation of the new Muslim middle class. No longer willing to take things lying down, they fought the zamindars in court, causing a steady drain on the estate's limited resources. The resulting tension also contributed to the worsening of relations between Hindus and Muslims. In our case, matters were worsened by the ongoing law suits against the Chhotahisya—some started by us, others by them. Sometimes the dispute was fought out by armed club men (the weapons used were often sharper than clubs) in the employ of both sides, leading to more criminal acts. Neither side could afford these luxuries. Mahals or revenue units had to be mortgaged and at times sold to meet the cost, leading to a steady decline in rental income. The net income from the estate was distributed as monthly allowance among the co-sharers, some of whom received truly derisory amounts. We, as owners of one-fourth shares in the property, survived a shade better, but only just.

The postures of grandeur which were neither sensibly given up nor reduced to any significant degree contributed to this impoverishment. As noted before, there were some hundred servants, male and female, in the employ of the estate. Many of them were not paid in cash but enjoyed rent-free land grants over many generations. These included our washermen, barbers and various other low-level functionaries like the women who came to paint the ladies' feet with alta, a red dye, an essential part of their toilette as well as a sign of marital happiness. Only unmarried and married girls were customarily permitted this luxury. The privilege ended with widowhood.

The expenditure incurred on behalf of the estate had long passed the point of what we could afford. Yet there was no curtailment in the expenditure on puja, or worship of the various Devis—embodiments of God the Mother—worshipped as Shakti or the creative power behind the universe. The most fabulously expensive occasion was Durga Puja, worship of the Goddess Durga, the presiding deity of the Bengalis in her role of Mahishamardini, the slayer of the buffalo demon. (Incidentally, since the days of the anti-Partition agitation, the demon, usually green in colour, was often painted white, sometimes with the face of Fuller, the hated lieuetenant governor of the newly created province of East Bengal; we however, did not indulge this particular fantasy.) On the holiest day of the Durga Puja, ashtami, the eighth in the bright lunar fortnight, 108 goats were sacrificed. The practice of buffalo sacrifice, a notoriously cruel business, had been stopped in our family. But Chhotahisya, the younger branch, even poorer than us, kept it up until they too were forced to migrate. On secular occasions like the day the annual collection of rent started, punyaha or the day blessed with religious merit (it was never very clear to me whose punya or merit earned through righteous action was being celebrated), the visiting ryots had to be fed in some style. There was also a shelter for guests. No visitor must go away unfed. As a young adult, I realized quite clearly that we could no longer afford most of these things. But noblesse, however tarnished, did oblige; only, it not only obliges, but can seriously impoverish at the same time. However, the show had to go on. On all auspicious occasions, when the zamindars trooped out from their rooms to meet the ryots and listen to their pleas, a brocade umbrella with a silver handle, called rajachhatra or royal umbrella, the symbol of claim to semi-royal authority, was held over the head of the seniormost person. I witnessed this charade for the last time shortly before the Partition of 1947 when we lost all we had. Few sights could have been more pathetic.

Our annual visit to Kirtipasha was quite an occasion. We had been taught that the town house where we spent some eleven months in the year was only a basha or nest, an abode for temporary shelter. The real home, bari, was the big house with palatial pretensions in the village of Kirtipasha where our family had lived for many generations. By the 1930s, the house was probably two hundred years old; some parts were probably older. The estate owned a somewhat luxurious 'green boat' plied by six oarsmen plus a helmsman. Despite such manpower, it moved very slowly taking some twenty-four hours to cover the sixteen miles from Barisal to the village. But it was a joyous ride. On our way we stopped at all sorts of places—fields growing cucumbers which we were free to pick and eat for a small or no payment, spots where the fishermen catching hilsa drew in their nets and, glory of glories, Shujar Kella or the mud 'castle' built by Prince Shuja, a fugitive from the fratricidal war for the Mughal throne, on his flight to Arakan where he was to meet his end. Nothing remained but a mound covered with grass, but climbing up that slope we had a sense of closeness to history. Aurangzeb's army was in hot pursuit: we could feel their breath on our neck.

The sight of hilsa nets being drawn was something else, the dark net shimmering with the silver-coloured fish struggling for their last breath. This was the only occasion when one could see the much favoured delicacy alive only for a few seconds, for the creature was delicate in every sense of the term. It survived outside water very briefly indeed. When we reached the narrow canal in our village, a reception committee of uncles, cousins, estate employees, etc., was waiting for us and we were greeted with joyous shouts of 'aiya gyachhe, aiya gyachhe' (they have come, they have come). Incidentally, the green boat with its luxury cabin had already gone out of use when we were children. Broken, discoloured, a ghost of its former self, it lay on its side on the bank of the canal where we used to land. It symbolized for me our own declining fortunes and our total ineptitude. No one ever thought of repairing it. Perhaps the estate also could no longer afford to retain the six oarsmen and one helmsman. After the green boat's demise, we travelled to Kirtipasha on hired boats called 'kosh'. The compartment covered with a bent bamboo roof had little space and we preferred to sit on its top rather than be cramped inside. The kosh had, however, one virtue. It moved faster, covering sixteen miles in as many hours at a mile an hour. That indeed was speed, relatively speaking.

The brief sojourn began with a visit to the bastu, the ancestral homestead, made of mud. We had to sit very properly, our legs covered with our dhotis, so that the holy water from the Ganges to be scattered in due course by the family priest did not fall on our feet, causing sacrilege. The same ritual was repeated when we left Kirtipasha. The last time we visited the village before leaving our home for good was a very painful occasion. My mother, a very strong woman, was weeping inconsolably and we shared her misery.

Our father, an uncompromising atheist, did not disregard the rituals. When the family priest asked us to bow down in honour of our departed ancestors, this atheist who had no faith in any life after death humbly did what he was asked to with a look of piety on his face. When I was old enough, I asked him to explain this contradiction in his conduct. He paid respect to a very moving system of belief, he said, not that he believed in it. The gesture of obeisance suddenly made the presence of the ancestors very real for him even though he knew for certain that they had long ceased to exist.

We entered the big house through the very long hall on the first floor. It had some oil paintings of our grandfather and his brothers, plus some other paintings depicting scenes from the Hindu mythology. They were in the style of Raja Ravi Varma. I am not sure if any of these were actually painted by him. There were also a few prints of European paintings, but none of these were in colour. The hall was furnished with marble furniture brought by my great-grandfather from Rajasthan. He had collected them on his restless journeys all over the subcontinent long before railways covered most parts of the country. They were brought into our canal, via Agra and the Ganges, on big seagoing boats, called bhars. Some very old men in the village remembered these occasions as indelible memories of their early childhood.

Besides the stone furniture, there was a row of bookshelves with glass doors containing books in several languages. Great-grandfather, Prasanna, was a Persian scholar trained by maulvis in Dacca. Knowledge of Persian was still a necessary component of a Bengali gentleman's upbringing in his days. There was one large bookshelf full of Persian books, some lithographed in Lucknow by Munshi Nawal Kishore; the rest were publications of the Asiatic Society in the Bibliotheca Indica series. Then there were shelves full of Sanskrit and Bengali books, mostly first editions published in the nineteenth century. These included the Sanskrit texts on Ayurveda in which one of my grand-uncles and later his son continued to take interest. Most of the shelves were stuffed with books in English, the great works of English literature, the Waverly novels, philosophical writings of Mill, Bentham, Hume and, in translation, the works of the French encyclopedists. There was also a set of Comte's works in the original which was later presented to the school named after Prasanna Sen, just to ensure, it seemed, that no one should read them. French was not a language on offer in the village school or known to many villagers. Besides, there were early editions of the *Encyclopedia Britannica* and a set of *Historians' History of the World*, pathetically tattered through long neglect.

Such high-minded stuff was adequately balanced by less improving reading matter like the *Mysteries of London Town*. These were prohibited reading, being considered pornography. That of course meant that we dipped into the volumes at the first opportunity. I was deeply disappointed. My feelings were similar when, much later, I tried to read the unreadable *Pearl*, the notorious Victorian pornographic magazine republished by an American university with a scholarly introduction. Who else would venture to do such a thing? The *Pearl* or the *Mysteries* would not excite a fifth former today. The repressed and easily excitable Victorian male was fortunate in this respect. They needed very little to titillate their appetites. Our jaded tastes have little to offer by comparison.

Two somewhat unexpected items were also located in the hall. In the closing years of the nineteenth century, an itinerant Englishman visited Kirtipasha with somewhat cumbrous equipment for photography. My enthusiastic grand-uncle, Rohini Sen, the eldest of the four brothers and the most famous member of the family, offered to learn the techniques involved and pay a fair amount for the service. This was too difficult an art for mere natives, he was told by the vagrant. Deeply offended, Rohini bought the required equipment from Calcutta, set up a darkroom and took pictures of everything and everyone within eyesight. A huge steel trunk in one corner of the hall contained thousands of his negatives. No one in the family, including his artist son, was interested in this strange hobby of the man. The negatives have perished through neglect, and thus a valuable source of Bengal's rural history has disappeared.

Close to the steel trunk containing Rohini Sen's photographic negatives were two more. These were filled with period costumes for amateur theatricals performed on the permanent stage facing the Durgadalan, the hall in the front courtyard where Durga and other deities were worshipped. Among the rooms downstairs there was one which served as the green room and also contained more of these costumes and weapons made of tin—a necessary part of the equipment for royalty and military characters appearing in the plays—besides sundry other objects needed for this very popular entertainment.

From the hall, one turned into an open corridor along a high wall separating the Barahisya building from its Chhotahisya counterpart.

A low door stood at the end of the wall. This was opened on festive occasions for purposes of communication with the Chhotahisya family, our kin as well as our enemy. Our mutual contact was modelled on that of the Pandavas and Kauravas except that we did not manage a grand war involving the entire subcontinent. On the happy occasions, there were formal exchanges of greeting which included close embraces and mutual gifts of sweets and snacks. Once these were over, our kinsmen returned to their house through the small door. If it happened to be a time when a battle royal was on between the two branches of the Kirtipasha family, on our kins' safe return home (there was never any question about that!) a steady shower of bricks and less acceptable stuff would begin to descend on us across the wall. The courtesy was duly returned. Any member of either family could have been killed by such fusillade.

The co-sharers had their quarters, two to three rooms per family, along the corridors at a slightly lower level. In the festive seasons hundreds of people from the neighbouring villages descended on the house and had a free tour of the place to see how the zamindars lived. Our lifestyle was pretty middle class and in no way spectacular, except for the chandeliers and marble furniture in the hall and a reception room where once music by great maestros from northern India and baijis, or professional women dancers, and vocalists from Benares and Lucknow entertained our forebears. By our time, these pleasures were no longer affordable.

But to the very poor visitors from the villages, our lifestyle was a matter for wonder. Fated to eat only soggy fermented rice called pantha bhat, with a bit of salt and chilli, dressed in threadbare clothes and sleeping on mud floors, they found the sight of four-posters, ladies dressed in silk sarees and men in fine dhotis, eating meals comprising many dishes off bell metal dishes or china, something incredibly marvellous. The rooms did not have doors or if they did, they were not closed during daytime. Curtains, meant to give us a minimum degree of privacy, were drawn aside by our visitors and we were not supposed to object. They watched the wonders they saw with a steady flow of accompanying comments.

'Have you seen her saree? It is shining like a hilsa fish.' (It did, because it was silk.)

'Look, look how many pots the babu has round his plate!' One, two, three, four, five—these were duly counted until they lost count, to my utter embarrassment. Sometimes the comments turned to our physical features. These were not always complimentary. 'He may be a zamindar's son, but his skin is dark like ours. Who knows how that happened? The mother is so fair!' A circumspect questioning of my legitimacy, and so on.

The estate offices, which also served as living quarters for some of the clerks, and the storerooms for the rent paid in kind and quantities of metal and stone utensils were all on the ground floor. These rooms, dark, squalid and very humid were somewhat scary for us children. Especially frightening were the andhariya kothas, the dark rooms where a variety of pre-modern weapons—swords, spears, clubs, javelins, shields, etc.—were kept. These rooms were once used to imprison recalcitrant ryots, some of whom never saw the light of the day again, or so whispered local tradition had it. Besides, these weapons were still in active use by the lathiyals, or club men, either in battles for land or when rent had to be collected by force from powerful tenants. The most grotesque symbol of extralegal power was a 'purpose-built' shoe, about a cubit and a quarter long, used to beat and thus humiliate the recalcitrant ryots who had been brought to the estate office especially for such purpose. In Bengal, a beating with a shoe is considered the ultimate humiliation. The memory of the long shoe endures in the folk songs of the region. Evidently, we are not remembered with a great deal of affection.

Yet, the zamindars' extralegal powers were often the only protection the ryots had. Nobody, I repeat, nobody trusted the police, and the courts were generally regarded as the high road to financial ruin which only the rich could afford. Hence both in disputes over land and in cases of criminal assault the estate offices were often the first, if not the only, port of call. I remember one occasion when a man with a ramda, a very large curved knife stuck in his skull, rushed into our hall and lay down on the large marble table. He had come to seek protection and justice. I do not know if his expectations were met. As land disputes were frequent, the estate offices and the zamindars were kept busy arbitrating disputes round the year. I have no idea as to the sort of justice they received, but at least they did not suffer total ruin which was the usual fate of those who sought redress in courts.

Ours was a Muslim-majority area and the majority of our tenants were Muslims. But even after some students from Aligarh came and planted the Muslim League flag in the village market and the Calcutta riots of 1946 had taken place, this dependence on the zamindars for rude justice persisted until the Partition. Besides, at night the guards, who were nearly all Muslims, took out the lethal weapons from the dark rooms when they did their rounds along the corridors. The doors to our rooms were rarely closed and their loyalty was never in question, even in the dark days after the first round of Hindu–Muslim riots in 1946–47.

The house had one peculiar feature. Basically two-storeyed and spread over two quadrangles, there was a single room on the terrace of the front quadrangle and another on top of it to be reached by a winding iron staircase. The top room with a wide vista opening before it was the one where we, the male cousins, gathered in the evening to have sessions of sing-song till the early hours of the morning. A word of explanation regarding Bengali kinship terms is perhaps necessary in order to avoid confusion. As my father had no brothers, all the male relations living in Kirtipasha were our cousins, if one used English kinship terms. But in Bengali usage, in fact according to the usage current throughout India, my father's cousins were our uncles, the only specification being that those older than him were jyathas and those younger, kakas. All older cousins belonging to our generation were dadas (elder brothers) and didis (elder sisters). In current 'President's English' the terms used are 'cousin brothers' and 'cousin sisters'. The terms dada and didi are shortened to 'da' and 'di'. Thus second cousin Kalu becomes Kalu-da and so on.

The single room on the wide terrace in the front quad was used by my grandfather and associated with many ghost stories. The one most endearing concerned a tamarind tree and its resident spirit. The Babus had ordered the tree to be cut down. But this had to be stopped, because two of my uncles then studying in London sent a telegram requesting that the tree be allowed to stand. Chhantu Pal, who had died recently, was living on it in his new identity as a Brahmadaitya, a Brahmin spirit, and appeared to them in a dream. This was obviously a ghostly miracle, because no way could the two young men know either about the order to cut the tree down or Chhantu's death. Their dream was evidence enough of the truth. The villagers celebrated their faith in honour of Chhantu. The Brahmin ghost acquired special sanctity by virtue of his visit to the imperial capital in the holy land inhabited by sahibs.

Of my two 'uncles' mentioned above, one was studying to qualify as a barrister and the other for an associateship of the Royal College of Arts. A third, to keep up with these two Joneses, went and probably trained to become a superior motor mechanic. I say 'probably', because his knowledge of relevant technology was not impressive. His own, very ancient car spluttered and stopped every few yards and he rarely succeeded to coax it back into motion. However, the barrister and the technician were two of the very few members of our family who earned their living by the sweat of their brow. The artist who took seven years to qualify returned to a life of leisure. He had specialized in portrait painting. But the one commission he had received from the maharaja of Mysore, he left unfinished. He found it too tiring—a tribute to the zamindari system which frowned upon all efforts to earn one's living through honest work. He was probably the only ARCA (Associate of the Royal College of Arts) who never painted a picture. Noblesse did not exactly oblige one to remain idle, but it surely approved.

I do believe that the Permanent Settlement of 1793 induced over time a permanent change in the outlook and attitude of the zamindars. Their forebears had to face the rough and tumble of either a commercial occupation or revenue collection and land management. Neither permitted a life of easy luxury. The latter was a gift of the Settlement. Financial security and total inaction produced a pervasive indifference to work ethic. Some of the zamindars actually considered the idea of earning infra dig. A few did emerge as patrons of literature and music, but very probably the majority were replicas of the ignorant country squires in England who really had no claims to distinction of any sort. I began to feel quite early in my life that this lot had no right to a livelihood sponging off other people's labour. Some of our cousins were very talented people. The eldest of them composed songs of some quality and did some very impressive translations from Kalidasa (in both English and Bengali) and Tagore (in English). He never tried to publish any of these. Three of them were skilled musicians, and when deprived of the income from the estate after 1947, managed to scrape a living in Calcutta by performing and teaching music. Excellence and resulting fame were well within their reach. But it never occurred to them to make the necessary effort.

The time spent in the company of our cousins during the festive season was, however, one of pure joy. On the sixth day of the bright fortnight in the month of Ashwin (September–October), when the sky had a very special tint of blue, the goddess appeared in the hall dedicated to her worship. One particular ritual brought her living presence into her clay image where she would stay the next four days. As our branch of the family were non-believers, this happening was not quite true for us. Yet, the literal faith of our cousins and the ladies had an overpowering effect. I often wondered if the goddess slaying the buffalo demon watched by her four children had not really come for a brief sojourn in our chapel. There were moments of terrifying excitement when animals were slaughtered as offerings to the goddess, but to be eaten by us in due course. The sight of poor goats being dragged to the scaffold and beheaded both fascinated and frightened me. The first time I saw the act, I developed high fever from the sheer shock of it. But the animal sacrifice was followed by sacrifice of vegetables, especially longish ones which could be easily 'beheaded'. The last item to be so offered on the bloodied mud pedestal was flowers. I watched this concluding act with a sense of profound relief. In the evening, there was arati or ritual dance and music with ear-splitting banging on huge drums. Kalu-da was an expert in the devotional dance, holding a clay pot full of burning incense either with his teeth or balanced on his head. We jumped around trying hopelessly to imitate his gracious style of worship. But these were unforgettable occasions, the highest of highs. No intoxicants were required.

The practice of buffalo sacrifice had been stopped in our family, but the Chhotahisya people continued it. I saw it once and that was more than enough. A strong man brought the buffalo to the scaffold single-handed. This was a prolonged action attended by very cruel torture to excite the animal until it was beheaded with one single blow of the huge bent knife, ramda. A deafening cheer with shouts invoking the Mother Goddess, 'Ma', 'Ma', went up. The truly devoted rolled in the bloody mud in a state of emotional intoxication. The act was a heady mixture of blood sport and extreme devotion. It was one of the many things which put me off ritualistic faith for good.

The puja was also the season for amateur theatricals on our permanent stage set up for the purpose. It had scenes painted in Western academic style, many of them the handiwork of Uncle Shital. Scenes from Mughal history were played against backgrounds of poplar-lined alleys and Swiss scenery. The plays were mostly historical; some drew upon our very rich mythology. My father, uncles, cousins and some of the more talented villagers dressed up for the various roles in extremely inappropriate costumes. The gods and goddesses were usually clothed in Elizabethan attire imported from Calcutta or further afield. That was OK since nobody knew the current fashion in paradise. There were tremendous battle scenes with noisy fire crackers booming in the background. The productions were excellent except that nobody had any sense of time. Eventually, only some of the most moving scenes were staged. Since everybody knew the story, it made no difference. These were indeed great occasions talked about for weeks afterwards.

Life in the village might lack excitement, but was in no way monotonous. The place was full of 'characters' whose ways could be perpetually amusing, though that was not the intention of the protagonists. Bihari Babu, a senior teacher in the school whom everybody addressed as 'Sir' because he had taught most of the villagers under the age of fifty at some point in time, was an extreme example. It was well known that he had acquired miraculous powers through his regular practice of yoga. These included the ability to fly. The truth of such facts could not be doubted because the information came straight from the horse's mouth and had been whispered by the horse himself as a great secret into the ears of a trusted few. The latter, of course, spread the good news at the earliest opportunity. In our 'adda' session beside the swimming pool one evening, headmaster Mahendra Datta asked Bihari Babu in a whisper, 'Did you go somewhere in the easterly direction yesterday night?' Bihari smiled mysteriously and responded, 'I had hoped no one would see me!'—implying that he had been on one of his secret flying missions. That evening he called on my father who was the secretary of the school and explained the stage he had reached in his acquisition of miraculous powers. It included the power to influence political developments. A little more hard work and he would have the power to make India free. An increment of five rupees in his monthly pay would give him the time required for this extra effort. The appeal to my father's nationalist sentiment proved fruitless. Failure to grant this measly increment delayed India's independence by several years.

In my boyhood and early youth I felt tied to my relations in the village by strong bonds of attachment. Back to Barisal after the festive season, I greatly missed their company and would write letters conveying my distress in the formal style appropriate in addressing 'elders' at the time. Mantu, who was older than me by six months and thus still an 'elder' according to generally accepted Bengali custom, replied with great gravity: 'Received your letter. Hope you are all well. Do accept my blessings. Thus, elder brother Mantu (Mantu-da), the bestower of said blessing.' At times, I would undertake the sixteen-mile-long journey on foot or bicycle. Often my companions were one of my Muslim classmates and a young English missionary at the Oxford Mission, Brother Catly, who spoke the Barisal patois with great fluency. He disdained the bicycle and preferred to walk the distance at four miles an hour or faster. The effort that this took did strain our friendship.

A major attraction in Kirtipasha was the superb food cooked by one of the great-aunts. The expected joy was so great that Catly would stop from time to time on our way and do a jig singing 'Aij thakumar ranna khamu!' ('We will eat food cooked by the grand-aunt today!') The grand-aunt in question was truly a wizard in the kitchen. As impressive as her cooking was her liberal outlook. In one corner of her largish room was a little 'shrine' with a small image of her favoured deity. In another, she had her chulli, oven, and we—a Hindu, a Muslim and a Christian—sat near it and devoured the delicacies she offered. The violation of the laws of pollution did not seem to bother her one bit.

The said grand-aunt was psychic and had a stock of blood-curdling ghost stories. She was the second wife of one of my grand uncles. The daughter of a very poor but genteel family, her widowed mother had readily agreed to marry her off to the local zamindar, older than her by several decades. One afternoon, according to my grand-aunt, she saw a well-dressed lady appear out of nowhere and congratulate her on her engagement. The words were followed by an act: the lady put some vermilion in the parting of her hair, the traditional sign of a married Hindu lady, wished her well and disappeared. When she went to live in the zamindar's house, she saw a photograph of her dead co-wife; the latter was the same person as the gracious lady who had visited her.

My grand-aunt, widowed in her youth with two children, was a victim of many misfortunes. After Partition, she had to leave Kirtipasha and spend her last days in a one-room flat in Calcutta with her son and his family. Her daughter, who had been married to a handsome young doctor, was abandoned by her husband who kept custody of their son. This son became insane and, eventually, so did she. Grand-aunt lived to see and suffer all these.

Only a small section of the refugees from East Bengal were really rehabilitated and regained a life of reasonable comfort in post-independence India. The majority were not so lucky. Some of our cousins who lived in Kirtipasha were among the less fortunate. Kalu-da, who had so many skills and was highly entertaining company, had great faith in the durability of our family's greatness and good fortune. His confidence in our prowess was certainly a shade exaggerated. A couple of months before the Partition, we cousins were having a typical Bengali adda around the large marble table in the hall. Adda is too Bengali a concept for the term to be translated into any other language. A chat-cum-gossip session is its closest description in English that I can think of. On the occasion in question, the emotional ambience was somewhat gloomy: we all knew that we were going to be dispossessed very soon. Kalu-da was, however, undaunted. 'Still,' he announced with some pride, 'if somebody farts in the Barahisya palace the entire village of Kirtipasha shakes in awe and apprehension.'

'Those days are over,' his elder Manu-da sadly commented with a sigh. I do not know when that happy time was in, but certainly it had left no vestiges.

Kalu-da migrated to Calcutta. He was among the refugees who forcibly occupied land belonging to developers and created shanty towns with their own hands. Several years later, I met Kalu-da at a family wedding. I tried to touch his feet as was the custom, an expression of regard from a junior to a senior relation. He shrank in horror. I shall never forget the look of utter defeat and consternation in his face. Living in a self-built hovel in a shanty town, this scion of a zamindar family had fallen from his class and hence the old rules no longer applied where he was concerned. Well, at least he had not been reduced to begging by the roadside. Some of our relations, whom I had once seen living in very considerable material comfort, were.

The zamindars as a class had once been very prominent in the social life of Bengal. In East Bengal, now Bangladesh, no vestige of this class has survived. Not a single person is left there representing the occupation or lifestyle of zamindars. Here was a social revolution which no one has bothered to chronicle. I think of myself as a member of an extinct species.

5

A Taste of the Sea: Cox's Bazaar

The Bengali middle class had discovered a new mode of pleasure-seeking, probably in the second half of the nineteenth century. In a certain season of the year, they started migrating to healthy places in the hilly and forested regions of the neighbouring province Bihar or to hill stations in their own province like Darjeeling, Kalimpong and Kurseong. A third choice, probably supported by the older practice of pilgrimage, showed some preference for seaside places like Puri, the seat of Jagannath. The practice may have had something to do with the spread of the anti-idolatrous reform movement, Brahmoism. Its real founder, Devendranath Tagore, escaped to the Himalayas when his Hindu relations and other benighted Bengalis celebrated the worship of the ten-handed Mother Goddess, Durga. The noise generated by that celebration was intolerable to the average human ears. It still is. The resulting propensity to migrate temporarily was further enhanced by the then popular medical belief that a 'change of air' helped with the cure of most ailments which afflict our species. In Anglo-Bengali, these seasonal withdrawals hence came to be known as 'going for a change'. It also became a status symbol: not everyone could afford this minor luxury.

In the category of places where one could 'go for a change' was the seaside town of Cox's Bazaar. One Mr Cox was the alleged founder of this semi-rural township on the Bay of Bengal in the district of Chittagong. I remember it as a place of exquisite beauty which has been effectively destroyed by the tourist trade in recent years. I last visited it in 1974 when the place was still suffering from the ravages of the war for the independence of Bangladesh and have no desire to return. The places for 'change' most favoured by my parents were, in that order, Cox's Bazaar, Shillong, now in Meghalaya, Kurseong and Benares. The holy city where we had gone by boat was a part of our family mythology. A sudden flood had nearly drowned the boat and killed the entire family. This is a story I had heard over and over again from Joti. The other mythical place was Shillong with its very green slopes, rhododendron forests and grandiflora magnolia trees with their large and beautiful flowers. Out of this brief list of places for change favoured by my parents, Cox's Bazaar and Kurseong are the only ones I actually saw in my childhood. For me that memory remains pure magic.

Very probably, the small rural town was once known as Roshang, the capital of the Arakanese kingdom. The ethnically Tibeto-Burman population are called Maghs, best known to Anglo-India for producing some of the finest cooks in the country. The Maghs are remembered in Bengal as pirates and slave dealers who, along with the Portuguese, devastated and depopulated a large area in southern Bengal now known to the world as the rainforest of Sundarbans, the home of the Royal Bengal tiger.

The Magh kings belonged to a hybrid religious tradition of Buddhists and Muslims at the same time. Their brand of Buddhism had some unusual features. During the fratricidal war for the Mughal throne, Prince Shuja fled to Arakan, tried unsuccessfully to seize the kingdom and got killed for his pains. The female members of the family were starved to death because the Blessed One, the Buddhist Arakanese believed, had asked them not to shed women's blood. Apparently, the Master had no objection to shedding male blood or so the Maghs understood his message. Given their general love of violence this was a considerable concession to the Buddha's preference for ahimsa, non-violence. But all this was some four hundred years

A Taste of the Sea: Cox's Bazaar

before our visit to Cox's Bazaar. By our time, pax Britannica had triumphed in that seaside town. Mr Cox had represented that pax and helped create this small resort by the sea.

The place had no harbour. We cast anchor at a point within reasonable distance from the shore where we climbed down a ladder from our steamship into gaily painted boats called shampans rowed by Magh boatsmen, dressed in equally bright-coloured lungis. This was my first encounter with people who were not Bengalis. Of course, one had seen white men and women—sahibs and memsahibs; but everybody knew that they were our rulers, like it or not, and so they did not really count. But Maghs! Great-grandchildren of pirates and slave dealers! They were rather fierce-looking! Would Jagadishya, Kalu-da, Mantu-da et al. believe that I had actually seen such humans? And then, of course, there was the sea. I had seen pictures of it in the illustrations of *Children's Ramayana*—Rama, bow in hand, conquering a turbulent sea. With Joti's aid, I had re-enacted that scene in our river often enough. But this was a somewhat different matter. The waves were too high for comfort and, unlike the river, the sea had no shore. But the water! Green near the shore and a deep blue further away. What bliss!

I was carried ashore on Noga's shoulder. New wonders awaited me there. Every wave brought with it a fantastic variety of shells for us to collect. What were those myriad red flowers which sprang into life and scrambled into the sand as we came near? Red crabs! How incredible and beautiful. Whoever thought that living creatures could be such a deep red in colour! And the sand dunes! What marvellously soft slopes for me to roll down! I soon learnt to climb them, equating my heroic effort with that of Mallory and Irvine. I discovered later that the sand dunes were not steady fixtures and could move to some other place overnight. This enhanced their wondrous nature. Then there was the other miracle of the receding sea water; it left behind little pools where one could catch a variety of small fish using a towel as one's net. The detritus brought by the surf also included a variety of sea creatures—jellyfish of many different sizes, translucent yet shot with different pastel shades, starfish and less attractive/more frightening creatures like the octopus and sea tortoises with a pointed hard sting sticking out of its bottom. No, I would definitely not like to encounter one of them in the water. Besides, I had heard of sharks. The sea, for certain, was not my place. But there were the little pools left behind by the receding sea. My practice trials, prelude to conquering the turbulent sea in Rama's footsteps, were carried out in these pools. At worst, the water, nearly three feet deep, would reach my neck.

Noga put me down from his shoulder when we reached a row of bungalows made of wood. This too was something new. An entire house made of wood! Will the wind blow it away? Noga said that was unlikely. I was not so sure.

Uncle Shital had accompanied us this time. That fact ensured an enjoyable time. He accompanied us every day both in our ventures by the sea and on window-shopping expeditions to the local market area. The last statement is somewhat inaccurate. Cox's Bazaar had neither permanent market area nor any shops to speak of. There were weekly 'haats' or mini-fairs where the locals from the neighbouring villages brought their wares. The one permanent feature beside such temporary phenomena was the kyang or Buddhist pagoda made of wood. The Magh priests called fungis, dressed in yellow, were the Buddha's servitors. A series of wooden statues represented the Buddha and the Bodhisatvas, or the Enlightened One in his previous incarnations before he had achieved enlightenment. My moment of glory came when the statues were given their ritual bath to the accompaniment of a chant which sounded like 'Om om om om'. As priests of an open-access egalitarian faith, the fungis allowed us to take part in the ceremony and pour water on the statues chanting as best as we could. Back home, the scene was re-enacted. Only, this time I took the place of the Bodhisatvas with Noga as my servitor. What bliss!

Visits to the weekly fair in the company of Uncle Shital were a treat. There was not much we could buy. Only, Uncle Shital consistently ignored our parents' proscription of locally produced candies and dried fruit. They regarded these as a short and sure route to cholera.

But not Uncle Shital. To him most parental restrictions imposed on children were modern superstitions invented by brainless sahibs in order to enhance the already heavy burden of misery suffered by their subjects. As a doctor, he knew. Looking back, I do believe that he was right, for we never fell ill in Cox's Bazaar and I, for one, happen to be still alive. One reason for our survival, however, was the inedibility of these local snacks. We spat them out whenever we thought Uncle Shital was not looking. But in truth he always was. This was evident from his brief and contemptuous comment: 'idiots' eggs'. Some items on offer for sale looked tempting. Chief among these were the beautiful lungis. Shital disallowed this with his all-encompassing comment, 'idiot's eggs', and promptly proceeded to buy one for himself. But when we woke up from our afternoon nap, the idiots' eggs found that two beautifully wrapped lungis had turned up near their pillows! Mysterious were the ways of Uncle Shital.

The visits to the weekly market turned into a grand occasion one morning. Under a pipul tree sat a woman vendor. Her wares included some very shiny and multicoloured objects. 'You know what they are?' demanded Uncle Shital. 'Diamond sticks!' he continued, without waiting for an answer.

'Rubbish,' said my cynical brother, 'They are made of iron and wrapped in coloured wires.'

'Idiot's egg!' commented Uncle and asked the vendor to wrap up one.

'What about me?' asked my agitated brother.

'What will you do with a mere iron stick?'

The poor chap burst into tears. Uncle bought one more stick, but his manner remained theatrically grim and disapproving. We returned home with these symbols of pride and glory. Years later, the day we were permanently leaving home for India, I saw that iron stick lying in a corner, its lustrous covering of coloured wires gone. Somehow in our new situation, I felt a sense of affinity with that pathetic-looking object. Like the Barahisya family, the diamond stick had been shown up for what it really was—something insignificant wrapped up in vainglory.

One morning we found standing at our door a seriously dilapidated car. It had arrived to take us to Himjhara, a forest resort famous for its wildfowl and pigs. Their presence had excited my father's hunting instinct. We picked up our modest luggage for a weekend stay and father, of course, took his gun with him. The car started but it seemed unlikely that it would get anywhere. By some miracle, it did—with a lot of stutter and splutter, covering the distance of a few miles in as many hours. It was evening and the fairly dense forest looked both mysterious and menacing. My father picked up his gun and said that he would go out for a stroll. 'Nothing of the sort', mother pronounced in a grim voice and that was that. The wild boars were supremely delicious on the table. But they had long sharp tuskers. The business in question was dicey: one could both kill and get killed. My mother did not fancy following in her mother's footsteps—being widowed in her twenties with two children to look after.

The forest looked familiar. I had, in fact, encountered it in the story of Ramayana and expected the ogres or rakshasas to step any moment out of the menacing darkness. The situation was quite hopeless. Neither Ram nor Lakshman was around. I myself had left my somewhat ineffective bows and arrows in Barisal. Could we make a fast escape by our car? It would be a very strange rakshasa that could not run faster than that unworthy scion of the automobile family. I went to bed with no hope of seeing daylight again. By some miracle, I did. And it was indeed a wondrous sight. Sunshine was seeping through the dense greenery. So many brightly coloured birds, especially green parrots, flew about in huge numbers. And what beautiful flowering trees! Why couldn't we stay on in this lovely place forever? The rakshasas had, after all, proved to be inoffensive. So what was there to stop us? I had already noticed that the grown-ups singularly lacked good sense and hence there was nothing to hope for.

Years later, on my visit to newly independent Bangladesh, I saw a locally produced film based on Bengali fairy tales. I instantly recognized that the ogre of the story was a resident of Himjhara. This was fine, except that the ambience was a bit disturbed when a huge truck momentarily hid him from our view—the coexistence of the modern and the mythical really did not work.

Our ineffective chariot did manage to take us to a charming waterfall in the depths of the forest. Father, impetuous as ever, jumped into its freezing water and proposed that we should join him. 'I have no wish to see my children freeze to death,' our mother declared with a determined expression on her face. Father had a mischievous look in his eyes.

'Then you better come,' he said and pulled her into that bubbling water. My mother shrieked with the shock of it and then added, 'Uncle had to give me in marriage to a total lunatic!' I still remember her look of ecstatic happiness. In her life, there was really only one person, her husband. I later used to think that she would have happily offered us as kebabs if her husband so wished. Who says that arranged child marriages did not work? She was ten and my father eighteen when they got married. That was a couple of decades after the passing of the Age of Consent Bill into law. Nobody seemed to take any notice.

On our last evening at Himjhara, I had a traumatic experience. It was not yet dark and the forest was suffused with a golden yellow light of supernatural beauty. A strong piercing sound suddenly rang through the forest. On a tree facing our bungalow sat a junglefowl. Its multicoloured feather shone like burnished gold. It sat with its chest puffed out, a proud monarch of the wild landscape. It was perhaps the most beautiful living thing I had seen in my short life. My father took up his gun and shot at it. A cry of anger and pain filled the entire space as the fowl flew away, wounded. We could hear that sound until the bird reached a fair distance. The echo rang through the forest for a while longer. I felt a wild anger against my father and started hitting him. That night I developed high fever which nearly killed me. My father never picked up a gun again.

Just before we left Cox's Bazaar, I was a participant in a very solemn ritual. One morning, when we woke up we were given an early bath and dressed up in khadi, the homespun which Gandhi had made the uniform of Indian nationalism. Father, who always wore khadi, had put on a Gandhi cap. Noga, as an accredited martyr in the cause, was strutting about, proud and defiant, in full nationalist gear. We all sat down on the portico of our bungalow and mother sang the anthem, *'Bandemataram'* and then another patriotic song, *'Balo balo balo sabe, shata bina benu rabe, Bharat abar jagat sabhay shreshtha asan labe'*. (Come and say it with pride, through a multitude of veenas and flutes, once again will India take her place of glory when the nations of the world meet.) Noga shouted *Bandemataram* and *Gandhiji ki jai* (Victory to Gandhiji). We set out for the seashore with pots and pans. There were a few other families gathered there. We took out some water from the sea and boiled it on a makeshift fire. The water dried up, leaving a small quantity of dirty looking residue which was salt. Noga again shouted his slogans. We had broken the evil Salt Act of the tyrannical British, my eight-year-old brother explained very proudly. A couple of policemen stood in the distance, looking at what was going on, without interest. Evidently, they were under instructions not to interfere. I learnt much later that at that very moment, a couple of thousand miles away, Mahatma Gandhi was making history at the end of his famous Dandi march. I, a totally ignorant child of four, had been sucked into the vortex of history though I had no clue as to what was going on.

A respected colleague commented incredulously on this episode which he saw as a claim to induction into the freedom movement at age four. No, I did not seek martyrdom as a four-year-old. Our father took us along to see what was going on, secure in the knowledge that the local authorities were not going to interfere. What I saw did only one thing for me—it gave me a sense of belonging to something very large that was going on, something related to Gandhi, the very great man who was to us what God is to most people.

6

Pains of Exile

My formal education began rather late for a Bengali child of our social class. It started with an ego-enhancing ceremony. I, of course, had to wear the gear appropriate for the occasion—a mini version of the adult dhoti and kurta or punjabi (so described presumably because this long loose shirt without collars had come from Punjab). As the occasion was sacred and dedicated to the goddess of learning—Saraswati, seated on her white swan—the dhoti was coloured a bright yellow, using the dried stems of her favourite flower, parijat or shefali, the name by which it was known to Bengalis. The family priest offered a prayer to the goddess and I bowed before her, though I already knew that no such being existed. A feeling of awe and sanctity filled my soul as I bowed. I prayed for her blessing and wished that she should never leave me. I had been brainwashed into believing that I would be her servant the rest of my life. I wished for nothing better. I still do not.

The priest made me write the letters of the Bengali alphabet with a shapeless piece of chalk on a thali made of black stone. From this initial discipline I graduated to writing on dried strips of palm frond, the traditional material on which books were written before the advent of paper in India. Even after that, the texts in Sanskrit and the local languages continued to be written on talpatra or palm frond, until printing made its appearance in India. The letters were dug out on this material with iron nails and I was made to practise writing on these with a quill pen until I was confident enough to write without such aid. Alongside such traditional instruction, I started reading my first book in English; learning English words and their meaning in Bengali. The word which fascinated me was 'ham'. It was translated in Bengali as 'shukarer labanakta shushka mangsa'—the dried and salted meat from a pig. I could not visualize the object but rejoiced in shouting out the description mainly because our more orthodox relations found it truly revolting: it was my first gesture of defiance against tradition, much of which was already more revolting to me than any dried and salted meat of pigs. Juran Babu who used to carry me to the riverside on his shoulders and promised to buy me a puppy and a lamb, was now my mentor for the English lessons, because my father had contacted some mysterious illness and was in no condition to look after my education.

That illness, which was eventually diagnosed as typhoid, was to be the source of multiple miseries for me. It was soon decided that we had to go to Calcutta for treatment. The news came to us, the two brothers, like a thunderbolt. How could we leave Barisal where we had all our friends, Uncle Bhuiya and his family, the two horses and the cows and Mena and Hashmatali? I had a brief experience at age five of that ghastly place, Calcutta, with its numberless buildings, fast-moving cars and millions of people not one of whom cared for me in the least. My father had taken me there to have my teeth extracted because over-consumption of sweets, encouraged by my doting grandfather, had led to pyorrhoea. I stayed with my aunt and uncle, Kiran Shankar Roy. Their very large house made of red brick, located in that strangely named street, European Asylum Lane, intimidated me.

The said Europeans who needed to be housed in asylums were subjects of the nationalist discourse in the nineteenth century. They were maintained from the Indian revenue and this, it was claimed, was an unfair burden on poverty-stricken India. That they had lost their sanity in the service of India was the official reply. Most people would.

My cousins found me very amusing because I was a yokel gawping without pleasure at everything I saw. There had been, however, moments of real wonderment, for instance when I went up an elevator to the dentist's chamber. How incredible! An entire room moving up and down! Nobody would believe me back in Barisal if I tried to tell them about it. I returned in triumph from the dentist's because the pain I had feared did not materialize, thanks to the anaesthetic. I truthfully told my cousins that I had not cried and was treated as a hero, even though I was considered abysmally stupid. But my moment of glory was short-lived. In the evening my father took me and my cousins to see an English film. Of course, I did not understand a word, but the sight and sound of pictures moving about on the screen and talking was compensation enough. In the interval we went to the brasserie and father ordered some ice cream for us. It came in shining white metal cups and the fragrance of vanilla ice was deliciously overpowering. This was my moment of bliss. But wait. I took a spoonful and the subzero temperature of the sweet hit my raw gums like fire. The resulting screams reached decibels which qualified it to be recorded in the Guinness Book of Records. My cousins burst out laughing. I had never known so much humiliation in my short life. Calcutta remained for me the city of my fall from grace. And now, we were to go and live there God knows for how long.

Here a social-historical note would be in order. The traditional Bengali looked upon his native village as his own country, 'swadesh'. Any place beyond its borders was foreign territory, 'bidesh'. The writer of the first autobiography in the Bengali language, Kartikeya Chandra Ray, records his sense of misery and alienation when he had to go 'abroad', to the city of Krishnagar, twenty miles from his native village. If I had read this when we were leaving for Calcutta, I would have understood perfectly the author's sense of total loss. I cried the whole time and was quite inconsolable. My brother tried to console me: he had already worked out how we would escape from Calcutta and how everybody in Barisal would be mightily surprised to see us back. He was a believer in forward planning. Only the plans did not usually work, had strong antisocial overtones and led to bouts of thrashing when they failed. But I wished desperately to believe in his plans because there was nowhere else I could look for comfort.

The evil day of departure eventually dawned. My brother seemed quite happy on the steamer. He was a lover of good food and, in the steamer's well-appointed dining room, tucked into the famous chicken curry of the Dacca–Barisal steamers with evident relish. As a person still averse to all food which was usually thrust on me by Joti, these were pleasures I was still to discover. We reached Sealdah station where my uncle Kiran Shankar Roy had come to meet us and take us to our rented house in south Calcutta. The journey was sheer misery. The dingy lanes, houses with discoloured walls closely huddled together, the hundreds of cars running at what seemed to me incredible speeds and, above all, the people, thousands upon thousands of them, filled me with a sense of profound revulsion and fear.

The house where we settled down for our sojourn faced a park. The only park I had known until then was Bell's Park in Barisal, named after Mr Bell, the collector famous in the district for his unforgettable forays into the Bengali language. His famous habit was to collect Bengali swear words and hurl them at his underlings, of which more later. It was a very green place which became all the more attractive on winter mornings when the race horses had their steaming haunches massaged by their attendants. The Kalighat Park, by contrast, was a miserable patch of scruffy land surrounded by dilapidated iron railings. There were a few swings and slides. These were inaccessible to us, thanks to hordes of scruffy and menacing children. Bawsha's brave attempts to establish our share of citizens' rights provoked serious aggression and for once in his life, the undersized hero found it wiser to beat a retreat. The atmosphere at home was stifling. We were not allowed into our father's room. Everybody spoke in whispers. That the menace of an unspoken and unspeakable threat hung over the family was evident even to us, the children. Once in a while, we were allowed into our father's sick chamber. His eyes were bloodshot and his face unshaven. He was not the handsome debonair person I loved so much. It was no pleasure being in his presence.

The one relief was the presence of Uncle Shital. He bought us the usual forbidden snacks and drinks and took us sight-seeing to the zoo, the museum, the Victoria Memorial and even to the famous Jain temple which was very far from our house. But he too had stopped joking and teasing us in his usual style. One day a very tall gentleman in a dhoti and shirt came to see father. This was B.C. Roy, the famous doctor, we were told. He came and left without saying much. Everybody looked even more anxious than before.

Then one day Uncle Shital came and called us into our father's room. 'Come, you idiots' eggs,' he pronounced. We knew that the worst was over. Father asked us to come near him and hugged us. I felt as if a great cloud had lifted and sunshine was breaking through.

But for us, the two boys, the worst was not really over. One of my father's cousins lived next door. He brought us ominous news. There was an outbreak of smallpox in the city. This item of information had little meaning for us. But the one that followed certainly did. We all had to have inoculation and a doctor from the corporation's local office was on his way to do what was necessary. We had probably had inoculation before this, but somehow this was not a part of our memory. Yet we knew enough about this menace and saw in it life-threatening possibilities.

My elder brother, always the man of action, went into his planning mode. We had to escape. It was a question of life and death. But how? That was simple. We just had to dress down and put on the gear of sanyasis, holy men and go out through the back door. But we had no saffron clothes! Not necessary. It was enough to go out in our undergarments. The best sanyasis wore nothing at all. But they smeared their bodies with ash. Well, we had a coal shed. Coal dust would have to do. This was a miserable prospect. Two child sanyasis in their undergarments, their bodies smeared with coal dust, begging in the streets of Calcutta! Would there be enough to eat? I liked my thin arrowroot biscuits with my ovaltine in the morning. Who would give me those biscuits as alms? Or ovaltine for that matter? We lacked even proper begging bowls. Besides, there were other dangers. Calcutta streets were full of kidnappers who broke the arms and legs of kidnapped children before setting them up to beg by the roadside. Some were sold to the tea plantations where they were regularly whipped as the sahibs watched while having their chhota hajri, that is, breakfast. Whoever knew that I, a son of the Barahisya family, was born for such a fate! Tears of self-pity rolled down my cheeks. Meanwhile, the man of action had dressed down as planned. I joined him in the coal shed and smeared coal dust all over my body. Soon there was a hullabaloo in the house. Where were the boys? Joti, always inclined to take a gloomy if dramatic view of things, quickly decided that we had been kidnapped. A piercing lament rent the air. 'They are gone! They will be killed! Perhaps they are dead already.' It is impossible to describe in words the sheer torture of that wail. Uncle Shital asked her to stop howling and with his knowledge of child psychology guessed exactly what had happened. He came straight to the coal shed and dragged us out by our ears. A huge guffaw went up when we were presented to the public in our sanyasi's gear. The inoculation hardly mattered after that inglorious end to our brief venture into Hindu spirituality.

But better days were indeed about to dawn. Dr B.C. Roy prescribed a 'change of air', that unfailing panacea for Bengali ill health, to help with father's convalescence. Kurseong, a minor hill station in the Himalayas, was chosen for this purpose, partly because Uncle Kiran Shankar offered their house in that town for our stay.

We reached Kurseong by the famous toy train. Again, here was a house made of wood, still something to wonder at. The round pillars on the portico were unbelievably cold. In fact, I had never been to a place so cold before this. But there were compensations. Straight in front of our house was Kanchenjunga, its snow-clad top dazzling white in the bright summer sunshine. It hurt your eyes if you tried to look at it straight. The gardener's son was a mine of information about everything local. He picked up a handful of dust and showed me how it sparkled. What were those shining bits in the dust? Mica, he explained. Mica? To be found on the road just like that? Wonders really never ceased! And those delicious roots he picked up from underground! Then the orange-coloured wild strawberries! Every Hindu child knew that the Himalayas were the place where God Shiva lived with his family. And for that reason, it was the favoured haunt of the sadhus who lived off fruits and roots. Well, if they were so tasty, who wanted to eat the insipid rice and dal, especially the thorny fish full of bones? I decided on my future career on the spot. I would be a sadhu when I grew up and live in the gorgeous Himalayas. That at least would save me from living in that horrid city, Calcutta, where most people seemed to go and work for a living. Nourished by roots and fruits I would, in due course, become a pot-bellied sadhu worshipped by thousands of devotees. No work and a lot of sweets offered daily by the disciples. What joy!

The sojourn in Kurseong was not risk-free. It was summer and occasionally the bears came up from the Terai looking for cool weather, our gardener informed us. It was safer to stay indoors after dark, he said. This fired the imagination of Uncle Shital and my father.

'I have never encountered a wild bear,' my father commented sotto voce, trying to make sure that my mother was not within earshot.

'Nor are you going to,' came a cryptic comment from the living room.

My mother never failed to remind him that after the arrival of my sister, there were three kids to bring up and the responsibility was partly his. But it never occurred to him or Uncle Shital that their survival till that date was partly due to the fact that wild bears also had not encountered them. This highly relevant fact was quietly ignored. Their return home from their afternoon stroll was increasingly at an hour by which time any wild bear worth the name could be expected to hit the dark streets of Kurseong. My mother gave up. One afternoon Shital offered to take us for a stroll. My mother pulled the end of the saree covering her head further forward as was appropriate when addressing an elder relation and quietly said, 'Shital-da, please don't take the boys to meet the wild bear.'

'Am I mad?' asked uncle in righteous horror. My mother had her ideas on this question, but thought it better to keep them to herself.

As usual, the first lap of our walk took us to the station where one shop sold luridly bright-coloured sweets which were strictly taboo for us.

'Idiot's eggs,' said uncle with reference to my parents and their stupid prohibitions and promptly brought us some of the scarlet and poisonously green stuff. They tasted like stewed armpit and the ghastly taste long lingered on our palate though we spat out the sweets from hell after keeping these in our mouth for only a split second. Well, we had hankered after them. It is for such occasions that poet Tagore famously wrote, 'What we wish for, we do through error, what we get we do not want.'

Now, on to the next adventure. It was already dark and we duly lost our way. This meant an extra couple of miles up and down the hilly road. Then it happened. In the distance we saw a creature the size of a large dog and very hairy. That is all that we could be sure of in the darkness. 'What is that?' we asked uncle in some trepidation. 'Probably a bear,' he answered with evident satisfaction.

'Probably a bear!' my brother whimpered, 'What will happen to us?'

'What do you think this stick is for, you idiot's egg?' Uncle responded with mock anger. We did not share his confidence in that walking stick. The animal came closer. It turned out to be a dog, probably a cross between a Retriever and a Great Dane. Thus, the efficacy of Uncle Shital's stick was not tested.

Back in Calcutta, worse news was waiting for us. Father was now in reasonable health and had decided that we would stay on in Calcutta for some years for our education. Did not Barisal have perfectly decent schools, in fact some that were quite famous? But nobody took any notice of our tears and we were duly admitted to Jagadbandhu School which was not very far from our house. It was a modest place. The teachers were kind and conscientious. I felt very happy there. Among the textbooks we had to read was one on how to keep good health. Its various advice included a chapter on how to keep one's clothes clean. The reader was instructed to wash the clothing every day with soda ash (soap was too expensive), dry them in the sun and then, neatly folded, place them under the pillow when going to bed. There were no references to ironing or any other alien practice. It occurred to me that our teachers had kept their dhotis and kurtas under their pillows the night before as instructed and put them on before coming to school. When they went home they would take in the clothes hung out for drying and the whole process would be repeated.

The most famous man among our teachers was our physical instructor, Jaga Shil, renowned for his skill as a boxer. He ran special classes in the evening for aspiring boxers and we watched the aspirants breathing fiercely while boxing. On our return home we tried to emulate their noble example, especially their fierce breathing. The highest object in life, it seemed to us, was to reduce all humans to pulp with heavy doses of boxing. Jaga Shil encouraged all the boys to acquire copies of his famous guide to good health, *Sharir Samlao*, translated as, 'Protect your body'. Nothing was neglected in this masterpiece. One chapter was entitled 'Ek nishwase malatyag', that is, 'Defecating at one go'. The end product of that noble effort was described with affection and scientific objectivity. The section on ideal crap read like Pater at his aesthetic best. The beauty, as we all know, is in the eye of the beholder.

During this happy time, my father had one of his escapades for which, according to my mother, he had a congenital penchant. She attributed this to genetic factors: his mother's family were noted for their eccentricities. On this occasion, however, the primary responsibility was not his. My youngest maternal uncle, the one who owned trucks, visited us from Comilla and father picked up from him the idea that procuring chicken from that city for the Calcutta market might prove to be lucrative. The uncle was a man of action. Without waiting for any further instruction from my father, he sent one thousand chickens for an experimental try. As there was not enough space for these winged visitors in our bed- or living rooms, they were kept on the flat roof of our flat. It is not clear if the agreement for renting the flat gave us the right to keep chickens on the roof, but what happened next was surely not covered by the said agreement. The chicken escaped and roamed freely in the rooms and kitchen of our Brahmin landlord for whom they were ritually polluting. Any contact with these bipeds was defiling, a threat to his twice-born status in this life and hereafter. In utter desperation the fellow began to scream. He regretted his fateful error in renting out the flat to a zamindar from East Bengal. The world knew of their profligate ways. The unholy chickens were the first violation of Hindu decency. Others would soon follow. Wine you know, and then the associated evils, wink, wink. His life as a sound-living twice-born was over. What would the ancestors in heaven say? He had lost his right to offer them food and drink. The man sounded as if the ten plagues of Egypt and all the misfortunes of Job had hit him simultaneously. Life in that flat became intolerable. Father somehow managed to get rid of the chickens at a loss. We had to move out to another rented accommodation. This time it was a bungalow, next to Uncle Shital's house near the new lakes. At last there was a silver lining to the miseries of living in Calcutta.

But wait. My father was one of those people who were never satisfied with anything merely good. Their eternal quest was for something better. As a part of that quest, he decided that Ballygunge Government High School was preferable to Jagadbandhu and thither we must move. Jagadbandhu had been a source of some comfort amidst the multiple miseries of Calcutta life. Now that respite was no longer to be a part of our vie quotidienne.

The new school was a much grander place. Some of the students were even grander than the school. Quite a few among the teachers came 'suited and booted', as we say in Anglo-Bengali. Those who came in Indian attire certainly did not wash their dhoti and kurta in soda ash, nor use their pillows as a substitute for ironing. The place was posh, to put it briefly. My persona as a country yokel felt both uneasy and revolted at the same time. Some of the students came in big cars and spoke fluent English. Their noses were most certainly in the air. One of these golden youth was Lord Sinha's grandson. He was famous for his recitations from Shakespeare. The students in the senior classes went near the school wall to smoke cigarettes, a practice which was supposed to be strictly prohibited. They were, I was given to understand, sons of Calcutta's wealthier citizens, professionally successful men or senior executives in the corporate sector. If they violated rules, teachers, it appeared, preferred to look the other way. A few belonged to the families of rajas and maharajas. Schoolboys can be terrible snobs and as the son of a mere zamindar from the countryside or mofussil, I felt quite inadequate.

One day I had a conversation with a fellow student which, looking back, seems priceless.

'Do you eat porridge?' he asked with a sneer. I was totally mystified. Eating porridge was one of the crosses I had to bear, a misfortune I attributed to multiple sins committed in previous lives and my grandfather's preference for Western habits.

'Yes,' I answered, 'but what a strange question to ask!'

Now he sneered with even greater contempt. 'You are fibbing,' he said. 'Bangals (people from East Bengal; the word also has a pejorative implication connoting a gormless yokel) eat muri (puffed rice) and panta bhat (fermented rice), not porridge. Porridge is consumed by people like us!'

'Of course I love muri and panta bhat', I responded. Now he looked satisfied.

'At last you are telling the truth. Why were you claiming that you ate porridge?'

I realized with a sense of shock that in this chap's world, the indigenous snacks could not coexist with the noble porridge. This curious dialogue began to make sense. Porridge was the food of Englishmen who were our rulers. Their Bengali imitators, as consumers of the same food, were thereby ennobled to the status of servants to the English. What greater honour could one wish for? This class of people who rejoiced in imitating the English were known to the average Bengali as Byangrej, or an Anglo-Bengali hybrid; the inclusion of the word 'byang' meaning frog, implied a subhuman identity. The species still flourishes in Calcutta's clubs and in the corporate sector generally and they take immense pride in their pathetic attempts to imitate 'English ways'. Their younger generation, of course, has opted for ways American, across the board. To me they are among the most pathetic leftovers from our experience of alien rule. The latter's worst consequences included a loss of self-respect among a section of educated Indians. Now, with globalization in full swing, erosion of all sense of pride in one's own culture is proceeding at a remarkably fast pace. By a strange irony, several decades after independence, the educated middle class in Bengal may well emerge as a hybrid, this time Byamericans rather than Byangrej; people bereft of cultural self-respect and, thereby, the essence of human dignity. This likely effect of globalization, though, is no part of the relevant discourse.

My unhappy days at our new school did not last long. One afternoon I was feeling very ill. The teacher came up to me, touched my forehead and said, 'You have high fever'. He summoned a rickshaw and sent me home. The doctor ordered a number of tests and diagnosed that I had paratyphoid. I was in bed the next three weeks or so and never went back to Ballygunge Government High School.

This was not because of my state of health or my dislike of that institution. One morning, when I was still bedridden, we had a visitor from our home town, Khan Ismail Chaudhuri, a Muslim zamindar from our district. He was a family friend and had come to warn my father about the situation in our estate. The employees, he told us, were making hay and we were in serious danger of losing our property. According to the land laws of the day, when a zamindar failed to pay the revenue to the government by sunset on a given day, his property was forfeited and auctioned. Some of our mahals (revenue units) had already been auctioned, Mr Chaudhuri explained, and the rest would follow unless my father returned to Barisal without delay and took charge. On hearing this, my father decided to leave for Barisal as soon as possible. As mentioned earlier, he had set up a company in partnership with Uncle Shital to manufacture dolls and manikins for the shop windows of the textile stores, making use of uncle's artistic skills. The business was doing reasonably well. But since the fate of our property was at stake, father decided to sell his share to Uncle Shital and return to Barisal. The decision was most welcome to my brother and me. We had had enough of the ghastly city.

This account of our unhappy sojourn in Calcutta would remain incomplete if I failed to mention one person, Ananta Sen, a friend and political colleague of my father. As a young revolutionary (described by the British as 'terrorists') he had gone through the usual experiences of arrest, torture and detention without trial. On his release, his movements had been first restricted to his native village by order of the government. Later, they decided that he would be less of a threat to the Raj if expelled from his home village. He came to Calcutta to earn his living as a schoolteacher. Given his reluctance to compromise, this was not easy, because many of these schools were owned by particular families who made a fair profit by running them. They were inclined to treat the teachers as their personal servants. Many of them were also strangers to the notion of honesty. Ananta Babu hence often quit schools he worked for. On one of these numerous instances of his quitting schools, it is reported, he was seen instructing two senior students to twist the ears of the secretary-proprietor. When he felt enough had been done to punish the miscreant he handed over his resignation to the man and left. He or the boys were not charged for assault.

This man, who had once hoped for the violent overthrow of the alien government and was happy to help with the relevant effort, had become a follower of Gandhi. When he came to our house at my father's request to be our first private tutor, he was clad in khadi or home spun, his clothes woven from yarn he had spun himself. I do not know if there are human beings whose morals are totally pure. If there are, Ananta Sen certainly was a member of that numerically negligible category. He would not, just would not, do anything he considered morally wrong nor was he willing to tolerate it in others. In his experience the worst example of moral turpitude was the British rule in India. He, like thousands of other young men and women, had dedicated his life to ending that evil.

He was an excellent teacher, but his forte was something other than academic instruction. He had made and stitched with his own hand little notebooks. On these he had written in bold letters 'Atmaparikshar khata', the notebook for self-examination. There was one page for each week of the year, the dates written horizontally at the top of the page. Vertically written was a list of possible offences against high morality that a child might be guilty of. The list included idleness, lies, inattention to studies, getting up late, disobedience, etc. In the evening, the first thing he would do on arrival was to check with us if we had violated the code in any way. A cross was put against the item where we had deviated from the straight and narrow. The day the 'slate' was clean, Ananta Babu literally danced with joy.

Nirad Chaudhuri told me that as children they too were subject to a similar moral regime. Only, their list of possible misdemeanour was longer and included one rather adult possibility, rupamoha—lusting after beauty. Nirad Babu's ten-year-old brother once had his ear twisted because he had admitted to this undesirable propensity on ten consecutive days. Not bad for a ten-year-old.

Ananta Babu was no humourless puritan. He took us on excursions to various places of interest and entertained us with refreshments which were normally out of bounds for us. We were really very fond of this fun-loving follower of Gandhi. His ethical regime gave us the first sustained lesson in morality. When I accepted Gandhism as my creed at a somewhat later date, it was the example of this man's spotless life which influenced me most. May be there are still people like him in independent India. I have not met any.

Strict in the observance of his duties, Ananta Babu was never late in arriving to teach us. He came exactly at seven without fail. One day he did not turn up. Several days passed. There was still no sign of Ananta Babu. My father concluded that something must be seriously wrong. Since neither Ananta Babu nor any of his neighbours had a telephone, father decided to call on him at his north Calcutta home and took us with him. This was our first visit to north Calcutta. Compared to the south where we lived, its streets appeared to be dark and dingy. We eventually found his house. The entrance door was wide open and the staircase to the first floor was barely visible in the darkness. Father asked in a loud voice if anyone was around. A middle-aged man came down to meet us.

'Ananta Babu?' he asked in a passionless voice. 'He passed away last night.'

The information took some time to sink in. I remember feeling a pang of intense misery and started whimpering. This was my first experience of bereavement and of the sorrow it can bring. Its memory survives as of a very fresh pain.

7

Nest of the Gentry

When we left Barisal for our long sojourn in Calcutta, I was seven. I was a very precocious child when we returned to our home town. The process of growing up involved, among other things, the discovery of a number of great writers. One of my favourite authors in adolescence was Turgenev (his *First Love* of course was at the top of the list). The title of one of his novels, *Nest of the Gentry*, it seemed to me, was a very apt description of the small district town (population one hundred thousand) where I spent my boyhood and early youth.

Iswar Gupta, renowned journalist and poet, visited Barisal in the fifties of the nineteenth century. He describes a town full of kutchcha houses—structures with walls made of mud or bamboo matting. Most houses had roofs of straw or bamboo. The relatively affluent homes had tiles or corrugated iron roofs. Houses with brick walls were a rarity. The roads too, like their counterparts in the villages, were made of mud which turned into slush during the monsoon months. Being frequently submerged under several feet of water, they were quite navigable during the rainy season. Those who ventured to walk had to negotiate roads which were waist-deep in water. People did not go out at night because they were likely to encounter tigers, the Sundarbans being not very far away. Wild creatures like snakes, monitor lizards, ferrets and skunks still visited the roads and homes of the town-dwellers in our time and crocodiles were familiar denizens of the river, but tigers had withdrawn into their forest home and the roads were no longer navigable even in the rainy season. Things had changed somewhat in one more respect. Brick had replaced mud in most of the roads. The enterprising municipal chairman, Barada Banerji, had macadamized the main roads in the heart of the town and further embellished them with rows of decorative palm trees. The road along the river with its row of jhau (fern) trees was especially attractive and so were the rice fields which lay between the road and the river. The canals along the town's roads acted as open sewers, but since they flowed at some speed, they were not sources of unbearable stench and less of a health hazard than they otherwise might have been. A large proportion of the town's inhabitants lived in brick-built houses. Later, when I briefly enjoyed the hospitality of our colonial rulers for my very marginal involvement in the Quit India movement of 1942, I discovered that the benevolent government treated with some respect the dwellers of brick-built houses. Prisoners, both political and criminal, were classified on the basis of the type of habitation they came from. Those who lived in pucca houses were treated as privileged, with a daily food allowance of one and a quarter rupee, a princely sum in those days and were provided with proper beds. Prisoners from less privileged backgrounds slept on bedbug-infested blankets spread out on the floor and had a daily ration of half a rupee. I should add that only a fraction of the sums prescribed by the government was actually spent for the nourishment of the prisoners, but one must acknowledge that the responsibility for such petty corruption did not lie with the higher authorities in Whitehall, Delhi or Writers' Building, Calcutta, or even with the district magistrate in his bungalow. Besides, the guardians responsible for our well-being certainly did not wish for us to grow fat.

For reasons historical and existential, both formal education and learning (the two of course are not to be confused) were highly respected in this town, as they were in Bengali bhadralok society as a whole. The British introduced in India the unfortunate preoccupation with degrees. The gentry acquired BAs and MAs in the forlorn hope that these would secure them jobs. As a second line of defence, some added two more letters to their name—BL—which entitled them to spend their sleepless afternoons in the local Bar Library. One's livelihood depended on securing a degree, for the masters had so ordained. The acquisition did not guarantee a livelihood. But its absence meant near-starvation in most cases. The respect for learning was rooted in an age-old social culture. The pundit was a person for whom the king got up from his throne to show respect. And as the former was usually a Brahmin, and hence a bhudeva, a god on earth, the king was also expected to wash his feet. Among the Bengali bhadralok the practice of washing the revered Brahmin's feet had ceased to be in vogue. But the respect persisted. Only, the seat of honour had passed from the scholar adept in nyaya (logic?) and smriti (normative codes of social and personal conduct, not 'law') to the BAs and MAs, who could actually read Shakespeare and rejoiced in inflicting large chunks of the bard's writing they had memorized on hapless listeners without any means of escape. I believe I had heard through such media a bulk of the tragedies before I could understand a word of English. It took me a long time to get over the resulting revulsion before I could learn to enjoy Shakespeare.

The majority of the middle-class bhadralok lived in kutchcha (made of material more flimsy than brick) houses, but one's dwelling was no clear indicator of either one's social standing or one's lifestyle. The very wealthy Sahas lived in a kutchcha house as did the highly successful and genuinely learned mukhtar (non-graduate lawyer), Manai Datta. And the dwellers of brick-built houses might be highly westernized like the barrister Jardine Roy whose wife was English or the zamindars of Lakhutia, who broke all existing social taboos by letting the lady of the house sit at the table with their guests, the English district magistrate and his wife. Alternatively, they might be barely literate country squires, Bengali style, with very little education and no different in their lifestyle from their rural counterparts who maintained a safe distance from Saraswati, the goddess of learning. But again, most male members of bhadralok society had some concern for literary education and many had genuine appreciation for what it conveyed. Increasingly, their brides had some school education, a few went to the local college in Barisal and one or two were famous for their academic prowess or literary achievements as well as involvement in revolutionary activities.

One expression of cultural interest was the collection of books in Bengali, English and occasionally Sanskrit to be found in most educated homes, both kutchcha and pucca (brick-built). The collection in our town house lodged in several book cases with glass doors reflected the overlapping interests of two generations—my father's and grandfather's. The most valued item in this collection was a set of Dickens's novels bound in half leather. Then there was a motley collection of English fiction and plays, some with claims to being considered classics like Fielding, Austen and, among the more moderns, Galsworthy and Bernard Shaw. Besides, the works of the romantic poets, Shelley, Keats, Browning and Byron were to be found in most educated homes, including ours. Popular writers of the day shared shelf space with these more august presences. Marie Corelli, Rider Haggard and Bulwer Lytton were powerfully present: I confess these less reputed writers provided a great deal more pleasure when I was growing up, though the first book I read in English was *Oliver Twist*. While we were encouraged to read virtually any book in English as these were considered 'improving' in so far as they helped improve our knowledge of English, the novels with a romantic core, 'love stories' as they were called, were looked upon with some disfavour though not formally proscribed, in the hope that we would not fully understand their content. This leniency was not evident in the case of books in Bengali. Bankim, the most famous among the nineteenth-century Bengali writers, was strictly taboo; since he wrote in our mother tongue it seemed unlikely that we would not get his meaning which he took good care to make very explicit. The works of Tagore in their first edition, holy of holies to literary-minded Bengalis, were of course open to us. The expectation probably was that we would confine ourselves to his poems for children and stay away from his novels and love poetry.

And then there were the bound volumes of the Bengali literary magazines, *Prabasi, Bichitra, Bharatvarsha*, etc. which we were not supposed to read.

One book case was full of somewhat unlikely material—books on theosophy and occultism. My grandfather, who was an atheist, continued to believe in the survival of the human soul. When questioned on this score, he used to answer with some irritation, 'Because God does not exist, it does not follow that ghosts do not.' His interest in the subject deepened ever since his wife's death when he was thirty. My father, who did not share the belief in the survival of the dead, considered the relevant literature unhealthy and discouraged us from reading them.

'Read them when you are grown up, if you will,' he would say with an implicit nod of respect to his dead father. Curiously enough, we were never forbidden to read the Bengali translations of the two Sanskrit epics, Ramayana and Mahabharata, which gave shape and content to my more lurid sexual fantasies in adolescence. We did not venture to read the Bengali notes on Kalidasa's works in Sanskrit. Consistently and highly erotic in style as well as subject matter, we would have found them both rewarding and improving, for they would have helped improve our Sanskrit.

My first encounter with Kalidasa came from an unexpected source, a man who helped shape my tastes and outlook on life in many ways. And incidentally, I shall always remain grateful to him for making me aware of the grandeur of Sanskrit poetry. He also unravelled for me the human value and exquisite beauty often to be found in eroticism and also the stupidity of judgements which equated it with pornography. The person was my father's first cousin and coparcener, Himangshu Raychaudhuri. In Bengali kinship terminology he was my uncle, not a cousin, in fact my father's elder brother.

Though the house in Barisal was the common property of all the twelve coparceners, our nuclear family, the owners of a 25 per cent share, had been allowed to monopolize its use before we left for Calcutta. While we were away, one branch of the family had moved to the town house to help facilitate their children's school and college education. They moved to the less attractive part of the house, leaving the rooms overlooking the river and the orchard for our use. Of the four brothers in that branch of our family, three lived as a joint or extended family (the relevant Bengali term ekannabarti, meant relations sharing the same food or kitchen) while one, a barrister, lived in Calcutta. At some point in time, my grandfather and his three brothers had lived together as a joint family, sharing the same kitchen. The arrangement had broken down long ago. The new arrangement in our Barisal house was in no sense that of a joint or extended family.

We experienced some of the disadvantages and advantages of that regime. The supply of water from the municipality was inadequate for two families. This could have been remedied by separating the arrangements for its supply, but nobody took the necessary initiative, which to my understanding was typical of the decadence which marked the attitude of twentieth-century zamindars. As a class, they had lost the energy to look after their mundane interests. The result in our case was an undercurrent of petty conflict and subdued bickering—we were too civilized to indulge in boorish quarrels. Fixed hours were allocated for each family during which we were supposed to use the water. But these arrangements were breached by both sides and the mutual ill will increased steadily. Yet, by a strange paradox, the relationship between the two families was far from unfriendly. One of the uncles and my father had been close friends in their youth and some of that closeness had survived. The ladies spent a lot of time together and there was much cooperation on festive or ritual occasions as also when there was any incidence of illness in either family. There were strong bonds of affection among the members of the two families in our generation. This was not affected by the silent friction between the elders.

One person unaffected by the tension altogether was Himangshu Babu—mejo jyatha (the 'uncle' elder to my father whose age ranking was in the middle of all the brothers) as we called him.

There has been a great deal of debate among historians of Bengal regarding the validity of the Bengal Renaissance. The cultural efflorescence experienced by the educated Bengali middle class in the nineteenth century, especially the great outburst in literary creativity culminating in the works of Rabindranath Tagore, was honoured by that description by an earlier generation of commentators on Bengali society. This description has been questioned by contemporary historians, especially of the younger generation. The very narrow class basis of the literary and social reform movements, as well as their shallow economic foundation, has been cited as reasons for such questioning. I have written elsewhere my views on the subject. Here I should note one fact. The colonial rule was a period of very limited opportunities for the educated middle classes. As late as the 1860s, the number of Bengalis earning more than seventy-five rupees (a little less than £6) a month was only a few thousand. One could just about maintain a small family on such meagre incomes (and many families were not that small), and it meant a life of deprivation. Yet there was something profoundly compensating about the cultural efflorescence—the discovery of concerns and new interests which were life-enhancing. Encounter with Western social thought and literature which inspired an outburst of creativity in the mother tongue was chief among these new experiences. Its by-product was a mood of self-criticism, generating in its turn what are known as the movements for social reform. Alongside these developments were new definitions of one's identity, a new pride in the religious community/caste, language group, etc., one belonged to and eventually a spectacular invention, the Indian nation. All these were highly charged with very positive emotions and there was a lot of talk about self-dedication to one thing or another—scholarship, literary achievement, artistic endeavour, social reform/service, religion and the nationalist cause. The number of people who found a satisfying respite from their lives of endless frustrations and material misery in one or other of these 'causes' was not small. There was something profoundly impressive about their lives. It was my good fortune that in the small town of Barisal I met several of these men and women. Mejo jyatha was one of them.

He was a very quiet man wedded to the traditional way of life with unquestioning allegiance both to its religious beliefs and ritualistic prescriptions. At the same time, he was a very modern man in his literary tastes and social outlook. It was in his collection of books that I first encountered Bernard Shaw's plays and the works of continental authors including the great Russians—Tolstoy, Chekhov, Dostoevsky, etc. One unlikely component of his collection was the novels by a number of Scandinavian authors—Ibsen, Knut Hamsun, and Johan Bojer among others. The award of the Nobel Prize in literature to Tagore in 1913 had generated a curiosity concerning the works of other Nobel laureates in Bengali literary circles. The interest in modern Scandinavian literature in translation was a by-product of that development. Mejo jyatha's collection of books introduced me to this unfamiliar world of literary experience.

Though uncle's literary interest was passive rather than actively creative, he did publish a slim volume of romantic poetry. It was deeply influenced by Tagore (the great majority of the latter's contemporary Bengali poets were), yet retained a measure of autonomy through the individuality of the emotions it expressed. But the concern at the centre of his life experience was religious. Perhaps 'mystical' would describe it better. The Hindu tradition promised the seeker the possibility of experiencing, under proper guidance, the unity of the individual soul with the Supreme Being. The paths to that experience were many. So far as I, a non-believer, could understand, uncle had chosen the path of bhakti, emotional devotion to the deity in the form of the Mother Goddess. As Durga, the goddess slaying the buffalo demon, she is the presiding deity in the Bengali vita religiosa, especially of those who worship God as Shakti, creative power manifest in the feminine form. A medieval Sanskrit text narrates the myth concerning Durga or Chandi slaying the buffalo demon, generally accepted as a symbolic legend. Uncle used to read it every morning, with tears flowing down his cheeks. How this somewhat crude if very powerfully written text could evoke such profound emotions in a highly sensitive man remains a mystery to me. But then, I was a stranger to the world of his beliefs. I have seen him similarly shedding tears when animals were sacrificed and when he recited the Karpuradi Stotra, a terrifying hymn to the dark goddess, Kali, which describes her as bedecked with a wreath of human heads at her neck and infants' heads dangling from her ears. What beauty and sublimity he saw in these descriptions of horror or the blood sacrifices was way beyond my perception. But I still remember the expression on his face on such occasions. Even as a child or an adolescent I could feel that he had reached a region of exquisite consciousness which was forever closed to people like us. Spirituality may well be a trick of the human brain or linked to the stimulation of some segment of that organ, but it has an existential validity beyond any question. As a young atheist, I came to believe this and ever since I have retained an active curiosity in religious/mystical experience, especially its Indian variants.

I had no access to the spiritual–mystical concerns of my uncle, but, as I have noted before, he introduced me to the aesthetic wonders of Sanskrit poetry. Uncle brought to his Sanskrit studies the new literary sensibility fostered by western contact. In the evening, he would often ask his children and us to join him when he read out from Kalidasa, translating and commenting for our benefit. We had no electricity and would seat ourselves on a bed while uncle read out from *Meghadutam, Abhijnana Shakuntalam* or *Kumarasambhavam* in the light of a kerosene lantern. In that half light, these evenings seemed strangely enchanted. We felt we had been transferred to a bygone age and were witnessing the joys and sorrows of men and gods who inhabited that distant and sunlit world.

Looking back, I realize that uncle brought a new sensibility to his appreciation of Kalidasa. The poet is famous in the Sanskritic tradition for his similes and metaphors and is described in one anonymous verse as the personification of the airs and graces (vilasa) of the goddess of poetry. In short, the ancients had admired his stylistic skills and what one would describe today as his poetic artifices. Uncle unravelled for us a very different dimension of Kalidasa's poetry—his awareness of human pain and joy and his spontaneous and highly personal responses to the beauty of his country's landscape and its wonderful change of seasons. His similes and metaphors excelled because they transcended the usual conventions in describing both nature and man. Sometimes in these evening sessions uncle would read out from Prabodhendu Tagore's beautiful Bengali translation of *Kadambari*, a prose work written in the seventh century which evoked in vivid detail the lifestyle of royalty and the aristocracy at that time. For me, Sanskrit literature, as presented by uncle, acquired the character of pure magic. I was truly shocked when an American Sanskritist described Kalidasa's writings to me as court poetry. The term suggested a degree of artificiality and soullessness which I would never associate with Kalidasa, Bhasa or Bhavabhuti.

When I was at school, appreciation of modern European literature as well as Sanskrit poetry was not confined to my uncle in our social circle. Among those who visited him on a Sunday or in the evenings were at least three other gentlemen who had a profound appreciation of Sanskrit literature. The Bengali adda or gossip sessions, often considered the bane of Bengali social life, were transformed into literary soirees of considerable excellence when these gentlemen visited uncle. A favourite theme at these gatherings, discussed by both Tagore and Bankimchandra, was comparison between Kalidasa and Shakespeare, especially their portrayal of two characters, Miranda and Shakuntala, the latter brought up by a sage in the innocent and sylvan surroundings of a hermitage. I knew Shakespeare only through Lamb's Tales. Being allowed to listen to these discussions was a life-changing experience. When I could read and understand Shakespeare many years later, memories of those discussions helped me see his meaning in an unfamiliar light. Among the participants in these 'soirees' was Manai Datta, a mukhtar with a very impressive legal practice, in whose collection one could find every newly launched Penguin and Pelican book as also every book published in the Everyman series and World Classics. Another frequent visitor, Bankim Raychaudhuri was a schoolteacher on a very meagre salary of which he spent more than half on buying books. His forte was knowledge of poetry—English, Bengali, Sanskrit and French. He could recite these from memory by the hour. He had very limited eyesight, but his collection of books included reproduction of great European paintings, from the Renaissance to post-impressionists. He held these close to his heart. The limited access this gave him to the world of Western art was a source of immense satisfaction in his otherwise sad life darkened by poverty and multiple frustrations.

Our small town in the middle of nowhere was enriched by its love of books. There were several private collections of impressive worth. The nawab of Shaistabad's library, managed by a librarian, was open to his friends and acquaintances. The local college and several schools had large collections, as did two religious foundations—the Ramkrishna Mission and Shankar Math, the latter a hub of revolutionary activity. The government-run district school had a library containing virtually every book relating to the history of the Mughals available in English, thanks to the initiative of one teacher. He was not a very effective teacher but made up for his inadequacy by reading out large chunks from these source materials. Thanks to his enthusiasm, by the age of thirteen I was familiar with the works of the famous seventeenth-century European travellers in India as well as the writings of Abul Fazl and Badauni, the two most famous historians at Akbar's court.

The men most respected in Barisal were those famous for their scholarship and/or people who had lived lives of great sacrifice in the nationalist cause. The best known among the scholars was Debaprasad Ghosh, a college teacher, who was reputed to have learnt eighteen languages and had a collection of several thousand books. He hardly ever wrote anything except to debunk others, especially the modern Bengali poets, but he took to knowledge for its own sake the way drunkards take to alcohol. The town had its internationally famous scholars as well. Two sons of Barisal, S.N. Sen and H.C. Raychaudhuri, were among India's leading historians. The historian R.C. Majumdar, who came from a different district, was also closely associated with the town. The most formidable among Barisal's scholars was the philosopher S.N. Dasgupta whose multi-volume history of Indian philosophy remains the standard authority on the subject. He was reported to be a jatismara, a person who retained memories of his previous lives. One evidence in support of this rumour was that he could recite the Vedas at age three. A likely mundane explanation of such precocious talent might simply lie in his family's tradition of great Sanskritic learning: the child may have simply memorized texts recited by his elders in his presence. Reading out or reciting literary and religious texts are a common practice in the families of pundits in India.

It was my great good fortune that I had free access to the presence of these very great scholars, thanks to the Bengali social mores which favoured such access. These men were role models to me though it is not my intention to suggest that I successfully emulated their achievements in any way.

As a political activist and a local leader of the Indian National Congress, my father was visited by a very different set of people. In 1920, he had joined the Non-cooperation movement initiated by Gandhi when he was a student in the postgraduate class, thus terminating his academic career. Later, there were plans for his visit to the UK to qualify as a barrister. These too had to be abandoned because of his father's illness. He too, like most zamindars of his generation, ended up earning nothing 'by the sweat of his brow'. We survived because our income from the estate was enough to keep us alive—just about, I should add.

The town of Barisal had a lively tradition of political activism ever since the agitation against the Partition of Bengal in 1905. Ashwini Kumar Datta, a leader of the movement, one of the first Indian nationalists to have suffered imprisonment for the nationalist cause, was a son of Barisal and a source of great pride to the people of the district. By the 1930s, the town was also very proud of its two generations of revolutionary leaders and cadres. The people who came to visit my father belonged mostly to this class of men and women. By this time Indian anti-colonial politics had become quite complex: it was by no means a seamless fabric of patriotism led by an ascetic with total faith in non-violence. During the anti-Partition agitation, revolutionary organizations had taken up guns and revolvers as legitimate weapons to fight for independence. Two of these, Anushilan Samiti and Jugantar, had strong bases in Barisal. It is far from clear if these revolutionaries believed that they could wrest independence from the mighty British Empire through their preferred means. More probably, they hoped to stir up consciousness through spectacular acts of courage and self-sacrifice. There is evidence to show that their acts of violence had some impact on the recruitment to the ICS. The last memorable revolutionary actions took place in the early 1930s. The most famous among these was the capture of the Chittagong armoury by a group of young Bengali men and women, some of whom died fighting. The leader of the movement, Surya Sen, was hanged. It is believed that by the time he was dragged to the gallows, he was actually dead from torture. The testimony of the hangman, generally accepted as true, is the source of this belief.

Many of the revolutionaries of the earlier decades had changed track and accepted less violent ideologies. As father was a follower of Gandhi, most of his political associates were Gandhiites, though many among the younger cadres, volunteers in the Civil Disobedience movement of the 1930s, were converts to non-violence only out of political necessity. As even the Indian National Congress made it clear, non-violence was not their creed but policy. Some of the former revolutionaries had accepted ideologies coloured by various shades of Marxism—ranging from socialism through 'revolutionary socialism' to the undiluted Marxism of the Second International. My father's visitors included people from this broad spectrum of political cadres and their local leaders, including those of the two Muslim parties, Krishak Praja Party and Muslim League. Some of the Congress activists stayed from time to time in our kutchcha outhouses. We talked politics and of their own experiences as activists. Most of the time, however, they were silent on one topic: how the police and the secret service had treated them. It was known that the said treatment included a record of physical violence, overt as also torture carried out in secret. One ex-revolutionary, who had later joined the Communist Party of India, had his backbone permanently damaged: he could walk only with considerable difficulty. Several others carried ugly scars on their heads or other parts of the anatomy as permanent badges of honour. They never talked about these things, partly to avoid heroics, perhaps partly because they did not wish to go over very painful memories. We knew that the scars were acquired during lathi charges, police firing on processions or, as some of them put it, in moments of more intimate converse with the police.

One afternoon there was a meeting in my father's drawing room of the Congress activists and the party's local leaders. The habitual informality of such gatherings allowed us, teenage supporters of the party, to be present. Unexpectedly, a haggard-looking person I had never seen before walked in and sat down in a corner. Every one stood up, evidently to honour the intruder. He sat there oblivious of others present mumbling to himself. After a while he left. Someone told me in a hushed voice that this was the famous Ullaskar Datta, one of the accused in the Alipur Conspiracy case. He had received a death sentence which was commuted on appeal to imprisonment for life to be spent in exile in Andaman. He had temporarily lost his sanity there, thanks to police torture.

My father's collection of books included a number of items proscribed by the government. Among these was a slim volume in Bengali, *Dyer o Punjab Kahini* (Dyer and the events in Punjab), which described the happenings in that province during and after the Jallianwala Bagh massacre as recorded in the report drawn up by the Congress Enquiry Committee. The volume was illustrated and carried photographs of young men being tied up on frames and whipped in the streets of Lahore and Amritsar. The narrative stated that schoolboys were selected on the basis of their good health: the idea was that they should be able to take the whipping without undue fuss and not die while still tied to the frame. I have found that in England there are very few people who know about the three-month-long reign of terror in Punjab in 1919. Those who know about Dyer and Jallianwala Bagh generally believe that it was a one-off incident, an uncharacteristic departure from the otherwise totally civilized record of the Raj in India. Hardly anyone has heard of the inhuman barbarity of what was done to innocent and unarmed civilians during the months of military rule. I have also not come across anyone, repeat anyone, who has read Lord Listowel's *India under the Lathi*, an account of extreme repression under a Labour government during Gandhi's Civil Disobedience movement in the 1930s. The photographs I saw in this volume made me realize what sort of colonial repression had provided the incentive to revolutionary terror. I was fourteen or fifteen when I saw those pictures. Many of the revolutionaries were recruited at that age. If somebody had tried then to recruit me into one of the revolutionary parties, there is little doubt that I would have been a very willing volunteer.

As stated above, the number of political parties with diverse ideologies had proliferated by the mid-thirties of the last century. In our small town most of these parties had their branches. Opposite the town hall, named after Ashwini Kumar Datta, there was a row of shacks with tile or bamboo roofs which housed their local offices. Most of them had small collections of books bearing on the history and ideology of the parties concerned. The Communist Party and one of the two socialist parties (Revolutionary and Congress) held regular classes for their cadres. They also had policies and some sort of programme for recruitment from among the older school and college students. There were agitations from time to time centred on specific local issues concerning the interests of the peasantry or civil rights of the middle classes (for example, the right to celebrate a puja in a particular place). Besides, observance of national days like 26 January, when the tricolour flag of independence was first unfurled, were occasions for nationalist propaganda. The party cadres and their local office played an active role on such occasions. Also, there was a great deal of talk about theory and future programmes, the acceptability of Gandhi's leadership, the class character of the national movement and the need for continued unity across the class barriers as a requirement of the anti-colonial struggle. As the war came close one could occasionally hear half-muted voices in favour of the Axis powers, especially after Subhash Chandra Bose had been driven into rebellion against the Congress high command and, a couple of years later, escaped to Japan via Germany in the hope of securing support of the Axis powers for a struggle for independence.

The cadres were also very active during the elections to the provincial assembly or the local representative organizations, the Municipal Committee and the District Board. In the town the Hindus were in a majority and the Municipal Committee was dominated by the Congress. Barada Banerji, not affiliated to any party, was long its chairman and had really done much to beautify the town and make it habitable. His tenure depended on the support of the Congress. When a local Congress leader coveted his chair, he had to vacate it. I recall his coming to plead with my father for his support and leaving in tears when he failed in his mission. He had been the municipal chairman for nearly two decades.

In the 1960s and '70s, a group of young scholars at Cambridge led by Professor John Gallagher and Dr Anil Seal offered a brilliant new insight into the workings of indigenous politics in India under the Raj. Though they have stoutly and consistently denied being members of any 'Cambridge school', their readership, both favourable and hostile, have persisted in finding in their writings one common thread: it consists in an interest-based explanation of political dynamics in colonial India, with competing interest groups fighting for the rulers' favour or alternatively seeking to build up support through opposition to the regime. This explanation (I have simplified a highly sophisticated thesis) has been reviled in India as a continuation of the imperialist explanation of Indian nationalism which was seen as cynical efforts on the part of atypical sections of the population to lead the loyal masses astray for their entirely selfish ends. When I first encountered the thesis of these historians, I saw much merit in it because it offered, to my understanding, a brilliant and complex explanation of the structure and dynamics of indigenous politics under colonial rule: the Empire in India was based on the active cooperation and acquiescence of the subject population, both the elite and the masses. The Cambridge historians showed for the first time how that cooperation actually worked. What I found unacceptable was the theory that the opposition to the Raj was only the other side of the coin, cooperation by other means.

My memories of local politics in an East Bengal town with strong nationalist traditions suggested serious questions about the acceptability of that proposition. The Congress volunteers owned nothing and aspired after nothing other than the country's independence (which brought them little material comfort when it did come). The volunteers, who mostly belonged to the lower middle classes—teachers, poorly paid journalists working for local papers, holders of intermediate tenures in land yielding derisory incomes—lived lives of serious material misery. This was true not only of the supporters of the mainstream nationalist parties but the communists and other political workers as well. The whole-time workers often lived in the party office on a pittance they received as monthly allowance. Partition and independence rendered most of these activists homeless, and totally pauperized them in the bargain. Men like Barada Banerji, non-party activists in social and political life, no doubt valued the public acclaim and prominence which they gained, but the quest for legitimate and not so legitimate material returns, the hallmark of post-independence local politics, was not a feature of political action in colonial India, so far as one could see. Corrupt men would have had problems finding popular support. People like my father, 'local notables' in the words of an eminent colleague, who often constituted the local leadership, gained nothing from their opposition to the government, except terms in prison and exclusion from the very limited economic opportunities of those days. Partition brought them further misery—homelessness, social alienation and total economic insecurity. Individuals and parties collaborating with the government of course had much to gain. That explains the success of the rulers in securing cooperation. But to say that opposition to the government was similarly inspired goes against the known facts and certainly my memories of anti-colonial politics, whatever they are worth.

Behind such misapprehension there are grave errors in the popular common sense in Britain concerning the Empire, the Raj in particular. Highly sophisticated academic analysis has not succeeded in escaping the implications of that pervasive error in understanding. I have come across in this country a deep-rooted belief that the British as rulers were dearly loved by the vast majority of the population in India. The exceptions were the small number of troublemakers, seeking their crooked ends. The Raj was ma-baap, androgynous father-cum-mother to the masses, and their departure is still bitterly lamented by them. Such simple faith is the gift of the British establishment to the people of the country, a brilliant act of brainwashing sustained over a very long period; only an atypical radical fringe rejects this simple-minded dogma. That nothing could be further from the truth was proved by the popular reactions to Axis victories in the first phase of the Second World War. There was something truly unholy about the glee with which every British defeat was greeted in India. A British police commissioner of Calcutta noted that if the Japanese came to the city, there would be a run on the city's flower stalls.

This hostility cannot be explained only in terms of anti-British attitudes, rooted in racism, though that element was not altogether absent: the popular description of Europeans as lal bandar, red monkeys, is evidence to the fact. But the hostility was not so much to the British as a people, as to their unwelcome presence as rulers. The individual Britisher, the missionaries in particular, were not at the receiving end of any significant hostility except at certain moments (my teacher, Dr C.C. Davies, described to me popular reactions in Amritsar after the Jallianwala Bagh massacre which I shall discuss later). But over time, the mass attitude to the Raj had moved from passive acquiescence to sullen resentment. Besides, throughout the history of the Raj there had been numerous localized popular revolts. The events of 1857 were a massive outburst of hatred which was fairly pervasive. At least one prominent Bengali journalist, Harish Mukherji, has recorded the extreme popularity of the rebels in 1857 in north and central India and questioned the truth of the Anglo-Indian propaganda regarding the atrocities committed by them.

The racist hauteur of the British, rooted in the total absence of any social contact with the Indian people and 'the illusion of permanence' concerning the Empire, were factors in producing this attitude of sullen resentment. The simple-hearted subjects of the Mughal Empire sought the emperor's darshan on the imperial balcony every morning. One hundred and fifty years after the death of the last great Mughal, admittedly an oppressor of Hindus in the latter phase of his reign, soldiers, feudatories and peasants, both Hindu and Muslim, were up in arms to bring back the rule of that empire. The viceroys did not offer darshan. It is doubtful that there would be many takers if they did. And it is unlikely that despite the multiple failures of the Indian democracy, Indians will ever rise up and pray that Prince Charles or his progeny pick up the broken thread of British rule in India. Very few felt that there was anything to thank the Raj for in their miserable lives. The humiliation which was the daily experience of Indians, both the politically conscious and the rest, was naturally wished on the rulers. Even if the average Indian had enjoyed reasonable prosperity and hopes for the future, the pervasive sense of insult would have been enough to generate this hostility. To look for hard, material reasons for anti-colonial nationalism is perhaps a mistake. Of course, such reasons were there in plenty in the daily experience of material misery which was the fate of most Indians. But as one French philosopher put it, if you give a man a million and then slapped him, he is likely to forget the million and remember the slap. No Indian had received any million from their colonial masters. Slaps, figuratively and at times literally, were very much a part of their daily experience. The delight at Axis victories and British humiliation is hence not difficult to explain. The sense of humiliation was a very solid basis for the anti-colonial element in Indian nationalism. The delight in the misfortunes of an unpopular ruling race was part of a characteristic moral degeneration which was a gift of imperialism.

All political parties opposed to the Raj found it relatively easy to recruit cadres though there was no material inducement they could offer. Idealism comes easy in one's youth and one hardly needs to look for special explanation as to why young men in a colonial society should seek to get rid of alien rulers. That they accepted the risks and suffering associated with such action can be explained partly by the absence of career opportunities in colonial India. Independent India is not famous for the ideologically inspired cadres of its political parties. Those who might have provided the social base for such cadres were absorbed in independent India in the fast-expanding tertiary sector of a developing country; only less desirable elements for the most part opted for the uncertainties of a political career. The absence of economic opportunities in colonial India allowed the ideologically inspired young people to retain their youthful fire. The example of men and women of extraordinary character courting suffering for the nationalist cause provided role models for political careers of great self-sacrifice.

In our small town, the uncrowned king of patriotic men and women was Satin Sen, an ex-revolutionary, once a member of the much feared Jugantar group, who had converted to Gandhism. Satin-da had no property and no income. The local Congress had a room in the Town Hall as its office. Satin-da lived there. Friends sent him his food and gifts of clothing. Of course, these necessities of life were often provided by the government itself because he spent long years as their guest in prison. It has not yet been suggested that such generous provision was one potent reason for opposition to the government (I should not be surprised if some day a foreign or anti-bourgeois historian of India decides that the comforts of prison life in India under the Raj was one potent reason for anti-colonial movements in the country). When the country was partitioned, Satin-da stayed on in Pakistan where he was repeatedly arrested. He spent his last years in prison and died there of tuberculosis.

The Indian National Congress had no active policy of recruitment in our area as it certainly did in the provinces it dominated politically. The appeal of the nationalist cause, enhanced by the example of men like Satin Sen and his followers, acted as the main draw for young people. As already noted, they were free to follow such idealistic impulses because material opportunities which might distract them were virtually non-existent for the vast majority.

The Congress held no classes for the political training or indoctrination of its cadres. Whenever there was a local conflict with the government agencies over some issue of civil rights or perceived injustice to ordinary men and women, the cadres were expected to organize and take part in agitations until some sort of solution to the dispute was found. Some of these episodes became famous in the annals of Indian nationalism as local 'satyagrahas' and were hailed as great victories for Satin Sen and his followers. One of these, the Patuakhali satyagraha, agitated about the right to take out religious processions through an area that the local mullahs, supported by the bureaucracy, had objected to. This incident had unfortunate communal implications, although that was certainly not the intention of the leaders. Besides, there were the various 'national' days, especially commemorating patriotic acts of martyrdom, where the ideology of the party was spelt out.

Not being a natural orator, Satin-da was rather shy of public speaking. In his speeches he repeatedly underlined one simple Gandhian message: We had no enemies, only a just cause to fight for. Since imperialism was degrading for all concerned, our struggle was as much to the interest of the British as it was to ours. Non-violence was essential because it was the only ethically acceptable way to fight for a cause. Violence was suitable for pariah dogs fighting for a piece of bone. Independence was too noble an ideal to be sought by such ignoble means. Non-violence empowered the weak: it gave them a sense of moral invincibility which was an immense source of strength. Later, when as a humble foot soldier of Gandhian nationalism one faced violent police action, one realized that there was a profound existential truth in this message. In such situations, one could have done one of three things—run away, resort to violence or be calm and resolute. The last was by far the most effective way to respond. It gave one a sense of deep peace, of a morally enhanced quality of life, rooted in humility and free of hatred.

The local Congress under Satin-da's leadership did attract a fairly steady stream of activists, some of whom worked for the Gandhian constructive programme, fighting untouchability and implementing plans for rural uplift. They also campaigned for party candidates in elections to the state legislature, a fact which perhaps boosts the validity of the 'Cambridge Thesis'. In 1942, they were at the forefront of the Quit India movement. There was nothing false about the ideological commitment of these cadres. One highly eccentric nationalist gave up using the means of transport run by the state or private British companies, i.e., railways and steamers in 1920 as an act of non-cooperation ordained by Gandhi. He stuck to this particular vow for the rest of his life, walking the couple of hundred miles to Calcutta when the need arose.

As I have indicated in an earlier chapter, adoration of Gandhi and some understanding of the nationalist cause were parts of our childhood upbringing. When at age four, I witnessed on the beach at Cox's Bazaar the symbolic violation of the Salt Act with which the police did not interfere, I did not become instantly a child freedom fighter (as one dear colleague once put it), but the message that a body of foreigners ruled over us and had no right to do so did get through. Two messages were integral to our moral upbringing—that we were victims of a grievous wrong and that we were immensely fortunate in having a godlike man as our leader who would lead us to freedom. Father used to joke that Gandhi was a very great snob because he was a member of the world's most exclusive club. It had only two other members—Buddha and Jesus Christ. The message that we had no enemies, only a righteous cause to fight for, was constantly dinned into our brains. With that went another—that the British were a very great people, the Raj notwithstanding. We were fortunate in coming into contact with this great civilization. One only wished that an act of conquest had been no part of the encounter.

There were two big gaps in the ranks of local nationalists. Even in the Civil Disobedience movement of the 1930s, there was a substantial Muslim presence in our district. By the late 1930s, there was hardly a single Muslim in the Congress ranks in Barisal. We heard that large sections of the peasantry did support the Congress-led agitation—the Civil Disobedience movement. But this was no longer true in 1942. The ineffectiveness of the party organization in the intervening years and growing complexity of intercommunity relations probably explain these later absences. In Bengal, wherever any constructive programme had been implemented with some success, the support for the Congress both in the elections as well as the Quit India movement appears to have been proportionately greater.

The British presence in our small town and our encounters with them were both minimal. So far as I remember, only the district magistrate and chief superintendent of police were British. I met the magistrates only twice, the first time when Mr Llewellyn came to lunch in our village home as a part of his visit to preside over the prize-giving ceremony at the school named after our great grandfather. The second encounter was more interesting, but of that, more later. I also had the pleasure of meeting the English police superintendent only once, after I was arrested for participation in the Quit India movement. Looking back, I have the impression that when such encounters occurred, the more decent British officers were rather embarrassed and ill at ease. If they were expected to project the might of the great empire, they did not do it very well.

There was one area where we met a few Englishmen under more relaxed circumstances. The Oxford Mission, I understand, had only one centre outside Britain and that was in Barisal. My father, despite his nationalist commitment, was very keen that we should have a good command of the English language. The Bible (authorized version), he believed, was the best source of pure English. He too, like his father, liked the English as a people. He had got to know them under rather auspicious circumstances—as teachers in Presidency College and missionaries of the Oxford Mission in whose hostel he lived in Calcutta as a student. He was on good terms with the missionaries of the Oxford Mission in Barisal (they visited him regularly in prison during 1943-44) and requested them to help me read the Bible. The young man who was entrusted with this task was one Mr Catly. He was a charming fellow, but not keen to teach anyone anything. My friendship with this young missionary helped develop my leg muscles but it did little for my knowledge of English. Brother Catly spoke the Barisal patois very fluently, in fact better than I did because at home we were discouraged from speaking this excessively vigorous dialect, free from all sense of obscenity. I picked up from Brother Catly's conversation words describing the human anatomy which were strictly taboo at home. But my English friend was a great walker at superhuman speeds. Association with this man has given me a permanent distaste for walking. Too much of an individualist, Catly could not accept the discipline imposed by the Mission for long. He left it to become a lone missionary in New Guinea preaching to, or more probably simply socializing with the aborigines. I had a clear impression that he found the restraints of civilization irksome. We used to visit the Mission every Sunday when they had open house for tea. I was immensely impressed by the way they dealt with wartime shortages. Sugar was scarce and so clarified molasses were used as a substitute. In place of teacups they used polished coconut shells. Their rooms were furnished with just one bed, a table and a chair. Books were stacked against the wall. And their few clothes hung from a string made of coconut fibre at one end of the room. Life could not be simpler. As I have always found 'things' bothersome, this simplicity had a great appeal. If the Oxford Mission accepted atheist novices, I should have joined them very willingly.

Perhaps the most significant development during our school days in society and politics which was to affect the country's future as well as our personal fortunes pertained to the relation between the two communities, Hindus and Muslims. There is a persistent popular impression, both in India and abroad, that these relations have always been adversarial. The British in India believed in this demonstrably false interpretation of the subcontinent's social reality. Even Churchill commented that if the two (meaning Hindus and Muslims) got together, the British were out of India. Well, the two did not get together and still the British were out of India. If one wants evidence proving the falsity of the popular impression, one has to go no further than the uprising of 1857 when Hindus and Muslims—soldiers, peasants, princes—fought together to get rid of the East India Company's rule and bring back the Mughal empire. The fact that ninety years later such joint action had become impossible suggests that what had gone wrong belonged to the history of the intervening decades. No, I am not trying to revive the somewhat naive thesis that inter-communal antipathy was the product of the British policy of divide and rule, even though that thesis has a hard core of truth in it. The relationship between colonialism and communalism is much more complex, but the causal link between the two is beyond reasonable doubt.

One British historian, analysing a few cases of intercommunity riots in the pre-colonial era, has concluded that 'communalism then was what communalism is now.' Nothing could be further from the truth. Colonial and post-colonial conflict between the communities is grounded in political competition and a pan-subcontinental sense of communal identity, engendered to a large extent by the executive policies of the colonial regime. The few violent encounters which occurred in the pre-colonial era—and they were indeed very few—had social causes which interrupted the normal rhythm of coexistence and cooperation, engendered by the existential compulsions of economic life and daily reality of encounter between two different ways of living. Colour thrown on unwilling beards, cows slaughtered in the proximity of Hindu habitations, music near mosques disturbing the prayers of the faithful—such were the sources of violent conflict before the nineteenth century. They were not comparable in scale to the events in Kanpur, 1924, Calcutta, 1946, and Punjab during the Partition; nor were they rooted in political competition arising from constitutional changes and executive policies, especially after 1919. The pre-colonial conflicts were insignificant in quantity compared to the overwhelmingly dominant fact of coexistence and collaboration in extensive areas of social and cultural action—ranging from food and dress to manufactures, architecture, art, music and matters of faith. Even more important is the fact that before the advent of British rule, there was no community consciousness covering the entire subcontinent any more than there was any sense of pan-Indian nationhood. Both nationalism and sub-national identities focused on communities were developments of the colonial era. The negative implications of the latter development were something we experienced during our years at school in Barisal.

I joined the Barisal Zilla School (i.e. the district school), a government-run institution, in 1937. Looking back, I realize that the standard of education imparted there was high. As some 90 per cent of all government jobs in Bengal until the 1930s were held by the Hindus, the very legitimate government policy of reserving 50 per cent of the said jobs for the majority community, the Muslims, meant that for years virtually all government jobs, including those of the schoolteachers, had to go to them. There was indeed a flaw in the argument behind the policy. Muslims might constitute a majority by a small margin, but they accounted for a small proportion of the people competing for the jobs which required academic qualifications like university degrees; immediately after the Partition, a fair proportion of posts which were normally filled by graduates had to have incumbents without any university education. Similarly, recruitment of Muslims in pre-Partition Bengal often had to be substandard. It is in this context that I remember with happy surprise the high quality of education dispensed by our teachers, the majority of whom were Muslims. Among the best teachers was our headmaster, Sirajuddin Ahmed, a person with green eyes, very fair complexion and an impressive goatee whose appearance reminded one of George V. He had an impeccable accent and the English he spoke was very elegant. I also remember the other teachers with affection and gratitude, especially Sa'adullah Saheb. Although ineffective as a teacher, he was the person who introduced us to the sources of Mughal history and thus helped create awareness as to how history is or should be written. As there was a quota system in the admissions policy as well, a very large proportion of the students were also Muslims. But if I remember correctly, the target of at least 50 per cent was not reached.

In our social life, Muslims were no strangers. In fact, we encountered them at many levels. Two of my closest friends at school were Muslims. Among our family friends was one family of Muslim zamindars, that of Khan Ismail Chaudhuri, zamindar of Charamuddi. Of Pathan descent like many of the Muslim zamindars of East Bengal, this family had been close to ours for some three generations. According to family legend, Ismail Chaudhuri's father, a fugitive from law on a charge of murder, took shelter in our village home in the days of my great-grandfather. Dressed in a saree, to avoid the suspicion of the servants, he stayed for months in a room in the ladies' quarters until the storm passed over. The Khan Chaudhuris were great gourmets in the grand Mughal tradition and invitations to dinners in their house were events we looked forward to. Their ladies did not observe purdah before our menfolk and in addressing the members of their family, we used the familiar Hindu kinship terms adding, in some cases, suffixes used while addressing the Muslim gentry. Ismail's eldest son Shahjahan and his cousin, Manik, were addressed as kaka, i.e., father's younger brothers; Mrs Chaudhuri was Dadi-saheba, grandma or grand-aunt; Chaudhuri himself was Dadu-saheb, respected grand-uncle. Shahjahan, until his conversion to the ideology of Pakistan, was the local leader of the Revolutionary Socialist Party. My first familiarity with Marxist literature was through his large collection of books on the subject. I remember the bitter tears Mrs Khan Chaudhuri shed when we were leaving Pakistan. The invectives she uttered against Mr Jinnah were strictly unparliamentary. Fazlul Huq, for some time the chief minister (the term in vogue then was prime minister) of united Bengal was a friend of my grandfather and a very close family friend. More about him later. Among the aristocratic Muslim visitors to our house, there was one remarkable person, nawab or rather nawabzada of Shaistabad whose library I have mentioned earlier. For reasons unknown, he stuck to his sonhood, rejoicing in the name of nawabzada, refusing to call himself nawab even in his fifties. He was always dressed in khaki and again, for reasons unknown, confined his visits to our lawn, firmly avoiding any entry into our house. Besides such august personalities, local Muslim politicians, some of whom became ministers in Fazlul Huq's cabinet, were also among the visitors in my father's drawing room. The visits could be purely social or for discussing the minutae of municipal politics. Their sons were our fellow students at the Zilla School. One of them, Abdul Wahab Khan, a lawyer, became the Speaker in the Pakistan parliament shortly before the military took over. I write these mundane details to underline one fact: the growing political hostility between Hindus and Muslims, especially after the formulation of the demand for Pakistan, did not mean any mutual social boycott or ill will at the interpersonal level.

Besides politics, one major source of intercommunity tension and bitterness in Bengal, to my understanding, was traceable to the social attitudes of middle- and upper-class Hindus towards less privileged Muslims as also the well-known exploitative relations between the zamindars and moneylenders, mostly Hindus, and the peasantry, a very large proportion of whom were Muslims. With the rising price of jute, a new middle class emerged from among the affluent Bengali Muslim peasant-farmers; the Hindu taboos against commensality with Muslims and a certain attitude of contempt that went with it came to be resented.

This resentment did not of course terminate overnight various social and economic links between privileged Hindus and less fortunate Muslims or the relations between Hindus and Muslims of the same social class. We had a cook, who along with his brother had been sent to the Andamans to undergo a life sentence for murder. There they met two sisters who had been similarly sentenced to exile for murdering their respective husbands. Appropriately, Afsar and his brother found their soulmates in these two sisters and acquired them in honourable matrimony. The wife of the British commandant of the prison in Andaman discovered Afsar's talents as a cook and trained him up to a high level of excellence. My British friends with Conservative inclinations (which most of them have) have often expressed disappointment at my lack of gratitude to the Raj. Well, my gratitude to the said British lady I never met is unlimited. If Afsar's cooking is any indicator of the quality of food in Anglo-Indian homes in the 1920s, I refuse to hear any criticism of the British cuisine. Her training imparted a paradisal quality to my boyhood years; mealtimes were located in heaven. Even centuries of alien rule may be acceptable for compensations of such quality.

I should like to mention one more instance of the irrelevance of intercommunity political resentment to social relations. Our sprawling village home had a body of night guards called mirdhas. They were all Muslims, and at night they went up and down the corridors, spear in hand, as a precaution against armed attacks by organized bands of dacoits. Even after the Hindu–Muslim riots of Calcutta and Noakhali in 1946 this practice did not cease. There was never any apprehension that the spears deployed for our protection from dacoits could be turned against us.

At school, there was never any overt tension between Hindu and Muslim students, but there were half-joking expressions of an undercurrent of mutual political hostility which gained in strength with the passing years. Two Calcutta-based football teams, Mohammedan Sporting and Mohan Bagan, were the mutually opposed symbols of communal pride. Matches between the two were occasions for the expression of mock or even not so mock mutual hostility. Unfavourable epithets were hurled at the other community, 'malayun' for the Hindus and 'nere' for the Muslims on such occasions. Mock heroic songs celebrating the glories of Mohammedan Sporting were sung by some of our Muslim fellow students, but the general mood was good-humoured rather than angry or bitter. Somewhat peculiar practices emphasized the divide between the two communities. Apparently out of respect for Hindu taboos on commensality, there were two separate tanks for Hindu and Muslim students to get their drinking water at school. Such tender concern for Hindu sensibilities, however, was only manifest in the government schools. But this dividing line was replicated in other areas of life not controlled by the government: in railway stations the tea vendors observed a communal divide. There was 'Hindu tea' and 'Muslim tea' on offer, the teas in question being evidently strict in their adherence to their respective confessional faiths. The practice disappeared almost overnight after independence. No one seems to have objected. The trade in vending tea continued to flourish as before, the loss of denominational labels notwithstanding.

We, 'reformed Hindus', of course were not bound by taboos against commensality with non-Hindus and freely partook of food in the homes of our Muslim teachers and school friends. At school, some of us made a point of drinking from the water tank for Muslim students with some bravado. As already noted, invitations to the home of Ismail Chaudhuri, a dedicated gourmet as well as gourmand, were eagerly awaited. Our Muslim fellow students, however, were under strict orders from their parents never to offer us beef. But tempted by their account of the joys of beef bhuna gosht (fried meat), I was among the first to taste the delicacy: it was truly a taste of heaven. When the father of the offending boy discovered what his son had done, the latter received a thrashing of a lifetime. 'What do I tell your parents?' the aggrieved gentleman asked me. Well, there was nothing to tell. My father, though very liberal, did stop short of eating beef. But I do not think that he would have taken me to task for this violation of an orthodox taboo. His commitment to liberal principles was too strong for that.

Politics based on communal identities was gathering strength in the 1930s, especially after the elections of 1937 which transferred some real power to the elected ministries in the provinces. The Indian National Congress continued to enjoy some support among Muslims and there were sundry groups described as nationalist Muslims who refused to go along with the increasingly separatist policies of the Muslim League. In united Bengal, especially the district of Barisal, the situation was further complicated by the fact that the party most popular with the Muslims, the Krishak Praja Party (the party of peasants and tenants on land), had a large lower-caste Hindu presence and remained non-communal in its avowed identity. Its leader, Fazlul Huq, was a son of the soil and enjoyed great personal popularity with both Hindus and Muslims. He had been a follower of C.R. Das, a highly charismatic leader of the Congress in the 1920s and when invited to form the government, had first offered the choice of a coalition with the provincial Congress party. The invitation was refused, and he formed a short-lived alliance with the Muslim League, but eventually went back to a coalition ministry which included the Hindu leader Shyamaprasad Mukherji and some disaffected members of the Congress. From that position, he was forced out by an English governor in a way which showed no respect for constitutional processes or for the famous 'provincial autonomy' allegedly conceded by the reform act of 1935.

Political awareness among students in the higher forms was quite intense for the simple reason that our material future was bound up with the developments in politics. Muslim students accused the Congress for the failure to unite against the British, and we, who supported the nationalist party, told them that their leaders were acting as stooges of the colonial government. One phenomenon was, however, singularly absent both among the teachers and the students: any obvious feeling of loyalty for the British rule. Among the recommended (but not compulsory, in the sense that we were not examined for our knowledge of this text) reading was a slim volume, *England's Work in India* by Ramsay Muir. Finding how many lies the book contained was a game quite popular with the students. Eventually, it was dropped from the syllabus. Only one poor teacher whose promotion was at stake, used to expatiate on the glories of British rule in India. He was not taken seriously. I also doubt if he believed in his own protestations.

Political and social attitudes did affect pedagogy in a different way. Some of the teachers had developed such an intense hatred of all things Hindu, that this ill will informed their teaching. Among them was one Kazi Saheb who was personally very kind to me and I reciprocated his genuine affection. I spent my first holiday away from home, after the school-leaving examination in his house in the seaside town of Chittagong. But Indian history for him was an object lesson in the multifaceted perfidy of the Hindus. Once, he set a question for the school test inviting us to expand on the many acts of chicanery and fraud performed by the seventeenth-century Hindu hero, Shivaji. On another occasion a Muslim boy, Johur, shouted 'Bandemataram', the famous nationalist slogan, simply to express his joy that the school hours had come to an end. Poor Johur was beaten within an inch of his life. The idea of a Muslim boy shouting a nationalist slogan was intolerable to Kazi Saheb. But the same man was kindness itself when I was his guest, despite my family's nationalist credentials. When I did rather well in the school-leaving examination, he was the first person to rush to our house with the good news.

Relations between Hindus and Muslims have never been an uncomplicated affair which can be explained in simple terms of ethnic hatred or seamless mutual amity. Most historians trying to analyse it have made the mistake of ignoring the complexity. During my school days I was witness to a spectacular and personally painful example of this complexity. Shahjahan Chaudhuri, son of Ismail Chaudhuri, uncle Shaju to me, was the local leader of the Revolutionary Socialist Party and a convinced Marxist. This very dear friend, who had introduced me to Marxist literature, turned up one morning at the head of a Muslim League procession shouting virulently anti-Hindu slogans. He stuck to his new allegiance the rest of his life, down to the time of the Bangladesh war. Trying to escape from Barisal, he was bombed out of an army boat and perished in the river. He is also reported to have taken part in the Calcutta riots of 1946. Yet he remained a friend of the family. The news of his miserable end was a source of much pain to all of us.

If one can generalize from the limited and highly subjective impressions of an adolescent in a small town in East Bengal, while there was a fair number of young people actively interested in politics in our part of the country, the nationalists accounted for a small proportion of the population and the intensity of involvement one had noticed in the older generations had become diluted by a sense of hopelessness. Independence, which most people wished for and some were willing to suffer for as well, seemed too remote a possibility to be a source of daily inspiration. I know I would not say this if I belonged to one of the districts like Midnapore, Hooghly or Dinajpur where the Congress was still very active and certainly not if I came from a Congress-dominated province like UP or Bihar, but belonging to a locality which was once at the forefront of the nationalist movement, I shared with many young people a sense of decline and defeat. By contrast, young Muslim activists, both the supporters of Fazlul Huq's party and the Muslim Leaguers, appeared to be more numerous, involved and hopeful of the fulfilment of their aspirations. Though we never imagined that the country would someday be actually partitioned, the young educated Bengali Hindu evidently suffered from a sense of hopelessness. For a social class dependent on jobs, the prospects of finding any were dismal. In constitutional politics the British bureaucrats of Bengal had distributed the seats in the provincial assembly in a way which had reduced the nationalists to a permanent minority. The Muslims in Bengal now had a vested interest in a separate electorate and a pro-government stance in the legislature. For Bengali nationalists, both Hindus and Muslims, there was hence nothing to hope for in constitutional politics. It is worth noting that the Krishak Praja Party that represented the majority of Bengali Muslims still avoided any identification with the colonial regime and was treated by the government as a virtually hostile organization, despite its support for the war effort. As to the prospects for the struggle for freedom, we did not expect independence to come in our lifetime. Living in a tunnel with no light at its end, the involvement of the local population in nationalist politics was limited and often half-hearted. In our part of the country, the intensity or duration of the Quit India movement of 1942 did not match those of the Non-cooperation or Civil Disobedience movements of earlier decades.

Politics always has its lighter side. Fazlul Huq, personally popular with most citizens of Barisal, could often be a source of exasperation. He formed a ministry in coalition with the Muslim League only after the Congress declined his invitation. But this latter action was not popular with politicized Hindus. As the steamer ghat was very close to our house and Mr Huq, a very large man, was in the habit of walking to his temporary residence when he came to Barisal as a part of his public relations initiative, he often stopped at our house for some rest. An especially large chair had to be provided for our eminent visitor. On one occasion there were a number of local people in my father's drawing room including Mr Huq's schoolmate, Indu Gupta, famous for his bawdy jokes. As Huq entered the room, Gupta commented in mock anger, 'Fazlu, you are acting in such a way that we, your friends, are too ashamed to show our faces in public.' Huq looked profoundly sympathetic and replied, 'That must be very hard. Why don't you show your bottom instead?' On another occasion, Jogen Mandal, leader of the Hindu scheduled castes (read lower castes), and later law minister in Pakistan, having won an election victory over his caste-Hindu Congress rival, came to visit us. There were a number of people present including Indu Gupta. 'Do come,' Gupta said in welcome, 'We are waiting for you in a mandal' (circle, one literal meaning of Mr Mandal's surname). Mandal was not too pleased with this reference to his caste status.

In 1940, when I was still at school we heard of the Pakistan proposal projecting an autonomous homeland for the Muslims in the subcontinent. Whether this meant a separate state or simply an autonomous area within a federal or confederated India was not clear. The progressive youth supporting the Pakistan idea shouted a hopeful slogan: 'Swadhin Bharate swadhin sthan, amra chai Pakistan!' ('An independent place in independent India, that is what we want, Pakistan!') But the demand was based on a strange theory: Hindus and Muslims were two separate nations from the beginning of time. Since majority of Indian Muslims were converts, the theory was based on no historical truth. Were our Hindu school friends, teachers, our Brahmin cook, the Hindu domestics members of one nation and Afsar, Ismail Chaudhuri, the mridhas, Uncles Shaju and Manik and our Muslim teachers members of another? This was a mind-boggling idea.

I asked my father, 'Are we, Hindus and Muslims, two nations?'

He replied without the least hesitation, 'Certainly not.'

'What are we then?'

'Brothers,' he replied with Gandhian certainty.

'Then what is all this talk that we hear?'

'Brothers fighting over ancestral property,' he replied, 'You belong to a zamindar family. You should have no difficulty in understanding what is happening. Have you not noticed how we, near-relations and coparceners, fight over pittances?'

'What is our future? How will this conflict end?' I asked.

'It will ruin us both,' he said. 'That is how all fraternal conflicts end. We are witnessing a new Kurukshetra war' (the war between the the Pandavas and Kauravas, first cousins described in the epic Mahabharata, which resulted in almost total mutual destruction).

I felt he was right. We did not know what awaited us. But I had nightmarish premonitions; anticipations of great misery for vast multitudes. But the horrendous consequences of intercommunity conflict I would live to witness went way beyond my most terrible dreams.

Politics had a large presence in our lives when we were growing up, but of course we were not indifferent to the more natural concerns of adolescence. Sailen Ghosh, an old revolutionary who had escaped to the USA in the 1920s, came back to Barisal as the principal of the local college with his American wife and two pretty teenage daughters. The latter's arrival caused something of a turmoil among the youth in Barisal. Boys and girls mixed freely enough in the town and incidence of romantic love was far from uncommon, but the advent of these half-American beauties was something else. Those affected included myself, then aged fourteen. My friend Manik Chaudhuri, a very scholarly and handsome romantic, older than me by some ten years, once recited for my delectation a lovely verse in Persian:

Pa-e sag busidah majnun
Shaks-e pusht—ye chisht
Goft—yeh sag gahe gahe
Rah-e Layla raftah bud

The lines translate roughly as follows: 'Majnu kissed the feet of a dog whereupon someone asked, "What is this?" Majnu answered, "This dog has, from time to time, walked on the road where Layla lives."' I found this romantic statement overpowering and decided to learn the language presumably studded with such gems. The Maulvi who taught Persian at our school agreed to teach me as a private tutor. Manik had thus unwittingly led me in a direction which would influence my future career. When my knowledge of the language had made some progress, he presented me a copy of Omar Khayam's *Rubaiyat* with the warning that this was not love poetry but mystical/philosophical verses. If I was keen on romantic verses, I should read Nizami. Later, over the years as a researcher in Indian history I had to dabble in a number of languages. My efforts to learn Persian stretches over many years. But somehow I failed to gain any proficiency in this language: it has been a case of frustrated love. But this introduction to Persian in my adolescence created a core of academic interest which later influenced my choice in selecting an area of research.

I took my school-leaving examination, matriculation, at the age of fifteen. The result was unexpectedly good and it made me a celebrity of sorts in Bengal overnight. Fazlul Huq sent a congratulatory telegram: 'Barisal ki jai' (Victory to Barisal). For a few days I felt I was walking on clouds. No success later in life has caused any comparable flow of adrenalin in my veins.

In July 1941, I left Barisal to live in a students' hostel in Calcutta for my college education. Duff Hostel on Beadon Street, one of the several dormitories run by Scottish Church College, became my virtual home for the next seven years.

8

College Days: 'Quit India' and a Taste of Prison Life

In the selections from Sanskrit prose which was our recommended reading for the language at school, there was a famous description of a great sal tree. Birds of many descriptions arrived from many directions and made that tree their home. On my arrival at Duff Hostel on Beadon Street in north Calcutta, I recognized the dormitory to be the tree described in my Sanskrit school textbook. Students from every part of India and some from beyond the country's boundaries chose that hostel as their temporary residence. There were large contingents from Kerala, Sri Lanka (then Ceylon), the northern hills, different provinces of the Indian empire and, after the Japanese capture of Rangoon, Burma. And to complete the circle, there was Murugaya or Murugan, a Tamil from Malay who was probably in his mid-thirties. The war had disturbed his academic career; hence his undergraduate status at a relatively late age. By our standards, he was immensely rich and treated with some regard partly because he was generous with his whisky, which, incidentally, was strictly taboo according to the rules of conduct prescribed for the college. No one paid any attention. The assistant superintendent in charge of enforcing discipline also partook of Murugaya's bounty and that, as the saying goes, was that.

College Days

The cosmopolitan nature of the hostel's residents was traceable to its Christian orientation. In the earlier decades of the twentieth century, the Scottish mission, in all probability, still entertained hopes of converting educated Indians to the true faith. Close contact with beef-eating Christians in violation of Hindu orthodoxy, it was perhaps hoped, might produce the desired result. Hence Hindu students who opted to stay in Duff Hostel with people of all faiths were allowed to stay free. By our time, this privilege had been withdrawn but its vestiges remained—students from other colleges were still allowed to stay there and this is how I stayed on for seven years even though I shifted to Presidency College in 1943.

Living in a metropolitan city away from one's parents and family was a new and liberating experience. The cultural diversity of the hostel's inmates was exhilarating, if somewhat baffling. The boys from Kerala, Syrian Christians, who claimed to be the oldest Christian sect in the world tracing their origins to St Thomas, had very distinct food habits which I came to find quite attractive. They brought from home a very pungent mixture of powdered spices to pep up the hostel food. A very thin brew known as dahi-pani, a minute quantity of yoghurt mixed with a large volume of water, was kept especially for them. They poured this liquid into their rice adding lashings of their powdered fire. That was the staple with which anything else on offer—meat, fish, vegetables, etc.—in short everything except sweets was mixed before being eaten. I tried this concoction and found it very satisfying. The refugees from Burma were all immensely rich by our standards. They looked down on the food offered by the hostel and went most evenings for their dinner to fancy restaurants like Firpo's or Grand, which were way beyond our means most of the time. They wore tailor-made suits, indulged in very pricey alcoholic drinks every evening (to repeat, strictly in contravention of hostel regulations) and were far from averse to rounding up their days with rewarding visits to the expensive brothels in and around Free School Street. This last mentioned practice generated great envy in our hearts. They also discovered the joys of French wine in the French colony, Chandernagore, an hour's journey from Calcutta. I am forever grateful to these young bucks for introducing me to this supreme pleasure which was still incredibly cheap though the war had stopped all supplies from Europe. It was an introduction to true civilization. A third ethnic group was the Ceylonese, all Buddhists, who formed a circle and danced Kandyan dances with great swaying of hips at the slightest provocation. Our puritanical assistant superintendent found their hip-swaying a bit too immodest and made an embarrassed personal request that they should keep it within reasonable limits, especially when there were ladies present. It might cause the latter disgust or arousal, both being undesirable end results. I also found the lifestyle of the boys from the hills impressive, to say the least. Converted by the Christian missionaries, they had a totally westernized lifestyle. This included very heavy drinking, in fact heavier than I have seen in any ethnic group west of Suez. I have always wondered if the practice was European in origin or derived from indigenous habit engendered by the Himalayan weather. For I have found that the taxi drivers in the hills prefer to get heavily drunk when negotiating a series of hairpin bends at above eight thousand feet; the drink gives them both the necessary courage and warmth. If it takes them rolling down the cliff side, presumably they die very happy men. Their sober passengers are denied such solace in the hour of their need. The main point of the above ethnological discourse is that at Duff Hostel I encountered, and occasionally participated, in lifestyles which were very remote from those of middle-class Bengalis and violated the prescribed codes of conduct in Calcutta colleges. This violation demonstrated to me the proverbial tolerance of India's high civilization. The college, in shutting their eyes to the entire goings-on, could not have been more tolerant if it tried.

Scottish Church College was one of the few academic institutions in Calcutta which still had a sprinkling of European teachers. Its standing was high and some of the teachers were justly famous. The reason why I decided to go there rather than the premier institution, Presidency College, successor to the old Hindu College, the first centre of higher Western learning in Asia, was the flip side of that college's reputation. It was a government-run college. One of its more famous teachers, Humphry House, later a professor at Cambridge, published a pamphlet 'I Spy with my Little Eye'. Its administration gently nudged individual members of the faculty to spy on the nationalist students. The practice did continue even after I joined the college in 1943. It was widely, and in all probability correctly, believed that one of our teachers spied for the government. I found the notion of teachers actually spying on students sickening. There was a positive reason as well for my choice. When I went to college, my intention at first was to study English literature. While Presidency College had some very famous teachers of the subject, I wanted to study it, if possible, with people whose mother tongue was English. The great reputation of Mr Mowat as a teacher finally clinched the matter. I opted for Scottish Church College and was admitted to Duff Hostel where Mr Mowat was the superintendent. I have never regretted that decision.

If my understanding of the person is correct, Mr Mowat was a sad man. Looking back I feel that he was one of the thousands among the ruling race for whom imperialism was a tragedy. No, he was not one of those Britishers who disapproved of imperialism on moral or political grounds. On the contrary, he evidently identified hundred per cent with the idea of a civilizing mission or at least service to the conquered people. Only, from his personal experience, he appears to have come to the conclusion that it was a totally hopeless task. The said experience did not derive from any encounter with horrendous Hindu practices like the burning of widows or the throwing of children into the sea as an act pleasing the gods. It consisted in his everyday task of dealing with his unruly students. Unfortunately, it also included a long strike which permanently damaged the college. His frustration derived from culture shock. He was what anthropologists once described as a 'culture-bound' person, congenitally incapable of empathizing with alien ways, which were often unattractive by any standard. He seems to have accepted his long sojourn in Calcutta as the cross he had to bear. He did so with patience and in a spirit of surrender, but could not bring himself to feel any Christian love for the barbarians whom it was his painful misfortune to teach. He was very kind to me personally and I felt for this man both admiration and affection. He had a comfortable life by Indian standards (a very large and well-appointed flat and several servants), but I did not envy his fate. Looking back, I think, many who served the Raj (Mowat did not ostensibly do so) had a similarly painful existence. It is not easy to live among people for whom you feel a spontaneous antipathy if you are a person of any sensitivity, having power over them probably does not make it any easier.

Livelihood in Calcutta was still incredibly cheap by contemporary standards. Exchange value of any currency does not convey any idea of its domestic purchasing power but let me try to explain how cheaply we lived in the 1940s. The hostel charged us 21 rupees per month for boarding (two square meals and a light breakfast) and lodging. The amount was equivalent to one pound ten shillings. There were sixteen annas to the rupee and the following price list will give a measure of the price revolution which has taken place in the course of six decades. A chicken cost six annas; its current price is about sixty to seventy rupees. Goat meat sold for twelve annas a seer (which is a little less than a kilogram); current price two hundred and fifty rupees. Prawn was sold at the same price as goat meat; their current price four to five hundred rupees. Hilsa, the favourite fish of the Bengalis, was available in the country towns at eight to sixteen fish for a rupee; its current price is four to nine hundred rupees for one fish depending on its weight. Cinema tickets cost nine annas, one rupee two annas for the more posh ones; current price eighty to one hundred and fifty rupees. A three-dish meal at the newly opened Chinese restaurant, Chung Wah, cost about one-and-a-half rupees (current price three to four hundred; more posh places may cost from about a thousand to several thousand). Even the poshest of posh restaurants, Firpo's, offered its famous three-course lunch for three rupees. Before the great famine, average-quality rice, the staple of Bengali diet, sold for two to three rupees a maund (about 37 kilograms). Its current price is over thirty rupees for a kilogram. When the price shot up to forty rupees a maund, approximately one-

College Days

thirtieth or less of its current price, some three million starvation deaths were the estimated consequence. I recorded these facts in the Bengali version of my memoirs. Many of my readers thought I was fibbing. Prices went up after the great famine of 1943. Still, when I left Duff Hostel in 1947, the hostel charged thirty-eight rupees (three pounds) per month for board and lodging.

Scottish Church was a co-educational college. The fact was a source of some excitement to the sex-starved youth of Calcutta. But the girls walked into the class with the lecturers and marched back with them—to their common room, strictly out of bounds to the boys. Hence there was a proliferation of societies and extra-curricular activities in which the girls were allowed to participate. Despite, or perhaps because of such multiple restrictions, the god of love did often smile on his local devotees and certain number of 'love marriages' took place regularly among the students. The men who achieved this feat were treated with high regard as modern Bengali incarnations of Don Juan or Casanova—for it rarely happened that these adventurous young men went into matrimony before trying their luck, usually successfully, in half a dozen places. Those who deserved and eventually acquired the fair were indeed brave men. The rest of us addressed our fellow students of the fair sex using the very formal Bengali equivalent of the French 'vous'—'apni'. Those who attained the more familiar form of address, tumi (French equivalent, 'tu') were considered members of a superior species.

On one hot afternoon in July 1941, we were attending a class taken by Mowat. He was engaged in the utterly thankless task of explaining the literary charms of 'Ode to Autumn' to a group of incorrigibly philistine hoodlums. Suddenly, there was a commotion outside. Poet Tagore, the most revered icon of Bengali culture, had been sick for some time and there was great anxiety regarding the state of his health. Mowat asked me to go and find out what the commotion was about. It was as I had feared. Tagore had died. I came back to the class bringing the sad news. A great scream of bewildered misery went up and the students rushed to the door. I shall never forget the expression on Mowat's face: 'This is how you mourn your great men,' he seemed to say without uttering a word. The Bengalis are a noisy people, Bengali youth especially so, and they are wont to express their communal sorrow loudly. Mowat never understood the Bengalis. To him their noisy response to a great tragedy was only further proof of their barbarism.

Since 1939, the war had been raging in Europe and also nearer home in East Asia. Chiang Kai-shek came to Calcutta to secure sympathy and support from the Indian people who, if anything, were sympathetic to the Axis powers, partly out of a visceral hostility to their rulers, the British, and partly because they took pride in Japanese victories seen as a triumph of Asia over powerful Western nations. Nehru had a clear understanding of the Fascist threat and was eager to have India fighting for the Allies, if given some real power and promise of freedom after the war. One thing he was unwilling to do: to fight for the survival of the British Empire. All left wing forces, excepting those led by Subhash Chandra Bose were in sympathy with this view. But, almost certainly, they constituted a minority. The whole world was fighting. Young people like us with left sympathies were really eager for action and believed that the Axis powers were a dangerous threat to everybody's freedom. The Cripps Mission aroused much hope. Most people including Cripps and his Labour colleagues in the British cabinet were unaware that Churchill and Linlithgow were undermining the Mission behind their back. Robin Moore's researches have established the truth of this proposition beyond reasonable doubt. No wonder the Mission failed. As Nehru put it in a famous statement, the British had offered them total control over military stationery during the duration of the war. Gandhi decided to launch a mass movement which was to be short and sharp.

On 9 August 1942 news reached us that Gandhi and the Congress Working Committee had been arrested and taken to an unknown destination. Bombay and several other towns and cities burst into flames. Calcutta was ominously calm. Around 10 o'clock that morning, a procession came to Cornwallis Square opposite our college. We had been milling around in the college grounds for nobody tried to hold any classes. Hundreds of us joined the procession and marched towards Dalhousie Square, the seat of the local government. After we had gone about a mile southward, the police stopped us and ordered us to disperse. When no one moved, they threw tear gas shells and charged us with lathis. When the shells burst, there was an intolerable burning sensation in one's eyes and some of those hit by the lathis were bleeding. The procession ended ingloriously—we ran for our lives. The scene elsewhere in the country was very different. Four years later it would be very different in Calcutta as well—at last a 'revolutionary situation' had emerged, the political cognoscenti remarked at that time. Of that, later.

All schools and colleges in Calcutta closed down and the residents of the hostels were asked to leave for their homes as soon as possible. On the evening of 9 August a man I had never seen before came and handed me a bunch of leaflets. These allegedly contained instructions from the regional committee set up to conduct the Quit India movement. Later, I met the chairperson of this committee, Kalipada Mukherji, who confirmed that they had indeed issued that leaflet. It asked us to go back to our homes and contact the local leaders of the movement who were still outside prison and would tell us exactly what to do. The movement, we were told, would avoid all violence against persons. But violence against government property was permitted this time. The main object of the movement was to obstruct the war effort by sabotaging all means of transport and communication. The activists were also to try and stop the procurement of foodgrains. The expectation was that such action would eventually force the hands of the government to negotiate with the leadership. The leaflet clearly stated that we were not against the Allies and would help in the war effort as soon as the government had conceded reasonable terms. But we would not fight to save the British Empire.

I left for Barisal with a bunch of these pamphlets in my baggage. On the steamer from Khulna I met many of our friends and other political workers. The atmosphere was tense, apprehensive and yet hopeful. The repression would be intense this time, the more experienced workers told us, because a war was on. Churchill had declared that he had not been appointed the king's first minister to preside over the liquidation of the British Empire. There were more British soldiers in India at the moment than ever before in the country's history. Yet the general mood was unrealistically optimistic.

On reaching Barisal we found that quite a few of the activists had been arrested. Others were in hiding. The communists and the followers of M.N. Roy were openly preaching against the agitators as misguided patriots. As many among the former groups were old revolutionaries, people hesitated to brand them as traitors to the cause. In any case there was much more talk than action. One afternoon there was a meeting in our house to discuss the course of action. Very few among the participants had any idea as to what the unprecedented type of resistance prescribed by the leadership could mean in practice. A ramshackle plan of action was drawn up along the lines laid down by the provincial leadership. We heard that Jayaprakash Narayan, the Congress socialist leader, and Aruna Asaf Ali had assumed leadership of the movement and were operating from underground; that there was a massive uprising in the provinces where the Congress had formed ministries and that the army and the police were in revolt. Unfortunately, there was no truth in the rumours concerning the army and the police though the acts of defiance in the erstwhile Congress provinces and some districts of Bengal were formidable enough. Nothing comparable had occurred in the country since 1857 and it took more than a year and very severe repression to crush the uprising.

In our district, lacking organiztion, comparable resistance was not possible. Soon after the workers had left our house that afternoon, most of them were arrested. The few who managed to melt away in the villages and a bunch of school students, including my brother, took charge of the action. There were a few incidents of arson involving the post offices, and an unsuccessful attempt to stop the foodgrains procured from the farmers being loaded on a Calcutta-going steamer in Barisal. But within three months the very ineffective embers of resistance had been crushed. By Christmas, the collector

College Days

Mr Bell could write proudly home that he was playing cricket with the students in B.M. College, the local centre of the agitation. The 'rebellion', such as it was, had been successfully crushed in Barisal. I heard this from Mr Bell when I later met him in the UK.

Barisal's involvement in the Quit India movement was thus very limited. The same can be said about our family's involvement in it, though my father, brother and I got our badge of honour: time spent in prison. My father left for our village home before the administration was smart enough to serve an order placing him under house arrest. Before the police arrived there, he tried to induce the peasants to refuse to help the government with their plans for procurement of foodgrains. This was not a success because there had been no previous effort to contact and politicize the rural masses in our area. My brother had tried to organize arson at a few of the post offices in the area and, to the best of my knowledge, taken part in an unsuccessful attempt to remove rail lines in another district. If caught in the last mentioned act, he could have been hanged. Since he was not, he was merely arrested at the Barisal steamer ghat and imprisoned without trial, as was my father. My involvement was confined to raising funds. I discovered with much joy that Indian members of the ICS were not reluctant to contribute to the cause of freedom. I was arrested on charge of 'wire-cutting and theft'. I asked the police what I was supposed to have stolen. 'Wire, of course', I was told. This sounded entirely reasonable, because it would be a pity to just throw away the costly telegraph wires I had taken the trouble to steal, when they fetched a good price in the market. As a matter of fact the local authorities had a simple policy. There were a few real and several fictitious incidents of arson and 'wire-cutting'. When anyone suspected of involvement in the agitation was arrested, they would be accused of participation in one or other of these cases. The word 'theft' was added to deglamorize their involvement and also to humiliate them. In the highly unlikely event of their being prosecuted successfully, they could be treated as common criminals. For three months the accused would be produced before a magistrate every fortnight, in theory until enough evidence had been gathered for formally charging them. As the latter never happened, after three months the accused was either released (if he/she was not considered a threat) or detained for an indefinite period under the Defence of India Act. My father and brother were so detained. I was released after three months, through the intervention of Fazlul Huq, or so we were told.

My brief introduction to life in prison unravelled for me some of the mysterious ways of the Raj. Technically, I was not imprisoned but merely in custody because I was not formally charged; even though I spent the statutory ninety days in prison just like those who were sentenced. The system of classification of the prisoners was based on due respect for social stratification, not the famous and inscrutable Hindu caste system which so excites Western anthropologists, but the allegedly more rational basis of class. Those who lived in brick-built houses, and hence considered relatively affluent (though, as stated before, this was not quite correct), enjoyed the privileges of 'B' class. They slept on proper beds and had a daily allowance of one rupee four annas for their food, a princely sum for those days. The jail officials never saw any point in wasting such huge sums on undeserving political prisoners, but the food for the 'B' class prisoners was adequate and edible. There was an 'A' class with the right of getting food sent from home. Inclusion in this privileged category depended on the goodwill of the jail superintendent. Since classification was a matter of social status, it would have looked very odd if my father had not been granted 'A' class. The superintendent hence graciously declared that he could have milk sent from home if he so wished. This generous offer was politely declined.

Those condemned to the lower category, 'C', slept on one blanket on the floor and had another to cover their bodies in winter. Unfortunately, the blankets were inhabited by numberless bedbugs; even if one kept a respectable distance from the said blankets, the bugs marched out in an orderly fashion and invaded one's body. The experience was not pleasant. The half-a-rupee allowance per day for 'C' class prisoners was far from inadequate. But the loyal servants of the Raj would not dream of spending such incredible amounts on the hoi polloi. Hence the food for the 'C' class prisoners was not fit for human consumption, I shall presently explain why. My father was allocated to 'B' class immediately after the arrest ('A' class followed later); it took seven days to determine in what type of house I lived. In my brother's case, it took one month. It is unlikely that the police did not know that all three of us lived in the same house. One was condemned to 'C' class treatment until that relevant fact had been established; evidently a few days in 'C' class was considered a wholesome experience for the very young and/or those suspected of involvement in serious acts of sedition.

A glimpse into prison life, 'C' class, is enlightening. The police arrested me in our house and after several hours in the police station where I was registered as an accused in a case of wire-cutting and theft, I accompanied a single policeman to the prison, walking the two miles. When I was taken to the juvenile ward, 'C' class, it was about seven in the evening. The place was filled with an almost unbearable stench. I thought the sweepers were removing the night soil but it was hardly the appropriate time for doing this particular chore. I was right on the latter but not the former point. The source of the overpowering stench was not any night soil but our evening meal. This requires some explanation. In our part of the country most people eat parboiled rice. Producing this type of rice from paddy involves a particular technique. The jail authorities, instead of buying parboiled rice from the market, tried to produce it from paddy inside the prison, using convict labour. The idea was to save money. But as the convicts had no knowledge of the technique involved, the rice rotted. Hence the stench I had encountered. No one possibly could eat that rice, not even the poorest convict. Of course, there was another choice for the evening meal—chapatis. These did not stink, but had a fairly thick outer layer of dust and sand. The prisoners assiduously rubbed the chapatis together to get rid of the coating of filth; then one washed them before eating. The prescribed daily diet included a given quantity of vegetables and dal. Usually the prescribed quantity of vegetable was served in one of the two meals as a single lump boiled with the dal. The vegetables were invariably too large to be boiled and hence inedible, unless one had a love of half-raw vegetables. And if the chosen vegetable happened to be arum or taro which can cause intense irritation if not properly boiled, the dal too became inedible through contact with the poisonous stuff. Hence, the meal often consisted of well-washed chapatis and nothing more.

After a week in the juvenile ward I fell seriously ill and had to be removed to the jail hospital. The district medical officer visited us, diagnosed my illness as jaundice and recommended a diet of cold water, coconut water and various cooling fruits. I must acknowledge that the authorities were very liberal with their supply of cold drinking water. The other prescribed items were too difficult to procure.

But what was truly horrific in that hospital was the way ordinary convicts were treated. Many of them suffered from venereal diseases or deforming skin ailments. They were made to lie down on the hospital veranda without any clothes. Then their bodies were scrubbed vigorously with coconut fibre and bucketfuls of iodine were poured over their raw wounds. Their screams reached the high heavens—to me it was a miracle that they did not die. Every morning some unfortunates were taken to one corner of the prison compound and severely beaten up. This was no random act of sadism but motivated by a very definite purpose. One of the least popular duties for those condemned to hard labour was cleaning the latrines: the night soil had to be collected by hand and carried to a specified place. In our caste-ridden society only sweepers would attend to such tasks and evidently there were no or not enough members of that caste among the convicts. Some of them had to be beaten on a regular basis till they agreed to do the unpalatable job. There was compensation of course. The jail sweepers were allowed a double ration of the inedible food. I should emphasize one fact—the food for the 'C' class prisoners I have described was unacceptable even to convicts from the poorest level of society. The district was known for its flourishing agriculture, especially its abundant output of rice and lentils. Rotten rice or dal which made your glands swell were no part of its vie quotidienne, even among the very poor.

The Indian empire, it is still believed in some circles, was acquired in a fit of absent-mindedness. I had one experience in prison which suggested that the atrocities committed under the Raj were far from absent-minded acts. I was still in the juvenile ward, 'C' class, when there was a lathi charge on the political prisoners. The latter believed that the situation which led to this attack was deliberately created by the jail authorities. The guards were becoming very chummy with the political prisoners and taking their letters to people outside the prison; hence a conflict was deliberately provoked. This was probably not the case.

The incident occurred before my eyes. One of the guards in the juvenile ward was addicted to opium and one afternoon the boys were indulging in horseplay with this chap who was in a highly intoxicated state. One of the boys tried to snatch his whistle whereupon he blew it. This was normally done only when there was threat of real trouble. The alarm bells in the prison began to ring and posses of police with lathis and guns rushed towards the wards. Prisoners with experience of such events asked everyone to sit down on the floor of the wards and put their heads between their knees. We sat in concentric circles, the stronger forming a cordon sanitaire as the outer ring of the circles. In a little while, the police and some of the warders with leather belts in their hands rushed in and for a few minutes thrashed us at random with great force. Several of the prisoners were severely injured. Some had their skulls fractured. This assault was far from necessary because no one was even standing up to face the police. They acted, I was told, according to their code. When the alarm bell rang, they were supposed to rush forth and beat up whomever they could find in whatever posture. This was no time to think and choose courses of rational action. In fact, thinking was no part of the Indian policeman's training. But the real fun began after this episode.

A few days after this event, very sizeable branches of big trees and huge stones which no human being could have moved from one place to another without the help of machinery appeared on many spots inside the prison. We were totally mystified by this.

The more experienced political prisoners smiled and said that the jail authorities were going to launch cases of jail rioting against the prisoners, especially those who had been badly injured. This was standard practice. True enough, some senior police officers descended on the prison and prepared their report on the basis of which the seriously injured and a few others were duly charged. They refused to take part in the proceedings and were sentenced to several years in prison. This terminated their status as prisoners under the Defence of India Act and the privileges that carried.

My high regard for the wonders of the judicial system under the Raj, so admired by its admirers, was greatly enhanced by these happenings. The events I have just described are also relevant to the reverence with which the records of the Raj are held. Anyone indulging in a bit of local history of my district during the period 1942–43, would have included in his/her narrative one infamous jail riot instigated by the political prisoners. He/she would do so on the basis of the most authentic source material available, the district police records, no less. And in the extremely unlikely event of anyone ever taking an interest in the life story of an obscure Oxford don and other comparable lowlife, he would learn that the man was guilty of theft. Only, a just regime intent on securing justice spared him because in a highly dishonest society, the truth is not easy to establish. Perhaps at times the said records have to be kept at a respectful distance, say, the length of a bargepole, if one is interested in what was 'ist echtelich gewesen' (what really happened).

Our very sanctimonious jail superintendent went to the jail hospital to visit the injured and told them with profound sympathy, 'You see, you should not have attacked the police. You know they are not very educated. And there was no point in trying to escape from the prison. The walls are much too high. Pity you have been so badly hurt. Just imagine how terrible it would have been if one of you got killed.'

One badly injured prisoner could take this line of talk no longer and commented sweetly, 'Yes indeed, that would have been a great pity. But if instead you got killed there would be rejoicing in heaven.

Your poor wife would have been the person most pleased, relieved that she would no longer have to put up with an obnoxious pig. Maybe she would have remarried, but this time a human being, just for the experience.' The superintendent beat as hasty a retreat as his enormous belly would allow.

My last few weeks in prison were spent in 'B' class which had amenities like a proper bed and reasonable food. The latter, despite the regular theft, was distinctly better than what we had at our college hostel. I had high fever when I was released. Fazlul Huq visited us soon after my release. He administered a friendly slap adding, 'There are lots of people for going to prison. You have other things to do.'

I did not know that close encounters with the Raj of a truly bizarre kind were still waiting for us. As the land revenue paid by the zamindars was one major source of the government's income, they took a natural interest in the management of the estates when the latter were in serious trouble. It saved a lot of complications when instead of auctioning the estates which failed to pay the revenue, the government took over their management by a court of wards returning the estates to their owners at an appropriate time. This temporary takeover was subject to the owners' consent, and in fact was often at their own request, but it was generally considered a humiliation. As mentioned before, our estate was owned by twelve co-sharers and was going steadily downhill. In 1941 it was entrusted to the court of wards with my father's very reluctant consent. Under this arrangement, the court administered the property and distributed the income net of expenses among the owners as monthly allowances. On my release from custody I found that this monthly allowance had been reduced by 75 per cent by order of the district collector as punishment for our alleged involvement in the Quit India movement. One could not possibly survive on that amount and we became dependent on the charity of friends who gave us modest sums pretending that these were loans. We did try and pay these back when we got back our estate.

I knew that the government had acted illegally because there were no charges against any of us for which punishment was due. Even if it was, no court could have ordered a total or partial seizure of property as punishment, because that would have affected innocent members of the family—my mother, my sister and my newborn brother. The supposed legality of British Indian law, whatever the reality on the ground, precluded such violation of natural justice. I was still naive enough to believe that the facts of imperial rule corresponded with the avowed ideals, forgetting the numerous instances of torture and physical violence of which I was aware. The district public prosecutor was a family friend. Still having some faith in the system of justice (for no good reason), I asked our friend if I should sue the administration. He advised against it because, he said, it was wartime, no lawyer would take up our case and if anyone did just for the publicity, no judge would dare give a decree against the government. Instead, he suggested a different approach.

The new district collector was a wrangler, and hence supposedly a person with scholarly inclinations. This incidentally was a serious error. Over the years, by pure accident I happened to meet several Indian wranglers none of whom showed any scholarly inclination. In fact two of these academic champions were, though highly placed, downright stupid. One of them described Nehru as the new Christ because what was Pancha Sheela (the five principles of coexistence) but the Ten Commandments divided by two? Anyway, the public prosecutor believed (for no good reason) that our wrangler collector had heard of my reputation as a budding scholar. If I went to see him (the public prosecutor was willing to take me along), he was likely to take a sympathetic view. Well, I took this advice. I was shown into the presence. No chair was offered. The collector barked, 'Your father is a fifth columnist. He deserves to be hanged. We have treated you very kindly. Now go.' I had a strong desire to slap the idiot. But I was in no position to indulge in such heroics. I have referred earlier to the profound wisdom the Raj was capable of at the very top of the executive ladder. That a petty official at the district level should regard a staunch follower of Gandhi as a fifth columnist was nothing to wonder at. One deputy king, after all, had decided that Gandhi was a Bolshevik. The record does not suggest that the rest of the bureaucracy, the links in the famous steel framework, were necessarily much wiser.

As a student of Indo-British history, I have often marvelled at the incredible stupidity of the British officialdom in India and concluded in sorrow, that we Indians must have been utterly gormless to let this dumb lot rule over us for so long. The frame which held the Raj together was, in my perception, made not of steel but unbounded insensitiveness and an almost deliberate lack of common sense, an ever ready willingness to believe whatever suited one's interest and stubborn reluctance to see the truth. Even an otherwise shrewd man like Lord Hailey believed as late as 1937 that the masses were loyal to the Raj and the landed classes, their natural leaders. When the Congress swept to victory in seven of the eleven provinces, men like him were genuinely surprised. Significantly, Linlithgow advised his guest, young Nicholson, not to try to be clever in dealings with the Indians. The British must depend on their superiority of character, the nobleman explained. Evidently, 'character' and cleverness were uneasy bedfellows. For 'character' read genuine obtuseness which is always a source of great self-esteem. No, it is far from my intention to suggest that stupidity is integral to the British national character, but only that the perceptions and attitudes which informed the Raj often had a persistent streak of unmistakeable idiocy. To sustain one's self-confidence in ruling a recalcitrant people, delusion is a necessary prop. Honest insights occasionally broke through the miasma of self-deception like when Linlithgow reminded his bosses in Whitehall that the Indians were a conquered people from whom empire loyalty could not be expected. But wait, recent historical research has 'established' that this is not quite true, because the Indians were no mere passive victims, but active and willing agents in the act of conquest. The reference, presumably, is to the traitors like Mirjafar and his co-conspirators who betrayed their masters. Using similar logic one could argue that the actions of Marshal Petain and Quisling prove that the French and the Norwegians were no mere victims of Nazi aggression but active agents in establishing Germany's temporary ascendancy over their countries.

My father sent me a note expressing his displeasure at my seeking an interview with the magistrate and collector. He made the point that since we rejected the legitimacy of the British rule in India, we could not appeal to their proclaimed legality to seek redress from their acts of oppression. And since we wished them to quit, we could not expect them to set limits to their aggression and should be ready to suffer any punishment they decided to impose on us. To expect justice from a body that was illegitimate was ridiculous and having courted punishment, we could not expect them to draw any line. But we had reached a point of near-starvation and these Gandhian moral judgements as well as the strength to live by them had eluded me. But as my father pointed out, if one was scared of bullets, one should not volunteer to join the army. He was, of course, right.

The Indo-British encounter always contained elements of the unexpected. I was soon to experience one which remains one of my treasured memories. After I was released I had to stay on in Barisal, as I was put under house arrest. But the government allowed me to sit for the intermediate arts examination which was roughly equivalent to the 'A' level in the English system. After passing this examination I was admitted to Presidency College. I had decided to study history as preparation for doing research on the subject. One of our teachers at Scottish Church College had suggested that, as a professional scholar, an Indian academic could hope to achieve little in the field of English literature. He cited the example of several great and famous teachers of English literature. I should therefore aim at working on some area like the economic history of the Mughal period, he said, following in the footsteps of Sir Jadunath Sarkar who had covered its political history in marvellous detail. His great oeuvre was produced over a period of sixty years. This idea appealed to me but my decision meant that I would move to Presidency College because the most renowned teacher of history in Calcutta, Professor Sushobhan Sarkar was on their faculty. As I enjoyed my stay in Duff Hostel and had many friends there, I wrote a very hesitant letter to Mr Mowat mentioning that I had been in prison for some time, a fact which was probably known to him, and asking if I could stay on in Duff Hostel though I had moved to Presidency College. His answer was something I had never expected; I realized that the person who wrote that letter was someone I did not know and had misunderstood seriously. I quote from memory: *My dear boy, you belong to us. Your room is there for you. Do come back whenever you are ready. I perfectly understand your moving to Presidency College to study history, though I had hoped to teach you.* Mr Mowat's view of the world and politics was certainly not mine. But my seditious associations had in no way undermined his evident affection for me.

That brief letter taught me a very important lesson. Political beliefs and affiliations belong to the externals of our lives and are determined by fortuitous conjunctures, the accidents of birth, nurture and social environment. They do not always affect the deeper streams of our existence, the often autonomous reality of our relationship with other human beings. This understanding has nourished many of my human relationships throughout my life. Difference in political outlook has not stood in the way of genuine friendships. Some of my very good friends at Oxford are people with whom I have hardly anything in common in matters of social or political ideology.

9

Presidency College: The Great Famine, Hindu–Muslim Riots and the Partition, 1943–47

In July 1943, I returned to Calcutta and the very room from where I had left for my traumatic experiences in my home town the previous year. But there was a big change. Now I was a student of Presidency College, Calcutta, and very proud to be so. It was the premier academic institution of India, a proud successor to the Hindu College where modern education had first begun in India. Its great reputation is now in eclipse, but it continues to produce brilliant men and women who flourish in different spheres of Indian life both at home and abroad. Many of the intellectual luminaries of nineteenth-century Bengal, the heroes of the nineteenth-century 'renaissance', were products of this college and it counted among its teachers some of the best known academics in the country. I opted to join the college mainly because I wanted to study with one of them, Professor Sushobhan Sarkar.

Like many of the other famous teachers of Presidency College, Professor Sarkar also was not a productive scholar. These men were devoted to scholarship: they spent their lives reading and teaching and had no ambition for scholarly renown. Professor Sarkar was an Oxford graduate and sympathetic to the Communist Party. He was a Marxist and believed in historical materialism, the Marxist interpretation of history. He wrote a small pamphlet in Bengali on the grand movements of history along Marxist lines. It was a rigorously argued volume, avoiding catch phrases and all forms of sloganmongering. In his lectures he did not however draw upon his faith in Marxist historiography. Instead, he presented a very lucid analysis of Europe's political history since 1648, the prescribed subject of our study. What we learnt from him was the clarity of explanations, the anatomy of the historical process as it were. His lectures showed how it was possible to extract from a plethora of details a clear pattern of structure and movement from one situation to another as also causal links which did not follow any preordained, theoretically determined patterns. His approach, if anything, was pluralistic. The only thing he questioned was randomness. Events and decisions had identifiable causes and mutual links. One task of history was to identify these. Narrative was important so long as one did not just stop there. I am a sceptic who does not believe in any particular interpretation of history. Professor Sarkar showed us how to look for causal links and patterns. He also suggested that all statements in history should be taken as being tentative—for the historian, there are no ultimate or absolute truths. As a professional historian I have found his teaching immensely helpful and proportionately difficult to follow. The proportion of historians who believe in the absolute validity of their conclusions and approach without saying so is unfortunately very large. We learnt from Professor Sarkar how to avoid that trap, or at least try.

The college was also famous for its succession of great teachers of English literature. The most famous among them in our time was Tarak Sen. We read *Twelfth Night* with him. His technique was to make Shakespeare's meaning at various levels as explicit as possible, drawing on his vast scholarship for this purpose. We studied English literature as a 'pass', i.e., subsidiary subject, concentrating on our 'honours' subject which was history in my case. Professor Sen's emphasis on 'meaning' for students at our level—he went into issues of literary criticism for students in his honours class—was invaluable.

He made it possible for us to enjoy Shakespeare and I dearly wish I had read all the plays with someone like him. If I still find reading Shakespeare a life-enhancing experience, the person I have to thank for this is Professor Tarak Sen.

Presidency College was home to intellectual snobbery. It attracted the very best students of Bengal and they were very aware of their relative excellence. Some of them, like Amartya Sen and Satyajit Ray, have become internationally famous. Others, like Siddhartha Shankar Roy and Pratap Chanda, made it to the front rank of politics in independent India as ministers in the state and Central cabinet or governors of states. People outside their circle must have found us awful. But our mutual contact was enriching in many ways. Long before interdisciplinary approach had become fashionable, we took serious interest in subjects which were far from the boundaries of our formal studies by earnestly dipping into the mighty and famous tomes our fellow students carried around, very demonstratively. On matters of politics and social philosophy there was always an ongoing battle of wits, especially on the two great issues of our time—Marxism and Gandhian doctrine, the question of the correct way to political freedom.

Opposite our college the new Coffee House, a workers' cooperative, came up when we were undergraduates. Some of us got all our education from our fellow students in that seat of learning without ever bothering to cross the street to attend classes in the other institution. Those who expressed their preference in this way were by no means worse educated. The college itself provided facilities for adda (a very Bengali institution, this term means gossip sessions, in some ways similar to what goes on in the French cafes on the Left Bank), especially in one rather derelict cafe known as Mr Ray's. There we spent many pleasurable hours until one smart-aleck decided that Mr Ray should be induced to provide beer, unbelievably still taboo, like every other alcoholic drinks inside the college. The profits on beer were good. Ray fell for the temptation. He was caught and that was the end of his cafe. Some of us now migrated permanently to the Coffee House. We did not encounter only our fellow students there. Many members of the creative intelligentsia, especially impoverished writers and retired politicians, came and settled down with a cup of coffee to enjoy for an hour the air-conditioned comfort the place offered. Its other branch on Central (now Chittaranjan) Avenue provided shelter to groups of intellectuals, one of which nurtured the talent of Satyajit Ray and really helped shape his first great film, *Pather Panchali*. I got to know two very interesting persons in the College Street Coffee House. One was Bhupen Datta, Swami Vivekananda's youngest brother, a famous revolutionary implicated in the Alipore Conspiracy case, who later escaped to Russia and worked closely with Lenin. Bhupen Babu had reached the extreme of poverty or so his one tattered-looking kurta suggested. We entertained him with a sandwich or omelette for the privilege of his company and he seemed grateful for the modest snack we offered him. Unfortunately for us, he refused to talk about either his career as an Indian revolutionary or as Lenin's co-worker. When invited to address our postgraduate seminars, he stuck to one subject—dialectical materialism. This was not very enlightening.

Our other acquisition in the Coffee House was our leading humorist in the Bengali language, Shibram Chakravarti. He lived in a low-down 'mess' or pension nearby and turned up for his cup of coffee at a regular hour. He too could not afford anything beyond that one cup worth four annas and was extremely reluctant to accept anything we offered. He had a standard response. He could not accept because he was in no position to return our hospitality. 'You provide us with such fun through your writings. Can we not buy a sandwich for you in return?' we insisted. But nothing would change his mind. For men like him, the air-conditioned Coffee House offered a brief but cool respite from the suffocating heat and squalor of the rooms they lived in. Shibram wished for little more.

In 1943, a new phenomenon hit the streets of Calcutta. Groups of men, women and children began to appear on the city's pavements who had little in common with the professional beggars and the destitute who had always made the streets their home. The new pavement dwellers were identifiably householders, not beggars, because there were entire families of these people; the beggars might have a partner or a child, but hardly ever lived as members of a family group. Only one thing did they have in common: they were very obviously starving and had that look of extreme hunger in their faces. At first, they did not beg—it is not an act that comes easily to people left with any vestiges of dignity. Price of rice and other edibles had been shooting up. Villagers who had no stock of foodgrains and could no longer afford to buy these had started coming to the city in the hope that they would find food and employment there. They kept looking vacantly at the affluent passers-by and said nothing. But extreme hunger and the sight of family members on the point of death are compelling forces and these people began to beg, very ineffectively at first. They asked for food and nothing else because cash was useless in a market where prices went up several points every day. Soon they realized that nobody had food to spare. The begging for rice, 'bhat', stopped. The hitherto unheard of plea, 'give us some gruel' (phyan dao go)—the water one throws out when cooking rice— was now heard on every street in the city. The half-dead soon began to join the ranks of the dead. We became used to stepping across dead bodies on the pavements. You could not avoid them.

Extreme calamity tends to coarsen our sensibilities. One morning we saw a miserable sight on the pavement opposite our hostel: a baby, all skin and bones, was trying desperately to suck at his mother's breast. The woman was dead. We rushed to the relief centre, which was located in the local ARP (Air Raid Precaution) office. A young man sat there, having nothing to do, because air raids cannot be prevented without resort to weapons, which he did not have. His duties which were to follow rather than precede air raids had not yet materialized. We described what we had seen and requested him to do something for the baby. He asked me on which pavement had we seen him. On hearing our answer, he commented distantly, 'Not my responsibility. Go to the other office.' He very kindly gave us the address.

It is easy to be censorious about this sort of behaviour. But it is strange to remember how continuous exposure to the sight of painful death—and few deaths are more painful than death from starvation—blunts one's sensibilities. The young man was no doubt brutish. But within his area of responsibility he was probably coping with several hundred deaths and near-deaths every day. We ourselves had got used to walking past dead bodies, holding our noses to block out the stench. We rarely stopped to see if the carcass still contained some vestiges of life. Our meals in the hostel had not suffered any decline in quality or quantity. Very virtuously, we fasted from time to time and gave our food to the starving. This was not even a proverbial drop in the ocean. I am also ashamed to admit that we did not stop going to restaurants from time to time. Strangely enough, restaurant prices had not gone up significantly. It was the basic staple—rice— that was seriously in short supply. I met an English doctor in Oxford in the 1950s who was in Calcutta during the famine. He showed me two items pasted side by side in his photo album. One was of a special seven-course menu of a gala banquet at Firpo's priced at 9 rupees (about 75 pence). The other was a photo of starving men, women and children outside Firpo's. I also discovered how more fortunate people like us were totally unfamiliar with the physiology of starvation. In occasional outbursts of public spirit, we would organize langarkhanas, i.e., charitable distribution of food, usually a very thin watery mixture of rice and lentils. The starving tended to develop severe diarrhoea within minutes of eating the food and died. The stomachs of starving people cannot cope with food, especially solids. The unfamiliar object has to be slowly reintroduced. How should we know how the physiology of that unfamiliar species, starving human beings, worked?

Historians attach a great deal of importance to 'eyewitness accounts' of important events. For big cataclysmic events like the Bengal famine which, to repeat, took some three million lives, eyewitness accounts have little value. People like us who lived through it, saw the incredible sight of dead bodies piling up on the city's streets. The government agencies dutifully removed them every day to be replaced by other carcasses in the next twenty-four hours. We also witnessed the price of rice shooting up. And we heard rumours. We learnt from the latter that as a wartime measure, rice had been procured from the villages to ensure that they did not fall into the hands of any invading enemy. All local means of transport, like boats and bicycles, had been confiscated for the same reason. This was the infamous 'Denial Policy', a sort of anticipatory 'scorched earth'. The rice procured by the government agencies were piled up in the Botanical Gardens. Part of the procured foodgrains was to be distributed through a system of rationing. There was an unfortunate time lag between the procurement and redistribution among consumers. As prices began to shoot up, unscrupulous traders and profiteers withdrew the rice from the market exacerbating the scarcity. Such black marketeering was severely punishable in theory. In practice, not one dishonest dealer was prosecuted. The people with limited purchasing power and no access to stocks of rice moved to the cities. What happened to these unfortunates was something we did see with our own eyes.

Well, we had no means of knowing if the rumours were true or false, though people were always ready to believe the worst of the government. When the dreadful shortage came to an end, the Indian Statistical Institute prepared a report which showed that the popular rumours were in essence correct. Only, its cold statistics revealed the full horror of the story. Besides the loss of human lives, a third of Bengal's cattle population was wiped out, permanently damaging the region's economy. Recent research has established that the district officials had been repeatedly warning the authorities in Calcutta, the governor and his advisers (who had virtually usurped the power supposed to be exercised by the elected ministers under the 1935 Act), of the impending danger and suggested modifications of the 'Denial policy'. Nobody listened. Recently, the son of the governor who held sway during the famine presented a paper in Calcutta based on his father's notes covering the period of his tenure. It hardly contained any reference to the famine for which the dignitary had a large share of responsibility and none to the various misdeeds attributed to him. Incidentally, Midnapore, a district where the Quit India movement had gathered some momentum, became a victim of a very destructive flood on top of a severe food shortage. The governor took a curious view of his duty in the face of this calamity. He visited the area by airplane three weeks after the flood had hit the district. Ministers of the provincial cabinet were prevented from visiting the affected region. The viceroy appealed to Churchill for a ship to bring foodgrains to Bengal. The great man was extremely reluctant to grant this request.

To repeat, I have hardly met anyone in the UK who has any knowledge of the Bengal famine of 1943 which occurred only four years before the transfer of power. I have also not come across any awareness in Britain that the colonial government was primarily responsible for that ghastly and totally avoidable calamity. The propaganda machine of the British establishment has succeeded brilliantly in hiding the facts from the British public. I often wonder whether the Soviet rulers would not still be ruling their totalitarian empire had they taken lessons in brainwashing from the said establishment. It took me some time to realise that the establishment does believe in its own propaganda. They do think that the empire from which their social class, but hardly anyone else, benefited immensely, was morally white as snow and a source of endless benefit to mankind. I have not come across any other human group with comparable capacity for self-delusion. This indeed was partly the source of the evident power, the much advertised 'character' which sustained the empire.

One thing which struck me about Presidency College, in contrast to what I had experienced in my home town and was later to encounter in the university's postgraduate class, was the relative indifference of the students to national politics. This is relevant because I am talking of the four years immediately preceding independence. There was a lot of discussion and brilliant analysis whenever the members of the intellectually outstanding student body met. But activism or any serious participation in the ongoing political process was minimal, and this despite the fact that some of our seniors were to figure in the state or Central cabinet after independence. The one striking exception was the communists who also had an active policy of recruitment. One of their student leaders was elected secretary of the World Federation of Democratic Youth, a communist front organization, and left for France to take up the post. He was Ranajit Guha, later to acquire fame as the founder of the Subaltern cartel. Most of the students whose academic achievements were outstanding were immersed in studies or were busy building their careers otherwise, which meant preparing to take up secure jobs or, less frequently, professions. The explanation is probably simple: concentration on building one's career had some meaning for the very best students, though a few of them were also drawn into anti-colonial activism. Most of our brilliant contemporaries joined the various cadres of the administrative services after independence and rose to the top of the bureaucratic ladder. For the vast majority, the career prospects were bleak under the colonial regime. Such men and women were less intent on career building because there were no careers to build. They were the potential recruits of the political parties, though some of our most brilliant students also became activists. After independence, the vast expansion in career opportunities no doubt partly explains the decline in the quality of recruitment into political cadres. I hope this statement will not be taken to mean that those who failed to get jobs took to politics both before and after the transfer of power. I only suggest that the unpromising material environment was one factor permitting idealistic young men and women to remain faithful to their chosen political agendas.

The transition from the Presidency College to the university's postgraduate department was academically an interesting experience. The courses for the BA (honours) degree were taught in the college by its galaxy of very famous teachers. Nominally, after our graduation, when we were working for our MA degrees, we were still students of the Presidency College, paying our fees to that institution. The MA degree was also the reward for success in written examinations at the end of two years of taught courses. But the academic atmosphere in the two institutions, Presidency

College and the postgraduate department of Calcutta University, was completely different. If the emphasis in the former was on the excellence of teaching, i.e., lecturing to cover the courses, the teachers in the latter were very famous scholars justly renowned in their respective fields throughout the world. Hem Raychaudhuri was probably the greatest Indologist India had ever produced, Suniti Chatterji the most eminent philologist and Suren Dasgupta, the world authority on Indian philosophy. The emphasis here was on the depth and extent of scholarly knowledge. Dinesh Sarkar and Sarasi Saraswati could literally recite from memory almost all the published epigraphs of Indological interest. Sukumar Sen had a comparable knowledge of all Indian literatures. Later, when as a very young lecturer of Calcutta University, I sat round the table in the teachers' common room of this august institution with these great and famous men (only one or two of the famous scholars had a room to themselves), I felt a due sense of humility.

The emphasis in this proud tradition was on scholarship and scholarship alone. The output of these undoubtedly great men was often weak in analysis and interpretation. The emerging influence of the social sciences was looked upon with some suspicion. And, with one or two exceptions, the scholars were not very good teachers, i.e., adept at expounding on their chosen field of knowledge in their class lectures. Some were distinctly weak in their command over spoken English, the language in which the lectures were delivered. Listening to the lectures of these famous men one often had a sense of being let down, especially in comparison with one's experience at Presidency College. I should add that in the 1950s, while listening to lectures at Oxford, I often had the same feeling. Many of the great scholars were not very good lecturers. But in Calcutta, the great emphasis on scholarship was very real beyond doubt. One took ten to fifteen years to acquire a PhD degree. This was partly because there was at most one research scholarship per subject. The researchers taught in some college or earned their livelihood otherwise, working part-time for a research degree. But there was no compromise on matters of scholarship while awarding a degree. Often, it could be earned only after several attempts. Later, the university tackled this problem by introducing an easier degree, not a very desirable step to my understanding. The old emphasis on genuine scholarship is a thing of the past.

There was another aspect to the environment of the postgraduate department which made it very different from the Presidency College. A large section of the student community here was highly politicized. Every political party had a branch among the postgraduate students. Many of the activists had been in prison in 1942. Some were revolutionaries who had spent years in exile in Andaman. One of them was the young man who had murdered a district magistrate in Midnapore (three had been assassinated in succession to establish the fact that the British could no longer hope to rule in peace without resistance). There is evidence to prove that these acts of terror did affect recruitment to the ICS. The revolutionaries did not hope to achieve independence by their stray acts of violence. But they did hope to render colonial governance virtually impossible. The young man who, at the age of sixteen, had murdered the district magistrate, Mr Burgess, had joined the Communist Party on being released at the age of thirty. He told us a strange story. In prison they were almost encouraged to read Marxist literature, made available in plenty, evidently in the hope that this would help weaken the main enemy, the Indian National Congress and its followers. With such fellow students among our ranks the political atmosphere was expectedly hot. The Quit India movement had failed. But the activists were preparing for another round of struggle with the colonial rulers. Whether we achieved independence in our lifetime or not, our hope was that we would not let them rule in peace ever again. Only, nobody believed in stray violence as the relevant means any longer. We hoped and pressed for a resumption of mass action. But it had to be under the leadership of that impossible old man, Bapu, our highly irritating father, in fact much more irritating than the usual run of fathers in the eyes of their young progeny. The Father of the Nation was a master in the art of indefinite postponement, while we, who knew better, wanted action yesterday if possible. Unfortunately, no one else had the necessary clout with the masses. Even his arch critic, Subhash Bose had waited for him to give the call.

Our direct experience of the war in which quite a few of us, antifascists, had hoped to take part was very limited indeed. The Japanese did not appear to have had any plans to invade India. Milan Hauner's exhaustive study of India in the calculations of the Axis powers proves this quite conclusively. The Japanese were evidently reluctant to stretch their front to unrealistic limits beyond the frontiers of Burma. The invasion of north-eastern India led by Subhash Chandra Bose's Indian National Army appears to have been partly a diversionary move and partly the result of Subhash Chandra's successful effort in inducing a military intervention. Before that, there had been a few air raids on Calcutta and Chittagong. Calcutta suffered from a mass hysteria of apprehension before the raids actually took place, leading to large-scale exodus. As the temporary refugees were far from welcome in the places where they had taken shelter, they preferred to brave bombing by the Japanese to the unfriendly treatment in the houses of friends and relations, mainly in eastern Bengal. They returned to Calcutta as they had fled from the city—en masse.

The first evening when the Japanese planes actually threatened the city, a few friends and I were returning from a cycle trip to Burdwan and neighbouring historical sites. We were in the business quarter of the city, Burrabazar, when the sirens sounded. The business people and shopkeepers were extremely reluctant to let us in. If bombs fell, they would have preferred us to perish on the road rather than, as potential criminals, endanger their security. This seemed entirely sensible; as a matter of fact much more sensible than the precautionary measures regarding air raids which mainly consisted in constructing brick shelters by the roadside, mostly used for purposes of sodomy, casual fornication and more legitimate activities like attending to calls of nature. One night, when we were watching a film at the Metro cinema, at last the bombs actually fell, killing only a few people, we were told. There were a few other incidents of bombing, two in residential areas and one, in daylight, on Kidderpore dock. The last incident is said to have killed three hundred people.

None of these air attacks killed anyone in the affluent quarters. Only two persons from the middle classes were victims of the Japanese assaults, according to my information. At night the city looked very dark, thanks to air raid precaution measures. But this was not merely an inconvenience: 'black out' had definitely its bright side for the city's wealthy bon viveurs.

For the privileged in Calcutta, the war provided a fairly enjoyable time. The news of Allied defeats brought vicarious pleasure. Muted cheers went up from roadside gatherings of people listening to the radio every time an Allied defeat or withdrawal was announced. Personally, I found these responses profoundly humiliating. They vivified for me the moral degradation of a subject people, their impotent weakness and stupid delight at the misfortune of a hated ruler whom they themselves could do nothing to dislodge. The Indian experience of the devastating war had nothing remotely heroic about it. The mercenaries did their duties, because they were honest soldiers and in a country as poor as India, recruitment is never a problem. In Calcutta, the famine had enriched further some of the very rich while many more benefited from the new and numerous massage parlours. First seen when the foreign soldiers arrived, these flourished during the famine. But their true glory days came after the Partition. Refugees from East Bengal far exceeded the famine-stricken in number. Besides, those who sought employment with the parlours were not yet starving or otherwise moribund. As masseuses, they were definitely of interest to those who could afford to pay them. Then there were lots of new restaurants though some of these were out of bounds to Indians. To be fair, there were others which were out of bounds to the soldiers. Thus a good time was had by many, but unfortunately not all, especially not the famine-stricken. But then, you cannot have everything.

In the very last years of colonial rule there were new and somewhat unexpected developments in politics which affected us, students, very directly. The Congress leaders were released after the end of the war and the newly elected Labour government opened negotiations with them and other political parties for an eventual settlement. The leadership did not really believe that any transfer of power was round the corner.

This is made quite explicit in the memoirs of Maulana Abul Kalam Azad, the chief negotiator on behalf of the Congress. They thought that the rulers were up to one of their multiple tricks. Nehru came to Calcutta and addressed an audience of some half a million people. As the microphones failed, we could not hear a word but only see his angry gestures from a distance. However, the newspapers next morning reported that the leader, as expected, had called upon us to be ready for the next round of action.

Meanwhile, something else was happening. Most people in India either knew nothing or had heard vaguely of the Indian National Army during the war. I remember one evening I was visiting my uncle Kiran Shankar Roy when a call came from the chief minister of the province, Nazimuddin. He said that Subhash Chandra was speaking on the radio from Singapore; we could tune in if we wished. As it was forbidden to listen to enemy broadcasts, this had to be done with due circumspection. The transmission was poor in quality and I could not follow a single word. After the war, the officers and soldiers of the INA were brought to India for trial. This aroused great emotion among the people and the trial at Red Fort in Delhi was abandoned only after countrywide agitation. But a fair price had to be paid to secure this decision.

In November 1945 students in Calcutta decided to observe INA Day, demanding the immediate release of the soldiers on trial. The plan was simply to go out in procession and take a petition to our elected premier (i.e., chief minister of the province), Mr Suhrawardy of the Muslim League. The one snag in the plan was that the premier's office was located in Dalhousie, still a 'prohibited area' under the Defence of India rules. The procession which was eventually joined by some hundred thousand boys and girls were stopped by the police on Dharmatala Street, about a mile from Dalhousie. When the students refused to move despite warnings, the police first threw tear gas shells and then opened fire. Unlike in 1942, nobody ran away this time. More students came and joined the demonstrators.

Some fifty students were killed. These scenes were repeated next day; evidently, in the three intervening years since 1942, the mood among Calcutta's students had changed. They were no longer in a hurry to run away when the police fired.

In February 1946, when the INA general Rashid Ali Khan was on trial, there was a repetition of the scene. Only there was a new element in the action this time round. The political situation had become more complicated because the Muslim League had taken up an uncompromising stand on the question of Pakistan. Progressive elements among the students were extremely worried about the worsening of relations between the communities on the eve of what looked like transfer of power in near future. As Rashid Ali, alone among the INA generals, had declared in favour of Pakistan the League leadership had approved of their student supporters participating in the demonstration demanding the general's release. The Students' Muslim League decided to join the demonstration. We saw an inspiring sight in Wellington Square which was never to be repeated. The nationalists, communists and League supporters among the students came to the square with their tricolour, red and green flags which were tied together in a melodramatic gesture. The unreal vision of unity seemed to be temporarily very real. We marched to Dharmatala Street in very high spirit, aware of possible danger, adrenalin rushing through our veins. The scenes which occurred on that spot in November the previous year were repeated. Tear-gassing followed orders to disperse. Then the police fired killing quite a few. This time, however, there was no running away. Premier Suhrawardy and the Congress leader, Sarat Bose, Subhash Chandra's elder brother, came to the spot. Restrictions were removed and the two leaders led the students to Dalhousie Square. One joined the charade with no feeling of victory, only a pervasive sense of emptiness and sheer waste, a bottomless depression with no light at the end of the tunnel.

I often look back on that scene and wonder what purpose was served by these incidents. Did it hasten the decision to transfer power which came seventeen months after this episode? The riots which followed some six months after Rashid Ali Day certainly contributed to that decision! What did the authorities gain from the events of February 1946? I cannot think of anything. An English friend who was in India during the war serving in military intelligence once showed me a photograph: its subject matter was the scene I have described above.

'I was there,' he said, adding, 'what a waste!' I told him that I too was there, only on the other side.

Often in the evening I remember some of the faces of the boys who got killed. What would have happened to them if they were still alive? Would they have ended their career as almighty secretaries to our government, or famous professors or journalists, or maybe even as clerks in our overpopulated secretariats? Who knows? The only fact is that they did not survive to build our country one way or another. And their parents? They probably just pined away.

My Gandhian faith was on trial that afternoon as it had been on the day of the lathi charge in prison. Part of that faith easily survives for I doubt if any human being feels any passionate hatred towards another trying to hurt or kill you, especially at the moment of confrontation. One's mind is too full of other thoughts at the moment—like how to save your skin. You also realize that you can do little to achieve that end. Pervasive hatred is produced by sustained propaganda and long-term circumstances of your life, not sudden impulse. If you have been exposed to the discipline of non-violence, you feel a certain calmness which I believe the soldier in action with a high morale also shares. In prison I had received one excruciating blow from a convict's very thick belt—the pain and the burning sensation left no room for thinking of anything else. On Dharmatala Street, I remember experiencing a measure of sadness for oneself as well as the aggressor.

'What a waste', I thought later.

The embryo of that sentiment was in my consciousness when the things were happening. There was not any great upsurge of either fear or heroic euphoria. I later asked my friend Professor Robinson, a much decorated teenage bomber-pilot in the Second World War, about the onset of fear. He said that there were butterflies in the stomach when the mission took off. Afterwards, one was too busy and then one was either shot down or came back. Not much time for numbing fear. We are indeed creatures of circumstances; we realize that fact somewhat vividly in the face of deadly threat. There is a sense of unreality, of detachment in relation to what is going on around one. Self-conscious heroism in any form is probably an apotheosis of extreme stupidity.

Things moved very quickly after this incident. Three members of the Labour cabinet, including Cripps, came to India with a constitutional proposal for resolving the impasse. In essence they proposed a somewhat loose federation with the Muslim-majority provinces in the east (this would include Bengal and Assam) and north-west, forming two semi-autonomous groups with certain matters like finance, defence and foreign affairs being in the hands of the Centre. Besides, the federating units would also have the right to opt out of the Union in the future. There was a reluctant acceptance of the proposal by all the major political parties, including the Congress and the Muslim League. An interim government at the Centre began to work, very creakily, on the basis of this understanding. Then something terrible happened. In a press conference in Bombay, Nehru declared that the Constituent Assembly, which had come into being as a part of the deal and would complete its work after the British had left, was a sovereign body not bound by any earlier commitment. Jinnah interpreted this to mean that none of the clauses in the agreement were considered binding by the Congress and hence they could not be trusted to respect the semi-autonomy of the Pakistan provinces. Nehru's repeated assurances that this was not what he meant proved to be fruitless. It does seem that Jinnah wanted Pakistan and had found the ideal excuse for this purpose. Only Direct Action would secure Pakistan, he declared. The sixteenth of August was declared to be the Direct Action Day. The nature of the said action was not explained except in the statement that this symbolic action would take place in the city of Calcutta.

The political scene had changed totally in India, especially where the Muslims were concerned. In 1937, nowhere had the majority of the seats in the provincial assemblies reserved for the Muslims gone to the Muslim League. The alliance holding power in Bengal included nationalists. In Punjab, the Unionists ruled and that party represented landed interests—Muslim, Hindu and Sikh. In the North-West Frontier Province, with a population more than 90 per cent of which were Muslim, the Congress was in power. Even Sindh did not have a Muslim League ministry. The 1946 election in the provinces changed all that. The League with its declared objective of establishing an autonomous Muslim state, Pakistan, swept to an unquestionable majority in the seats reserved for Muslims. This meant that they could form ministries in the Muslim-majority provinces. Suhrawardy was the prime minister in united Bengal and the European members of the assembly, in other words the colonial government, supported him. And it was in the capital of that province that Direct Action would be launched.

The afternoon of 16 August 1946 saw the first Hindu–Muslim riots on a very large scale which firmly opened the door to Pakistan as a separate independent state. I was one among the several million who saw what happened that day. Some Hindu readers of my memoirs in Bengali have been deeply upset by my alleged pro-Muslim bias in describing the horrors. Let me explain the basis of this allegation. Here again, the old problem of the limitations of all eyewitness accounts become relevant. The habitation pattern in Calcutta has one peculiarity. In some areas the population is overwhelmingly Hindu, in others Muslim. In the midst of these areas inhabited mostly by members of one community, there are small pockets of habitation by people of the other community. To my understanding, what happened on 16 August 1946 was not rioting, i.e., violent conflict between Hindus and Muslims, but acts of butchery against the small number of men, women and children of the other community marooned amidst a sea of Hindu or Muslim population. If you were a Muslim, you would see Hindus being butchered; if a Hindu, then Muslims. Living in a Hindu area I saw acts of butchery performed by Hindus and described them in my memoir. It was not my intention to provide excuses for the Muslim acts of brutality, some of which I saw only after the first three days of intense killing: some ten thousand were killed according to official estimate but the number was probably closer to 50,000 as a matter of fact. A very large number of bodies were thrown either into the river or into the sewers, the manholes being opened specifically for this purpose. These of course could not be counted. The official estimate was based on the bodies in the morgues. I should add that during the first three days of horror no one was brave enough to move out of one's area because the chances of being butchered in places where the majority were members of the other community were very high. When on the fourth day buses began to run, we ventured out. Open manholes everywhere were one of the sights which greeted us.

For at least two weeks before the outbreak we heard rumours that supporters of the Pakistan demand were preparing for riots on a massive scale and weapons were being distributed for the purpose. These rumours were probably true. Circumstantial evidence proves that there was similar preparation among sections of the Hindus, especially the Marwari traders of Burrabazar whose darwans or security guards are known to have played a prominent part in the murderous attack on Muslims returning home from the Maidan meeting. But there was one curious fact regarding these rumours. Bengalis are a habitually excitable people. Rumours of possible Japanese air attacks had driven hundreds of thousands from Calcutta in search of safer places of refuge. One would have expected that the rumours of an impending communal riot, if believed in, would have similarly driven the denizens of the small Hindu and Muslim ghettos to safer places. This did not happen, a fact which partly explains the very high death toll. But there were some strange facts which cannot be explained away. Shortly before 16 August several senior police officers were replaced by persons known to be sympathetic to the League cause. The commissioner of police was British but that did not affect the total inactivity of the force during the first three days of the riots. In fact they were not to be seen on the streets. At the meeting in the Maidan, Suhrawardy made one curious statement: those who wanted Pakistan had twenty-four hours to achieve it. This might be simply rhetorical flourish, but the action on the ground and the inactivity of the government do suggest more sinister possibilities. The army was shut away in their barracks outside Calcutta for three days with evident approval of the governor who had shown no hesitation earlier in intervening in executive decisions. It is reasonably certain that in 1946, Whitehall or Delhi did not favour the idea of Pakistan. It is almost equally certain that some British bureaucrats, inspired by their deep hatred of Indian nationalism, welcomed the possibility. Both Wavell and Linlithgow had countenanced the idea. Frankly, I do not know how to interpret the acknowledged facts I have mentioned above. Was there a tacit understanding between Suhrawardy's government and sections of the British bureaucracy, including the governor, which rendered the mayhem possible? Liberal Muslims refuse to believe that Suhrawardy, who had called upon them to attend the Maidan meeting with their families, would knowingly expose Muslim women and children to the danger of being massacred; the riots started before they could return home and the participants in the meeting were among the first targets of attack. And of the ten thousand killed according to official estimate, six were Muslims. Well, politicians rarely show much scruple in their efforts to attain their objectives and there are frequent errors in their calculation. The precise causation of the riots on the Direct Action Day will remain an unsolved mystery until and unless the police records and governor's papers are thrown open to researchers. This has not happened yet and it is uncertain if it ever will. The well-known Bengali author, Annadashankar Ray, a member of the ICS, recorded a conversation with the governor in his memoirs. Asked why he had ordered the army not to intervene during the first three days, he answered: 'The Hindus and Muslims were having it out. Why should we get involved?' Well, the British still had the ultimate responsibility for law and order! The accusing finger does point firmly to the provincial cabinet and the British bureaucracy. It is simply not true that the killing could not have been prevented. It stopped as soon as the army and the police were on the street except for casual acts of violence which continued for a year. Professor C.H. Philips commented that there was an administrative breakdown: of the ten thousand acknowledged cases of murder there was prosecution for only one. The last mentioned fact can only be explained as the result of deliberate decision, not inadequacy of bureaucratic power. Nobody has so far tried to establish who were the initiators of and parties to that decision.

My direct experience of the riot was limited but painful and very humbling. I had a certain pride in the non-communal outlook of educated Bengali Hindus. What I witnessed during those three days destroyed that self-regard forever. Around ten o'clock on the morning of 16 August a Muslim procession manned by the slum dwellers from the other side of the main street, Lower Circular Road, came and looted our street corner sweet shop. They destroyed no lives and quickly went back where they came from. This event was followed by horrendous rumours—of murder and rape all over the city perpetrated by Muslims on Hindus. A daily tabloid of no importance shot into great popularity by manufacturing blood-curdling rumours; it was known that the editor produced these without venturing from the safety of his home. And so far as we knew, the paper had no reporters. The rumours, some of which were true, incensed the Hindus in our area including some of our fellow residents in the hostel. Around midday there was a hullabaloo outside our hostel, and shouts of 'a Muslim, a Muslim'. A shrill scream followed. From the roof of our hostel we could see a crowd of men with sticks in their hands, quickly running away. I rushed out and found the body of a ten-year-old boy lying on the road, his head crushed. I had a closer look and recognized him. He was Osman, who used to come from a suburb to the south of Calcutta to sell mangoes in the season. I had got to know him because he used to entertain us with songs. He had a good singing voice and had ambitions of learning vocal music properly from a private tutor some day. He had only one parent, an invalid mother. But his hopes were high. He would save money and some day have a vegetable and fruit stall in the Gariahat market. And then, he would add shyly, he would take music lessons. I had promised to help him when that unlikely hope materialized. Well, if heaven is meant for innocent victims of fate, I trust Osman would reach that blessed place and have his vegetable shop as also his music lessons from some suitable angel. What happened to his immobile mother, I have no idea. Begging by the roadside and eventual death from starvation? Maybe.

That night some students from the hostel went out and burnt the slum from where the morning's procession had come. Were people killed? I do not know. When the arsonists returned, the expression on their faces was more sheepish than heroic. Among them were some with leftist leanings. One could still talk to them. The rest had reached a state of fanatical excitement where no reasonable dialogue was possible. I asked my 'pink' friends what they thought they had achieved by their action.

'Aggression is the best means of defence,' they answered. When the news of what had been done to Muslims in their area reached their co-religionists in the Muslim-majority quarters, they would stop their aggression against Hindus. Well, had they stopped their attack on Muslims on hearing of the latter's misdeeds elsewhere in the city? They had no answer to this query.

When the rioting stopped and the police was again on the street, one rainy morning we took out a peace procession but were attacked by a mob after we had gone a little distance. Bombs were thrown at us. We dispersed, realizing the futility of our efforts. Not very far from our hostel there was a hostel for Muslim women students in the postgraduate classes of the university in the very heart of the Hindu area. Deeply concerned for the fate of those girls, some of whom we knew very well, we went to that hostel as soon as normal transport had been restored. As we approached the place, our hearts sank. Suitcases, books, papers, items of clothing, etc., were strewn all over the road. The hostel was lying empty. Some people looked at us balefully, probably thinking that we were Muslims. One gentleman came forward and said that no one had been molested. A police vehicle had come and taken away the girls to safety.

A few days later when the classes were resumed we went and met our friends in the university. They looked traumatized. Only one or two of the girls were willing to talk about what they had gone through. A mob, consisting mostly of the bhadralok and a few slum dwellers had forcibly entered the hostel. The girls were abused in the filthiest language imaginable. But nobody touched them. The attempt to do so was frustrated, interestingly, by the slum dwellers. The assailants then concentrated on destroying their belongings. Among the intruders were a few men personally known to the girls. One of the girls was so traumatized by the experience that she could not talk normally to us, her Hindu friends, ever again. She had lost all faith in the civilized Bengali Hindu bhadralok, the species to which we belonged.

If before the return to 'normalcy' we were witnesses to atrocities committed only by the Hindus, once we could move about relatively freely this limitation to our experience of the riots was adequately corrected. The administration took some time to remove the cadavers which were literally piled up in places. The murderers had taken good care to ensure that the communal identity of the victims was obvious to the viewer. At times the uncircumcised limb was stuck into the corpse's mouth in a celebratory spirit. The first Hindu corpse I saw belonged to a Brahmin: it had its sacred thread proudly displayed round its neck. Female corpses were disfigured in ways which the sensitive onlooker would find 'disturbing', to quote an oft-repeated phrase now used by TV announcers in describing calamities in different parts of the world. What struck me was the fact that the artists of horror took quite a bit of time over their handiwork. They were evidently in no hurry to run away in revulsion from the ghastly things they had done. Some of the miscreants became heroes in the eyes of their community and were discussed adoringly. In fact the glories attributed to them were often far in excess of what they had actually done. Human imagination can always run ahead of the limited action we are capable of.

For one whole year stray acts of inter-communal violence continued. Every day, at one point on the bus route to the university, hooligans of both communities made it their practice to throw acid bulbs on public transport and/or stab unfortunate individuals. Among the people so killed was one well-known Gandhian political worker, Sachin Mitra. 'Sachin has become immortal,' Gandhiji wrote by way of consolation to his devotee's poor widow. A number of people were killed in different parts of the city trying to protect individuals of the other community. Again, no one was arrested, no one prosecuted. Law and order, it seemed, had collapsed for good.

I should like to record one curious fact here. I passed through the danger point I have mentioned at least twice every day. I often saw small crowds discussing excitedly some act of violence which had occurred only a few minutes earlier or heard of such acts having taken place shortly after our bus had passed the danger point. A dead or injured human body lying on the road was a frequent sight. But I was never at the receiving end of this aggression. In a city of several million, the laws of statistics ensure that however extensive any civil disturbance, only a small percentage of the population is directly affected—one more reason for caution regarding 'eyewitness' accounts. Eyewitnesses in most cases are really 'ear witnesses' and need to be treated as such, especially since people very often 'see' what they wish to see.

During these unhappy months I had one experience which I cherish. The Constituent Assembly was in session in New Delhi. My uncle, Kiran Shankar Roy, leader of the Congress party in the Bengal Assembly was a member of the Constituent Assembly. He invited me to come to Delhi with him. 'History is being made,' he told me one day, 'maybe a sad one, but history nevertheless. Fate is producing a cruel joke. We are about to achieve what we have sought all our lives, but in a bitter, unacceptable form. Our lives will never be the same again. Come with me to Delhi and see what is happening from the ringside.'

The years when I grew up into adulthood constituted a time totally different from the age in which we now live. It was a time of manifold aspirations sustained within an ambience of very little hope. The aspirations structured around multiple interests gave meaning to the lives of many an individual and generated a degree of transcendence when one had little or no expectation from one's material existence—there were writers, poets, musicians, artists, political activists, men of faith seeking God—all living in relative poverty and squalor, a constant inadequacy of material resources and limited hope of escape from obscurity, but their lives vivified by whatever it was that had captured their souls in their youth. The devotion to chosen tasks, the exposure to human culture covering a wide spectrum and the mildly romantic bohemianism generated by relative if not absolute poverty together produced a great variety of fascinating personalities. In an age when life is much easier for the Indian intelligentsia, the creative individuals one encounters are not interesting in the same way.

I have mentioned earlier several persons, mostly scholars and politicians, who answer to this description of unusual characters. Kiran Shankar Roy was surely a most unusual person and one I got to know very closely during my years in college. By occupation a zamindar, he really believed that there was nothing immoral in living off other people's labour, for civilization in order to develop has always required a leisured class and others who had to provide for their needs and luxuries. Examples are the Greek society which was based on slave labour and nearer home, ancient Hindus dominated by Brahmins who could afford to spend their time meditating exclusively on the nature of the Ultimate Reality while the Kshatriyas fought off unwelcome intruders and the Shudras attended to the daily needs of the privileged. I found this notion horrendous yet fascinating. Expressed by this Oxford graduate with great elegance and a touch of cynical humour, it did not sound as revolting as it was in fact. His social outlook was altogether unacceptable to me for it was rooted in extreme reaction so far as I could see. He had been active in nationalist politics ever since his return from Oxford after the First World War. He made no bones about one fact: the independence he was working for was intended to transfer power to people of his own class. The best that the hoi polloi could expect was to be treated decently and assured a reasonable livelihood. It was absurd to expect that the masses should actively share power. Later, when I read Churchill's comment that the 1892 Reform had undermined the structure of British politics, I was reminded of this particular opinion of my uncle. He had trained as a barrister, went to the Calcutta High Court just once and then gave up because he found the stiff collar suffocating and the gown too uncomfortable for Indian weather. Besides, a gentleman should not have to earn his living, even if he had to live in poverty as he certainly did, relatively speaking. He was an extreme conservative in all matters. He lived as a member of a joint family by choice. Not that he was particularly fond of his brothers and their families, but this is the way things had been ordered for centuries and that justified its continuation forever. His seven years in England did not induce him to alter his life habits. Meals were still taken seated on flat wooden seats, pidis, and with one's fingers off bell metal plates. And worst of all, women were an inferior subspecies and should be treated with kindness but not undue respect. He had three daughters and there was no question of letting them marry by their own choice. When the time came, they had to be married off into affluent homes, because that is all that they understood. This part of his social ideology did prove rather unfortunate for his daughters' personal involvements were firmly ignored.

The person I have just described sounds fairly repulsive. It is difficult to imagine how kind he was in fact and how exquisitely refined were his humane sensibilities. He was a writer belonging to an avant-garde group developed around a magazine, *Sabuj Patra* (the Green Journal). Their contribution to Bengali literature consisted in the sustained use of the colloquial language for literary purposes. And the handful of short stories he wrote were very fine specimens of that genre, marked by elements of parody and a much understated angst. He introduced me to his favourite authors, Anatole France, Thackeray and Fielding. *Crime of Sylvestre Bonard*, *Four Georges* and the *Ordeal of Richard Fevrel* became my favourite reading. And I read with him long chapters of the Mahabharata which to him was the greatest work of literature. He could not stand Romain Rolland, then very popular among the Bengali literati, partly because of his close friendship with poet Tagore. He found Jean Christophe too verbose and sentimental. In fact he just could not stand sentimentality in literature. Kiran Shankar was a devotee of the poet. He described as the happiest time of his life an evening when the poet came to their Calcutta house and sang some of his songs sitting by the pool in their back garden.

I consider it my great good fortune that this relation by marriage, older than me by some thirty years, became a close friend. Again, I learnt from this friendship to love and respect someone whose world view was totally abhorrent to me. To repeat, perhaps the most outstanding gift of the cultural efflorescence in nineteenth-century India was the advent of unusual individuals; unusual in their creativity, but even more in the striking excellence of their personal characters, the surprisingly wide variety of their personalities. In the afterglow of India's nineteenth-century culture, such men were still to be found in many walks of life. Their potentialities, often unfulfilled in a colonial environment, were manifest in a quality of transcendence, of dedication to varied endeavours and philosophies of existence with little or no expectations of material return. This volume of reminiscences is partly meant to record my impressions of these often obscure men and women. I should use the adjective 'great' to describe their personalities without any hesitation. I find the very valuable works of my British and American colleagues on India somewhat lacking in so far as I never encounter these exceptional human beings in their writings. As a result, their highly sophisticated contributions often seem to lack any blood and are very distant from the human reality I encountered at very close quarters.

By the time I accompanied my uncle to Delhi, there had been significant developments in the politics of India. Some of these had grim implications for our future. Both the Congress and the British government had accepted the proposal for the Partition of India. The twenty-four hours of Direct Action on the streets of Calcutta had served their purpose. The Congress leadership, all excepting Gandhi, were convinced that there would be repetition of those horrors if

Partition was not conceded. But as Gandhi foresaw, the horrors were repeated on an unimaginable scale even though Partition had been conceded. As a part of the deal, the two provinces of Bengal and Punjab, which would go to Pakistan, were also to be partitioned. West Bengal and East Punjab which had non-Muslim majorities were to go to India. One British civilian, who had no knowledge or experience of India, was to draw a line on the map demarcating the precise frontier of the two countries. He had to do the preparatory work in a few weeks which did not allow time for any visit to the areas concerned. And he was also supposed to take into account the history, culture and local traditions of the areas affected. Of such matters, he was more innocent than a newborn baby. The British were hell-bent on leaving as soon as possible. Their commitment to maintaining law and order until they had left was quietly ignored. But I am getting ahead of my story.

When Partition was only a few weeks away, the Congress and League leaders in Bengal—Sarat Bose, Kiran Shankar Roy and Suhrawardy—came up with a new proposal, that of United Sovereign Bengal to be secured by treaties with both India and Pakistan. Jinnah blessed the idea. Perhaps he hoped that a sovereign Bengal, the majority of its population being Muslim, would eventually join Pakistan, maybe with the aid of a few more Direct Actions. The Congress was far from enthusiastic—the Marwari traders of Calcutta, including Birla, it was rumoured, were a major factor in their negative preference. However, the occasion when Kiran Shankar invited me to accompany him to Delhi, his mission was to lobby the Congress leadership as also meet the viceroy to try and sell their project of united sovereign Bengal.

One morning in Delhi, he told me that he was going to meet Gandhiji and I could, if I so wished, accompany him. I was more than a little surprised. These were very tense times and Gandhi at the moment was one of the busiest persons in the world. Anyone and everyone who had a political plea were at his door. Especially active were those desperate men and women in East Bengal and West Punjab who were pleading for the inclusion of their particular district into India. Kiran Shankar was on his way to explain to the leader their case for a united sovereign Bengal. What would a young man of twenty-one, a nobody, do there? Uncle explained that Gandhi did not believe in secret diplomacy and then smiled, adding that he departed from this principle of transparency only very rarely. Since he was opposed to the proposal of sovereign Bengal, this would be an occasion for open discussion. In other words, he had already made up his mind on this matter and nothing was going to change it. This meant that other people would drop in while the discussion was going on. Therefore, it would make no difference if I tagged along. The matter had been cleared with Gandhi's secretary.

Gandhi was living in a mud-built room in a sweeper's colony at the time. There was nothing ersatz about that. It was a one-room shanty typical of the Bhangi Colony. Only the advent of the Mahatma had induced a cleaning up of the place. It was terribly hot and no air conditioner had been installed for the great man's comfort. Only, a khus khus mat was hanging at the entrance to the room which had no doors and some devotees were watering the mat every hour or so. This kept the room reasonably cool. This was the only luxury Gandhi permitted himself, one not accessible to the bhangis or sweepers. There was no furniture. He was seated on a quilt covered with a spotlessly white bed sheet. In a corner there was a spinning wheel, a Wardha charkha (I recognized the flat instrument, because since age fifteen I had used one as a committed follower of the Mahatma, producing exceedingly thick and totally unusable yarn) and, somewhat incongruously, a pot of Pond's cream on the niche. I wondered if the Mahatma's beautifully shiny skin owed its lustre to that foreign product.

I have stated before that we were an atheist family. The man who now sat facing me had virtually taken the place of God in our consciousness. By age twenty-one, I had many criticisms of his politics and even some doubts about his saintliness. Yet being in his presence was an overpowering experience. I touched his feet in accordance with our social tradition. He did not object. Nehru would have been furious if I had tried to touch his. The fact that I was permitted this small gesture was deeply gratifying. For a man without religion, it was an epiphanic moment. Where would I meet another man like him? There was no one. Such men are born once in a millennium, if that often. At that moment, I almost believed in the Hindu doctrine of Karma, the results of one's actions, good and bad, in previous existences materializing in one's current life. I was in the presence of Gandhi, an incarnation of God to our Noga and many millions. The good deeds of many previous existences were at last resulting in this supreme good fortune. I had a feeling of fulfilment and deep humility. I felt blessed. Perfection was no part of the human destiny. This was the closest to that impossible objective our imperfect species could expect to attain.

Kiran Shankar presented his plea. Gandhi said what had been expected. He was still not reconciled to the idea of partition. What choice was there? Nehru, Gandhi's secretary Nirmal Bose had told us, raised the same question.

'Another mass agitation for independence,' Gandhi had replied.

'After the Calcutta riots, we do not have the courage,' Nehru had commented.

'You think India will be free without a million deaths? That will come, whether in a good cause or bad will depend on you.' This, according to Bose, was Gandhi's response.

Suren Ghosh or Madhu Babu, as he was popularly known, an old unreconstructed revolutionary, came and joined the discussion. He said that after partition, widespread violence was feared in East Bengal. He and his old comrades would resist any attack on Hindus with even greater violence.

Gandhi smiled and said, 'Madhu Babu, you people have tried that before. What have you gained?'

The interview ended. We came back. I was in some sort of a daze. I knew that nothing significant had happened in that past hour. Whatever had occurred was inside me, in a strange medley of my conscious and my subconscious I had a sense of great elation which was no part of all my past experience. I am forever grateful that this had happened. I had met and touched one of the greatest men of all times.

The day of the Partition drew near. We urged our parents to come away to Calcutta. After the riots of August 1946 and the continual violence of the year that followed we could no longer believe that life for the Hindus would be safe and peaceful in eastern Bengal. And we entertained no stupid hope that our district would be included in the Indian Union. My father was extremely reluctant to leave Barisal. Satin-da was staying back; he was destined to end his days in a Pakistani prison. He urged our father to stay back too—in times of threatened trouble, leaders could not in all conscience leave the rank and file to face the music without them. We told Satin-da that he was an ascetic for all practical purposes. Father had to think of his family—especially his wife, daughter and the little son. There was danger for them and no possible future for us in Pakistan. We had to leave. There was really no choice. Our father, a very proud man, feared among other things that if he migrated to India, he would become financially dependent on us, his sons. This possibility he found altogether unacceptable. Yet eventually with great reluctance, he agreed to come but not until after the Partition.

On 14 August 1947, Pakistan was established at the midnight hour. The fellow dominion of India was born twenty-four hours later. There were rumours that there would be riots. At midnight the steamers, motor boats and the steam launches on the river sounded the advent of Pakistan with a tremendous blast. The skies resounded with the slogans we had become familiar with—'Allahu Akbar', 'Pakistan zindabad', 'Quaid-e-Azam zindabad'. Father sat quietly the whole night holding in his hand the one gun we possessed. I do not know what use that gun would have been if a riot had actually broken out. He had joined the movement for independence as a young postgraduate student twenty-seven years ago and scrupulously followed Gandhi ever since. He never told us what he was thinking on that night of independence, an independence which was to drive him out of his ancestral home of many generations. And we never asked him.

The following day at midnight India had her 'tryst with destiny'. Despite widespread riots, there was wild jubilation in the streets of Delhi and the other towns and cities of the Indian Union. Calcutta witnessed something very strange and almost incredible. On the morning of 15 August, Muslims from some of the worst riot- affected areas of the city poured into the Hindu areas in joyous procession with music and happy slogans, scattering rose water and distributing sweets. There were wild scenes of fraternization. People embraced one another and shouted in joy while tears flowed without inhibition. The gates of the Government House, the governor's residence, were thrown open and the crowds poured into the palace unchecked. What was happening was incredible yet real. This new-found brotherliness did not last, but it was something to cherish so long as it did. I did not see these heart-warming scenes except in movie documentaries which were shown in all cinemas for some days. One of our most famous poets, Bishnu De, greeted the event with a very moving poem *'Ananda aaj ananda ashim'* (Boundless, boundless is our joy this day). But alas, miracles do not endure. I have often wondered who were the unknown men and women responsible for this short-lived miracle. Nobody has tried to find out and we will never know.

10

Homeless in Calcutta: Early Years in an Academic Career

Exodus or migration en masse from one country to another has a tragic/prehistoric ring to it. The image of vast numbers moving to escape threat of violence which is following close behind them had a reality about it in the western part of the subcontinent where millions were driven from their ancestral homes marching into unknown territory in columns stretching up to fifty miles. In the eastern part of the region the tragedy was a shade less dramatic. Here too people left their homes in millions but under less imminent threats. The injured and the dead were fewer in number and the process of migration was spread over years rather than months. The intensity of violence was of a lower order. Many, like us, left without any immediate threat to our lives and limbs, more from an apprehension and sense of insecurity than the urgent need to escape in order to survive physically. When we left Barisal and our village home for good, the district was peaceful.

Migration for us was a very mundane and somewhat shoddy affair, a sudden descent into an impoverished and inglorious lifestyle, taking up residence in a place where we were unknown and without honour.

The exodus had its element of tragic drama. The small boat in which we left our village home for the last time went down the familiar canal towards the river. On both sides, the village folk, mostly Muslims, stood shedding tears (the very virile peasantry of East Bengal are given to high drama and are prone to shed tears at the slightest provocation).

I felt an overpowering sadness which I tried to fight in the full knowledge that there was much worse to come. I also knew that I was leaving our ancestral home of many generations for good. I returned to Kirtipasha as a visitor after fifty-two years by which time the palatial building was half in ruins and the mud-built shack which we piously treated as our original homestead was razed to the ground.

Finding a place in Calcutta where one could live involved petty and somewhat humiliating negotiations, material adjustments rendered necessary by the lack of funds. From the high status of respected zamindars we suddenly became members of a social class to which we really belonged by virtue of our very limited material resources, namely, the urban lower-middle class. The Partition reduced us to the level of the unwanted. Looking for a place to live in we discovered that rents in Calcutta had shot up sky-high, way beyond our very limited means. The beneficiaries of the boom, the house owners in Calcutta who had rooms/flats/houses to let, looked upon us as undesirable elements of the human species, Bangals, i.e., uncouth yokels from eastern Bengal whose arrival had pushed up prices of every consumer good. The sooner this lot was driven back to the wilderness from where they came, the better for the urbane Calcuttan. The little fact of phenomenally increased rents at black market rates which puffed up their pockets was overlooked in these animated discussions. With great difficulty we found three rooms, to be shared with a friend of my elder brother—a highly unsatisfactory arrangement which collapsed within a few months. The landlady refused to give any receipt for the rent. She had given us shelter out of pity, she claimed. The cash transactions were our humble tokens of gratitude not to be confused with mundane matters like rent. This was the usual prelude to further enhancement of rent and to being thrown on the street for failure to pay it. Law suits followed and life became generally insufferable. The landlady would stand on the public road outside the house and pour out streams of abuse to the general amusement of a sizeable audience. It was indeed a very impressive performance.

We were poor enough in Barisal in terms of our cash income. Now we were even poorer. Transfer of income from Pakistan to India was prohibited. But in the early phase (we left Pakistan about a year after it was founded), the restrictions were not very strictly imposed. Our estate employees had arranged with a Marwari businessman to send our very modest monthly income to Calcutta. He charged a commission of 40 per cent, that is, as reported by our employees, some of whom had assumed the surname Raychaudhuri indicating proprietorship of zamindari property. We heard that they had also adopted the lifestyle appropriate for Raychaudhuris. We had no choice but to accept these alleged terms. One fine morning this meagre flow of funds stopped: the Government of Pakistan declared such transfers a cognizable offence punishable by rigorous imprisonment. As we never had any savings to speak of, we were rendered literally penniless. My brother had a small business. The latter chose precisely the same moment to collapse. Our family of six now had only one source of sustenance: my salary of one hundred rupees a month from the small college in the suburb of Howrah where I had found a job as a lecturer.

My ill-considered choice of an academic career at a time when opportunities for employment in the state sector were opening up on a large scale was considered by my well-wishers an act of self-sacrifice in the service of Saraswati, the goddess of learning, and a very noble, if foolish, act as such. I was duly admired and pitied for this spectacular stupidity. In 1948, when I began my career after getting a first division in my MA examination, the hangover from the glory days of the Raj still haunted India's academic life. The subcontinent had seventeen universities as compared to the current figure of some 350 in the Indian Union alone. There were some three hundred colleges; the current figure is twenty-one thousand. This meant that academic jobs (read lectureships) were scarce. In the small number of government colleges where the pay was marginally better, the highest position one could aspire to was equivalent to that of a deputy magistrate, a fairly lowly position in the provincial bureaucracy. You had to be very fortunate even to get that far. The majority of teachers in the government colleges were lecturers enjoying the same rank and pay as the lowest gazetted officer, just one level above the clerks in the secretariat. Their jobs were aptly described as Subordinate Education Service—underline subordinate. Men and women with brilliant academic careers were happy to remain members of this glorious service all their lives because the choices were grim beyond ordinary imagination. There was an All-India Education Service almost equivalent to the ICS. But this was strictly for the sahibs and a few fortunate young men who had benefited from an Oxbridge education. The very famous and undoubtedly great Indian scholars who taught in the Presidency College and comparable institutions elsewhere in the country hardly ever rose above the rank equivalent to that of the deputy magistrate in the Provincial Education Service. But such men and women were objects of envy, for they had steady jobs with a regular pay received at the end of each month. Only a small percentage among those who had opted for/been forced into the academic profession owing to the absence of alternative careers were so lucky.

The majority of the academics had to face prospects which were horrendous. The topmost level of the academic ladder was the postgraduate departments in the universities. The ultimate reward of a lecturership there was a gift of fortune not to be hoped for by ordinary mortals. Full professorships were exceedingly rare, at most one per department in the universities. One could hope to reach that highly unlikely goal if one lived longer than one's colleagues and/or one's predecessor obliged by dying at an appropriate time. Professorships, in other words, was no part of normal human expectation. One usually taught in a private college, full- or part-time, and had a loose connection with the university's postgraduate department. My first appointment in that revered institution was as an honorary temporary part-time lecturer. The qualifying adjectives, if you were indeed very lucky, fell off one by one until you were admitted to the gloried rank of a full-time lecturer actually receiving a pay in the scale of 200 to 400 rupees per month. Incidentally, the salary at the lower end of the scale was not enough to support even a small family: one had to supplement it by various means ranging from private tutoring to writing cribs. The sterling equivalent of two hundred rupees was about fourteen pounds. I was exceptionally fortunate and the object of many people's envy that I graduated from the much adjective-d status to a full lecturership in about three years. The usual wait could extend to ten years or more and some never made it to that ultimate Valhalla of academic reward.

But I am still talking of the elite level of employment in academia. The majority who taught in the private colleges established by altruistic individuals and often not so altruistic families with an eye on potential gains were paid seventy-five to two hundred rupees a month. Highly qualified scholars often remained unemployed for five to seven years and then got one of these lecturerships. The pay, according to the formal agreement would be Rs 75 per month. One was lucky to receive Rs 50 at the end of the month and that on a regular basis.

When I entered the profession I did so in the full knowledge that the material prospects were poor. But I had no idea how poor they were in reality. My teachers in the postgraduate department were not discouraging when I told them that I wished to start research on the Mughal period. But they made it quite clear that I should not expect any financial support. There was only one research fellowship per department. The one in history was, of course, 'occupied' and would be so perhaps for the next couple of years. Well, I could look for a lecturership in one of the private colleges. I did and was told that I was overqualified. Young men with firsts in their MA taught in one of these colleges for a year while they prepared for the competitive examination for the Central government services. The consequent high rate of turnover was unacceptable. Eventually, one college in suburban Howrah relented and appointed me on Rs 100 per month after making sure that I was not preparing for the service examinations. This indeed was good fortune, the latter enhanced by my appointment as an honorary temporary part-time lecturer in the Postgraduate Department of History of Calcutta University. What more could one expect?

Before our family migrated from East Pakistan, six young men, including me, had rented a flat in the Muslim-majority area of Park Circus. It had been abandoned during the riots by the owner, Sarat Das, famous explorer and Tibetologist, and very probably a secret agent of the Raj. The flat contained, inter alia, one four-poster and a grand piano, also usable as a bed. We took turns in using these facilities thus enhancing the quality of our life. We paid ten rupees per head for the rent and another twenty rupees covered our other material needs including a Buddhist cook from Chittagong who was a wizard in the kitchen. Contrary to our apprehensions, he did not object to fish or meat, but would not countenance bloodshed. The latter he avoided when he bought live fish or chicken, by burying the creatures for a few minutes. The arrangement was mutually satisfactory, so far as we were concerned. We did not, of course, seek the opinion of the fish and chicken on this matter. When my parents came to Calcutta, I had to leave this abode of happiness and move to Tollygunge. And there one morning I found that I had become the sole bread earner of the family with my income of Rs 100 per month as the only available resource.

Narasimha Datta College was named after the Diwan or finance officer of a nineteenth-century Portuguese merchant, Mr Belilios. He made his money exporting sheep to Singapore. On the demise of the merchant, his good lady took a friendly interest in the Bengali Diwan and endowed a college named after the latter. But the pious wife had not forgotten her dead husband. The college displayed with due honour a photograph of Mr Belilios as well. The college was a modest affair—it offered no honours courses and hence its academic routine could be covered easily during the morning hours, ten to one. After one, we teachers and students were free to go our respective ways and earn extra cash by performing other tasks if necessary.

The necessity was of course there, but the tasks were not always available. The college had a science department and the subjects covered included biology. The teachers, it was rumoured, dissected prawns instead of frogs and the dissected prawns were duly fried and consumed. This gave the teachers of biology a marginally higher real income compared to ours. We had to be content with our Rs 100 per month or seek other means of supplementing it.

Here I was again fortunate. My old college Scottish Church had a temporary vacancy and I was invited to teach there in the afternoon hours for a few weeks—not more than ten hours a week, the maximum which this missionary college prescribed. When I joined, I was first told that I would be paid only Rs 100 instead of the statutory 150 because I was already being paid elsewhere. And as for the limit on the number of hours I had to lecture, one of my old teachers promptly fell ill on my arrival (I believe this was due to some allergic reaction caused by my presence and I had to take his classes, pushing my total to sixteen per week not including the ten hours at Narasimha Datta College. My income from the two appointments and twenty-six lectures per week came to Rs 200 per month. Even this princely sum was not enough to sustain a family of six. The rent alone was Rs 150 and in 1948 fifty rupees could not buy much by way of food and other necessities of life. I had to fall back on the ultimate resort of poor lecturers—private tutoring. As I was a novice, my fees never exceeded Rs 25 a month and so I had to coach four students to earn the minimum of the extra hundred we needed. I was grateful to the family of one student who gave me a substantial tea, thereby increasing my real income. I used to leave home at 8.30 in the morning, reached the college in Howrah, strap-hanging all the way in a very crowded bus, had my lunch at the Howrah railway station, taught till 4.30 at Scottish Church College and then did another four hours of private coaching, returning home around 10.30 at night. But believe me, I enjoyed it and never felt that I was overworked even though one had to put in another three hours or so at night and work during the weekends to prepare the lectures.

The enchantment that kept me happy was that of youth. I was twenty-two, had a roof over my head, enough to eat and doing what I had always wanted to do, though the circumstances were not ideal. True, I could not afford to go to any decent restaurant or buy cinema tickets except at the lowest price. I also had to do with the minimum of clothes, just enough not to violate urban notions of decency. But books were still cheap. Penguin books were available for 10 annas each (there were sixteen annas to the rupee which was one-thirteenth of a pound), one hard-bound Everyman's cost a rupee and two annas. A forty-rupee book prize enabled me to buy forty volumes of Everyman's classics covering a fair section of the Greek and Latin classics in translation. I was, in short, a happy young man. Only, I had no time for research though I had registered to work for a PhD degree.

Relief came sooner than I had expected. Partition had induced a mass exodus of Muslim government employees including the college teachers. The vacant positions had to be filled up quickly. I got a job as a lecturer in the Islamia College, renamed Central Calcutta College after the Partition, on the incredibly high total pay of Rs 300 per month including the dearness allowance. I could now afford to give up private tutoring and had at last some time for serious research. After months of insecurity and back-breaking drudgery, I felt I had attained the paradise of my dreams.

One thing which made me appreciate my good fortune was the fate of some of my close relations and acquaintances. Some of my cousins from Kirtipasha who used to live in the ancestral home had ended up in a slum built by the manual labour of the refugees themselves. A very close relative, who had come and settled in one of the small towns, was cheated out of the meagre capital he had managed to bring over to India. He was actually reduced to begging by the roadside. This was the man in whose home we had once enjoyed the fabulous fishy meals and milk products described in the first chapter of this book. In this context, to complain of one's limited privations would have been obscene. Among the refugees from East Pakistan, we were indeed very lucky.

Teaching in Central Calcutta College was an interesting experience. My personal friends, Kalyan Sen and Arun Dasgupta were among my colleagues and so was Amalesh Tripathi, famous as a polymath since his student days. Our principal, Mr Pereira, taught English and was a distinguished alumnus of Cambridge University. He was something of a strict headmaster and kept a vigilant eye on some of us teachers, who had a penchant for spending time in nearby restaurants when our prescribed duties demanded that we should be in the classrooms doling out precious knowledge to our students. One of our colleagues, a teacher of mathematics, came to the college from afar and was usually late for his first class. He suffered reprimands from the principal on a regular basis. His command over the English language was less secure than his knowledge of mathematics. After patiently swallowing Mr Pereira's words of admonition he would come to the senior common room, looking for tea and sympathy.

'Mr Pereira drives in from his quarters next door. What would he understand of the travails of poor teachers like us who come straphanging in a bus and then have to tackle the terrible "pederastian" traffic on Dharmatala Street?' We did express sympathy as was right and proper for we too shared his experiences except for one thing. We failed to recognize the 'pederastians' on Dharmatala Street; otherwise we too would have been partners in his enhanced anxieties.

One nineteenth-century French sociologist/philosopher noted the penchant for self-praise among intellectuals of the Third World (the expression had not been invented yet). Denied what was very much their due both in material life and in terms of international recognition, they felt a degree of psychological compulsion to declare themselves their undoubted excellence to the entire world. I have known a very large number of highly talented South Asians given to this often very embarrassing habit. Their common sense, dignity and natural self-restraint seemed to fail them once they launched on the subject of their own extraordinary merits. Such performances were both very sad and at the same time comic occasions. Our vice-principal, an economist and a very effective teacher, was a nearly terminal victim of self-adulation. He would catch Kalyan and me by our ties as we entered the college. He seemed to materialize from nowhere leaving us no chance of escape. Held firmly by our ties, we were subjected to third-degree treatment. It is my firm belief that the wizards of Guantanamo Bay have somehow got hold of our vice-principal's secret notebook on 'how to extract confessions' and put it to effective use.

'I hear you two are having a very good time under my wings, my protection?'

'Ye-e-es,' we managed to splutter, our lives nearly quizzed out by twists in our ties.

'You heard my lecture the other day. Tell me honestly. Have you ever heard anything better in your entire lives?'

By then there was hardly any life left in our respective bodies and it took some time to spell out 'N-n-o'. Such delays were not to be tolerated. The ties were held in the right hand, but the left hand was free. It was used to poke our respective bellies to great purpose. There was no choice but to confirm desperately his self-knowledge, the evident fact that we were in the presence of a paragon. We gave up wearing ties. But he still turned up in front of us from unexpected corners and we were hard put to it to protect our bellies. It was no use. Kalyan left to join his Central government job. I stayed on to live out the results of my sins in many previous existences.

One of our colleagues was the famous poet Bishnu De. His poems were not easy to comprehend. One of our colleagues was in the unfortunate habit of teasing him on this point. This was not appreciated.

The poet would hit back, 'I have no problems with women and children. It is the half-educated middle class with whom it is difficult to communicate.' As members of that half-educated class we accepted the admonition, but I still think that children who easily understood Bishnu Babu's poetry were not numerous.

The poet had some unusual skills. He came by the bus from Ballygunge, the passengers tightly packed like sardines in a very small tin. He emerged from it without a crease in his dhoti or kurta. If we complimented him on his exceptional skill he would smile and tell us that his father would go to bed in his dhoti and kurta and wake up in the morning without a crease in either. He implied that this particular skill of his, like his poetic genius, was genetically determined and hence not any reason for undue vanity.

We often accompanied him home to share in his feasts of Western civilization—Bach, Beethoven, Eliot and Pound, reproductions of the great paintings from Giotto to Picasso. He stretched himself on a well-quilted bench leaning against the wall, his back protected by sumptuous cushions. Once he had attained this nirvanic posture, there was no further physical movement for a few hours. Pranati-di, his good wife, rushed about attending to the mundane duties of a middle-class household. These activities were happening in another planet so far as the poet was concerned.

'Don't you feel embarrassed leaving every chore to your wife?' I sometime ventured to ask.

He would smile an indulgent smile and reply, 'My wife is extremely embarrassed that I have to earn a living.' Yes, truly the good lady would have preferred her prodigy of a husband to spend all his waking hours writing poetry or meditating in preparation for the creative act.

Bishnu Babu introduced us to Jamini Roy, the most famous artist of Bengal who left the Western academic style of painting to seek inspiration from the folk art of Bengal. His paintings now sell for the equivalent of a million rupees or more. When we were introduced to him, his pictures sold for a couple of hundred rupees, that is, when they did sell. Bishnu Babu whispered to us that the artist was passing through a difficult time and he would get the paintings for us for very little money, Rs 150 or so for a picture. I did not purchase any, partly from ignorance of their worth, partly because I could not afford to. After all, the amount was half a month's salary.

Simultaneously with my work at the Central Calcutta College, I started lecturing in the postgraduate department of the university. This was a highly satisfying experience. It was a privilege rarely granted to a man of my age without any experience. The students were indulgent towards their very young teacher. Some of the girl students expressed a coy interest which was gratifyingly non-academic. And my relations with my teachers, now my colleagues, who regarded me as an eccentric with limited understanding of his material interest was based on genuine respect on my part and affection on theirs. My brief years as a teacher in Calcutta University were probably my happiest, despite the continual struggle with penury.

Working for a research degree in Calcutta University was a highly unstructured activity. When later I worked for a second doctorate in Oxford, I found that the conditions were not significantly different there. In Calcutta, every candidate for a doctoral degree was assigned a supervisor. You might meet him occasionally or you might not, again a situation very similar to what I found in Oxford except for the fact that my supervisor at the latter place was exceptionally kind and helpful. But then he was not one of the Oxford 'greats' who would rarely stoop so low. I had decided to work on the social history of Bengal in the early years of Mughal rule, an unexplored field with very limited source material. It was an unpromising subject and my supervisor, an authority on the history of the Sikhs, was not very interested. But I did get guidance from other scholars. Professor Nihar Ranjan Roy had recently published his voluminous history of the Bengali people before the advent of Islam—a highly original and innovative work drawing on the insights of the social sciences like anthropology and sociology. He helped me to formulate my questions and work out some tentative hypotheses. Professor Sukumar Sen, the historian of Bengali literature, provided me with all the bibliographical information I needed. The man was a walking encyclopedia and would not tolerate any manifestation of ignorance or stupidity. Even after I became his colleague as a lecturer in Calcutta University, he would tell me off in no uncertain terms whenever he found any unacceptable gaps in my knowledge. His main point was that at my level of ignorance it was sheer impudence to undertake research. Plumbing or road building would be a more suitable occupation. But he was unstinting in providing scholarly help, doled out with appropriate admonitions. He taught me, among other things, the lesson of humility though he himself was not an exemplary practitioner.

I drew upon a wide variety of source material including the scriptures of the various religious sects of the period, written in Sanskrit and Bengali, as well as Bengali literature. Indian scholars were still debating whether literature was an acceptable source material for any branch of history. To my understanding, contemporary literature, especially the biographical texts were rich in information on the life and values of those times and I used literary texts as source material ignoring that debate. I was gratified when later, Sir Jadunath Sarkar, the ultimate authority on Mughal history, approved of my decision.

I have stated earlier that to my understanding the most notable feature of the Indian renaissance, a justly criticized thesis, was the advent of exceptional human beings. It was my great good fortune that I came into close contact with one of them, Sir Jadunath Sarkar, the doyen of Indian historians, in course of my effort at research on the Mughal period. Sir Jadunath decided to work on the latter phase of the history of the Mughal Empire when he was twenty and finished his work by completing his multi-volume *Fall of the Mughal Empire* in the eightieth year of his life. His model, needless to say, was Gibbon. His *History of Aurangzeb* in five volumes is in fact the political history of the subcontinent in the latter half of the seventeenth century. His *Fall of the Mughal Empire* brings the story down to the fall of Delhi to the Company's forces in 1802.

This mammoth undertaking spread over sixty years was the sole concern of his life and he pursued it with single-minded devotion through a series of personal tragedies which would have broken the will of any lesser person. A son, a son-in-law, a daughter and a grandson died under tragic circumstances. His family life was beset with other serious problems. He endured it all like a yogi as described in the Gita, *duhkheshvanudvignamanah sukheshu vigataspriha*—unperturbed by sorrow, indifferent to happiness—and stuck to his chosen task. Every hour of his life, all the details of his material existence were worked out with a view to facilitating that central concern. He made a point of going to the market every day because servants could not be trusted to buy the right food for the nourishment of his brain, a subject on which he had some idiosyncratic ideas. Summer months had to be spent in a cool place like Darjeeling, and after he was sixty, the Western Ghats where his friend Sardesai, the leading historian of Maharashtra, had a house because heat was unhelpful for intellectual work. He also believed that it reduced one's longevity by a given number of years. When I accepted a job in Delhi, a decision he favoured, he warned that I would lose some ten of the years I was likely to live owing to the extreme heat of that place. To ensure that his annual sojourn with his friend remained productive, he presented his entire collection of material on the history of the Mahrattas to Sardesai. Every morning he would seat at his desk near the window and work the number of hours he had prescribed for himself (eight till he was sixty and six after that) ignoring the punishments life inflicted on him. I was present on the occasion when his disciples and well-wishers called on him to offer condolences for the death of his daughter who had committed suicide in London. He opened the door and said, 'So you have heard the news. I received a telegram at midnight. Well, there is nothing to be done. Thank you for your concern.' The visit was terminated. He closed the door and returned to his desk. This was in accordance with his usual style. He never asked anyone to come in and sit down if the visit was during his hours of work. That rule applied to all circumstances. This occasion was no exception.

He needed a research assistant when a new edition of Blochman's translation of *Ain-i-Akbari*, revised by Sir Jadunath was in press. Professor N.K. Sinha introduced me to the great man and I helped him with the minutiae of proofreading, etc., both for that work and the final volume of *The Fall of the Mughal Empire*. In return I was given access to his wonderful library which contained, among other things, a handwritten copy of the *Baharistan-i-ghaibi* which he had discovered in the Bibliotheque Nationale, Paris. This was the history of the Mughal conquest of Bengal written by one Mirza Nathan who followed Islam Khan, the general leading the conquering army. For reasons unknown, the author conferred on his opus an unlikely title—*The Spring Garden Written by an Unknown Author*—and then proceeded to announce his authorship in the very first paragraph of the work. It was one of the major sources for the social history of Bengal I was working on. I told Sir Jadunath about my project. He was not discouraging, but warned me that the source material was scanty and it would be difficult to reconstruct an adequate picture of life in that period. I developed my own method, first picking up bits and pieces of information from chronicles like the *Baharistan* and fitting them together as in a jigsaw puzzle. When I wrote an account of the Mughal administration in Bengal on the basis of such data, I gave my draft to Sir Jadunath with a truly fearful heart. He read it and arranged for me to present it as a paper in the Asiatic Society. This was much more than I had expected and I felt reassured that my project was not to be trashed.

I think the said project became something of a burden to my friend Arun Dasgupta, who later became professor of Southeast Asian history in Calcutta University. He was one of the few among my contemporaries who opted for the academic profession in spite of getting a first class in his MA. As noted earlier, people with any prospects sat for the examinations leading to government jobs in the early years of our independence. The exceptions were, quite rightly, objects of pity. Arun, like me, was a beneficiary of the Muslim exodus from government jobs and thereby my colleague at Central Calcutta College. He appreciated my excitement over my work and, misreading the signals in all probability, I inflicted large chunks of my draft chapters on this unfortunate young man. He had recently got married to a cousin of his despite stiff resistance from his family as was to be expected in a traditional Hindu home. Under the circumstances, the man was entitled to some privacy and uninterrupted marital felicity. The thickness of my skull precluded any appreciation of these facts. I regularly turned up with substantial sections of my magnum opus and read them out relentlessly to Arun, who listened with helpless resignation. His good lady, Manashi, had a look of apprehension in her eyes whenever I turned up at unpredictable hours. Arun's patience with me was, however, unlimited, something that helped me push ahead with my work. He passed away last year. It is a loss I have not been able to accept yet.

Working on the history of the Mughal period required a sound knowledge of Persian and though I had started learning the language when I was at school, my command over it was far from adequate. So I decided to take more lessons and found a wonderful teacher, one of my contemporaries in the postgraduate class. Abdul Alim Razi, the son of a pir and educated in a madrasa, had joined the postgraduate class in Islamic history because he had ambitions to become a modern scholar and something more besides. He was fluent in Arabic, Persian and Urdu—very unusual for a young man from East Bengal and would have been a very great scholar if he had stuck to his métier. But he had other ambitions—to go to England and become a barrister in addition to acquiring a doctorate from the SOAS. Modernization is not always something desirable. But for me the real problem lay elsewhere. Abdul Alim Razi had literary ambitions as well. He spoke Persian fluently and taught me using only the language itself and hence my progress under his guidance was fast. But, alas, he was engaged in writing 'the great novel', the one to put all others in the shade. Published and sold at half a rupee a copy, to the best of my knowledge, I was the sole buyer of this great work of literature depicting the travails of a group of refugees from Burma on the Arakan Road. When asked to comment on its worth, I said very truthfully that I had not read anything like it in any language and it was highly unlikely that I would in the future. Alim saheb shook my hand, agreed with my judgement and said that henceforth he would concentrate all his energies on purely literary endeavour. That was the end to my Persian lessons. Subsequent arrangements I made for instructions in the language were unsatisfactory and eventually I had to give up my plans for work on the Mughal period because of the inadequacy of my knowledge of Persian.

Work on Mughal Bengal presupposed a range of linguistic skills; ideally a knowledge of a number of languages besides Bengali and Persian. The quest for teachers who could teach me Portuguese and later Dutch, opened doors to interesting social experiences.

Calcutta is a truly cosmopolitan city with people from varied ethnic backgrounds. But the ethnic mix in Calcutta was like a badly cooked curry—the different ingredients remained separate, refusing to be parts of a harmonious mixture. I found a Goan teacher who agreed to teach me Portuguese. He worked for a firm as a clerk and lived in what was described as a 'mess', in other words a dormitory inhabited by people from the colonies ruled by European nations other than the English, namely, the Portuguese and the French. It was a curious place and until then I had no idea that such places existed. There were some forty beds in a longish room and long tables and benches in another where food was served. The residents all came from Pondicherry or Goa. They spoke French or Portuguese. None of them had any contact with the Bengalis or anyone outside their respective communities. I do not know whether this was due to the insularity of the people concerned or the ethnocentricity of Bengalis. But through them I discovered a social world whose existence was totally unknown to me before this encounter. They were the flotsam and jetsam of Europe's imperialism that seemed to have no clearly defined identity except for the fact that they took an enormous pride in their command over a European language. French and Portuguese respectively were in fact their mother tongue.

I met a very different type of person in my quest for Dutch lessons. Dissatisfied with my poor progress in Persian, I was looking for some alternative source material of socio-economic history which had not been explored in depth as yet. The bibliographies in the works of W.H. Moreland and K.M. Panikkar suggested that the records of the Dutch East India Company could be such a source. Unwittingly, I had stumbled on a gold mine. Only after I went to the Dutch archives did I discover that these records were even more systematic and voluminous than those of the English East India Company and ran into well over a million manuscript pages.

The man who agreed to give me Dutch lessons was Father Van Exem, a Jesuit missionary from Belgium who was in charge of the Catholic Church at Howrah. He was a polyglot with knowledge of eighteen languages. His Bengali was perfect but his real forte was Arabic. His mission sent him to Hejaz to try and bring the Budouin within the fold of the true faith. This was in the thirties of the last century, long before the advent of jet planes and package tours. The mission gave him a one way ticket to Hejaz and three months to acquire an adequate knowledge of Arabic. Incidentally, converting a Muslim to another faith was an offence punishable by death according to the Sharia. There can be no exceptions. But Van Exem was assured that once they had broken bread with a guest, the Bedouin would not dream of doing him any harm. What might happen in the time between the infidel's arrival and breaking of bread was not explained. Martyrdom is a much valued fate to true Christians. Van Exem took a vow and shut himself up in a room with an Arabic grammar, an Arabic–French dictionary and a copy of the Holy Keran. Water and bread was passed to him through an opening in the wall. Working eighteen hours a day, he emerged from his self-imposed incarceration with a fair knowledge of Arabic.

With this noble tale to inspire me, I launched on my project to learn Dutch. The task proved less arduous than learning Persian. I wish I had followed my teacher's example and shut myself up with the relevant material and a vow to learn Persian. My temperament and circumstances rendered such an exercise in asceticism impractical. My knowledge of Persian hence remained half-baked, but in six months I had a fair command over Dutch. Van Exem warned me however that seventeenth-century Dutch in which the Company records were written was a very different language, unknown to him and I would need to learn the calligraphy of the period as well. Having no idea of how difficult those tasks would be, I went off in a very buoyant mood elated by my success in picking up a language which would prove vital for my projected research.

I got my DPhil degree in history, less prestigious than the tough PhD, from Calcutta University in 1952 and, most inadvisably, published the thesis the following year. My Indian publisher had a somewhat unusual perception of his trade. He invited his authors to publish 'one books' through him. This to him was not an error, but carefully chosen words. He saw his publications in editions of one thousand or more. He knew he was publishing a book, but how could a singular noun cover a thousand books? Hence the justified plural, the 'one books' we were invited to publish through him. Well, looking back I feel more than a little embarrassed that I accepted that invitation. It was a half-baked piece of research based on very shallow scholarship. But it had a few new ideas and somehow appealed to the readers, though it did get a stinging review from the famous archaeologist, Dr Dani. He was of course right. But altogether, the book was a succès d'estime. And to my great embarrassment it is still reprinted and continues to sell, especially in Bangladesh. Some unknown entrepreneur in the said country has done me the great honour of bringing out a pirated edition, because the book is on the recommended reading list for undergraduates. Extreme shortage of books on the history of medieval Bengal explains this embarrassing anomaly.

My father, Amiya Kumar Raychaudhuri

Our family, at Barisal (from right to left): Elder brother Arun, Mother Pratibha Devi, Sister Sujata, Father and I

Rai Bahadur Bhudhar Das (seated on a chair fourth from right) with family; Grandmother Tillotama Devi is seated extreme left in the same row

From left to right: Father, Arun, Grandfather Binod Kumar, I and Mother

The Chandi Mandap of our ancestral house at Kirtipasha

Barisal Zilla School

My first school, Jagadbandhu School

St Antony's College

Duff Hostel on Beadon Street which became my home after I left Barisal to study in Calcutta

Punting with Ido Lelie

In front of Christ Church College (from right to left):
Rabi Chakravarty, Kumar Mukhopadhyay and I, 1956

With friends at Oxford

After being conferred the DLitt

My wife, Hashi

Mahatma Gandhi and Rabindranath Tagore at Santiniketan; my wife is seated on the floor in the centre

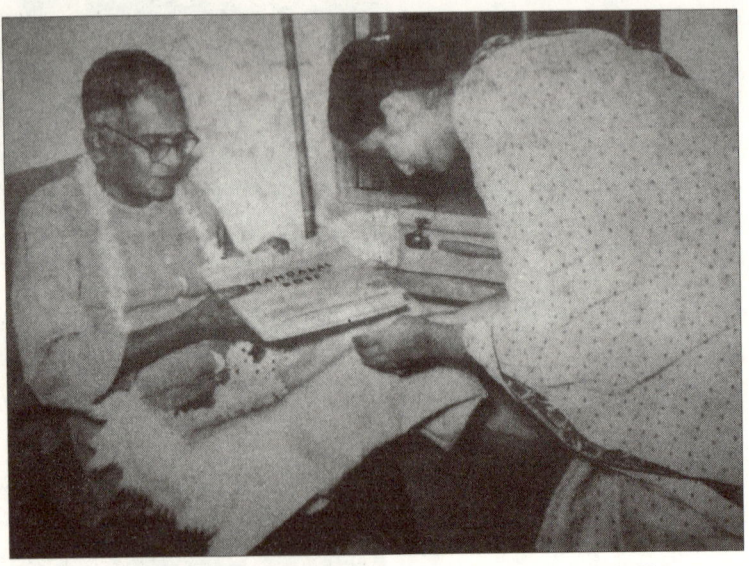

My wife, Hashi, handing over a commemorative edition of his paintings to Nandalal Bose

Part II

11

Oxford, 1953–57

The road to 'gurukula'

In 1953, I got a state scholarship to study at Oxford. I would have preferred to do a first degree which I still feel is the best education the place has to offer. But I was too old (though I found, to my surprise, a retired policeman working for a degree in PPE among my fellow students in Balliol) and already had a doctorate, whatever its worth. I opted for work leading to a research degree. I was admitted to Balliol College to work for my second DPhil degree, supervised by Dr Colin Davis, the reader in modern South Asian history.

On my way to Oxford, I met some young Indian academics who were later to win name and fame. I took a train from Calcutta to Bombay where we were to board the ship for England. Among my fellow travellers on that train was young Amartya Sen, then nineteen or so, and his parents who were going to see him off. The fellow passengers on the boat included Parthasarathi Gupta who achieved a great reputation as a teacher when he became professor of history at Delhi University. Another passenger was Romila Thapar, whose reputation as a skilled ballroom dancer reached us. But I did not meet her on board the ship, because she was a first-class passenger and I was in the economy class along with a large group of Indian students. Incidentally, the class in question was not called 'economy' but I have no memory as to its actual designation.

The life on the boat SS *Strathnaver* of the P and O Lines was my first direct experience of Western life and also of racism. I do not count the slights which were a part of the experience of dependence: how would we know that we were a subject people without those? When I first visited Calcutta in the 1930s, one afternoon we were refused entry into the Botanical Gardens because the military band was playing for the entertainment of the sahibs and memsahibs. During that holy hour, the place was out of bounds to natives because the transparent dhotis worn by the Bengali men, through which their dark legs were visible, were offensive to the memsahibs. I remember my father's face went red at the racist insult, but I was too young to understand the implications of this blatantly offensive measure. On the very first day on the ship, the captain came to see me (I believe because I was the oldest among the students) and asked if we had any objection to their usual arrangement—putting all the Indian students at mealtime around one single long table instead of grouping them four to six persons around each table, regardless of race, like the other passengers. I talked to someone who travelled by the same boat a decade later. The same arrangements still continued, I was informed, no doubt out of tender concern for the well-being of the Indian students travelling to England. I had no idea as to how things were arranged on the ship and agreed without consulting anyone else.

The results of the decision looked extremely odd, with the Indian students piled up like garbage at one end of the dining room while the rest sat in small civilized groups around reasonably sized tables. I have no idea why the captain did this. In all fairness, it could be from the mistaken belief that the young Indians would feel more comfortable this way or that the European passengers might feel ill at ease sharing their tables with uncouth Indians. There is some inconclusive evidence to support the latter conclusion. In course of the nineteen days it took to cover the journey from Bombay to the Tilbury docks with two shore excursions, no European passenger was ever seen talking to any Indian and, of course, vice versa. I should, in fairness, mention one exception. One of our fellow Indian passengers also on his way to Oxford to do a degree in English literature (he got a first in schools) had been in the army. He had some familiarity with Western life habits. He made friends with some young Englishmen and used to flaunt the fact to his less urbane Indian fellow travellers. But his exceptional good fortune derived from his own initiative, not any effort on the part of his British friends. The informal apartheid meant that the rest of the Indian travellers hardly participated in any of the numerous leisure activities on board and acted as if they were the denizens of some ghetto. A few pretended noisily as if they were enjoying the journey, but so far as I could see, this was far from the truth.

The behaviour of the waiters in the ship's restaurant, who were still all white, was openly offensive and on one occasion I felt constrained to complain against the steward to the captain. This was far from a pleasant task, but I felt I had to. The steward who had given offence apologized but in as guarded a fashion as possible. 'You and I understand each other,' he said loftily. To my eternal shame I snubbed him invoking class. That the vice of snobbery was alive and kicking deep inside my socialistic soul was a fact I had not been aware of. I had acted in a way which went against everything I believed in. I have never been able to forgive myself for this act because I do not see any difference between racist intolerance and class snobbery.

Life on the ship provided several experiences of culture shock. In the morning we lined up for a shower. Quite a few among the European men stood calmly in the nude, their only contact with textile provided by the towel on their shoulders. I was to find later that most European men are not embarrassed by the fact of nudity in the presence of their own sex.

Most Indians would die of shame in such a situation. I remembered Swami Vivekananda's sociological explanation of this difference in attitude. I also recalled Herodotus's famous observation that the Persians, being barbarians, wore some clothing while engaging in sports unlike the civilized Greeks who of course went into the arena naked like newborn babies. I was soon to discover that in European culture the sense of bodily shame had suffered a serious decline by the mid-twentieth century. Among our fellow passengers were three women's hockey teams from Australia, India and New Zealand. When we reached the Red Sea, admittedly a somewhat warm spot, they appeared publicly in attires which would not be recognized in India as clothes appropriate for either sex in civilized society. In fact if the purpose of clothes was to cover bodily shame as was the old antiquated belief, their dress or absence thereof singularly failed to serve that purpose. It would be hypocritical to suggest that the situation was entirely unwelcome to us younger male passengers. I cannot vouch for the responses of older men.

Some of the Indian passengers, the only ones I got to know, were highly interesting specimens of humanity. The man who made the maximum impression on my mind was one Mr Chatterji (not his real name). An exceptionally orthodox Brahmin, he wore a talisman on his arm, a gift from the family guru meant to ward off all evil, especially dangers of succumbing to the charms of some white beauty. Dutifully every morning, he would plunge his talisman in a glass of water and start the day by drinking the liquid thus purified. He loved his ice cream but would not touch it if the previous dishes contained any meat, not taboo to Bengali Brahmins. According to his understanding of the scriptures, the meat became beef if followed by milk or milk products. I have no idea whence this notion was derived. One day at lunch I found him ordering 'veel'.

'What on earth are you doing?' I asked in horror, because unwittingly he was becoming a candidate for excommunication, beef in any form being taboo to the orthodox Hindu today, though it was the preferred meat of the Vedic Hindus who knew a thing or two about tasty food.

'Why?' he responded, 'It is delicious.'

'What sort of meat do you think veal is?'

'Sheep's meat of course! Try it, it is very good.' I was entirely in agreement with the last part of his statement and preferred to remain silent on the first.

Some months later I ran into one of our fellow passengers in India House. He took me aside and asked in whispers, 'Remember Chatterji?' How could one forget him, I said.

My acquaintance lowered his voice several decibels and asked in a virtually inaudible voice, 'Any idea what he does every evening these days?' Now I was really worried. The poor fool must have got involved with some crime gang. I expected to read very soon in that august journal, *The News of the World*, about the doings of an Indian student, typical of his class, as the leading figure in some drug racket. But no, it was much worse, I was told.

'You won't believe it,' whispered my fellow passenger. I listened in hushed silence. 'The fellow, can you believe it, actually dances, and that too with women and every evening.' The news reassured me. Chatterji was not engaged in activities likely to bring shame on the Indian community. But nobody can escape the results of such heinous action as dancing every evening and that too with women. Chatterji, I was to learn later, returned home a Roman Catholic and that too with an Italian wife. Wonders never cease.

There was a brief stop at Cote d'Or for a shore excursion to Cassis and La Ciotat. I felt enchanted. I had never seen any place as beautiful as these. In the fifties of the last century, Europe's seashores were still far from overcrowded and even the less famous beaches like those of the two villages mentioned had the power to charm despite their shingles which rendered them unpleasant. Crowds of tourists and ugly-looking hotels disfiguring the bounty of nature have really ruined these places of great beauty. Even in 1962 when I revisited Cassis and La Ciotat with my wife as part of a sentimental journey, they were no longer the places I had seen in 1953. It was love at first sight for me so far as Europe was concerned. And I have not yet recovered from that emotional affect.

I have wondered with sorrow in my heart why the grand inheritance of India's past and the great scenic beauty of our hills, seashores and vistas are so often shrouded in ugliness. People in the West spend vast amounts in quest of sandy beaches while our long coastline provides numberless spots where beaches of every variety are easily accessible. Now tourism, both domestic and foreign, has made this rich treasure a source of some enjoyment to people who love beautiful spots and the remains of man's heritage. But in most places you approach them through spectacular ugliness and squalor. The plethora of four- and five-star hotels, rising above the slums and the accumulated garbage, simply enhance the pervasive squalor. This is no necessary result of urbanization. India's roads and cities in the remote past were of course not paved with gold, but the travellers' accounts of the remote past from Megasthenes to Hiuen Tsang offer a picture of cleanliness and quiet beauty. The contemporary ugliness is no result of mere poverty. One has only to see the Santhal villages to appreciate the fact. India's urban squalor and revolting ugliness are perhaps due to what late Nirad C. Chaudhuri described as re-barbarization—the sad experience of a highly civilized people lapsing into barbarism in their vie quotidienne.

We reached Tilbury docks one dismal September morning. The sky was the colour of dirty water and a continuous drizzle added to the ambience of melancholy without any charm. This was not the green and pleasant land I had read of. My heart sank at the thought that I would have to spend more than three years in this awful place. A middle-ranking official from the Indian high commission came to lecture us about the ways to survive in this country. He told us, bursting with self-importance, how awful it had been to study in England in the days of the Raj when the shoeshine boys used to ask, 'How do you like our rule, sir?' Now of course under the tender care of our own high commission it was a very different story.

We were lodged for a few days in a government hostel near the London University. It was a place of exceptional shabbiness, much worse than the hostels we were used to back home. My enthusiasm for studying in England went down several points and I did my best to summon all my capacity for endurance invoking once more the Yogic ideals of transcending multiple miseries. Parthasarathi Gupta was staying in the same hostel and we decided to visit Oxford before actually taking up residence there.

Oxford, Oxford

It was a mild morning, overcast but not rainy. We walked from the railway station to High Street. I felt we had stepped into the middle ages, especially when we walked down Merton Street. My depression lifted. I told Partha that I wished to live in this city the rest of my life. Several of my whimsical wishes have been realized in highly unlikely circumstances. If I were superstitious, I would have attributed such good luck to the Deity's personal and favourable interest in my affairs. This particular wish also came true—some twenty years later. That is one stroke of luck I have never regretted. I told myself later that this place did not belong to any particular country. It is part of man's heritage. I feel exceptionally privileged to have spent the greater part of my adult life here. I have loved it in spring and summer, but no less in autumn and winter and through its modified version of the monsoons which marks its weather at all times. People from all over Asia came to Nalanda, the great Buddhist university which once elected a Chinese monk as its rector. Here in the Far West, I had stumbled on the Western Nalanda—my reward for good actions in past lives!

I turned up at the gates of Balliol a few days later. My knowledge of British social habits was limited and hence I took the gentleman in a three-piece suit, a pocket watch in his waist coat pocket, to be a don and was about to address him, Indian style, as 'Sir' but something told me that a more neutral address would be appropriate. The personage in question was Cyril, our head porter. 'Mr Raychaudhuri?' he asked when I entered the porter's lodge, pronouncing the name correctly. How did he know my name? Nothing mysterious. He was expecting me, the only Indian who was going to turn up that morning. I had a very sizeable trunk filled to capacity, thanks to my mother's tender concern for her sickly son's probable fate in the arctic climate of Oxford. After looking around for a coolie I soon remembered that I was in the wrong country for such facilities.

Cyril understood my predicament and produced a trolley for my benefit. It was beyond my ability to place my trunk on it. I stood outside the lodge, baffled when a man in rather shabby clothes with a leather patch on the elbow of his tweed jacket came and offered to help. It was not an easy job. But between the two of us we managed to drag that very sizeable trunk up to the first floor on staircase nineteen. I was not sure who my saviour was and unsure if I should offer him a crown or not. My guardian angel was looking after me: on mature consideration, I decided not to tip this unknown person. At the master's party that evening I met him again. His name was Christopher Hill. I happened to be familiar with his writings and his very great reputation. His rooms in college were next to mine. I got to know him reasonably well. Several weeks later I told him of my intended action of tipping him. 'You should have,' Christopher said, 'I was passing through rather difficult times.'

My rooms in Balliol offered luxury without comfort. The large bedroom with its stone walls was unbearably cold for me during the months of autumn and winter. A measly electric heater was supposed to warm up that room. Well, it did nothing of the sort. The scout who looked after the denizens of the rooms on staircase nineteen left a jug of hot water for my use and a basin. I was familiar with this arrangement from the dak bungalows built primarily for the use of the functionaries of the Raj. As these facilities were probably left in our bedrooms around dinner time, by the time we entered the place the water had gone cold. When we woke up in the morning, there were chunks of ice floating in the jug. An interesting experience, but not one which brought any comfort. The sitting room overlooked the inner quad. In spring and summer I could see a decorative cherry tree in full bloom from my window and the lawns were indeed very green. I had very distinguished neighbours. Christopher Hill had his rooms on the floor above, but we shared a bathroom. As the bathroom was privileged to have a tub, I unwittingly caused problems for the famous man by spending rather a longish period in that facility when other students, I could see, walked painfully across the lawn to the communal bath room. Since people bathed there in the nude, I should have preferred to go without baths rather than share the joys of communal bathing. Having a study in addition to a bedroom was of course incredible luxury so far as I was concerned, but the level of comfort remained somewhat low. This was because I had to depend on a gas fire for heat and the latter in its turn depended on a steady supply of shillings to keep going. I could never manage to stock up the right number of shillings to ensure adequate heating. This was partly because my command over the supply of British coins of whatever denomination was somewhat limited.

Besides Christopher Hill, I had two other very distinguished neighbours—E.H. Carr whose bedroom was next to mine and Tommy Balogh (later Lord Balogh) whose office shared a wall with my study. I got to know Dr Hill who often asked me over for a glass of beer. This was a privilege for which I had to pay a price on my return to India, a curious story which I shall narrate later. Through him I got to know some of the luminaries of the extreme left, like Eric Hobsbawm and Gordon Childe. But my other neighbours remained strangers. I was too shy to take the initiative in talking to these eminent men and they, of course, never bothered to pick up an acquaintance with an obscure Indian. Balogh had a formidable reputation as a tutor. Words attributed to him vis-a-vis his women students would have dragged him to some feminist court of justice had he uttered them in more recent decades. Once in a while, he would call out in my direction, 'Boy, Boy!' I am not sure if this was appropriate description for a person of 27–28. But there was one good reason for this strange mode of address. Once a friend knocked at his door by mistake and asked which one my room was. 'Raychaudhuri! Ah, that is how it is pronounced,' he said with some relief, adding, 'I have always wondered.' Dr Balogh was in the habit of addressing most people he knew as 'darling'. He visited Delhi School of Economics when I was teaching there and became especially enamoured of P.N. Dhar, then director, Institute of Economic Growth, and later political advisor to Indira Gandhi during the Bangladesh war. Balogh marginally changed his usual form of address to suit the occasion and called P.N. 'Dhar-ling'.

Teaching at Oxford: My Teachers and My Friends

On my very first day at Balliol, I was asked to see the senior tutor. For reasons not very clear to me, the 'interview' took place in the front quad and hence necessarily standing. May be the object was to keep it suitably brief. The senior tutor (whose name I forget) explained to me that the life of a graduate student at Oxford was a somewhat lonely one. I would have to do almost all my work on my own. I have hardly ever heard a truer word. In the fifties, the instruction for graduate students was totally unstructured. Some supervisors, especially if they happened to be one of the luminaries of the university, rarely met the students working under their guidance. Some of them explained to their lucky pupils that they would read 50 per cent of the thesis and not more. Some did not bother to read that much and the student would meet their supervisor once a term if he was lucky. Some of the professors/readers/lecturers ran graduate seminars, but I am not sure if this was part of their prescribed duty. In short, for the most part the graduate student was left to himself/ herself to swim or sink. The rate of failure was very high, but nobody seemed particularly bothered by that.

Dr C.C. Davis, once a major in the Indian army, supervised all students working for research degrees on Indian history, irrespective of subject or period. Irfan Habib, who worked on the agrarian history of the Mughal period, Dr Puri, whose thesis concerned the rule of the Kushanas and I, who worked on the Dutch East India Company's trade, were all his supervisees. His own work was on the north-west frontier and Warren Hastings (the latter to justify his readership in modern Indian history which required lecturing on Warren Hastings, the only course on Indian history included in the history syllabus). This arrangement was justified on the assumption that to supervise, one required only a command over historical method and a broad knowledge of the history of the region/period in question. Specialized knowledge of the relevant area of research of course helped, but was not essential. In principle, one cannot object to this assumption. And I should add that Colin Davis did his duty by us conscientiously and to good purpose, and that I did learn much from him about the craft of historical research.

He was a rather sad and embittered person, a victim of the social snobbery endemic in British society in his days and, at Oxford, of a pattern of intellectual snobbery which did make exceptions but only in favour of those who enjoyed the support of powerful cliques within the university. In the army he was told very plainly that he could not expect to go above the level he had reached because he did not come from the right social class. At Oxford no one told him what was wrong with him but he was never elected a fellow of any college, but only given dining rights at Balliol. He was elected to his readership in modern Indian history for five-year periods at a time. Only towards the fag end of his career, I believe, this absurd arrangement was rectified and Colin Davis given a permanent post till retirement. He felt deeply humiliated by this twofold discrimination. He came to see me and took me out to lunch when I succeeded to his readership but did not accept my invitation to come and dine with me at my college. He had not entered any Oxford college in the preceding ten years and did not intend to do so for the rest of his life, he explained. I felt extremely sorry for my old teacher for I was convinced that he deserved better.

Dr Davis was an old-fashioned political historian who had certainly achieved a level of excellence within those limits. He was not an intellectual familiar with modern approaches to historical interpretation or with the social sciences. But both as a student and a teacher at Oxford I have met many scholars here who suffer from these limitations without losing out in their careers as a consequence or being denied fellowships in the colleges. He had a certain mastery over the archival source material for the subjects of his research, took a legitimate pride in the fact that he had swam in every river mentioned in his monograph on the north-west frontier of the Indian empire and wrote an elegant narrative, using his common sense as the tool for interpretation. Would it be too much to say that most poltical historians of his generation could be covered by similar descriptions? He appears to have been almost singled out for humiliating treatment for reasons unknown to me. Oxford, like any other human institution, has notoriously never been free from battles royale between powerful individuals and cliques. I do not know whose ire poor Colin had provoked with such bitter consequences for him and why. But knowing his work as a teacher and scholar intimately, I am convinced that he did not deserve it.

He was a plain-speaking person given to telling home truths. After serving as an officer in the First World War, he won a scholarship to Cambridge where he got his PhD degree. His election to the readership at Oxford, he told me, was partly the result of political considerations. His competitor for the post was Thompson, but the latter's attitude to the Indian national movement was too sympathetic to allow his election, Davis used to say. One of the 'scandals' in India's academic relations with Oxford was the denial of a DPhil degree to S.N. Sen, a leading Indian historian. Years later the University made amends by conferring on him a BLitt degree, honoris causa. Colin would say, sotto voce, that the time was inappropriate for giving doctorates to Indians. Hence a BLitt for S.N. Sen. I do not know how far these bits of information were based on facts, but Davis had no doubts regarding their credibility. He had no illusions about the nature of imperialism and its horrors. 'Had I been an Indian gentleman, I would have joined the Indian National Congress,' he would say. He had some simplistic equations: a nationalist Indian (he identified me, correctly, as such a person) would naturally be 'anti-British'. The fact that I, very obviously, was not, he found somewhat unnatural. I failed singularly in my efforts to convince him that wishing one's country to be independent did not imply hostility to any people, especially after the desired freedom had been attained.

He was an officer with the Gurkha Regiment in India and told me horrific stories about their actions which I have not read or heard about from any other source. When they were posted on the frontier on missions of pacification, in peaceful times they would make friends and play with the local children being truly childlike in their nature. But if there was any uprising, they would happily behead the same kids with their kukri, laughing merrily as they did so. In narrating his memories of the first World War, he again mentioned horrors I have never read or heard of anywhere else. The very young tommies would at times light a hand grenade, he told me, and thrust it down the trousers of captured Germans and split their sides with laughter when the unfortunate creatures were blown up. He and my friend Richard Symonds were the only British people of my acquaintance who had served the Raj without claiming to believe in the absurd myth that the Indians looked upon their rulers as their 'ma-baap'. Colin passed through Amritsar shortly after the Punjab disturbances. The people on the street, he told us, looked at him in a way which suggested that given the chance, they would love to tear him to pieces. I was reminded of this when later I read in Nirad C. Chaudhuri's memoirs that on VJ day the crowds in the streets of Delhi wore expressions that reminded one of tigers who had been deprived of their prey. Davis was no political radical and had happily fought for the empire because he knew it to be to the interest of the British, or rather, his own class. He had a commonsensical understanding of the class basis of the imperial project and never believed that the Raj was for the benefit of either the Indian people or the poor tommy who gave his life in an unbearably hot climate for twenty rupees a month, ostensibly to enhance the glory of his king and country. And he never fell for the inane propaganda that the Indians dearly loved their alien rulers.

I have often been asked if it had been worthwhile to travel all the way to Oxford to write a thesis under the supervision of Colin Davis. I have two answers to that question. First, the graduate student at Oxford did not come only for the benefit of supervision by one academic. Secondly, while for sure there were much greater scholars in India who could have supervised me, I am not sure that anyone would have done for me what Colin did.

He read his students' drafts very carefully; in my case, more than once. I do not know of any other Oxford don who took so much trouble over his students' thesis. As I shall presently explain, I had virtually discovered a new and copious source of information for the economic and political history of India, the records of the

Dutch East India Company and went through thousands of folio pages of manuscript material which probably had not been touched by anyone after their addressees had read them. Consequently, my enthusiasm for the material I unearthed far surpassed my sense of judgement as a historian. I was inclined to include in my narrative every fact I had discovered. Davis taught me to identify and weed out what he called 'dead facts'. Writing history, to my understanding, is more a craft than a scientific undertaking. In his old-fashioned way, Colin had mastered that craft. No, he was no Marc Bloch, but he was capable of meticulous scholarship, careful sifting of evidence and had a narrative style which I can only describe as fat-free. He was not an intellectual identifying structures and causalities underlying surface data with the aid of the social sciences. But he was, contrary to general impression, a man of strong common sense and held no brief for any particular body of opinion. In his work on Warren Hastings, he made no effort to justify the latter's action. This negative virtue is often absent from the works of well-known historians of British India. Objectivity, he used to tell me, was not possible because it is no part of human nature. But one had to try hard to reach that goal. One's degree of success in this effort was the measure of one's quality as a historian. I found this an excellent and humbling maxim. I remember Colin Davis as a fine research guide, despite his intellectual limitations.

As I have noted before, the university made no other formal provision for the instruction of graduate students working on Indian history beyond appointing a supervisor. But the institution catered for an ongoing intellectual feast and one was free to partake of it as one wished. I sampled happily some of the lectures delivered by the very famous. Most of these were rather disappointing, perhaps because I lacked the background knowledge necessary to appreciate them. I am not, however, sure if that diagnosis is correct. There was one scholar, Professor Windt whose lectures on European art from the days of the Renaissance down to that of abstract art I found immensely enjoyable and instructive, though my knowledge of the subject was less than that of a sixth-former. These lectures drew such large audiences that they had to be delivered in the university's theatre, the Playhouse, and people stood on the pavement listening to him speak with the aid of microphones. I particularly remember one series entitled, 'The Mask in Modern Art'. His thesis was that artists like Picasso, and in some ways, Braque and Klee were really in the tradition of la petite maniere, which they covered up and presented as a new grand vision by distorting reality using their consummate skills as painters. Knowing little about the subject, I felt he had hit upon a correct insight. I often have similar feelings about postmodern thought: very clever men and women have distorted the language of common sense to create an opaque complexity which covers up ideas that are essentially very simple and could do without much of the verbiage and painful assaults on Queen's English.

A seminar series repeated every year should have been of interest to any researcher. These were arranged by Professor Vincent Harlow and entitled, simply: 'How to write a thesis'. Starting with the way to choose a subject for research, it went step by step through the many facets of thesis writing. One I remember particularly well dealt with punctuation. Living in a time when punctuation has been virtually given up in favour of rolling prose interrupted only by the full stop, I now particularly appreciate the difference a comma or a semicolon can make to the meaning one tries to convey. But one cannot hope to stem the tide of history and hence must live humbly with sentences that have no comma or semicolon and others which probably have some meaning, the meaning, however, being accessible only to the sacred bands of the initiated.

I benefited from the human resources of the university in two other ways. I took lessons in seventeenth-century English calligraphy which proved to be of some use in my work on the Dutch records. More important, Davis sent me to Sir George Clarke, the great authority on the seventeenth century to seek advice on relevant developments in cognate fields. I recall his asking me whether I had seen and knew the uses of the spices which were the staples of Dutch trade. This down-to-earth pragmatism of his approach I found very attractive. He continued to take a kindly interest in my work and read a fair portion of my draft chapters. This is the sort of instruction I had hoped I would get when I came to Oxford. I was not disappointed. Professor Harlow, who modestly denied any knowledge of trade history, also helped in the same way. But to repeat: such access to the great scholarly resources of Oxford was no part of any structured academic programme.

While the undergraduate at Oxford had to write one or more essays per week, to be commented on by a series of very learned men over the nine terms of his/her stay, the graduate student was free to do as he liked except for the rare encounters (not so rare in my case) with their supervisors. This way one indeed learned the very worthwhile lesson of intellectual/academic self-help. The vast holdings of the Bodleian and one's college library were there at one's disposal. And besides one's supervisor, there were one's contemporaries who, directly or indirectly, helped shape one's intellectual and academic interests.

Late Rajeswar Dayal, India's permanent representative to the United Nations who assisted Dag Hammarskjold in his mission to Belgian Congo, has recorded in his memoirs that during their time in Oxford (as a trainee ICS officer, he was at Christ Church College in the 1930s), the English students did not talk to them. We were far more fortunate in this respect, though a group of our contemporaries did keep to their own circle. Those excluded from the pleasure of their company were by no means exclusively non-white. I got the impression that this was more a matter of class than race. Nowadays, undergraduates who have been to the great public schools are not exactly eager to declare the fact. Even aspirants to the prime minister's chair, if they have been privileged to be students at Eton, are at some pains to justify the fact. In the fifties of the last century, the public school boys still tended to hang together. The truly smart set was members of the students' clubs specializing in ridin', shootin', huntin' and of course wining and dining. Occasionally in summer, one saw them at the breakfast table, bleary-eyed and still in evening dress, partaking of champagne breakfast. One member of this tribe took a brief liking to me. He once took me along to a party at Christ Church College thrown by the son of a Greek shipping tycoon who owned a 'plane, allegedly parked on the Christ Church meadows'. There were some two hundred guests there. The refreshments on offer were simple and unostentatious—lobster, one per head (more if desired), caviar and champagne cup—that is, champagne enhanced by cognac, VSOP (Very Special Old Pale) of course. It was a humbling experience.

Some of our contemporaries have justly achieved great fame later in life. Professor Sir Keith Thomas and Professor Charles Taylor from Canada are the best known among them. Maurice Keene, FBA, who looked like and in fact was a little boy fresh from school is no less well known. I stood in some awe of the luminaries whose brilliant future was easy to foresee even when they were undergraduates. Later I have tried to learn from Keith Thomas's marvellous contributions to the discipline of history, but as a student I had only a nodding acquaintance with him and Chuck Taylor, though neither of them was in the least unapproachable. My social awkwardness, manifest among other things in my eating habits which made me something of a laughing stock in some quarters (for reasons unknown, I could not manage a quarter-boiled egg and treated it with prolonged tender care for fear that I would spill its contents all over the table: this caused a great deal of mirth expressed in loud laughter and very audible comments) restricted my friendships and contacts to a relatively small circle. Most of my friends were radicals, some in fact members of the Communist Party, until the brutal action of the Soviet authorities in Hungary, which led to their resignation en masse.

Among those I got to know best were Ralph or Raphael Samuel, founder of the History Workshop, Peter Sedgwick, well known as a biographer of Trotsky and the Trotskyite activist, Michael Kidron. Ralph introduced me to the rich body of Marxist historical writings and also to the Annales School of history. Outside this circle of radicals, young Maurice became a good friend despite the difference in age. When I returned to Oxford to teach, he was one of the few contemporaries with whom I could resume contact. Two Sanskritists, Vladimir Zwalf and Cyril Lewis were also among the people I got to know well and so was a student of Persian. John (name changed) had a somewhat exaggerated admiration for Indian ladies which nearly got him into serious trouble. On the occasion of the Indian colour festival, he put some red dye into envelopes and mailed them off to all the Indian girls at Oxford wishing them a happy Holi. This had unfortunate consequences: when the envelopes were opened the dye got into the eyes of the girls and as abir, the coloured powder used in Holi, was not available in Oxford, John had used the nearest substitute—chilli powder. We could stop the girls from going to the proctors only with much difficulty. The road to romance is rarely very smooth. John's journey in quest of it, unlike Alexander's quest for glory, did not take him east of the Indus, but he did travel eastwards in hope and eventually married an Iraqi lady of great charm.

Kidron and I had a shared interest in the Dutch language and needed to improve our knowledge of it. As people who could help were not easily available, we wrote to the local representative of the British Council hoping that he could put us in touch with one of the students from the continent who had come to learn or to improve their English. We received a charming reply: 'Yes, we have a few Dutch girls in stock. One is rather plump and the other has a slight squint, but I trust that they will serve your purpose.' The writer would have got into trouble for writing this in our more enlightened days of scrupulous concern for women's dignity and political correctness.

When I moved to Holywell Manor, situated near a graveyard, Cyril Lewis was a fellow boarder. On his way back from pubs somewhat late at night, he could hear the clanging noise produced by the shackles which hampered the movement of the damned souls. I argued that this was opposed to Christian dogma because the condemned souls would suffer their punishments only after the Day of Judgement and, as far as I knew, that day had not arrived yet. The clanging noise Cyril heard hence had to be from some source other than the chains of the damned. This theological argument cut no ice. Cyril stuck to his strong belief. The fact was that he liked his beer strong, export quality, and in reasonably large quantities. And so he continued to hear the sad noise from the chains of the damned.

Russell Meiggs, the famous historian of the classical world who had excavated the ancient port of Rome was the warden of Holywell Manor. The Manor was originally a medieval nunnery where the fallen women of the aristocracy were made to wash other people's dirty linen by way of penance (this bit of historical knowledge I picked up from mere hearsay and hence cannot vouch for its authenticity). At some point in its unhappy past the Manor got burnt. There were persistent tales of it being haunted and it was rumoured that Mr Meiggs had seen the disembodied spirit in question. He used to ask over the residents of the Manor in batches and invited four of us, including Cyril, to dinner one evening. I decided to commit a social faux pas and ask him about the ghost after due apologies. He answered my query very politely. Yes, not only he, but several members of his family had seen the ghost, not once but many times. The apparition usually stood on the steps of one of the buildings, the classic woman in white, and slowly walked away in the direction of the graveyard whence Cyril's famous clanging sounds tended to emerge. There was a look of triumph on Cyril's face. I gently pointed out that the apparition was not bedecked in chains. But Cyril would not quibble over such insignificant details.

My friends and acquaintances among the students included, of course, a number of Indians, some of whom were at Balliol. But the most spectacular Indian contemporary was the maharaja of Dhrangadhra, a small princely state in Gujarat. His letterhead articulated his self-esteem. It read:

Court of Dhrangadhra
Camp Oxord
Christ Church College
Oxford.

He had two secretaries—(1) private (female) and (2) military (appropriately, male), both Oxford graduates. It was not clear what military advice he received from number two, but I have often seen the young man in question emerge from his study with a very serious expression on his face. We feared some war was about to break out on the borders of the city of Oxford where the king's camp (like Charles the First's in an earlier age) was temporarily located while the potentate worked for his BLitt degree. Secretary number one had a hard life. The maharaja was in the habit of dictating his letters seated on the throne inside his toilet while the poor girl sat outside on a chair and took dictation, her face the colour of beet root. I feared she might have a stroke some day, but what could one do? Short of a revolution, there is no way to alter the ways of royalty. And rebellion was out of the question, because the cussed Nehruvian state had already abolished princely power and privileges, providing only for a pitiful annual allowance. The raja could still have a camp, but he no longer had any subjects who might produce a decent rebellion. I was privileged to meet quite a few future members of the House of Lords and a substantially larger number of honourable young ladies in the maharaja's spacious rooms at Christ Church. And when he threw a party for his brother-in-law, the maharaja of Jodhpur, the reception room was chock-full of British aristocracy. After all, the latter were not, unlike the honoured guest, descended directly from the Sun (or was it the Moon?). I do not know about love, but snobbery certainly conquers all—certainly in the sceptred isle.

Another Indian student who will go unnamed was of a reformist bent of mind. He strongly disapproved of the shameless Western practice of kissing and smooching in public. But the reasons for his disapproval were altruistic rather than puritanical. He would catch hold of the errant lovers and tell them off, 'Don't you have any consideration for other people? Can you not spare a thought for people like old men and children who do not have these facilities? How do you think they feel when they see you indulging like this? Shame on you!' People thus confronted walked away sheepishly, the reformer in a mood of triumph.

Among my contemporaries were several persons who later rose to prominence in Indian academic life. Barun De and Parthasarathi Gupta emerged as highly respected historians. A.N. Kaul long chaired the department of English literature in Delhi University.

But deservedly the most famous among my Indian contemporaries was Irfan Habib, the leading historian of Mughal India. I know of no other case where a doctoral dissertation becomes a classic in the subject. Irfan's 'Agrarian System of Mughal India' achieved this rare distinction. Colin Davis used to tell us that this was by far the best thesis written under his supervision. Evidently, the man had a clear sense of quality in historical research, his alleged limitations notwithstanding.

But in our time, the most famous Indian at Oxford was Raghavan Iyer who is no longer with us. He achieved all that a brilliant undergraduate at the university is expected to achieve, except for the blues. He got a top first in PPE, became president of the union (Heseltine was the librarian of the union when Raghavan presided) and it was widely believed that some day he would succeed Nehru as India's prime minister. Raghavan, influenced by the Theosophical Society in his boyhood, had strong mystical beliefs. When the news of his victory in the election for the post of president was announced, Raghavan, allegedly seated in the lotus posture, looked skyward and humbly thanked the Lord of the Universe with the words, 'The victory is thine, oh Lord, not mine.'

The 1950s saw the beginning of the Cold War and also of the war in Vietnam. The wind of change, Harold Macmillan was the first to acknowledge, had already started to blow. Anti-colonialism and, as its sub-theme, anti-Americanism, were very much in the air. Afro-Asian solidarity was a slogan often to be heard at meetings addressed by radical intellectuals. The al-Mahdis of Sudan, uncle and nephew, were among the leading protagonists of the said solidarity. They would stretch out their hands, shouting 'Afro-Asian solidarity' whenever one tried to attend these meetings. Taking those hands, stretched out in abiding friendship, into yours carried one small risk. If you had an attractive girlfriend or partner, she might disappear with the owner of those hands the moment your attention was distracted. There is always a price to pay for worthwhile political alliances.

My relative isolation at Oxford as a graduate student was enhanced by my aversion to all forms of sport. But in that great seat of learning,

I acquired one sporting skill. My area of excellence was 'shove ha' penny'. This parlour game was once the joy of pubs in the UK. Alas, I have not seen these life-enhancing tables in the pubs in the last three decades, much to my sorrow. Many an afternoon was spent in the Balliol junior common room engrossed in this charming game in which Ralph Samuel was declared one night to be the unchallenged king. One time-wasting pleasure I much cherished consisted in the highly un-English practice of gossip sessions which often lasted till the early hours of the morning, usually over cups of coffee. I think I probably owe the curse of my life, the distressing ailment of insomnia to this particular indulgence. Some of my companions in this harmless (except to oneself) vice, I encountered again as members of the faculty. But alas, they were by then respectable householders no longer given to such degenerate habits. Maybe, that is why I retain a sneaking preference for the social life in Calcutta where long sessions of adda, pointless conversation covering every topic on earth, remain the central concern to people in all stages of life. The sheer luxury of wasting our most irreplaceable asset, time, is something to experience.

I had already made up my mind before I reached Oxford that I would work on a topic which would allow me to concentrate on the Dutch East India Company's records as source material for the economic history of India. After long discussions with Davis and Sir George Clarke, I decided that the most viable project for the purposes of a thesis would be a study of some phase in the history of the Dutch Company's trade with India. I decided to focus on the Coromandel or south-eastern coast of India which was one of the major props of the Dutch trade with Asia. There was one problem I had to solve before I got on with this work. The Dutch I had acquired bore very limited resemblance to the language of the seventeenth-century documents, and the English calligraphy of the period I learnt at Oxford was very unlike their Dutch counterpart. This implied that I would have to go to Holland and start from scratch, settling down first to learn the old language and calligraphy which would cut into the strictly limited period covered by my scholarship. Well, one could only hope for the best.

A Dutch Interlude

One sunny morning I set out for Holland via Harwich and crossed the North Sea by boat. Holland is not famous for any spectacular natural beauty, but its old towns and cities, green fields and sea beaches charmed me. In April and May there was the unforgettable sight of tulip fields, a business enterprise emerging as a thing of great beauty. And my first stay in the country was in an unlikely place, the Dutch royal palace in The Hague which had been donated (rather lent, for it was later taken back by the next queen) to the newly established Institute for Social Study. Their three hundred years of colonial experience had given the Netherlands a substantial body of expertise on Asia and Africa. Some of these experts got together and with financial assistance from the UNESCO established this institute. The queen 'donated' her palace in The Hague to house it. Members from other universities were welcome to stay there if rooms were available. The cost of board and lodging in the palace on Molenstraat was 200 guilders; the equivalent in English currency was twenty pounds. This gave me a comfortable surplus and when I moved on to Amaliastraat to live as a paying guest in the house of Mr Lelie, a leading architect of Den Haag, the cost was reduced by another fifty guilders or five pounds. I had a very enjoyable time in that beautiful city and formed a liking for the gentle and highly cultured people of the Netherlands. Among other things, I developed a liking for the Indonesian food available in Holland. Meals were served in the restaurants in set number of dishes, ranging from twelve to forty. I have seen corpulent Dutch men and women sitting by themselves with a determined look on their faces ploughing diligently through a meal of forty dishes. Later, when I was staying in London, close to my rented flat in North Ealing was a shop named Young Outsizes. I discovered that their oversized items of dress were meant mainly for the Dutch market. In that land across the North Sea, the young ladies supplemented their Indisch-Chineesch meals of multiple gerechten (dishes) with pastries or gebakken covered in slagroom, whipped cream. Slagroom was also sold by the litre from moving roadside stalls. The ladies, young and old, who rejoiced in these delicacies, however, were careful to avoid one major item in the Dutch diet, gekookte aardappelen, boiled potatoes. The object was to avoid obesity. In my case, the fondness I developed for slagroom later led to triple bypass and, when I was eighty-two, the replacement of a heart valve with bovine tissue. But it has been worth it. How my body has escaped emulating the happy Dutch ladies remains an all-time mystery.

At the impossible to pronounce Algemeen Rijksarchief, surrounded by cafes, government offices, bars and night spots, I found the academic help I badly needed. Mr and Mrs Japikse, both archivists, helped me learn seventeenth-century Dutch calligraphy: I would copy out a page of documents every day and they would check it letter by letter, refusing to accept any payment for this work. They also procured for me a set of Pieter van Dam's multi-volume history of the Dutch East India Company written in the seventeenth century. The language was the same as that of the documents and they found a teacher of English, Mr van Veelo who struggled jointly with me to make sense of its text. These efforts proved fruitful. One morning I opened a volume of documents and suddenly I found I could read it. The limited vocabulary of these commercial documents was a help.

I also got to know at the Algemeen Rijksarchief two of my famous colleagues who were working on the Dutch records—Professor Holden Furber of the University of Pennsylvania and Dr Kristoff Glamann from Denmark. Taking advantage of the frugal habits of the Dutch, we three would often meet for lunch at the nearby cafes that allowed us to take our sandwiches there so long as we consumed their beer/coffee. I have not come across such generosity in the cafes of any other country. Along the nearby canal, the lunchtime crowd of Dutch men and women were sprawling while they consumed their sandwiches or the snacks like spring rolls (lumpia) and croquettes bought for 25 cents from the roadside machines. Once I went to one of the many pubs and around 1.30 in the afternoon was accosted by a streetwalker who spelt out in English for my convenience the service she was offering me. Her English was not perfect. She used the letter O in place of U in describing the activity under discussion. The girl was genuinely surprised when I declared my lack of interest in her wares and concluded that I must be crazy.

Around the square where these pubs were located were a number of nightclubs. An American friend from Oxford who had a lively interest in such places once came to visit me and wanted to take me out on a nightclub crawl. Frankly, I was too scared to go because I had heard that such places were often scenes of violence even in the peaceful Netherlands. But his insistence triumphed. The first thing I noticed was that the musicians were the assistants from the grocer's shop next to the archives. Only they had changed into scarlet costumes probably leaving their workaday clothes back in the shop. This fact gave the place a somewhat homely ambience. Presently, the ladies in scanty clothes (which they soon discarded) appeared to loud music. Sadly, they appeared to be somewhat past their prime. After some fifteen minutes my American friend got up and said, 'Let us go. I now know where the strippers go when they retire.' My friend's profoundly humane curiosity satisfied, we were now free to move to less exciting places.

The Plaats, as the square was called, had other things to offer besides striptease joints. One building, once the home of a Dutch count, Mauritchuis, housed a small but exquisite collection of the great seventeenth-century Dutch artists. Some of the finest early Rembrandts (including the *Anatomy Lesson* and early self-portraits), Vermeers (including the *View of Delft* and *The Girl with the Pearl Earring*), the great landscapes of Ruysdael—they were all there. Admission was free and after a few hours' back-breaking work I could walk into this building on an artificial lake, Vijverburg, and feel my fatigue just drain away. I can now close my eyes and see all these very beautiful things shine forth in my mind's eye. I am a person of very limited culture, but this close acquaintance with Dutch paintings has permanently enriched my life. If I had got nothing else from my three years in Europe except this, I should have considered the enterprise worthwhile.

My stay in Den Haag, where I spent all the vacations plus one term, had other things to offer. The Lelies with whom I stayed had three sons. The middle one, Ido or Idotje, pronounced something like Ido-ch-cha (the Dutch reduce everyone and everything to their diminutive forms: even elephants become olifantjes, the dear queen koningintje was the same age as I). Though living a bourgeois existence, he was one of the anticipators of the philosophy of alternative lifestyle. He expressed it in terracotta figurines whose expressions embodied a profound disenchantment with life. He had fallen in love with a very pretty Indian lady at the Institute for Social Study, but she went away with a Danish poet. Ido was no renouncer and liked his glass of genever or beer. Only, he found any obsession with consumption and acquisition utterly pointless. This was very un-Dutch.

There was a dark shadow on the life of the Lelie family. One of Mr Lelie's parents was Jewish and the Germans occupying the Netherlands offered him a simple choice: work for the Nazi reich or Auschwitz for the entire family. Being no hero, he accepted the former alternative to save self and family from the gas chamber. His eighteen-year-old eldest son was carried away by Nazi propaganda and joined the Wehrmacht. His military career was brief. On his first day of action, in fact the very first hour, an enemy shell blew off his right leg. After the war, the family went to prison as collaborators and were released only after thorough de-Nazification. Ido's American girlfriend and later wife deeply disapproved of the family's 'Nazi' past. I have never been able to empathize with that level of political correctness: would it have been morally correct for Mr Lelie to send his family to the gas chamber to sustain his political morality? I wonder. As far as I am concerned, the Lelies too were hapless victims of the Second World War.

They were a typically upper-middle-class Dutch family. Through their lifestyle and attitudes I had access to something very valuable in Dutch culture which I continue to cherish. The Dutch interiors celebrated in the seventeenth-century paintings projected an ambience of cosy contentment, a subdued pleasure in the little joys of our vie quotidienne, a sense of delight in what life has to offer—made up of the many small things which shape the texture of our existence as we experience it. I had a sense of closeness to that pleasurable reality in the Lelie home and the homes of their friends. It is summed up in one word—gezellig (not easy to pronounce unless you have a sore throat) which probably occurs more frequently than any other in Dutch conversation. Gezellig is everything pleasant, pleasurable and comforting—a burst of warm sunshine on an autumn morning, the feel of a fluffy blanket round your bare feet in winter evenings, the boterhamtje (sandwich) made of Gouda cheese in your school lunch box and the fatigue you feel when you sit down for a borreltje, a glass of gin or genever that is, with a funny sounding he, he or oh-God-oh-God-oh (prononced oh-khotoh-khotoh–khotoh) after an hour of fast walking or when you share with a friend the pleasure of looking into reproductions of Rembrandt or van Gogh. Life is gezellig, in fact the act of living is, for it is made up of many things that are leuk (nice), lief (dear) and lekker (delicious). To use the last adjective, the object in question does not have to derive from any haute cuisine. If a child learns to take deep pleasure in his boterham which rarely contains ham, but most likely, the same edam cheese day after day, then who needs caviar, truffle or champagne? A natural sense of deep physical pleasure in the everyday things of life seems to be central to the experience of the human condition in the Netherlands. No, there is no grandeur about it, no angst concerning the profound tragedy underlying our brief tenure on earth, only a spontaneous joy in the sheer physicality of life as we taste it day by day, minute by minute—in a warm room, from carpets spread on tables, and the warmth one receives from other human hearts. It is a culture without any high pretensions, yet it has given us not only wonderful paintings but this-worldly thinkers who have tried to make human life more sane and liveable with the aid of nature's one gift which cuts a passage of light through surrounding darkness—our common sense and unencumbered intellect. We owe to this unassuming culture, to Erasmus and Hugo Grotius, the beginnings of humanism and international law. It also provided safe and secure homes for two other champions of common sense and this-worldly wisdom, Descartes and Spinoza. I found the people of this country gentle and accessible, though never effusive. The physical and human environment suited me very well. I enjoyed my stay there and learnt much that has informed the rest of my life. The rhythm of hard work, interrupted by a glass of beer or a cup of coffee and time spent in the Mauritshuis, returning in the evening to the pleasurable domesticity of the Lelie home was deeply satisfying, exceedingly gezellig to say the least. Even the gekookte aardappelen, boiled potatoes, contributed to the gezelligheid.

When there were no visitors, the highlight of the evening was the afwassangen, a song-and-dance session focused on washing up the dishes after dinner. Somewhat plump Ellie, an afficianado of gebak met slagroom, was our impresario. Ellie was the fiancée of Jantje, the youngest of the Lelie sons. He was a bit of a disappointment to Mr Lelie who had attained high social status despite his working-class origins. His eldest son was a lawyer, the second, Ido a trainee architect. But Jan had returned to factory work and found a mate from that environment. Mr Lelie was polite but stiff with his future daughter-in-law. But Ellie did not mind. She had a large heart full of fun in an appropriately large body which made her the natural leader in our song-and-dance session. Her repertoire of songs, however, was limited. It consisted mainly of two gems. The first went:

Wie heeft suiker in the erwtesoep gedaan
De heele compagnie heeft het eten laten staan

Rough translation:

Who has put sugar in the pea soup?
The entire regiment has stopped eating it.

The second was more personal:

Daar gaat Jantje naar de bliksum toe
Naar zijn alle laaste rendezvous

Rough translation:

There goes Jantje to his doom, literally, crashing thunder; to his very last rendezvous.

Jantje or little Jan being her future husband, this should have been a matter of some concern to Ellie, but she seemed truly delighted by the prospect and we, the fellow dancers and singers, shared her joy.

The Dutch, apparently unknown to the wider world, has a large stock of highly amusing poetry which has truly enriched my life. Anti-romanticism comes to them naturally. Mr Lelie's favourite book of poetry was a verse epic entitled *Dievertje Dikkema*. The first word means little thief, the second fatsy. The two together denote a picaresque heroine modelled on nineteenth-century Europe's romantic heart-throb, Carmen. It is a heart-rending story capable of tickling the most morose misanthrope.

Two verses in the tradition of quizzical poetry have stuck in my memory:

Zeker Achmat van Baghdat
Lag met zijn gat op zijn badmat
En zo hij las zijn dagblaad.
Iedereen zag dat
Het is raar, maar in Baghdat
Daar magh dat.

[A certain Ahmed of Bagdad, lay with his arse on his bath mat. And thus he read his daily paper. Everyone said, 'This is unusual, but in Baghdad, it is possible'.]

Under Bush this inimitable verse has acquired a measure of topicality in that such luxury is no longer accessible to the war-worn Baghdadis, not even the immortal Achmat.

My second Dutch poem is the ultimate comment on the human condition, the infinite loneliness of the alienated individual:

Ik zit bij de vensterglase onnoemelijk te vervellen
Ik wou dat ik twee hontjes was zo dat ik kon samen spelen.

[I sit by the window immeasurably bored. I wish I were a pair of puppies so I could play together.]

One day in 1956, I had to bring to an end my researches at the Algemeen Rijksarchief. My scholarship was running out and with the amount of data I had collected there was little chance that I would be able to finish writing the thesis within the allocated time. I said goodbye to The Hague with a heavy heart and returned to Oxford.

The Thesis and the Degree

There I sat down with my pile of notes to write my thesis—and could not write a line for six months. Davis had repeatedly advised me to write draft chapters to lighten my task. I had blithely ignored his advice and was now paying the price of my stupidity. Eventually, I did begin to write, but had to seek an extension beyond the three-year period. I got the extension, but not a penny in additional funding. Towards the end, I had to stay up nights and sought the help of the energizing Benzidrine to help me do so. This had marvellous consequences. Suddenly, my brain cells became hyperactive and I was blessed with revelations. High on Benzidrine which helped me to keep awake, I made, what was in effect, an earth-shaking discovery for my area of research. It is well known that in the trade between Europe and Asia in the pre-colonial period, bullion, not manufactured goods or agricultural commodities, were the main exports from Europe while in return the imports consisted of manufactured goods like textiles and a range of agricultural products, including spices. One night, while revising my chapters, I made a startling discovery. The received wisdom was false. The truth of the matter was in fact the exact opposite. It was Europe that exported manufactures and a range of agricultural products to Asia receiving mainly bullion in return. I sat up and rewrote my conclusions and, excited by my discovery, showed the results, the unsuspected new truth revealed to me, to my friend Barun De next morning. He went very quiet and commented after a while that there was a small error in my calculations. I had read the data on import as those for export and vice versa. To correct this minor error, I had to stay up more nights. Barun came and slept in my bed to prevent me from using the facility: the date for submission was nigh. I had to reinstate my more humdrum conclusions which were in accord with the received wisdom.

This insignificant incident has one small lesson for the generality of mankind. If you have made any startling discovery, treat it with some circumspection. You, very probably, are mistaken.

Well, the day for the viva voce examination dawned. The examiners told me that I had, in effect, passed though it was not for them to tell me this. That night I decided to celebrate. I invited three of my friends to join me for dinner at the renowned restaurant, Elizabeth. This incredible luxury which I could think of only as one last reckless fling cost me all of four pounds in toto—three courses a la carte plus wine. The last time I ventured on this luxury before the revered restaurant closed down to be replaced by a Chinese one—an indicator of the changing balance of power in the world—it cost me seventy pound sterling, per head. As a student, our average cost of binges in the High Street restaurants was a shilling and six pence, five shillings on the very rare occasions when we were in a mood for reckless spending in places like Cafe de Paris, Indian-owned.

Before I left Oxford I was witness to a magnificent display of Britain's democratic tradition. France and Britain, at the instigation of Israel had attacked Nasser's Egypt to punish him for nationalizing the Suez Canal. There were strikes and marches in protest all over Britain. Faculty, administrative staff, students, virtually all members of the University came out in a mammoth procession. I was told that the last time such a thing had happened was during the general strike in 1926 when G.D.H. Cole brought out the workers at the University Press in protest. In 1956, the prime minister resigned. The opposition to Blair's Iraq adventure was probably not less strong. I have not met anybody in this country who supported that action. The demonstration in London was a million strong. Blair did not resign.

    I had induced the Indian high commission to let me use my travel money for a journey by land instead of the usual passage by boat from Tilbury to Bombay. They made one condition however. They would not be responsible for my treatment in case of illness. And if I died, I would have to pay for my funeral expenses. It was not clear how they would make me stick to the last-mentioned condition of our agreement. But no matter. One October morning I said goodbye to Oxford, marked by the usual rain with occasional sunshine, and the following day took a train from St Pancras hoping eventually to reach Bombay in about three months' time. I was sad and excited.

12

The Journey Home

The Road through Europe

I have travelled a great deal on business and for pleasure and thus seen a very large part of the planet we inhabit. Nowadays travel is easy and frequently gift-wrapped as package tours which take away much of the hassle but also the excitement. Most of my travels are singularly unadventurous and contains little that is new/unfamiliar in these days of mass tourism. Yet, I decided to write at some length about my journey home, mostly by land and partly by sea. I did so because on this occasion I travelled as a poverty-stricken student, spending altogether about one hundred pounds (which I had managed to save during my stay with the Lelies) in as many days plus the fare. I was a backpacker and met many whose financial situation was comparable to mine. There was, as a result, much more excitement than my later travels under more comfortable conditions. I shall focus on people and situations that interested me rather than places of beauty and antique grandeur.

On the boat from Dover to Calais I met a committed protagonist of Western romanticism. In recent years the late Edward Said has been hailed/blamed as the inventor of the notion that Orientalism was a by-product of imperialism, identifying the varied civilizations of Asia as one ectoplasmic mass, one of Europe's many inferior others, a projection invented to embody and maintain a given relationship of power. I humbly submit that this is only a half-truth without wishing to join Said's many critics. Herodotus, the Father of History, talked of two entities, Europe and Asia, and their millenia-old conflict. No imperialism there. Crusading Europe admired the high civilization of the Arabs summed up in the adage ex oriente luxe, luxury comes from the East. The above-mentioned person, a charming Belgian lady, somewhere in her mid-forties and plump like the women in the paintings by her countryman, Rubens belonged to that attractive tradition: she just loved the East, or Oost as she put it in Flemish. She did so because she had tasted that unique gift of God to mankind, Oosterse liefde, zoo diep, zoo zacht, Eastern love, so deep, so tender. She told me this within five minutes of meeting me because she knew that the 'Oosterse man' was naturally 'sympatique' and would appreciate the depth and tenderness of her own feelings. She owed her unique knowledge to the love of a good man, an Iraqi who had studied engineering in Brussels. More than twenty years had passed since then. The good man capable of such deep and tender feelings had duly returned home and acquired one wife and several children as demanded minimally by the social code of the Orient. But still he wrote regularly and 'hij denkt aan mij, denkt aan mij, ik weet niet warom' (he thinks of me, thinks of me, I know not why, oh, I know not why). Eternal love comes easy when it does not interfere with the mundane realities of existence. By the time the boat reached Calais, I had heard the story several times over. Such is the nature of true love—totally impervious to other people's boredom. As I said goodbye to this romantic donna, her eyes were dreamy with exquisite memories and she had passed into another world, perhaps of the thousand-and-one Arabian nights.

On my way to The Hague on this nostalgic journey, I stopped briefly at Antwerp, the home of my Flemish friend, the very beautiful blonde Rika who had livened my days at the Rijksarchief. We went back to our old haunts, Bruges and Ghent, before saying a final goodbye. I was sorely tempted to quote Browning at her, the 'Last Ride Together', but my sense of the absurd saved me from this silly gesture. Instead, we indulged ill-advisedly in the earthly pleasures of poffertje and waffelen, guaranteed to lead you in the direction of obesity. She was already showing signs of progress in that direction. I do not know what has happened in the years that followed.

At The Hague I went to all the familiar spots, to Mauritshuis and the beautiful beach at Scheveningen, with an aching heart, because I had little expectation of revisiting these places in the foreseeable future. The evening before I left for my next stop, my friends threw a party for me. There was a great deal of music and dancing. Lena, the wife of Ido's friend Fred, had brought a quantity of records, mostly Strauss, especially popular classics like the Blue Danube. Fred had one look and dismissed the lot with one scathing adjective, Romantisch, to him the ultimate in the line of pejoratives. His preference lay in a different direction and he was like a force of nature. So we danced to the tune of 'come Mr Tallyman, tally me banana'. Lena gave up with a sigh and a brief comment, 'Fred is a brute.' Unfortunately for her, she was hopelessly in love with this brute.

I can take ferocious dancing and calypso, played at an ear-splitting level of sound, only up to a point. When the noise level went way beyond my capacity for endurance, I decided to produce my ultimate weapon. As is well known in the West, all Indians are expert astrologers and palmists. You may take your oath on any holy book that is produced denying all knowledge of these ancient 'sciences', but nobody will listen. And if you declare yourself to be an expert, you can dine off that claim the rest of your life, unless the police intervenes. I had formulated a simple principle as a life-saving device: whenever in trouble in the West, invoke your identity as a born astrologer. I declared that I would read a few palms. Calypso is no competition for an Indian yogi. The music stopped. A dozen hands were stretched forth. I picked up Lena's, partly to soothe her damaged ego. Believe me, if there is anything to palmistry, I am as innocent of it as a newborn child. But that fact is irrelevant. I had had several glasses of brown beer and was feeling quite high;

so I babbled whatever came into my head. I do not know why, but I told Lena that she would inherit great wealth, but this good fortune would have something to do with death. Either some wealthy relative would die leaving her a lot of money or maybe she herself would enjoy her wealth only briefly. Six months later, I got a letter from Ido with unnerving news. Lena had indeed received a million dollars, but at a cost. Fred and some friends were celebrating the completion of a bridge—he worked as a civil engineer for the government, when their jeep fell into a ditch. They were all killed. The million dollars were paid in compensation. I have never played that stupid and deadly game of palmistry again.

My road homewards led from The Hague to Paris, a journey I had made many times assisting the truck drivers who carried herring from Holland to Paris. The joints at which they stopped were a revelation. I had no idea that simple food could be so delicious and purchasable at such low prices. I had tried my hand at assisting the herring boatmen on sea. But their exclusive diet of raw tea and raw herring had defeated me. The weekend trips to Paris were a very different story. And with my proletarian comrades I had seen sides of Paris life not accessible to the ordinary tourist. On this journey of farewell I revisited my favourite spots, in and around the impoverished arrondissements.

Next stop was Germany—still half in ruins eleven years after the war had ended, thanks to the allied bombings of the Second World War. At Dusseldorf, I saw houses in which a single room had survived. There was light in that half-destroyed room and a man sitting at his table, hard at work. At Karlsruhe I met my famous Indian friend, the altruist who discouraged kissing in public to ensure that people lacking such 'facilities' did not suffer from frustration. I was very pleased to find that he had solved the problem of these 'facilities' in his personal life. He introduced me to his beautiful German fiancée. Then I tried to do the usual tourist things, inter alia, a trip on the Cologne-Dusseldorfer. I am glad I did. The Rhine, its industries ruined by the war, was still very beautiful. When I did the same trip again with my wife and daughter several years later, reindustrialized

Germany had ruined this natural asset. The Rhine I had first seen made both the Rhine maidens and Rhine gold entirely credible. If the former were still around, by the 1960s they had probably taken jobs as senior executives in the reborn industries. At Cologne Cathedral, I encountered an unusual expression of German sensibility. There was a prominent notice listing various things that were strictly verboten. The list was long. Shorts and miniskirts of course fetatured in it. But there was one item which still has me confused: no hands in your trouser pockets. Why was this innocent action considered inconsistent with permissible behaviour? Well, one understands that in Victorian drawing rooms the word 'leg' was taboo.

At Heidelberg I was witness to a painful encounter between human dignity and boorish insensitivity. The latter, I am afraid, was manifest in the behaviour of some of my countrymen. They belonged to the new generation of technicians who had trained in Germany and other Western countries. It is my belief that traditional India embodies a very high level of human decency, but the same cannot be said of the country's urban culture today. Delhi is probably the world capital of contemporary barbarism. It is known to be the capital of rapes and assault on women in India. This particular lot I met in Heidelberg was very fluent in German and asked the owner of the cafe where I was having my lunch to recommend a decent eating place because his food was not edible. The man said with great dignity that he knew he was not a good cook and pointed to a restaurant down the road well known for the excellence of its food. And it was not expensive, he added. This was greeted with a triumphant guffaw signifying the barbarians' victory. I have rarely felt more ashamed of my countrymen and made a point of telling this generous man how much I had enjoyed his food which was in fact very edible. I lacked the courage to tell the boors what I thought of them.

The purpose of my overland journey was both to revisit the places and people I had known in the course of my three years' stay in Europe as well as to see places I had not yet seen. Switzerland was one of the countries which belonged to the latter category. I am not ashamed to admit that I was philistine enough to be fascinated by the natural beauty of the place. I stopped at a small village, Rigi, at the foot of Mount Rigi and then at Interlakken. I found these places and Lake Lucerne quite exquisite. I was at Interlakken again in the 1990s. The place had been choked into ugliness by a plethora of hotels and cheap accommodation. It was no longer a place I would dream of visiting a second time. Similarly, in 1957, the Isle of Capri was a place of great romantic charm, still recognizable as the place described by Axel Munth. I revisited Capri a few years ago and wondered what the tourist today found to attract him/her to that suffocating, overcrowded and overbuilt place. The damage mass tourism has done to Europe's nature is evident to anyone who saw the continent even half a century ago.

I had visited Austria in 1954 as a delegate to a university lecturers' conference on behalf of Calcutta University. There I had made friends with an American couple attached to the embassy and I decided to visit them on this journey. The reception was cordial and communication easy though we had had little contact in the previous three years. Contrary to an impression popular in Europe, I have found my relationship with individual Americans enduring and in no way superficial. This couple was no exception. But it was the early phase of the Cold War and the conversation turned inevitably to politics. In this period of international relations the Soviet Union was India's ally and though our country's formal position was one of non-alignment, in fact, the political attitudes among Indians were distinctly more favourable to the socialist bloc and had a strong flavour of anti-Americanism because of the Vietnam War and American support for Pakistan in the dispute over Kashmir. In Indian eyes Americans were unquestionably ugly. Needless to explain, I did not share this extreme attitude, otherwise I would not have taken the trouble to visit this patriotic American couple. At some point, the conversation inevitably turned to the Cold War and I commented in good faith that I could not accept the image of Soviet Russia as unmitigated evil and asked how the West could forget the Russian contribution to victory over Nazism but for which Europe would almost certainly have been taken over by

Germany. My friend exploded at this remark. Europe and the world for that matter had been saved single-handedly and at great sacrifice by the USA, he asserted, adding that the Asian intelligentsia were the most ungrateful lot in human history. Despite all that America had done for them, their neutrality was still heavily in favour of the Soviet bloc. They would learn their lesson only when they became victims of Soviet aggression. He went on and on. I realized that this was the end of our friendship and that the line between the private and the public concerns of individuals was often thin to the point of non-existence. As I said goodbye, my friend's mild-mannered wife wished me well and expressed the hope that we would meet again. I knew that this was highly unlikely. Personal relations, something I greatly value, do not always survive political disagreement. In the early years of their world domination, the decent American, reacting to pervasive criticism, took it as something almost personal. I have come across comparable responses among British men and women to any criticism of their imperial past. Such criticisms are often regarded as a personal insult. This makes any conversation on the subject and life in general somewhat difficult, because the topic is brought up by the people in question who expect to hear only unstinted praise and expression of eternal gratitude. Like most human beings, I tell my fair share of lies but to stretch my mendacity that far is beyond my capacity.

From Austria I went to Italy, another country I had not visited. If any of my countrymen asks me to suggest one country they should visit in Europe as a tourist, I mention Italy. It has everything—great natural beauty, relics of history covering many ages, art and architecture unsurpassable in excellence, delicious food which is both simple and affordable and singularly free from the fussy complexity of French haute cuisine, beautiful people and great style. It is a land with unfair advantage over all other countries. Three weeks of my planned hundred days in the journey back home I spent in this God's own country, spending the nights in not very clean youth hostels, carrying my backpack sometimes fairly long distances, taking night trains to avoid the expense on lodging. I cannot pretend that these three weeks were spent very comfortably. But I managed to stop at almost every town and city I had heard of as places worth visiting and I am ever so glad that I did this. By the end of that period I was tired beyond words, but a deep sense of satisfaction suffused my consciousness. At Brindisi I took a boat which would take me to Crete via Athens and then bring me back to Athens. My plan was to take the train from Athens to Istanbul and then further trains to Baghdad and Basra, whence the Gulf boat would carry me, very slowly, to Bombay.

From Brindisi to Athens the boat carried a number of tourists. It had a proper dining room and three-course meals were served at lunch and dinner. At Athens, the tourists left. Their place was taken by locals who would get off at various islands where the boat would stop to be replaced by others who would board carrying their luggage and often accompanied by their livestock, especially chicken and goats. The goats were a friendly lot, but their body odour was not entirely acceptable to humans. The problem was probably mutual, but the goats had no votes. I, the only surviving tourist on board in a dense crowd of natives, at first welcomed with retsina, as a specimen of that strange and distant breed, Indos, soon ceased to be acceptable to the majority of passengers owing to a sharp difference in lifestyle. As there were no other tourists on the boat, the captain decided to close the dining room and my meals were to be served where I had my seat for the rest of the journey. When the first course at lunch was thus served, my fellow passengers watched with interest as they opened their 'lunch bundle' and brought out their souvlaki. When the second course came, there was some excited and amused murmur. On the arrival of the third and the last, the bounds of courtesy failed to hold any longer and a huge guffaw burst forth. My fellow travellers, mostly of sturdy peasant stock, were evidently unused to seeing one's meals served (except, perhaps, by housewives) and the notion of two courses followed by a third was distinctly alien. As the available choice was to accept the arrangement or starve, a stiff upper lip was my only recourse. But by the third meal, my fellow passengers had got more or less used to the improbable sight of three dishes served sequentially. The guffaws had been replaced by a distant and indifferent look of contempt. But the friendly offer of souvlakis, several days old, had long stopped. I had ceased to be a part of the temporary retsina-swigging goat-loving community.

In Crete, I was privileged to see with my own eyes the light-hearted vandalism perpetrated by the great archaeologist Evans who reconstructed what he had decided were Minoan antiquities using garish colours when it pleased him. The description which persists assumes that there was a king called Minos and, very probably, a monster called the Minotaur. Hence the naming of the palace as the Labyrinth. These were attractive thoughts as were the identification of particular rooms as the king's and queen's. But the antiquities which the great man spared and hence survive as he had found them were impressive enough. And as Crete had not yet become a tourists' haven, I could enjoy the sights in peace having a monopoly of the services provided by the guide. It was a rainy day and I was the only tourist. The guide appeared to claim a personal acquaintance with the Minotaur and after seeing Evans's atrocities, this seemed entirely plausible.

That night, nature provided me with a painful insight into human nature, especially my own. I spent the night in the boat because, being poor, I could not afford a hotel room. Sometime around midnight I woke up to realize that the boat was being tossed about like a cockle shell and so was my feeble body—right to left, north to south, diagonally, up and down, in short in every possible way that a material object can be thrown about. The storm had struck suddenly and the boat was in the worst possible position for such a situation, namely, moored near the shore. Having thrown up whatever food I had consumed since childhood the body was trying to get rid of the guts themselves. A cabin boy came along to see if I was still alive and assured me that if it got worse the captain would take the boat to mid-sea position, apparently the best place in a serious storm. The danger of capsizing was a shade less serious there. This seemed entirely logical. But I took a vow that in the unlikely event of my surviving this monstrous freak storm; I would not get within a mile of a seagoing vessel ever again. But the sun rose, the storm ceased as suddenly as it had begun and the world with its blue sea shining in the sunshine looked supremely acceptable. I forgot my solemn vow and vastly enjoyed the journey from Crete to Athens. Mankind learns nothing from history, Hegel taught us. They learn nothing from personal experiences either.

Back in Asia

In Athens I felt that I had already reached the East. This was not because of the alleged affinities between Greek and Sanskrit or the similarities between the deities of the Greek pantheon and the ones I was familiar with back home, but more mundane things. In front of a grocer's shop on a fairly dusty street, I saw gunny bags full of onions and potatoes. They caused a huge gush of nostalgia. Sharp memories of the business area in Burrabazar, Calcutta, its distressing sights and suffocating smells, filled my senses. I suddenly became aware how I had missed these sights and smells, revolting though they were to normal human sensibilities. The streets in Oxford, even those in Cowley, were distressingly clean and smell-free. The realization dawned that man did not live by cleanliness alone. Squalor was a necessary component of the human condition. Absence of squalor was probably one contributory factor to the distressing phenomenon of British aloofness. After all, proximity to other humans, mental or physical, can imply acceptance of a certain degree of squalor: it is better to stay aloof. I soon had further evidence of the likely links between squalor and the ease of communication between humans. I had taken a bus ride to the suburbs of Athens one very sunny morning. As I was walking along, I came across an orchard full of luscious oranges and stood for a moment to admire this unfamiliar sight. The owner or the gardener emerged, said something by way of greeting and asked me to wait using sign language. He came back in a few minutes with a whole bag of freshly picked oranges. I tried to recall when I had last encountered a gesture like this from a stranger and realized what I had missed in the human ambience of Oxford. There is a great deal of debate now regarding Orientalism, the Western perception of the East as different. That supposedly artificial construct may not be all that artificial after all. My overland journey home convinced me that there were basic differences between Europe and Asia in matters relating to inter-human contact. Only, in this particular sense, Asia began in Greece or perhaps southern Italy. And perhaps the difference I noted had more to do with the development of industrial civilization than with cultural ethnicities.

From Athens, I took the train to Istanbul, a sad remnant of the Orient Express. The train was virtually empty partly owing to the Graeco-Turkish conflict over Cyprus. As there was no one else in the compartment, I decided to indulge in a little luxury. I took off my shoes and put my feet up. Presently the ticket checker came, looked at me with profound distaste and made a sign roughly ordering me to put my feet down. As there was no other passenger, I thought that this was entirely gratuitous, but presently realized that this intolerant act was the product, not of racism but contemporary politics. 'Turkeya?' the man asked with a distinct note of hatred in his voice. I shot back the only Greek word in my repertoire, 'Indos.' 'Indos? Indos!' suddenly the compartment was filled with sweetness and light. I got the general impression that this gruff person, so rude one minute ago, had suddenly reached the epiphanic moment of his life. This is what he had been waiting for all these years! To meet a live Indos, the dream of his childhood, the aspiration of his youth! Alas we shared no language. He gestured inviting me to place my feet back on the seat. In fact, it was obvious that he would have been happy to have them on his head—or so it seemed to me. Why this untoward friendliness? Krishna Menon was being quite unfriendly to the Greek claims in the UN debates. Soon, all was revealed. A string of names poured forth from the lips of this admirer of things Indic. Meena Kumari, Madhubala, Helen, Raj Kapoor, Dilip Kumar—the litany went on and on. The man had a beatific expression on his face. I was saved. These countrymen and women of ours have repeatedly guaranteed a secure status for me in remote and unlikely corners of the world. In China, I have been treated to renderings of '*Main awala hoon*', in Moscow to dance numbers learnt at the feet of Amitabh Bachchan, in Sami tents in Lapland to songs by the Mangeshkar sisters. We waste our limited resources on embassies for no good reason. Our film stars are our true ambassadors, the real harbingers of true globalization. Long live Bollywood.

At Istanbul, I felt I had come another giant step closer to home. Ah, the sheer joy of noise in the bazaars, the joyous abandon of shouted conversation, the dashing and pushing in the bazaars with total disregard for the discomfort of other humans! And what am I talking about? Whoever felt any discomfort at people dashing and pushing past you when social mores guaranteed your right and privilege to do the same to others? Wasn't that the essence of Asian democracy, especially Indian style? And this was true freedom, the freedom to dash and push, not your mealy-mouthed Western-style democracy at the ballot box. And above everything else the overpowering smell of kebabs, the glorious sight of doner kebabs going round and round on their spit. I had nostalgic visions of Delhi's Chandni Chowk and the old kebab and biriyani shops around the Jama Masjid in Delhi. I loved this city of many civilizations, even the tourist bits which are often very boring. The Blue mosque and Aya Sofia, like the Taj, could bore only the extreme philistine. And Top Kapi, where we were told the sultans carried out regular spring cleaning by throwing the spare begums past their shelf lives into the sea through holes in the marble floor. The treasures—rubies, diamonds, sapphires, emeralds, amethysts and the like—heaped up in glass cases or studded on thrones (the imperial bottoms must have been especially sturdy to be able to cope with their supremely unsmooth surface), sword handles, hookahs and other articles of daily royal use, some for the sultans to handle casually when they attended to boring royal tasks. The jewels in the Tower of London are almost insignificant by comparison and those in the royal collection in Tehran come a poor second. The eyes began to hurt after I had looked at that overpowering collection of precious stones for some time. I wondered what the Mughal imperial collection of jewels must have been like before Nadir Shah, Ahmad

Shah Abdali, the Jats, the British and sundry others had had a go at them.

In Istanbul, I was staying in the YMCA at a rent which virtually was next to nothing especially as I had taken the trouble to change my hard currency before I entered Turkey, a strictly illegal action. But there was a small price to pay for it. One slept in a dormitory with some forty other people in cots laid out as in a hospital, but without any space between them. And it became soon obvious that God had decided to punish this atheist and at the same time give him a glimpse of true faith. On either side of my bed was strategically located two Indian Christians who were touring the world in order to 'climb the heights and plumb the depths of Lord Jesus Christ'. During the hours when the rest of mankind slept they woke up from time to time and very loudly declared their faith in the Lord: 'Our Lord who created us is a gracious Lord', 'Our Lord who punishes sinners is a just Lord', etc. This litany went on till sunrise when the two devotees got up to wonder at the beauty of nature created by the same gracious and just Lord. My punishment was enhanced by the fact that they took upon themselves the sacred duty of saving this sinner by sticking to him like leech. They accompanied me wherever I went constantly singing into my years the varied excellences of the gracious Lord who made them. I refuse to believe that the same Lord was my maker for even in my thoughts I had done nothing to deserve such excruciating punishment. However, their effort to save my soul was at least a partial success, for I learnt the virtues of patience and resignation. After three days with these children of God I could have left Job cold at the doorpost in any trial of endurance. Now I had on my lips the fixed sweet smile of the saintly indicating the level of spirituality I had reached. But my hope that this would lead my tormentors to believe that the process of saving my soul was more than complete proved vain.

One morning the three of us were standing at a stop to take the bus to Aya Sofia when a civilized-looking person with some English books in his hand started talking to us. He told us that he was a professor of mathematics and within a few minutes invited us to lunch at his place. His looks and manners suggested that the food would be good and hence I promptly accepted the invitation—but with some apprehension. The man was a bachelor but he assured us that his mother was an excellent cook and just loved to entertain. I had serious doubts that the mother would be beside herself with joy at the arrival without notice of three lunch guests whose origins were uncertain, at least so far as she was concerned. On arrival at the professor's very elegant flat my apprehensions proved to be more than correct. The old lady started to curse his son in a manner which left one in no doubt as to their meaning: no knowledge of Turkish was necessary to interpret her perfectly understandable response to our arrival. But no. The professor smiled and told us that we had quite expectedly misunderstood his mother's intended meaning. And then he began to summarize that very eloquent flow of words as follows.

She wondered whence she had found an unworthy son like this, a shame on the memory of such a worthy father. She had never even known another human so mean and miserly as this one, the son of a noble father, the most generous among the children of Adam. She knew for certain that this unworthy creature was his father's son (oh, those joyous nights!), otherwise she would have wondered whence he had come. He always behaved like this with the express purpose of humiliating her. Bringing guests without notice so that he did not have to spend on a proper meal of ten to twenty dishes! She had cooked only six that morning. How could a daughter of gentle folk, good Muslims, she descended from the prophet on her mother's side, offer such a mean meal to guests, especially foreigners! What would they think of her, of Turks in general! What insult to the memory of the father of the nation, Ataturk. We tried to communicate to her through the son that we were truly gratified by their hospitality, but she was not to be pacified. The six dishes were served with lashings of abject apology. It was a gorgeous meal. I left wondering if this scene could have been enacted in any Western country. I hope Turkey has not qualified in her social conduct for entry into the European Union.

The day before I was to take the train to Baghdad, the devotee twins left by bus for Iran to further plumb the depths of Christ. I accompanied them to the coach station and helped them take their very sizeable trunk to the coach. They too were returning to India by the same boat as myself. But when I boarded that boat owned by the India Steam Navigation Company, a name I was familiar with since childhood, there was no sign of them. I had given up my original intention to travel through Iran because there was some trouble brewing on the Turko-Iran frontier. I concluded that their Lord in all His mercy had gathered His devotees into his arms somewhere on that disputed border. No doubt, they were at peace. And so was I.

My train started from Haiderpasha station which was on the other side of the Bosphorus. As I queued for my ticket to take the boat, a student with a bundle of books in English and German in his arms began to talk to me. Before I could say anything, he pressed the boat ticket into my hand and refused absolutely to accept the fare he had paid on my behalf. On the boat he kept pressing on me very hot bell-shaped glasses of raw tea, totally undrinkable so far as I was concerned. At Haiderpasha, he helped me find my compartment and again pressed on me ten packets of expensive cigarettes. My helpless objection on the ground that I did not smoke made no impression. 'Give it to someone who does', he said, 'it will help you make friends. You will need them on this long train journey.' Then he told me the story of his life and its problems. The latter, needless to say, concerned his love life. He had, expectedly, met the most beautiful woman in the world, but the parents refused to accept her because she did not belong to their class. If they did not change their mind, he had only two alternatives before him—to join an order of dervishes or kill himself. Like a good Bengali, I suggested that such extreme measures might not be necessary. The parents would change their mind when he got a job and especially after the grandchildren arrived on the scene—the classic Bengali solution in such situations. He thanked me for my invaluable advice and walked a few steps with the train after it started. There were tears in his eyes. Well, after all,

I had saved his life. It suddenly struck me that I did not know his name and was unlikely to meet him ever again.

The journey was indeed long—some seventy-two hours. There was only one other passenger in my compartment, a Turk or an Arab, I never found out. The train stopped at all sorts of small stations. At one of them, a formidable-looking lady accompanied by a multitude of children boarded the train. Soon she opened a huge bundle and out came the roasted carcass of some huge bird. Judging by its size, it was either an ostrich or some comparably proportioned specimen of the avian race. The children fell on it like a pack of wolves and tore out chunks of meat using their fingers and teeth. The mother looked on with a benign expression in her face while feeding her infant son at her breast. Presently, the infant got interested in the ongoing orgy of eating and decided he should have a share. The mother let him join the feast. He did fairly well with his toothless gums. I got some idea as to how Genghis Khan must have been brought up.

I had been warned that as and when the train entered the Arabian Desert, there would be no food or water. Used to living rough, I ignored the advice hoping to scrounge at the railway stations. But station after station came and went: no food, no water. No, that is not entirely true. There was water for sale, but with a thick layer of insects floating on top. My companion bought and drank the stuff, casually removing the insects. He also offered me shares of his food, a kind of sausage, but after first having taken a bite probably to prove that he was not trying to poison me. To a Bengali, food purified by other people's saliva is highly unacceptable. But I was starving, so I started at the unbitten end of the sausages and sheepishly threw out the end which had been bitten into. And one was forced to drink the insect-infested water. The desert heat probably killed the germs for nothing went wrong.

At Baghdad, I had to share my room with a local who lived in that room on a more or less permanent basis. No, this is not the prevailing custom in the city, but simply the result of my poverty. The hotelier had decided to take advantage of my two deficiencies—lack of money as well as linguistic skill, to push me into this uncomfortable

The Journey Home

situation. But my fellow guest was kind. He always offered me a share of his kebabs brought by the hotel servant from some source outside. And sure enough, he never forgot to take a bite before offering the kebab to me. I declined and ordered my own lunches and dinners which came from the same source. One day I discovered the source: it was the pavement outside the hotel. The bread was neatly laid out on the pavement and so were the kebabs. No cloth or paper intervened between the pavement and the food which happily coexisted with dog shit and less easily identifiable excreta. I began to go to cheap-looking restaurants. There at least I did not know whence the food came. There were other joys on offer there. I sat and had glassfuls of tea brought to me while I smoked a hookah and a serviteur polished my shoes. This imperial style of entertainment in the erstwhile capital of the Abbasids cost me all of four annas—one-fourth of a rupee, the latter being one-thirteenth of a pound. The joys on offer included camel meat. Strictly not recommended. It was tough and disagreeably fatty. Besides, it stank.

Talking of the Abbasids, I went forth in quest of their palace. No one could tell me where it was. As I was going into the local museum, I asked a student standing outside the building and was treated only to a vigorous shaking of head denying all relevant knowledge. Well, as I entered the museum, I saw a small notice indicating that this was the old Abbasid palace or what remains of it after the Mongols had had a go at it. How fragile indeed is worldly glory. My visit to the remains of old Babylon, by bus to a site covered in nondescript ruins known as al-Hilla, was equally disappointing. This was partly because the famous palace, or what remained of it, had been moved to the Berlin Museum long ago. I wish imperial Europe had completed the job it had started, viz., removing the antiquities of the past from Asia, Africa and Latin America to various European cities. Would it not be wonderful if one could see the Pyramids, the Taj Mahal, the glories of Machu Pichu and the like by simply buying a season ticket to the museums of London, Paris and Berlin? It is merely the false vanities of the nations in question that prevent such action beneficial to all mankind. Incidentally, the Baghdad I saw in the winter of 1957 looked to me like a ramshackle north Indian town except for the posters advertising the charms of numerous oversized ladies, belly dancers as they are called in Europe to the utter disgust of people in the Middle East who perceive them simply as dancers. Their sizeable and exposed bellies are no essential part of their art, though the audience are appreciative when these quiver. The Baghdad I have seen on television in recent years, thanks to the humane interest taken in the city by Bush and Blair, is a very different and much grander place. And as to Babylon, Saddam following in the footsteps of Evans, has recreated the hanging garden and tower of Babylon far surpassing the achievements of the old Babylonian kings. Even the Baghdad of post-Bush-Blair enterprise stands grand in its ruins compared to what I remember. The world must forever remain grateful for the many blessings it owes to the West.

Prior to boarding the ISN-IGN company's boat at Basra I had to spend a couple of nights in the town. Again it was like a small town in north India, but dustier and poorer with only the ubiquitous posters displaying the charms of fat ladies relieving the dreary monotony of life. Where indeed was that city of romance or, for that matter, the famous red roses of Basra? I was sitting in a riverside cafe, beside the Shatt al-Arab, feasting off a fish which had been kept in a net in the river so that the customers could choose their victims and eat them fresh. A person with obliging looks joined me without any invitation on my part and ordered some more food because he felt that what I was eating was inadequate for my needs. Of course, he insisted on paying for the meal. I asked him about the rose gardens. He had not heard of them. Instead, he very proudly hired a taxi and took me to see the city's new glory, a pathetic little aerodrome. He gave me his card. I learnt from the card that he owned a shoe shop. He had learnt English at school, he informed me and of course we vowed to write to each other when I parted. Like my Turkish friend at Haiderpasha, he too was quite tearful at the moment of parting.

Deck Passenger on a Gulf Boat

At the jetty on the river where I boarded the ship, an unexpected scene awaited me. A fierce struggle was on between two groups—the passengers and customs officials, as I learnt later. The former insisted on their democratic right to get on to the boat, their luggage unexamined, while the latter were keen to perform their official duty because this boat had a notoriety for gold smuggling. Eventually, some sort of compromise was worked out. I am not sure who gained, but one presumed that there was some friendly exchange of cash.

We third-class passengers were described as deck passengers. This was inaccurate, because no one was supposed to sleep on the deck, partly because one was likely to be swept into the sea if there were high winds. But as a matter of fact we did sleep on the deck when the weather allowed, partly because it was almost impossible to sleep in the beds allocated to us in the hold, owing to the great heat. Passengers preferred to risk being drowned to being suffocated in that hellhole and spread their bedrolls on the deck. At mealtimes, we had to go back briefly to our berths where we were given our meals on metal plates which looked dirty and overused. We promptly returned to the deck with our food where again there were great scenes of hospitality. Both the Arab and Pathan passengers carried their own supplies. These were wrapped in fairly dirty-looking cloth, and consisted for the most part of flat bread, dry kebabs and dates, which were freely exchanged in the high oriental spirit of bonhomie, people freely partaking of one another's food and saliva. I failed to take part in these jollifications because of my superstitious inhibitions regarding other people's saliva. The feasts were followed by entertainment. The Pathans led the choir singing, with full-throated ease, what sounded like fierce war songs. I asked timidly about the theme of their grand music. 'Ishq', I was told. The word means love. The Bengalis have a reputation for cowardice. It is rumoured that the last independent king of Bengal, Lakshman Sen, fled through the back door when only seventeen Pathan (read

Afghan) horsemen entered his palace. I suppose they were singing their love songs. Any sane man would have run on hearing the first notes. I persisted only because I had no choice.

We stopped at almost every possible port, the centres of the now famous emirates which were hopelessly poor at the time. When the boat anchored, dozens of sailing boats turned up bringing a variety of kitsch, products of the sea. Little boys came swimming to do their turn, picking up coins which were thrown into the water. The boat carried a large number of people working as coolies. There was a large contingent of people from Dubai who evidently suffered from home sickness and extreme patriotism. As we approached Dubai, they sang in unison, 'Wah wah Dubai, wah wah Dubai', though at the time there was little to wah wah about in the said kingdom. The gulf was exceptionally calm. There was nothing to indicate that we were sailing on the sea except for the shoals of flying fish accompanying us. Some of these in their flight landed on the lower deck and were promptly captured by the sailors—to be fried and eaten in due course, especially by the ship's officers.

Among them was a Bengali doctor by whose grace I was an occasional guest at the captain's table where I had my share of fried flying fish. Excellent stuff. The doctor's fate was not enviable. The Arab passengers believed that they had claims on his time twenty-four hours each day. He would be woken up at midnight by a patient who complained in inadequate Urdu that he had saliva in his mouth: 'muh me thu ata'. The doctor's attempt to convince him that this is where the stuff came naturally, anywhere else would be a matter for concern, did not work. The patient regretted that he was not getting the service that was his due because the ship did not have an Angrej (English) doctor. This dark-skinned native was of no use. He was considered a total failure by the long queues of Arab patients who hoped to enhance their virility by the magic of Western medicine. The doctor tried to tell them that their virility had reached the ultimate limits vouchsafed to the males of our species. They shook their heads and said that Western men satisfied unlimited number of women, thanks to the wonders of their medicine. This was common knowledge. The doctor was keeping all that medicine for his own use so that he could sleep with all the courtesans of Bombay and Calcutta. The poor man sighed in despair. Like all good Bengalis, he bitterly missed his home and family. And then to be told that he was a habitual whoremonger was, for him, the ultimate in degradation.

When the boat reached the open sea, the waters were no longer calm. The last two days of my nine-day journey from Basra to Bombay were turbulent. A very bad sailor, I took to bed and left it only when we anchored in Bombay.

Joys of Homecoming: A Lesson in Self-knowledge

Cyril Lewis's scholarship included the expenses of a two-year stay in India and he was waiting for me outside the dock area. But there were ordeals to go through before I could reach him. The customs area looked like a refugee camp with luggage opened and scattered around for purposes of inspection. The official who examined my luggage, on hearing that I was a student returning home, assured me that he would treat me 'like a brother'. The brotherly treatment consisted among other things in tearing apart my holdall in the belief that smuggled gold might be hidden in the linings. When the ordeal was over, I walked out and was relieved to find Cyril waiting there with two tickets for a Hindi film. *Jhanak Jhanak Payel Baje*, a musical with good classical Indian dance numbers, had caught his fancy. He had seen it six times. He wished to share the joy with me. This sharing duly done, I took the train to Calcutta.

But before I finally left the dock area, I was witness to a minor (not for the victim) tragedy. One of our fellow passengers on the ship had a curious memento with him—a lion skin complete with a formidable head. He had entrusted it to a coolie after customs clearance. The latter guessed its true content from its excessive weight and quietly melted into the Bombay crowd. The lion's head was stuffed with gold, the broken man now confessed to us, shedding profuse tears. The customs people had suspected the truth but that problem was sorted out on the market principle propounded by Adam Smith and now, in our age of globalization, accepted as the universal religion of mankind. For the shrewd coolie, this was the chance of a lifetime and, naturally, he had no intention of sharing his good fortune.

I must mention one episode on that insignificant journey because it enhanced my self-knowledge. We had our lunch in the dining car and were waiting for the train to reach the next station. It suddenly stopped in the middle of nowhere and a number of passengers got off the dining car. As the train seemed in no hurry to move, I joined them to walk back to my compartment. Whereupon, the train did restart. When I realized what was happening I began to run because the station was visible from where we had got off.

Well, there was a welcoming party at the station waiting for me. I was red in the face. There was no reason for embarrassment, the station master assured me. Where I had prematurely detrained, was a spot known as the ticketless travellers' station. The said gentle folk, who lived in neighbouring villages, pulled the chain. As the train waited a while to start again (presumably owing to an amicable arrangement with the railway employees) everyday, the station master assured me, some idiots got off the dining car just as I had. They allowed a bit of time to let the said idiots catch up.

The episode taught me two things. One, that by generally accepted standards, there was a case for classifying me as an idiot. Two, I had potentialities to emerge as an Olympic runner. After all, I had outrun a train, an uncommon feat. If I was humbled by the first lesson, the second restored my self-esteem.

Next day, I reached Calcutta—to restart my career as a professional academic.

13

Unemployed in Calcutta

Back in India, I found myself in a peculiar situation. In Calcutta, I was interviewed and selected for a professorship in Presidency College, but owing to a peculiar decision of the Public Service Commission was in no position to accept it. Someone senior to me as also a personal friend with whom I had worked as his junior in Central Calcutta College was placed second in the interview conducted by the said Commission and hence was to be my junior if I accepted the post. It was an odd and inexplicable decision, probably initiated by a senior bureaucrat to humiliate my friend, Professor Amalesh Tripathi. In the bureaucratic system of which the Education Service was a part, these rankings mattered a great deal. Professor Tripathi, humiliated and damaged by the decision, threatened to resign. The academic community in Calcutta was naturally sympathetic to him and wished I should go away. The latter course was, in theory, open to me because I had also been selected for the post of deputy director, National Archives of India, located in Delhi. I was not very happy at the thought of leaving the teaching profession, but given my strange predicament, was willing to accept the Delhi job. Unfortunately, I was not free to do so, because I had an agreement with the Government of West Bengal to accept whatever job they offered and work for them at least five years. Failing that, I had to repay a specified amount. Eventually, I agreed to do so, paying the money in instalments. But the process of getting the necessary clearance took six months. With two jobs on offer, I was in effect unemployed during those months and hence penniless. As I was staying with my parents, I was not without food or shelter, but this state of total dependence was something new in my experience and rather humiliating. Besides, I did not have a penny of my own and had to beg even the bus fare from my father if I wished to go anywhere.

These months in limbo gave me the chance to indulge the most favourite pastime of the Bengalis, namely adda, or gossip sessions where one discussed everything and everyone.

My efforts to do some useful work, like revising my thesis for publication, made no progress, because I did not have a room where I could sit and work. Besides, I felt rather uncomfortable just hanging around at home doing nothing financially rewarding. I could for the first time empathize with the millions of young educated Bengalis who had spent a substantial part of their lives in comparable situations.

But the addas I participated in were high-quality and hence educative. One was located in the flat of Ranajit Guha, now famous as the subaltern guru. And the chief participants included Amartya Sen, the great economist and Nobel laureate, then in his twenties. When I left for Oxford, Ranajit had just returned from Europe after spending several years in Paris as the secretary, Federation of Democratic Youth, a Comintern front.

In that capacity he had met all the leading figures of world communism, including Stalin, Mao, Chou-en-lai, Castro and Che Guevara. But this was a subject on which he was entirely taciturn. I extracted a few facts using virtually third-degree methods. He inherited my humble job in the Subordinate Educational Service when I quit and was promptly sacked on discovery of the well-known fact that he was a communist. When I was suffering from forced unemployment, Ranajit was teaching at the then new University of Jadavpur. To my dismay, Ranajit was at the time going deep into Hegel and the like, which I, congenitally averse to abstract thought, found exquisitely painful. But he was a kind man and spared us any discussion of his favourite themes. His first wife, Martha, a Polish lady who had learnt to speak Bengali fluently, was an important member of the adda and provided endless cups of tea, an essential element in this degenerate institution. She also helped to keep the fire burning for the hookah which Ranajit had introduced to enhance the quality of adda.

Another important member was late Paramesh Roy, mathematician and economist, who was at Oxford at the same time as I. He was famously innocent. An Oxford undergraduate who was a universal heart-throb, was especially kind to Indians, particularly Paramesh. Paramesh did not catch on and was rather puzzled by what was happening. Once he came to me in high agitation to report an inexplicable episode and seek advice. The young lady had descended on him after dinner and asked, ' What do you think of my figure?' Paramesh mumbled something. 'How can you have an opinion without having seen it first!' the lady commented and undressed, to facilitate an objective assessment. 'What do you think now?' she asked. 'Well, nice. May be a bit masculine, like the Michelangelo sculptures of *Day* and *Night*.' Being a truthful person, Paramesh was unable to lie. 'Then she dressed and left,' Paramesh informed me, utterly confused. Had he done anything wrong? he asked. No, I assured him. He had ensured for himself, by virtue of his evident saintliness, a secure place in heaven; only, it would be a heaven unpolluted by houris.

Amartya Sen, having won all the prizes and honours available to an undergraduate at Cambridge, had been elected to a junior research fellowship at Trinity College and was working on his doctoral dissertation while spending time with his parents in Calcutta. There was something unique in the way he organized his time accommodating the institution of adda, so central to Bengali social life. I have come across this unusual ability in only one other person, Satyajit Ray. In the latter case, however, adda was a part of the director's serious work, namely observation of middle-class Bengali ways which was after all the main theme of his films. Amartya used to turn up at Ranajit's flat around 10.30 in the morning, having done a couple of hours' work, stay there till midday, go home for his lunch and another couple of hours' work and returned for the afternoon adda session punctually at 4.30. Incidentally, the end product of his research, interspersed with regular sessions of adda, was his famous monograph on choice of technique which is still read half a century after it was first published. Later, when I encountered him again as a colleague at Delhi School of Economics, he was already far too important and busy to have time for adda. I do not know if this change in lifestyle had any effect on the quality of his work.

Eventually, my six-month-long period of forced unemployment came to an end when the state government accepted my offer to pay back the stipulated sum in instalments and I left for Delhi to take up what many considered a somewhat glamorous post, even though it was pretty low in the bureaucratic hierarchy. Except for the confusion in the minds of the experts, there was no reason why this job should have come to me. The experts were historians and believed, quite incorrectly, that the specialization required for archival administration was a good knowledge of history. As I discovered while working for the National Archives, the old Imperial Records Department, nothing could be further from the truth. The man who literally taught me whatever I learnt about archives, Shourin Roy, was the person who should have got the job. But again bureaucratic machinations were at work and I was its unintended beneficiary. In the early days of independence, the most popular slogan at leftist rallies declared: 'Yeh azadi jhoota hai' (this independence is a lie). This was inaccurate. Some people had certainly become independent, a great deal more than others. This was especially true of the bureaucrats. Even the minor ones exercised a degree of authority which could be converted into solid cash whenever the opportunity occurred. And as for the politicians, their independence knew no limits. If the ordinary citizens suffered a little in consequence, that was of no consequence.

The point of the above comments refers to the circumstances which led to my getting the job in Delhi. Shourin Roy was justly famous for his great scholarship and generally recognized as the leading authority on matters archival in India. But he was not popular with the authorities because he had the unwelcome habit of making fun of them, often to their face. A couple of examples follow. In the blessed days of the Raj, the sahibs moved to the Simla Hills during summer so as to give the natives the full benefit of their valued service. The high-ranking native officials who accompanied them treated this as an indicator of status and prestige. The conversation of their wives was studded with references to this movement up and down. 'When are you going up?' and 'When are you coming down?' were questions which featured prominently in the said conversations. If Roy was around, he was in the habit of asking sotto voce up or down which tree were the august personages intending to go.

The panjandrums of the Central Secretariat hated Roy. One of them, a joint secretary, had a special reason for doing so. An assistant director at the Archives who had relieved the panjandrum of his three sisters in succession (the law would not have objected if the necessary rituals had been simultaneous instead, for this gentleman shared the Islamic faith with his highly placed brother-in-law) was innocent of matters archival and Roy had pointed out the fact several times. The post of deputy director had been created, it was understood, for the obliging brother-in-law, but with Roy as competitor there was no chance that he would get it. Hence an enquiry into Roy's personal life which established, prima facie, that he was living in sin. Sin is something not tolerated by the Government of India (crime is another matter) and preparations for charge-sheeting Roy were afoot. The selection committee for the post was given a note on these matters which made it impossible for them to select him. They found the obliging brother-in-law unemployable and hence decided at the suggestion of one of the experts, quite illogically, to nominate me instead. When I had no reasonable choice but to accept that job, I wrote to Shourin Roy apologizing for my presumption. He wrote back to reassure me that I was most welcome and that there had never been any chance of his getting the job. I felt relieved though many well-wishers assured me that Roy was a dangerous man and that I should be very careful. His sharp tongue and mordant wit had not won him many friends. I went to seek the blessings of my mentor, Sir Jadunath Sarkar. An ardent admirer of British rule in India, he almost revered the institutions created by the Raj as well and was happy that one of his disciples had got a senior post in that set-up even though under their unworthy native successors. He congratulated me but added that I would lose ten years of my longevity owing to the heat. I am sure he was right about the said loss but it was due to reasons other than heat. He also told me that the human and political environment in Delhi resembled that of the eighteenth-century Mughal court and quoted Tulsidas, 'Han ji han ji karke sab kam karke lo' (say yes to whatever is said and thus get your job done). I do not know what the conditions were in Tulsidas's time, but no self-respecting person could have followed his advice in post-independence Delhi.

14

A Bureaucrat in Delhi: Sharing the Joys of Freedom

On arrival in Delhi by train one warm September morning, I took a taxi to my allotted accommodation in Constitution House, one of the hostels for the accommodation of the members of the Constituent Assembly (later Parliament) and single officials, male and female. These were barracks for the accommodation of GIs during the Second World War which had somehow managed to remain erect years later. Some unfortunate family men in the service of India's independent government also had temporary accommodation there and fumed while they waited for the more long-term allotment.

Incidentally, the Raj had entered into the spirit of the Indian caste system and put it, as was their wont, to new innovative uses. The accommodation of government officials was strictly on the basis of the neo-caste system. The sahibs, as the Brahmins, of course lived in the bungalows with acres of green lawns and gardens in the middle of the city, an invention of the great and famous Lutyens. The Shudras (the clerks, that is) had to cycle in from a distance of several miles. The untouchables (that is, the menial staff), however, lived in close proximity to the Brahmins, mostly white ones with a sprinkling of the brown-skinned, so that these VIPs were never to suffer any shortage of domestic service. The fifth caste (Class IV staff in officialese) was accommodated in servants' quarters on the slip roads invisible to the generality of the population so that there was no danger of pollution.

But the cussed Nehru caused a problem (even though he did not interfere with the principle of caste itself, bless him) by suddenly expanding the size of the bureaucracy manifold in the name of development. The accommodation required for the new servants of the independent state could not be provided with comparable speed. Hence there was varna-sankara, the mixing of castes—so utterly condemned in the divine Gita—in matters of accommodation. Those entitled to B class accommodation had to live for months in C or even D class accommodation, causing insufferable agony. In the good old days of the sahibs, one's status was evident from one's address. Now there was unhappy confusion. I once went to another officers' hostel to look for a friend and committed a solecism by knocking on a door to find out where exactly he lived. Out came a bald-headed man, his face blood-red with indignation. How would he know where people entitled to D class accommodation lived, he, an official entitled to B class accommodation, condemned to live in this hellhole for months. I realized that I had violated a basic principle of social stratification and made my escape with mumbled apologies.

The majority of the denizens of Constitution House were young officials, men and women, living alone and with a measure of freedom. We were a happy lot and our behaviour at times crossed the limits of self-restraint expected of A class officials and some of the older men living there took it upon themselves to surreptitiously keep an eye on our conduct. Our behaviour on the occasion of the colour festival, when we happily sprinkled coloured water on the girls who looked in consequence like Bollywood heroines, their saris completely drenched and hence see-through, was the special object of severe judgement. One evening I found our critic-in-chief, a bald-headed and middle-aged bachelor, walking along the corridor at a fast pace, peering into the rooms through the windows but with due circumspection. 'On your usual round of inspection?' I asked politely.

A Bureaucrat in Delhi

Not prepared for such an encounter, he blurted out, 'Just three more rooms—91, 92, 93,' and fled in confusion. Room No 93 happened to be my room.

Room 92 was occupied by the very famous dancer, Madame Simki, once the prima ballerina in Udayshankar's troupe. Now she worked for the Indian government in the ministry of culture and was accommodated in a modest room of Constitution House. Unfortunately for me, I was her neighbour. Unfortunate because I had to share a bathroom with her. This was one of the most curious arrangements in the place. Each bathroom was shared by a pair of rooms. While using the facility one latched the door leading to the other room. Unfortunately for me, I always forgot to unlatch the door on Simki's side while leaving for my office. Within a few minute of my arrival at my destination, I would receive an angry call from her and, with a thousand apologies, send the key back to her. My offer of a duplicate key was sternly refused. To my request for a change of room I received the standard reply so dear to India's bureaucracy, 'Dekhenge' (we shall see). What they were 'seeing' was a highly amusing drama and they would not be deprived of their innocent fun. Once, Amartya Sen came to spend a few days with me, sharing the room. When I returned from office, he had a bemused look on his face and asked me to explain a strange episode. A lady had told him not to shut her out of the bathroom like her friend because it was supposed to be shared. This was a warning, not an invitation, I explained.

It was still early days of independence and some of the MPs who came to stay at the Constitution House were highly conscious of national honour. One of them was outraged by the Western-style arrangement for meals—sitting at a table and dining off china with knives and forks. He entered the dining hall, solemnly sat down on the floor and demanded that his lunch be served there. When this request was turned down with due apologies, the man who made our laws climbed and squatted on the table. It required a delegation of fellow MPs to induce him to agree to his meals being served in his room.

Sir Jadunath's bit about the Mughal court was certainly right. As there was no director of National Archives at the moment, I had to act as director for the time being. I had as my office an enormous room where one could easily play tennis (the British loved to do things in style and neither the bureaucrats nor the politicians of independent India showed any inclination to abjure that happy inheritance). The first file I had to deal with was a strictly confidential one concerning Mr Roy's sin. I was to report on the matter in a week. I wrote back to my superior (the aforementioned joint secretary, popularly known in the secretariat as the saala sahib, the respected wife's brother, a pejorative rather than a term of affection in Indian vocabulary, especially if the 'sahib' is dropped as was usually done in this instance) stating my lack of experience and training in matters like enquiry into private lives which was not included in my list of duties. However, as a faithful servant of the government and a dutiful citizen of independent India, I would of course do whatever I was asked to, but I did need advice and instruction in this case. I never got a reply. I understood that when the full-time director was appointed and took charge, he was asked to attend to this urgent duty. He recommended that Mr Roy be suspended for his sins ('moral turpitude' was the word used) and, after a full-fledged enquiry, as was right and proper in the world's largest democracy where truth always triumphed ('satyameva jayate' was the motto adopted by the Government of India, the words emblazoned on its letterheads), dismissed in due course. As this was a complicated process, it was not undertaken. Meanwhile, Mr Roy took charge of me and carefully monitored my progress in archival knowledge. I remain forever grateful to him for the time he gave me, because the technical expertise in archival management sharpened and deepened my awareness of the use and, more important, limitations, of archival material as a source of historical knowledge. I learnt why and how such material, especially those of a colonial regime, has to be taken with bucketfuls of salt. Their surface meaning is highly suspect, a fact which many historians of India, inclined to treat the colonial archives as gospel, often tend to forget. Management of archives taught me the all-important relevance of provenance and what it meant for the evidential value of archival evidence. During my stewardship of the National Archives, I can lay claim to one minor achievement. I initiated an agreement with the Dutch government to secure microfilm copies from the Rijksarchief of all material relating to India. This project took several years to complete. The Dutch were so pleased with this agreement that they gave India the microfilm copies free of charge.

All first-class officials of the government were expected to call on the minister of his department as a part of his formal duty. As my minister was Maulana Abul Kalam Azad, president of the Indian National Congress at the time of the transfer of power, I was more than happy to perform this duty. In my boyhood and early youth, year after year I had followed with great interest the elections to the presidentship of the Congress. In our eyes, the Congress Working Committee was the legitimate Central government and its president, the true head of the state. Now that this had become everyday reality, despite the many disappointments there was a sense of pride and satisfaction in the fact. And Maulana Azad was not just any minister. Since the days of the Khilafat agitation he had almost symbolized Hindu–Muslim unity. He was also the person who, as president, had negotiated the transfer of power on behalf of the Indian National Congress. I was greatly excited at the prospect of meeting this charismatic figure.

The minister's personal assistant received me in his office at the Central Secretariat. I forget his name, but remember the fact that he was a member of the national hockey team and had participated in the Olympic Games. He was a very handsome man and spoke to me in beautiful Urdu. I apologized and said that my spoken Urdu was execrable but I had no difficulty in following the language. I was shown in to Maulana sahib's office. It was a vast room and he was sitting at one end beside a table with a shining surface which had no papers on it. It was his practice, we were told, to have the files read out to him by his secretary and then he would dictate his decision, always in Urdu and sign the file, again in the Urdu script. The usual sight of a mountain of files piled on the minister's table was hence absent in his case. I repeated my apologies that I spoke Urdu too badly to try it in the presence of a recognized master of the language, but translation would not be necessary. Maulana smiled and asked me to sit down. Though he was known to be fluent in English, he always communicated in Urdu. It was a matter of nationalist pride.

Maulana Abul Kalam Azad made an overpowering impression on me. There was a grandeur about his looks which made me feel as if I was in the presence of the Mughal emperor. I imagined that I was surrounded by the mansabdars and ahadis in the Mughal imperial service and the office had momentarily been transformed into the diwan-i-khas, the private audience hall of the Mughals. I think the Maulana, used to dealing with hundreds of people over many years, guessed the impact he had had on this greenhorn of a bureaucrat. There was an amused and indulgent smile on his lips. He asked the usual polite questions and added while I was taking leave that he understood I came from a family of nationalists. Now I was not a bureaucrat, he said, but a servant of the people. Even the most mundane work I had to do was service to the nation which had at last come into its own. This awareness could transform the quality of one's work and one's life, he said. I knew he was speaking, not as my minister but my leader, a man who had given his entire life to the nationalist cause and suffered greatly in consequence. Nothing much happened during the few minutes I spent with him, but in an inexplicable way I felt this man had touched what was most worthwhile in my own consciousness. If in the days of the nationalist movement he had asked me to risk my life, I knew I would have obeyed without hesitation. That I suppose is what one understands by the word charisma.

I was destined to have one more contact with the Maulana in my official capacity before I left my job. In the centenary year of the great rebellion of 1857 (which was certainly not a mutiny, whatever else it was: for one thing, none of its leaders was in the service of the Company), the government had commissioned an authoritative history of the event. The person entrusted with the job was the well-known historian S.N. Sen. The book was reviewed by Penderel Moon (still a plain Mr, not Sir) for the journal *Indian Archives* of which I was the editor in my capacity as acting director, National Archives. Mr Moon of the ICS had criticized the actions of the Indian government during the Quit India movement in a private letter. This being wartime, the letter was opened by the censors and its content editorially criticized by one of the English-language dailies. Moon resigned from his post, but was invited back by Nehru to serve as an advisor to the newly established Planning Commission. Incidentally, he was a great admirer of Soviet planning and many of his ideas concerning the economic reconstruction of India tallied with those of Nehru.

There was great commotion among the staff of my office when the contents of Moon's review of Sen's book was revealed. The reviewer was full of praise for the book itself. But he severely criticized Maulana Azad's introduction, which did not really conform to academic standards of historical criticism. How could we publish a review criticizing the views of our boss? I consulted my colleagues and asked for an interview with Moon. At the same time, I sent a copy of the review to Maulana sahib. I explained to Moon our predicament and asked very hesitantly if he would mind modifying, not his views, but the undoubtedly severe language he had used. He curtly stated that there was no need to publish the review. I told him that if that was how he felt, I would publish his review as it was. Moon, fortunately for me, compromised and sent a revised version while on the very same day I heard from the minister asking me to publish the original version without altering it in any way.

The contact established with Moon, later Sir Penderel, survived over the years. He used to come to our seminar on South Asian History when he was a fellow of All Souls. Once he made some jokes concerning the members of a certain Indian community, without meaning any offence, and then realized that several of them were sitting in the front row. He was so embarrassed that he never came to our seminars again. He was too old, he told me, and no longer knew what he might end up saying.

I was soon to be treated to an insider's view of the ways of the bureaucrats in two countries, India and the UK. The director of Archives, whose post was vacant while I held fort as the acting director was eventually selected from the ranks of the senior clerical officials in the Central Secretariat. His claims to be so selected were twofold. He had once been a technical officer at the Archives. More important, he was a friend of the son-in-law of a powerful cabinet minister. He had other accomplishments. He came to the office with a small bundle of paan or betel leaves duly garnished with varied ingredients, popular all over India. He would invite me to his room in the Archives and dole out generous quantities of the bundled paan. After an early lunch around twelve he would move to the Central Secretariat to pay his respects to various ministers and senior secretaries with whom he was on friendly terms, partly by virtue of his alleged skill as a palmist and astrologer. Occasionally, he asked me to share the roti and vegetables made by his good wife. These were not very tasty. The director was aware of this and would occasionally give vent to his desire to remarry, not because his wife of some twenty-five years was a bad cook (he was, as he was keen to point out, ever a humane person), but because she had aged while he, thanks to all the ghee he had consumed in his youth and the wrestling he had regularly practised, was still very virile. I pointed out very gently that ageing might not be an adequate reason for divorce in the eyes of the law in India. Who was talking of divorce, he would say. He was too kind a person to divorce his wife of many years. He would simply take a second wife, as his ancestors had done before him. In fact some of them in their virility had taken several. Now that happy practice was a criminal offence, thanks to Nehru, so indifferent to the great traditions of our country. The director smiled. Five cabinet ministers and seven senior secretaries to the government virtually ate out of his hands, he said. What could the law do to him? Well, there was the principle of independence of the judiciary written into our constitution. He smiled at my naivety. The prosecution for bigamy had to be launched by the executive. He knew everyone who was anyone in the Delhi police. If he wished to

A Bureaucrat in Delhi

take a second wife, he would and neither Brahma, nor Vishnu nor Shiva could stop him. The man had thought out the whole matter very carefully.

His self-confidence derived not merely from his worldly influence but his great spiritual powers. Once, his wife was ill and he was doing his puja. 'Presently the gentleman arrived on his bullock.' The gentleman in question was Yama, the god of death. He made a sign asking the director to accompany him as would his wife. He bowed in obeisance and made a sign requesting the deity to leave. Yama now descended to mean tricks. He threw his favourite weapon, a snare, at Bhargava. The latter defended himself with his open palm. Yama, frustrated by the man's great spiritual power went back. But after all, the director had been hit by a divine weapon. He showed me the deep cut it had made on his palm. By the time I got to know him, he had reached new heights of spirituality. If he picked up a stone it was transformed into a lingam, Shiva's of course. Professor Basham was visiting Delhi at the time. He also had been told about this newly acquired miraculous power. 'Sounds sort of rude to me,' he commented laconically.

The last chapter in the directorial epic is truly an improving tale. The denouement happened after I had left government service. The Archives needed two hundred thousand rupees worth of cartons every year to replace the old ones. As this was a specialized and only moderately profitable business, the same small company had supplied the cartons over the years. But when tenders were called under our yogi's directorship, he himself submitted a tender in the name of a non-existent firm and also accepted the same against the advice of his technical staff. He then proceeded to set up a manufactory in his own courtyard using the services of some peons from the office and began to produce the cartons. The matter was expectedly reported to the vigilance department and their report confirmed that a serious crime had been committed. The ministry issued a 'show cause' notice. But there the matter stopped, perhaps because the senior officials wished to avoid the hassle of a dismissal procedure and the court case which would inevitably follow. Or maybe, the five cabinet ministers and seven senior secretaries who allegedly ate out of the great man's hands had put in a word where it mattered. The man continued to be in the pay of the government and retired honourably in due course. The last two years of his service, he did not come to office at all because the home ministry who, as his real employers, had granted him extension, had no suitable posts for him and the education ministry refused to have him in the Archives, a department under their authority. But for my eighteen months' work as a Central government employee, I would have remained a stranger to these deeper mysteries of the Indian bureaucratic world.

Even before the advent of the great director, strange things had been happening to my brief career as a bureaucrat. I received a friendly phone call from the minister of state, Mr Shrimali, one morning asking me to drop by at my convenience. The protocol strictly proscribed such informality. On arrival at his office, I was astounded to hear what he had to say. Apparently, there was a police report against me. The government hoped to clear it up but it would take a few months. Meanwhile, would I like to move to the Central Secretariat? He guaranteed my return to the Archives. I asked for a few weeks' time and explained that to the best of my knowledge I had committed no crime and the only party I had ever joined was the Indian National Congress at the age of sixteen. He smiled and said he knew all that. The report was from the UK and he was confident that this could be cleared up. As I had no intention of moving to the secretariat, I began to look for a job and eventually Dr V.K.R.V. Rao, vice chancellor, Delhi University, decided to appoint me reader in economic history at the Delhi School of Economics. In February 1959 I moved from the Constitution House to the Delhi University campus to begin a new phase in my career.

What I discovered over time was reassuring and full of charm. The charm consisted in the close and happy relationship between the Commonwealth countries and the UK. In the British days, as was well known, the government kept an eye on the Indian students in the UK where they picked up most of their seditious ideas. Apparently, this happy practice had continued after independence. The government of Britain was glad to oblige the Indian high commission. The latter had learnt from the former, in fact the formidable MI5 no less, that I was very close to the top leadership of the British Communist Party, almost a member of the Politburo. Such a person was unsuitable to be in charge of the National Archives of India. He might in fact sell the entire archival collection to the Soviet Union any day. I looked back and realized that the occasional glass of beer I had with Christopher Hill, the rare encounters with Eric Hobsbawm and my friendship with Ralph Samuel were not appreciated by MI5. I developed a deep respect for their perspicacity. Ever since the threat of Muslim 'terror' has darkened our horizons, I have lived in fear that my friendship with my Pakistani grocer may any day lead to my arrest as the chief agent of Osama bin Laden, in charge of destroying Oxford and Cambridge, the infidels' intellectual headquarters. I have often wondered why the secret services are described as 'Intelligence' when in fact that is the one endowment they frequently lack. A fool, as the saying goes, is born every minute. A large proportion of them evidently find refuge in the secret services of the world, the myth of James Bond notwithstanding.

May I suggest 'stupidity', instead of 'intelligence', as the generic name of the world's secret services.

15

Return to Academics: DSE and Delhi University

Delhi School of Economics: Glory Days

Dr Khaleeq Naqvi of Aligarh also joined the Delhi School of Economics as reader in economic thought the day I did. His wife, Zubaida, taught botany in Aligarh. As he was to live in Delhi as a grass widower and I was still a bachelor, he suggested that we rent and share a flat. We found a very spacious one by the side of a man-made pool in a northern suburb of Delhi, Model Town, inhabited mostly by refugees from Punjab. Manmohan Singh, India's present prime minister, also rented a house in Model Town when he joined our faculty. I was very pleased to live near a stretch of water, which for me is a sine qua non for a state of happiness. The cook we had the good luck to employ was a true wizard and I began to live by the poolside very happily. Ismail, our cook, also happened to be a stern man and helped keep us on the straight and narrow. He tried his best to ration our consumption of beer and whisky. In the case of Khaleeq Naqvi, Ismail's efforts succeeded about 5 per cent. In short, these were happy times.

As to my professional life, I discovered that I would have to create my own work and felt assured that I would have the full cooperation of my colleagues in this matter. There was one course in the economics syllabus on patterns of economic development for me to teach and I was asked to draw up more courses for the following year. The School was in its glory days at the time. It had on its staff, K.N. Raj, one of the architects of India's Second Plan, M.N. Srinivas, India's leading sociologist who had taught earlier at Oxford to be succeeded by Dumont and sundry luminaries who were soon to be joined by the three whiz kids, Amartya Sen, Sukhamay Chakravarti and Jagdish Bhagavati, all as full professors, and all at the age of twenty-seven. Others who joined the School as reader or lecturer around the same time included Andre Béteille, now a famous sociologist, and Arjun Sengupta, later financial adviser to Mrs Gandhi and India's ambassador to the EC. One could drop several more important names, including that of our present prime minister who left the World Bank to join our faculty but let me desist for the moment.

In winter, the great economists of the world descended on Delhi to study the country's experiment with democratic planning. Besides, Delhi in winter is a place of great charm, full of bright sunshine and never too cold. I found during my brief career as a bureaucrat that my colleagues in the profession had a curious preference for having the professional conferences in summer but, whenever possible, in Kashmir, known popularly in India as Bhusvarga, Heaven on Earth. Our visitors from abroad seemed to divide their time between the Central Secretariat and the Delhi School of Economics, but presumably found the latter place more congenial. They were also frequent guests at Nehru's official residence and the home of whoever happened to be the finance minister at the moment. In season, there were frequent parties in honour of these famous visitors in the houses of the great and the good in New Delhi where our famous economist colleagues were regular guests.

One regular visitor was Mrs Joan Robinson who never failed to spend some time in the People's Republic of China either on her way to Delhi or on the journey back home. She had great faith in Mao and, presumably, his famous Thoughts. During the Cultural Revolution, she once remarked, 'I know you people won't believe this, but you can take it from me that this is true. Several of my students from Cambridge who were professors in various Chinese universities are now working as landless labourers. Believe me, they are much happier, much much happier.' Of course they were. Mao must have advised them personally to be so. I met a son of one of these demoted (promoted?) professors later at St Antony's when China started her policy of opening up to a limited degree. His father used to teach English at Beijing University and, during the Cultural Revolution, was employed to clean the public lavatories of the city. The poor man died in a few months, probably from an onset of unbearable happiness. But the son, who had been sent to Mongolia as a teenager to become a shepherd, was truly quite pleased. There was no boring college education. Besides the climate was bracing and the food, which came mostly from his own herd of sheep, had protein content much higher than what he got in the capital. He returned to university education and a year at Oxford at age thirty. This was acceptable though the food in Mongolia was better than at St Antony's. That was no matter for surprise though we are quite proud of our chef and sous-chefs. But he did not complain.

The atmosphere at the Delhi School was intensely intellectual. As a friend of the institution once described it, the place was like an intellectual hothouse. Even the small talk at the place, including the jokes, had a hard core of very high-powered theoretical economics. I felt lost and realized that I had made a mistake in coming here. My colleagues could not be more accommodating. In 1964, a chair in economic history was created and I got it in due course, being raised to the status of a senior professor soon afterwards. The University Grants Commission created a few Centres of Excellence in the Indian universities and the department of economics at the Delhi School was one of the first to be recognized as one of these. My colleagues decided that it would specialize in economic history and economic development which allowed me, first, to create a readership in economic history (late Dharma Kumar was appointed to the post and she succeeded to the chair I held when I left for Oxford) and second, set up a visiting professorship to which I could invite some of the top economic historians from the UK (including Professors Postan, Habakkuk and Mathias), the USA, Japan and the USSR. The visitors from the USA were funded by the Rockefeller Foundation which made it possible to have at least two eminent visitors each year. I think my colleagues were aware of my predicament, the professional isolation from which I suffered, and did their best to make me feel at home.

My economic history, such as it was, belonged to the historical branch of the subject and was peripheral to the interest of the faculty and the students in the department. Econometric history or statistical arguments were not within my expertise. And I had no knowledge of mathematical economics, all the rage at the time. My lectures were popular with the students but in course of the fourteen years I taught at Delhi, the last two in the department of history, I got only two students who came to write their thesis under my supervision. One of them was Dr Om Prakash who later succeeded to the chair in economic history. I felt what I had to offer was of interest to the students as some sort of light entertainment, but they were reluctant to take up the brand of economic history I taught as a serious academic pursuit. My colleagues who also happened to be good friends did their best to help me. At their suggestion I was elected director of the School and given powers which would enable me to have some impact on the life of the institution. But the problem from my point of view was too basic to be solved in this way. My sense of isolation persisted and I ceased to be productive.

Attempts at Research

Not that I did absolutely nothing. My Oxford thesis was published in a totally revised form in 1962 by the Dutch Royal Institute for Anthropology, Geography and Linguistics in their series of Proceedings. I did a new edition of my first book with an anthropological introduction. In this I was influenced by Keith Thomas's famous article on anthropology and history in the *Past and*

Present. I took lessons in anthropology from Srinivas and Béteille and was very pleased when Keith Thomas published a note on the new edition of the book in the *Past and Present*. With the help of Dharma Kumar I launched a new journal, *The Indian Economic and Social History Review*. Many a scholar in the field of Indian economic and social history, now well known in the field, cut his/her first academic teeth in this journal. Then Professor Jack Gallagher invited Dharma Kumar to undertake a two-volume *Cambridge Economic History of India*. Dharma asked me to join her as a joint editor of the volumes and I brought in Irfan Habib to co-edit with me the first volume covering the pre-colonial period. Meghnad Desai (now Lord) agreed to assist with the work of the second volume, covering the British period and after, especially the statistical bits. All this may not sound like absolute zero in terms of academic productivity, but I was doing very little research and felt deeply depressed.

Matrimony

In the last years of my bachelor days I became aware that the institution of arranged marriage was very much alive and kicking even in the highly educated circles of Indian society. As an eligible bachelor (an Oxford degree could still confer status in the early days of Indian independence; now, it has more or less ceased to do so, the ideal groom being an employee of some American company or at least of the Ambanis or the Tatas, thanks to globalization and the triumph of the market forces signalling, as we know, the end to all history) I was frequently targeted and the young ladies in question were often not unattractive. What saved me was the proverbial poverty of the teaching profession which discouraged would be fathers-in-law. My growing reputation for unacceptable behaviour also helped. Sharing a flat with a Muslim colleague was bad enough. But there was worse. One evening, when Khaleeq and I were having a few glasses of beer to the accompaniment of Ismail's memorable roasted chicken drumsticks on the terrace of our flat, a friend arrived unannounced with an uncle by marriage. The last-mentioned gentleman had more than one marriageable daughter and he had decided to survey the ground personally before making any actual offer. Drinking beer in the evening was still not acceptable behaviour in potential sons-in-law. I did not feel like hiding our bottles and, after considering several alternative scenarios, decided to invite the might-be father-in-law to join us. The look of horror on his face was indescribable, but there was no way I could withdraw from my honest gesture, morally sound according to the ethics I believed in. My friend and his uncle left soon. A kindly Providence had saved him and his daughter from a dire fate, the uncle commented. This I learnt from my friend the following day. If I believed in any Providence, I too would have thanked Her/Him in some appropriate manner, perhaps by offering a goat at some suitable shrine.

In another instance of similar parental initiative, I got interested because the young lady in question was very pretty. But the father, a famous academic, put me through a third-degree cross-examination about my financial situation. I disabused him of the entirely wrong idea that my family had brought great wealth from our estate in East Pakistan. When told that we had never had any money to speak of, his face fell. The next time I called, the mother took me aside and explained sympathetically that they had not brought up their daughter in a way which could enable her to survive on a teacher's salary; hence the courtship better be nipped in the bud. I felt like asking how she, the daughter of a famous doctor, had managed on her husband's salary as a college teacher, but guessed that the father had helped out.

I got married in 1960. I met my wife through my colleague and teacher in Calcutta, Dr Pratul Gupta, the son of a very famous lawyer, Atul Gupta, well known as a literary critic and a person at the vanguard of every progressive social movement. The Guptas were distantly related to us. My wife, Hashi, was married to Pratul Babu's younger brother Amal who died at a very young age. I met and married her two years after that tragedy. Widow remarriage, originally not permissible among Bengali Hindus, was legalized in 1856 at the initiative of the famous reformer, Iswarchandra Vidyasagar. It of course is a major civilizing act of the Raj, as claimed in the textbooks written under their rule. This is also one of the glories of the nineteenth-century Indian reform which every school child in India reads about. Though such remarriage never became popular among Bengali Hindus, I had not expected any opposition to what we were doing, such marriages being one of the sacred cows in the modern Hindu's perception of their recent social history. Iswarchandra Vidyasagar was undoubtedly a very remarkable man and legalization of widow remarriage is always presented as his crowning glory. In India, accepting this reform had become a clinching evidence of rational modernity since the late nineteenth century. But I was sadly mistaken. Hashi's mother-in-law by her first marriage kicked up a tremendous fuss, feeling that her family honour was threatened by our action. No one tried to stop her in her track. Since she was the wife of a very eminent person, she was surrounded by an expected number of sycophants, who took up the battle cry as if we were committing a major crime. This gave me an unexpected insight into educated Bengali society: its pretence of modernity was but skin-deep. One of the leading lights of Bengali literature even took the trouble to publish a short story very obviously parodying our decision to get married, apparently an opportunistic act of treachery to the famous and saintly father-in-law and his family.

Indo–US Relations

During my work at the DSE, Indian academe, Delhi in particular, got into a tangled relationship with the USA, particularly with its great philanthropic foundations, Rockefeller and Ford. Both had appointed permanent representatives located in Delhi University. We were ambivalent in our attitude to these foundations, though very clear in our attitude to the USA and their Western allies. These were imperialist powers that had fought the Axis countries to preserve their empire and/or their worldwide influence. We did not for a moment believe the US pretension to be the saviour of democracy. Until Pearl Harbour, they were happy to let Europe be dominated by Nazi Germany. And as to the western European nations, Britain had done her best to regain Burma and Malaysia (the latter no doubt out of concern for saving the world from the threat of communism); the Netherlands, helped by the UK, to reconquer Indonesia; and France Indo-China, leading to the US entry into the Vietnam War. Many of us saw US interventions in Asia as the most potent source of our misery, their very unfortunate support for a variety of scoundrels including the military bosses in our neighbouring country, Pakistan. We did believe that but for American support to the Pakistani dictators democracy would have had a chance there. Their pretence of being defenders of democratic freedom looked very hollow to most thinking citizens of India. Their past belied such claims and their present did not look particularly convincing either. To us, the Western powers were wolves in sheep's clothing. The USA seemed quite happy to appear on the world scene in her original wolf skin without bothering about the woollier cover.

As in India's foreign policy so in the attitude of the country's leftist intelligentsia, there was an element of hypocrisy as also lack of clarity in relation to the Soviet Union and the Eastern bloc. We of course knew of the Stalinist purges, though perhaps not its full horror. But somehow, to us these belonged to a past unlikely to return. We certainly did not believe that once Europe had been divided into two zones of influence (this is how the map of Europe looked to us, not as a division between democratic Europe and the Soviet Empire), the real threat to the world's freedom was the Soviets, surrounded by American military might on all sides, but the USA itself. The latter's conduct in Asia, Africa (to wit, Belgian Congo) and Latin America confirmed our suspicions. Hence while we were loud in our condemnation of US foreign policy in Vietnam, Korea and the like, our criticism of Soviet action in Hungary was somewhat muted. And China, to the Indian radical, was beyond criticism. Even the brief war in 1962 did not change many attitudes. Our awareness of the great inequities of our own society was so acute, that China by contrast seemed to be a heaven of social and economic justice. In all fairness, this refers to the period before the forcible annexation of Tibet, claimed to be a part of China. But even after the full horror of that story became evident, very few in India were loud in their protests. We should not have given political asylum to the Dalai Lama, many whispered. Underline 'political' in this context.

What I have said so far constituted the background to our attitudes to the American foundations. The Rockefeller representative, Chadbourne Gilpatrick, became a good personal friend. But he had at his very first presentation at the university explicitly stated that he was on the CIA payroll during the war. We were told that once a CIA person one remained a CIA person for ever. What was our attitude to be to this ex-CIA man? We could of course take him or leave him. But it was not so simple. Should we not accept the funding for visiting professorships which enabled us to bring to Delhi the good and the great in the field of economics and economic history? Besides, somewhat embarrassingly, his Foundation was offering Indian academics a series of visiting appointments to American and British universities. Should we or should we not accept them?

There was little doubt that these initiatives were meant to soften the attitudes of the Indian intelligentsia towards America and negatively influence our favourable perceptions of Soviet and Chinese policies. Our students would brand us American agents as soon as we accepted any American grant. But the Foundations, in their wisdom, had never once asked us for anything in return. One of their beneficiaries, a leading historian, remained a very vocal member of the Communist Party of India (Marxist) throughout his life. But things got even more complicated when it became known that the Asia Foundation, the leading American grant-giving body in India, had in fact been funded by the CIA. Nearly all of us had accepted funding from them for one thing or another and we felt we could not lose our virginity twice. When a heated discussion was going on about such matters, Mrs Robinson gave us a very cynical advice: Take money from wherever it may come, because money carries no ideological brand. But be careful not to do anything which may help the policies or causes which we found objectionable. Well, so far to the best of our knowledge we had not done so. When offers came to me, first of a visiting appointment at the School of Oriental and African Studies (SOAS) and then visiting professorships for two semesters at Duke and Berkeley, I did not refuse. I, in fact, accepted these offers without hesitation. But when a couple of years later, we objected to the proposed US–India cultural agreement and succeeded in blocking it in the democratic phase of Mrs Indira Gandhi's prime ministership, I was not sure we were being consistent. We were afraid that once America with her vast resources was allowed entry into the decision-making processes of Indian academe, we would in effect lose our autonomy. From certain things that had already happened, this apprehension did not appear baseless.

A Year at SOAS

In 1960, I came to London with my wife to take up my assignment as a research associate at the School of Oriental and African Studies and was temporarily accommodated in a house rented by an American friend who was away on holiday. My wife was expecting and our only child, a daughter, was born in June that year. We had to look for an accommodation for the entire period of our stay. This was a very revealing experience. The Race Relations Act was not yet on the statute book. We went to one of the leading housing agencies and were given a list of eight hundred accommodations in the price range we could afford. Only two of these would accept non-whites with children. One of the two was in a state of extreme dilapidation. The other was actually a brothel owned by a very canny Indian. We eventually found a satisfactory accommodation through friends.

A word about our experience of racism in England may be relevant here. When I was a student at Oxford, we were sheltered from racist behaviour both in the college and the authorized digs many of which belonged to the college domestic staff. We did encounter offensive behaviour in shops and railway stations. The employees at the till or the ticket office would often make a point of being offensive, thanking the customers who preceded and followed and omitting the courtesy in our case. The waiters in restaurants were frequently offensive. I must add that they were not particularly polite to white customers either. There has been a change in this respect over the years. For the last six months of my stay at Oxford I opted for unauthorized accommodation which happened to be cheaper. Sometimes the owners who advertised these would guess from our accent that we were not English and say that their rooms had already been let out. We would then ask one of our English friends to call and found that the rooms were very much available. Sometimes we were asked to come and see the rooms and be told that these had been let out, as soon as we turned up. It seems that violent racist crimes have increased in recent decades. Immigration as a political issue, exacerbated by right-wing elements in British politics, has indeed consolidated negative attitudes on the question of race all over Europe but the general public attitude in these matters have certainly changed for the better, especially in Britain. The British-born Asian today is hardly distinguishable from local whites except for their skin colour, and the locals are much more welcoming to non-white people, even though we have had racist abuse shouted at us on rare occasions. Familiarity has indeed bred indifference, racist crime and occasional conflicts notwithstanding. Enoch Powell was fortunately mistaken. There have been no rivers of blood.

Here I should also like to enter a caveat, though it is in no way a startling discovery. As a student of differing social attitudes over time and space with regard to the basic concerns of life (echo of Keith Thomas's famous essay), I find that British attitude to children is rather different from that of most other cultures, one reason why out of eight hundred accommodations only two would accept children as well as non-white tenants. There is often a feeling of relief when one's own children leave the parental home. As to grandchildren, while they are of course welcome for a period, their departure in most homes is not unwelcome. It is too much work for most elderly people, a thought, which if it did occur, would never be given expression in an Indian family. This is as true in London as in Delhi. The availability of home help is not what makes the crucial difference. I have noticed any number of times people stopping on the road to treat other people's cats and dogs to tender baby talk, but never, repeat never, any expression of demonstrative affection to other people's babies or small children. If one shows any interest in a cute child on a bus, his/her guardians stiffen up and assume a look of indifferent sternness to imply that they had not noticed the misdemeanour. Nowadays one might be in danger of being reported to the police for paedophilic tendencies. I found that the Dutch, the Italians and even the Nordic nations are very different. When I have talked to friends about this, it became clear that they had never given any thought to this matter and hence could not explain these disparities in their conduct. However, the implied suggestion that they perhaps lack human warmth does cause offence. Over the years I have found that the British are perhaps the most generous people on earth. Charities flourish in this country as nowhere else. But the kindness is dispensed preferably at arm's length. Proximity of other humans is rather embarrassing and hence not very acceptable. When one encounters members of one's species one is not especially fond of (which is generally the case), one is at a loss as to which way to look. The Chinese allegedly invented the wonderful practice of waving a fan. When an acquaintance waves it on seeing you on the road, the gesture is to be interpreted as indicating that he/she has not seen you. So it would be an excellent idea if this custom was adopted in Britain by an act of Parliament. Besides, it would help if the Oxford University Press (OUP) published a dictionary of common sayings in England. This would contain phrases like 'we must meet soon' (meaning, 'please cross over to the other pavement if you ever run into me'); 'you must come over one day' (meaning, 'for heaven's sake, don't you ever even dream of bothering me') and so on.

At the SOAS I had an academically profitable time. Professor Philips, the director and Professor Basham each ran a weekly seminar and the papers presented were of a consistently high quality. Ranajit Guha, who was sharing my flat, and Kirti Chaudhuri, still a student working on his doctoral dissertation, were participants in these seminars. That did enhance the quality of the discussions. There was one painful feature in Basham's seminars. Some of his very numerous Indian students were in the habit of interrupting others. When Basham tried to stop them, they complained loudly of racist discrimination. Over the years, the professor had learned to treat these comments with yogic insouciance. But, identifying as Indians with these boors, we felt acutely embarrassed. I came to value greatly my friendship with Kirti and Basham. Kirti in his twenties was already a formidable scholar, partly thanks to his early training under the guidance of his famous father, late Nirad C. Chaudhuri. In one session of Professor Philips' seminar, he outlined his long term plans of research, virtually covering the trade of the Indian Ocean over many centuries. Philips advised him to be more cautious, in fact less ambitious to start with. Ranajit disagreed and said that a young man capable of such academic ambition should be encouraged. Years later, the Cambridge University Press asked my opinion regarding his proposal to write a book on nine centuries of trade in the Indian Ocean. I replied that if it had come from any other person I would have rejected it as an extreme example of megalomania. But since it came from Kirti Chaudhuri, I supported it whole-heartedly.

Basham, I feel, is one of the neglected figures in the field of Indology. He was a poet and a linguist and what is even more important, a humanist with the rare capacity of empathy with a very different culture. His work of great scholarship, *The Wonder That Was India*, has come to be treated almost like a coffee table introduction to ancient India, thanks partly to its very unscholarly title. If one remembered that almost every statement in the book was based on original source material, not secondary sources, perhaps one would treat it with greater humility. His knowledge of modern Indian languages, both northern and southern, was formidable. He did a great deal of work he never bothered to publish. He had translated many Sanskrit texts, just as finger practice. These included a marvellous rendering of *Mrichchhakatikam*, *The Little Clay Cart*. He had done it for a group of school children who wanted to stage a play. The Government of Greece had invited him to set up a course in Indological studies. He decided to learn modern Greek to facilitate communication. In a few months he translated Kazantzakis, but never even thought of publishing it. He belonged to a tradition of Indology which went back to William Jones. At its heart was a shared pleasure in a very special understanding of the human condition, its joys and its tragic fate. He was of course a scholar, but literary enjoyment rather than just hard-headed scholarship was perhaps his central concern. Scholarship to him was a pleasurable game. He felt no compulsion to convert all he did into some currency to enhance his career. Among other things, he was a great defender of the Hindi cinema, what we sneeringly describe as Bollywood. He saw as its core an undying tradition going back to the great epics, the theme of victory of good over evil mingled with a highly civilized voluptuousness. I cannot entirely agree because I do not find the lechery so manifest in that genre very civilized.

At SOAS, I was paid a monthly stipend of one hundred and fifty pounds net. It seems mythical when I remember what we could do with that modest amount. We could hire the services of a nanny twice a week on which evenings we went to a West End show, usually a play or a ballet and rounded off the evening with a meal at one of the restaurants recommended in the weekend newspapers. We could thus see the performances of Margaret Fontaine and Nureyev and of the great British actors, Lawrence Olivier, John Gielgud and all the famous ladies of the stage. I remember this as a privilege which would have been way beyond my means but for this fellowship. Interestingly, we never managed to see Agatha Christie's famous play, *The Mousetrap*. It is still going on, but we lost interest.

Miss Amer, our nanny, was an 'old India hand' and often asked us if we knew the manager of a certain British bank for whom she had worked: her former ward was by then a bank manager himself and treated her with affection and respect. Her next question might refer to Ram the grocer. Her social range was truly impressive. She referred to the 'natives' with a certain condescension; but then she knew that 'they' knew no better. She took great pride in the fact that our daughter, her ward, was British-born. That, certainly, had redeemed her. Miss Amer always recommended Lyons' Corner House when we went out for dinner, but added that she had never been to a cinema. One never knew what went on there and she did not wish people to cast aspersions on her character. At seventy, she was still careful on this point. We kept in touch with this gracious lady for many years, but then we lost track. I am sure she has moved on to some heavenly version of the British Empire. There was one problem there. To Miss Amer, the Empire was the ultimate heaven. There was no higher or better place to go to. What she really needed was a time machine. People sharing her simple faith run into millions in this country.

The fellowship at SOAS allowed me to spend a few months in The Hague where I collected some data later used for my chapters in the *Cambridge Economic History of India*. I also started work on a press list of the Dutch documents on India modelled on William Foster's *English Factories*. My volume covering the initial years would just be a starter for other volumes to follow. But I never got round to publishing the work I had done. We took the opportunity of our sojourn in the continent to visit a few other countries. These travels followed the usual pattern except for one chilling experience which I should record.

We had decided to spend a few days in some village by the Rhine. Our boat ticket allowed us to stop where we liked and we got off at Konigswinter which was a beautiful place, like something out of a fairy tale. Now the place is a very unattractive suburb of Bonn. Some owners of bed and breakfast places were waiting near the landing in the hope of catching stray tourists. One of these, a person who had a few words of English, picked up our luggage and we followed him to a charming cottage. The owners were a childless couple and the wife treated a doll as her child substitute. Poupa, as this object was called, was dressed, washed and fed exactly as a human baby would have been. The poor woman was overjoyed to see my one-year-old daughter who became her poupa for the three days we stayed there. When we left, she was quite heartbroken. The husband had fought on the Eastern front and showed us his war photographs kept in a very fat album. It was a worm's-eye view of the war and gave us an insight into that monstrous reality we have not found anywhere else. There were photos of cafes deep inside the Soviet Union, especially Ukraine. The expression on the face of the waiters serving the German soldiers was one of pure hatred. I have not seen anything like that before or after. Then, he said, he would show me the piece de resistance of his collection, something he felt sure I had never seen before this. He turned the page of his album. There was a large photo of a dozen Russians hanging from the gallows, their eyes gouged out, their bellies gutted. Those hanged included a couple of children. He loved that photo, the man explained. I stopped myself from throwing up with great difficulty.

American Interludes

The grants from the Rockefeller Foundation paid for a visiting professorship at two American universities, Duke and Berkeley. James B. Duke was a local boy from North Carolina, who had started his life as a newspaper or cigarette vendor, I forget which. Cigarette is what eventually made his fortune. He offered his money, I understand, first to Harvard and then Princeton on a simple condition: they had to change their name to Duke. Since they were reluctant to make this small change, he gave the money to his home town to set up the university named after him. The very beautiful campus was arranged in the shape of a cross with a statue of Duke at the centre. The buildings were very 'Oxbridge'; the stones looked like Cotswold stones. It was rumoured that they were chosen with an eye on their likelihood of quick deterioration, so that the university would look venerable without having to wait eight centuries. A pine forest nearby had been chosen to provide homes for the faculty. We were allotted the home of a professor who was on leave. The day we arrived, we found a small cake and a toy waiting for our daughter and tea laid out for us as a gesture of welcome. I have often heard that the

Americans were rather superficial in their friendships. Well, we had gone there for some six months not looking for abiding friendships (though we found those too) but this little gesture welcoming us at the end of a long journey was deeply rewarding. A people to whom such small acts of kindness come spontaneously are anything but emotionally superficial in my judgement.

I was deeply impressed by certain aspects of the American university system. Research rather than undergraduate teaching has a centrality in it. The system of term papers is an excellent introduction to training in research. A student is thrown into the middle of a subject he/she knows nothing about, suggests a topic for research in a fortnight, draws up a bibliography with the teacher's help and by the end of the term produces a paper which at its best is publishable. In fact, several of the articles published in our journal in India were term papers to start with. The little eccentricities in the system were not unattractive. I was allotted a workroom which had a huge mirror on one wall. The mirror, I later learnt, was see-through. Fortunately, I did not indulge in any unacceptable activity in my workroom. On one occasion, I was introduced to the professor of horse-judging from a land grant college nearby. These chairs were not to be pooh-poohed. The man's salary was way above those of his colleagues in the great universities, simply because there was a high market price paid for the services of their graduates. Whether horse-judging is an appropriate subject on the syllabi of a university, the way Greek literature or Western philosophy is, is another question. I asked the highly paid professor what courses he offered. 'Horse-judging and advanced horse-judging,' he answered.

Of course! I understood that at the University of Miami one could take doctorates in swimming and circus clowning. I did meet one young man whose PhD was in butchering technique. It is not clear if Bush used his discoveries in Iraq.

The year I first went to the USA was important in the country's history. It saw the beginning of the Civil Rights movement. A white activist was killed in Durham—bleaching powder was poured down his throat. I was deeply impressed by the seriousness and dedication characteristic of American political movements. I thought, here was a remarkable culture which brought its tremendous energy and organizational skills to whatever it did. Later, when a million people marched on Washington to demand an end to the Vietnam War, one of the little details to which attention was paid referred to the provision of mobile toilets. I know of no other country where radical groups would have the practical sense to attend to such details as also the ability to provide for an essential necessity for one million people. I found a degree of seriousness in campus life which I had not encountered either back home or in Europe. Young people seemed to be aware of their role on the world scene as citizens of the world's most powerful country. Their sense of power and responsibility had a humane orientation thanks to their liberal inspiration which can be traced back to the puritanical tradition and of course to the War of Independence and the Civil War.

Here I should like to underline one fact. While deeply suspicious of American foreign policy and the right-wing establishment in US politics, I should take strong exception to being described as 'anti-American'. Finding people like Bush, Cheney or Wolfowitz and the typical 'ugly American' deeply repulsive is probably an attitude people like us share with the majority of politicized Americans who have repeatedly rejected extreme reaction as an acceptable plank of policy. It does not imply a failure to appreciate the greatness of a very great nation. My first sojourn in America made me intensely aware of that greatness. And a certain simplicity of conduct and ease of access which goes with it charmed me. I do not know of any other people with comparable acquisition of power (of course, no other nation has acquired such power and wealth in the history of mankind) who have remained so unspoilt and basically unpretentious in their outlook. Snobbery, to my understanding, is a singularly un-American vice. Their alleged naivety and materialism are more than counterbalanced by their great cultural achievements, the excellence of their academic institutions and their record of spectacular philanthropy. I admire profoundly the civilization that is America. Only, that admiration does not extend to the country's foreign policy in Asia, Africa and

Latin America or to politicians like George Bush and his cohort. That does not make people like me anti-American.

Perhaps this is the appropriate point where I should clarify my attitude to Britain and all that she stands for. As I have stated before, I come from an Indian nationalist family who were great admirers of the English and their civilization. It is well to remember that Indian nationalism began with a class of people who were among the few actual beneficiaries of the British rule—as their most important collaborators. Empire loyalty came naturally to such people despite the humiliations and frustrations they suffered until they realized that their aspirations could in no way be realized under the Raj. Over time, they also came to empathize with the horrendous condition in which the vast majority of the Indian people lived and to believe that an end to alien rule was the sine qua non for any amelioration thereof. Indian nationalism, enthusiastically loyalist to begin with, became strongly anti-imperialist in its more mature phase. Again, anti-imperialist, not anti-British. It is a serious mistake to treat the two as synonymous. One can scour the entire body of nationalist writing and not come across anything criticizing the people and culture of Britain. You do not have to be anti-German to be anti-Nazi or anti-Russian to abhor the Stalinist terror. At the heart of every imperialist regime, the British very much included, is a hard core of undiluted evil. People do not go out and conquer other people's lands for the latter's benefit. Compared to the absurdity of the notion that they do, the belief that the moon is made of green cheese seems entirely reasonable. The level of overt oppression may vary from empire to empire, and the British one was certainly mild unless provoked by serious opposition (but as vicious as any other when that happened; to wit, the 1857 rising) but these fine distinctions between different shades of darkness have little meaning for the victims. Yet the politicized Indian was deeply appreciative of Britain's high civilization. The Clives, the Dyers, the O'Dwyers, the famines which killed millions, the harsh repression of 1857 and later political agitations even under a Labour government and the misery that was life under the Raj for the vast majority did not cloud one's admiration for Shakespeare, Newton, the Parliament, the Industrial Revolution and the humane culture which had produced such great gifts to human civilization. The long tradition of tolerance and sobriety in intellectual judgements at the heart of the Indian culture had something to do with this, but the reality of this admiration even among the most extreme critics of the empire is unquestionable. A quirk of history produced the regrettable phenomenon of empire which benefited a small section of Britain's, especially England's population (it is known that in battle, Welsh and Scottish regiments were first thrown into the fray but the history of Britain we were taught at school was exclusively the history of England). Their sustained propaganda over the centuries has produced the belief that the empire was to the benefit of all mankind, and the glory of the British people, who are not even aware of the endless misery it caused to many hundreds of millions of men and women. The black book of the empire is no part of history lessons in schools or colleges in Britain.

Since the educated Indian's understanding of Britain's greatness was contradicted by their experience of British rule and the conduct of the British in India, a new paradigm emerged regarding two types of Britishers—the unspoilt and highly civilized British at home (as encountered by the Indians visiting the UK, though they were not shielded from being abused as blackies or niggers) and their unworthy fellow citizens who went out to rule India and behaved like monsters of racism. Even that great admirer of the Raj, the late Nirad C. Chaudhuri commented that the nineteenth-century British in India were the Nazis of their time. Of course, the paradigm I have mentioned was a crude simplification. The British in their role of imperial masters could not have behaved very differently from the way they actually did. The logic of imperialism induced certain responses and patterns of behaviour. Evil was integral to the phenomenon of foreign rule. Individual conduct might vary and the ruling race in India was the usual mix of good, bad and nondescript one encounters in any community. Genuine dedication to the welfare of Indians was not uncommon among the missionaries and sections of officials, though they too were not free from the regime of informal apartheid which was a necessary part of imperial rule. But the domination and exploitation which the Raj was all about and the highly offensive attitudes that went with these were unavoidable consequences of imperialism.

The pirate ship of empire has never been short of chaplains. Now that ship has sunk, but the unholy race of its propagandists still flourishes. In the media, in scholarly works, in schools and colleges they continue to preach their gospel of imperial beneficence and the British public remains largely convinced that the empire was a source of infinite benefit to mankind. It is curious that none of the alleged beneficiaries are appreciative of the fact. Recent research has further established that only a fragment of the British population itself actually benefited from the empire. Half the world was exploited for the advantage of a small fraction of the British people, happy to keep in misery the underprivileged in their own society as much as the non-white populations whose lives they controlled in distant lands. The establishment which projects highly sophisticated falsehoods regarding the empire's benign character is probably the greatest con artist in the history of mankind. They have succeeded in enthroning a pathetic lie as the noblest truth. It will take many decades before that lie is rejected by the people of Britain. Meanwhile, the chaplains continue their unrelenting effort. They are a powerful force to be reckoned with. Now that Britain is unlikely to regain her empire, some of them are urging the USA to take up the white man's imperial burden exactly the way Kipling had done nearly a century ago. Meanwhile, people like me must defend their claim to be admirers and hence friends of Britain and her many-splendoured culture. Given our tangled history, this is not simply a matter of intellectual conviction, but a belief with a sharp emotional edge to it. Our abhorrence for the imperial tradition and its present-day defenders does not make us 'anti-British'.

To return to my first visit to the USA, I went from Duke to Berkeley, where I got to know most of the historians working on India who had come there for a conference. Some of them became very good friends. Later, when Tom Metcalfe came to Delhi, I had the honour of giving away the bride, Barbara, at their wedding in Skinner's old church. At Berkeley, I also got to know very well Bob Frykenberg, who invited me to contribute to his volume *Studies of Land Control in Indian History*. I wrote a piece based on my experiences of the zamindari system in my home district. I had already met Morris D. Morris in the UK. Here, at his invitation, we had a symposium centred on his article in the *Journal of Economic History* which had projected a positive image of the British impact on the Indian economy. I questioned some of his assumptions. Again, at his suggestion, we had a debate on his paper in our journal, *The Indian Social and Economic History Review*. While this debate attracted some attention among the historians of empires at the time, I have never been very happy about that initiative. It was interpreted in some quarters as an attempt on our part—ultra-nationalists—to damage Morris's scholarly reputation. This is the last thing I would have wished for. A radical in his outlook, paeans of praise for empires were the last thing he had intended. In effect, his was an argument first put forward by Karl Marx; he simply extended it along neoclassical lines. I fear that our relationship was affected by this controversy, even though the symposium was his idea, not mine. I have limited faith in scholarly commitment and care much more for inter-human relationship. I should have happily given up my effort to establish an academic 'truth' if I knew that it would in any way damage a valued friendship. I have often found to my sorrow that academic criticism of a colleague's statements is seen to be an 'attack' on him or them. The fact that you may genuinely respect and like an individual but be critical of his/her particular ideas is rarely appreciated. To repeat: I do care for historical 'truth' as I see it but I value interpersonal relationships a lot more.

In Berkeley, I became aware of another side of American culture, which was amusing to say the least, though one must remember that the practitioners of alternative lifestyles were in earnest, as committed about their fads as the political and civil-rights protesters. On the very first day of my lectures, a young girl faced me with a poster which had a single four-letter word written on it. I told her that neither the word nor the action was unfamiliar to me. Why did not she go elsewhere? Her purpose was to decriminalize such words, she said. Well, one could not object to that. Another day I found a young man stretched on the floor of my class playing with a gas balloon which kept going up and down. I asked him what he supposed he was doing. He was merely doing his own thing, he said. I told him that I also had my own little thing to do, namely lecture, and that the two things could not really coexist. He had not thought of that, he informed me, picked up his balloon and left—presumably to find some other location where he could continue doing his own thing. Evidently, these fighters for a freer and nobler way of life had not lost their regard for individual liberty. On another occasion, I went looking for a friend in a block of flats in San Francisco. Unable to find it, I knocked on a door behind which there were sounds of human existence. It had a nameplate declaring that the occupier was a warlock. Well, the warlock opened the door. There was not a thread on his robust body. I decided to respect his privacy and beat a retreat. Since everything about this man was so public, I am not sure that the word 'private' has any relevance in his case. A certain tolerance towards nudity was necessary for a sojourn in California. Girls came to the class in bikinis with surfboards under their arms. But they did not neglect to take notes from my lectures. I got the feeling that they attended lectures and went surfing with an equal degree of seriousness.

I remember one memorable evening when Joan Baez was singing on the campus, with a lone guitar. One of the songs she rendered was the famous song of the civil-rights activists: '*We shall overcome*'. It was a moonlit night. The words and the music flooded my consciousness. Yes, I said to myself, yes, you certainly will. Again, I was deeply impressed by California, notwithstanding the many negative things I had heard. Its innocence, its vast energy and eccentric joy in the act of living were things I had not come across anywhere else.

In 1969–70, I visited the USA a second time and taught at Pennsylvania and Harvard Universities for one semester at each place. At Harvard, I was allocated a room in the Widener Library.

It was a twofold privilege. The person I shared my office room with was Theodor Zeldin and an office in Widener meant a free access to its collections. The latter facility became a time-waster for me, but never have I wasted time more gloriously. And getting to know Zeldin also was a rare privilege. I soon found that his approach to history was completely original. It was not something anyone else could emulate. Harvard was rather unlike any other American university I had been to. The democratic openness and accessibility characteristic of all American universities were powerfully present here as well. You could pick up the phone and make an appointment with any member of its highly illustrious faculty and you would be asked to meet him or her for lunch. But in general, it was extremely individualistic, the famous and not so famous intent all the time on pushing forward their career as well as their research. I have never come across a less relaxed group of human beings. Small talk seemed to be virtually unknown. From my experience of other American universities, I felt encouraged to invite my very distinguished colleagues to dinner at home. When they came, I realized that they had never met before this outside faculty meetings. And the younger faculty could be a bit of a pain. Even on social occasions, they could not but indulge in high-powered academic discussion completely ignoring faculty wives if they happened to be non-academic. I realized that it was possible to attain great eminence intellectually and remain a barbarian or an egotistic child at heart.

In Pennsylvania I encountered an aspect of American life I had been spared until then, though later, during my fellowship at the Woodrow Wilson Center in 1993–94, I ran into it again and again. I am talking of the violence which lies under the surface of American urban life as an ever-present threat. First, the campus was at the heart of the inner city. We were warned to move cautiously if we came there in the evening. On one occasion I heard that there had been a rape followed by murder the previous evening at the centre of the campus. I had rented accommodation outside the city in the beautiful town of Swarthmore and used to come to the campus by train. One morning, I saw an African American boy of about twelve in our compartment who appeared to be sozzled. He had, rather ominously, a long knife stuck in his belt and was muttering words incomprehensible to me. Other passengers in the compartment looked scared and, for reasons I did not understand, they were looking at me somewhat furtively from time to time. The boy got off the train at one of the midway stations. Everyone seemed to heave a sigh of relief. One of my fellow passengers addressed me directly and said that I had had a narrow escape. For reasons unknown, the boy had taken a dislike to me and was threatening to kill me. If he had attacked, nobody would have tried to stop him. For that would have meant risk of death for the person trying to intervene. Walking through the streets of Philadelphia, I often had a glimpse of the inside of black people's homes. I have never seen such abject poverty outside India. Since this was the world's richest country, the sheer horror of that poverty was all the more overpowering.

Fatherhood and Reasons to be Happy

My visits to the UK and the USA interrupted for brief periods the tenure of my stay in Delhi. There was a lot of personal happiness in my life there. The university allocated for my use one of their beautiful houses in Cavalry Lines (named thus because the cavalry was stationed there in 1857). The house, which had a number of very big margosa trees, was located just below the Ridge, an extension of the Aravalli Range. The campus was one of the most beautiful parts of the city. Many of the buildings were part of the temporary capital created when the seat of government shifted from Calcutta to Delhi in 1911. The vice chancellor's office and the adjoining rooms which accommodated the university offices had originally been the viceregal residence where Mountbatten had proposed to his lady.

The Ridge was still a wild area with a lot of birds and animals, including deer, rabbits, peacocks and jackals. There was a hunting lodge from the pre-Mughal period and the flagstaff where British civilians had taken shelter during the 1857 rising. As late as the nineteenth century, British officials had hunted lions on the Ridge. It was a place of great charm, especially in the early morning when I went there for walks with my daughter who was only a few years old. She was absolutely delighted with the fauna, especially the rabbits and the peacocks. Once these very flamboyant birds obliged her by descending in a group of seven in our garden. These beautiful creatures were however not very friendly, with sharp beaks which they were ready to use without notice. But when they took flight simultaneously, it was a wondrous sight. I was a happy father living in a lovely, large house with my small daughter and very beautiful wife. We built up over the years a very fine garden which contained more than sixty varieties of roses. I bought a car from an innocent-looking economist. He assured us that he had never taken it to a garage for repairs. This was certainly true. To be fair, the car did occasionally move. But it needed help. Going up the ridge even on a low gear it would give up at some point. I carried some bricks in the boot for such occasions. These were put behind the rear wheels to stop the car from rolling back and then we had to appeal to the goodwill of my passengers and any passer-by who had the misfortune to be around. One hard push and we were again on our way. Many an eminent person, including V.K.R.V. Rao, were thus dragooned into pushing my car. My daughter, greatly embarrassed by this old lemon, which was a source of mirth to her fellow students in the primary school, used to advise me to sell it. She did not know that to do so her father would have to find someone more stupid than himself. That would not be an easy task. Given that there were so many things going for me, I should have been, and was in a way, a very happy man.

I did have some very good friends on the campus. Andre Béteille often accompanied me to late-night shows of Hindi films in low-down cinemas. I stopped going to this favourite haunt only after a fellow customer at the cinema tried to pick my pocket. If my limited worldly wealth was at such risk, could I relax and enjoy the pleasures of Bollywood? The Mughal cuisine offered by the cheap restaurants in and around Chandni Chowk, the kebab shops around the Jama Masjid, chat or snack shops of the Bengali Market and India Gate, the Chinese and Punjabi eateries in Connaught Place and the parathas served on dry lotus leaves in the Parathawali Gali, as also the world famous jalebis produced at the corner shop of that narrow street were sources of deep delectation. Often Andre and I would round off our journeys with a visit to a paan shop which rejoiced in the photograph of a customer—Rajendra Prasad, then the President of India. Here I used to indulge in kimam, a tobacco paste enhanced into an experience of paradise by the addition of various spices. Andre, who had never tried it before, once had a go. He swallowed the first mouthful of juice which is not advisable. It is alleged that thereafter he warned me that I should not take any more of this stuff because I was fading away. I have no memory of this perhaps because I had faded away.

Another good friend was Arjun Sengupta. There was a problem there. He was a bachelor at the time and his factotum, deeply suspicious of our motives and character, informed us whenever we called that the master was in the toilet. Either this was a ploy to fend us off or his master was more ill than we imagined. The great economists, our colleagues, were very busy men but they did have time for an occasional adda. The most realaxed of the lot from this point of view was Sukhamay Chakravarti who found in me a patient and interested listener to the outpourings of his encyclopedic knowledge. Chamu Srinivas was a neighbour and invitations to south Indian breakfasts in his house were very welcome. His two daughters, Lakshmi anf Tulsi were friends of my daughter as well as myself. After a visit to the USA, they had ceased to be pure vegetarians. They were allowed to have meat and fish at our house. But basically they remained vegetarians, Lakshmi once informed me, though they were occasionally allowed sausages. But what she liked best was steak. Lakshmi was a young lady of great culinary discrimination. Her father too was a strict vegetarian. When he came to lunch with us, he looked with barely disguised disgust at some of the dishes on the table. 'Is that fish?' he asked, his aversion hardly concealed. 'Cooked the Bengali way?' On receiving affirmative replies, he would say, the disgust still manifest in his tone, 'All right, let me have a piece.' In fact, he had several pieces.

The great concentration of resources and patronage in the capital had attracted a fantastic range of talents. Great musicians, writers, academics, actors, dancers and of course politicians and diplomats had been drawn to Delhi by the policy and munificence of the Central government. Some American scholars had settled near the campus. They had huge resources by our very modest standards and could afford to throw lavish parties which did, to some extent, alter our lifestyles. And there were parties in New Delhi—at the houses of diplomats, bureaucrats and politicians—at which we were frequent guests. On the campus, there were national and international conferences of very demanding standards as also lectures by very famous visiting scholars. At the New Delhi parties, we met some very worthwhile people who became good friends. Among them was Ebrahim Alkazi, director of the National School of Drama, and Hiranand Vatsyayan 'Agneya', probably the greatest writer in the Hindi language and his wife, Kapila Vatsyayan, a powerful bureaucrat and a great scholar. And the cultural life of Delhi was indeed rich. There were great musical soirées, plays, films, dance recitals, art exhibitions and all the usual components of a high culture one associates with an old civilization as well as a very important modern city. All in all, it should have been a full and happy life.

But it was not for me. My profound professional frustration began to produce physical symptoms. The human ambience of Delhi, despite my luck in having very good friends, I found almost stifling. Let me give a couple of examples to explain what I mean. Once, I ran into an old acquaintance at a musical soirée. He invited me to tea at his place. After a few minutes, he seemed rather restless. I asked him if he had any other appointment in which case he should feel free to leave. He apologized and said, no, he had kept the afternoon free for me. But I had not told him why I had come. I was mightily surprised and said he had asked me to tea. Yes, he said, that of course, but I had not told him the purpose of my visit. When I explained that I had no other purpose, it was his turn to be surprised. In Delhi, he explained, no one dropped by just to have a cup of tea. My acquaintance was a person of some influence and he was always willing to oblige.

On another occasion, in Chittaranjan Park, where I had built a house for myself, I had gone for a walk, when I saw a familiar name on a nameplate. I knocked at the door and the owner, a secretary to the government, opened the door. An old sinner from my days in the Constitution House, he was very pleased to see me. But again, the same question cropped up: why had I called? Just to see him, I explained. Come on, he said, I did not have to stand on ceremony with him. He would do for me anything possible within his remit. When I convinced him that there was no ulterior motive behind my visit, his amazement knew no bounds. In Delhi, people did not call on secretaries to the government just for the pleasure of a chat. To repeat, I found this social milieu stifling.

My life in Delhi University was not sheltered from the impact of happenings in the wider world. We were enthusiastic supporters of Mrs Gandhi in the first phase of her government and some of her close advisers were among our friends. Things began to change in 1969. The Congress government in West Bengal had become highly unpopular and was defeated at the polls by a coalition of leftist parties. A breakaway section of the Congress party was in that coalition. Their leader, Ajay Mukherji, became the chief minister of the state, but soon found it impossible to work with the left parties. When he resigned, Mrs Gandhi decided to impose President's rule on the state. This was strictly unconstitutional, but the lady was beginning to reveal her autocratic tendencies in a variety of ways. At her behest the governor, Dharma Vira, an old member of the ICS, dismissed the elected government. We were horrified. The senior members of our faculty, including Amartya Sen, Sukhamay Chakravarti and K.N. Raj demanded that I, as the director of the School, should call a protest meeting. I had my doubts about this. I, as an individual, was of course free to protest, but could I do so in my official capacity? Besides, could the premises of the School, a part of the Delhi University, an institution funded by the Central government, be used for a political action critical of the government.

Was this legitimate? I still have doubts about the correctness of our action but I went ahead and called the meeting. We used, of course, very severe language criticizing Mrs Gandhi's action. She had not stood forth as a dictator yet and our words and action did not attract any repressive measures. Be it said to her credit that later, when her Emergency, a legitimizing name for her acquisition of dictatorial power, provoked strong protest from members of the Delhi School, that too did not attract any repressive action. One explanation of such tolerance was simply that she did not feel that the academics could have any mentionable influence on public opinion. The politic thing to do was to let them be.

But my action did have some consequence for me. When two years of my directorship was over, I suddenly got a notice from the vice chancellor informing me that it had been decided to change the nature of the directorship. The period of incumbency was to be limited to two years, a new director being appointed at the end of the period from among the members of the faculty. This came as a surprise, because such a radical change had not been discussed in any of the decision-making bodies. Of course, the vice chancellor had the power to make such change and none of us objected. Later, I came to know that our vice chancellor, Dr B.N. Ganguli, a very good friend, had been constrained to take this decision owing to the pressure of the Hindu chauvinist party, BJS (Bharatiya Jana Sangh) which had just captured the Delhi municipality. They were still a long way from aiming at power at the Centre. But since they hoped to recruit activists from among the students and the faculties, they were not happy to see a person with radical sympathies at the head of the Delhi School of Economics. The decision to make the directorship and headships of department for two-year tenures was in effect a good one and I had no complaints. But it was not any concern for democratizing authority within the university that led to the change.

The finger exercises in a grim political game were being played out during the last years of my stay in Delhi. The Rashtriya SwayamSewak Sangh (RSS), ostensibly a cultural organization whose ideology projected the future of India as a Hindu state, was very probably implicated in the assassination of Mahatma Gandhi. His assassin, Godse, had left the RSS over differences regarding his preference for an openly political stand. But he went to the gallows with an RSS shloka on his lips. Its top leader, Guruji Golwalkar, was released after being kept in prison for some months. He was an open admirer of Hitler and his policy towards the Jews. In the case of India, read Muslims for Jews. The organization was banned for some time after the Mahatma's death and the RSS assumed a low-key posture for a period of years when legalized. But they were building up their political front, the BJS, and the student activist organization, the Akhil Bharatiya Vidyarthi Parishad (ABVP). The Delhi campus was a level ground where the ABVP fought for supremacy with the Youth Congress. Behind them, very interestingly, were two other forces—Coca Cola and Pepsi. Those who controlled the students union controlled the franchise for the supply of soft drinks to their cafeteria, a highly lucrative business. Hence the active interest of the two soft drink giants. There was little to choose between the two student organizations, except that anti-Muslim propaganda was no part of the Congress agenda. I forget the exact year when BJP captured the Delhi state, but they were steadily moving in that direction. There was no formal ban on RSS activities on the campus except that one was not allowed to further any political agenda in one's official capacity. We were aware that this wholesome convention was being ignored in practice.

All the professors were on the governing bodies of the constituent colleges as representatives of the university. On a visit of inspection, I found a very impressive map of India hanging in the office of a college principal. I lifted it admiringly. Behind the map of India was another, a map showing all the shakhas or branches of the RSS in the country. I told the principal that we were aware that he was the Sar-sanghachalak or top leader of the Delhi branch of the RSS, but we expected him to play his political role outside the college. As the BJS prospered, his fortunes steadily rose.

Back to the Department of History: Wonders of Academic Life in India

I felt that professionally, I had done what I could in the department of economics and it was time to move. In 1971, an opportunity opened up. A chair fell vacant in the department of history and I applied. On being selected, I moved to that department located in the Arts Faculty and was appointed head of the department. I had one foolish hope—that I would be able to build up a department of all talents, getting together people who would constitute a spectrum of ideological and methodological orientations. The development of historical research was dominated in India by one school of politically radical thought. The coexistence and clash of varied beliefs and approaches to history would, I hoped, stimulate fresh ways of looking at the subject. I had entirely misjudged the situation. There was a firmly entrenched group in the Indian academia, very reluctant to let in people they did not agree with. Hence my efforts did not succeed.

There was an unfortunate and very unhealthy convention in Delhi University in the matter of appointments to college posts. The head of the postgraduate department in the university virtually had the last word in all appointments in the subject. Since the final choice was from among equals, nobody could claim that his or her judgement in the matter was above criticism. The disappointed candidates were often very bitter and saw themselves as victims of injustice. This much makes perfect sense, but what some of them did was unacceptable in any civilized society. I started receiving dozens of abusive letters every morning. Their language was filthy beyond belief. When I took no notice of these letters, those who wrote them set up a cartel and sent out copies of this sustained abuse to all the two hundred teachers of history in the colleges. They almost flaunted their identity as a challenge almost to say, 'Let us see what you can do.' The only thing I could have done was to go to the police, but that was not on.

To date, I have not come across any academic institution free from cliques and pointless intrigues. And I would like to emphasize that what was happening was not typical of Indian universities or, for that matter, even Delhi University. The whole thing was organized by two very frustrated and sick individuals, incidentally both educated in England. One of them, much favoured by the establishment, went on to be a vice chancellor. They recruited a small number of their very young colleagues to help with the hostile propaganda. I have one tentative social explanation for their behaviour. I do not think it could have happened in any other Indian city. Delhi, since the Partition, did not have a stable local population with firm roots in the soil. The gracious tradition of the Mughal imperial culture, charming even in its decay, had been destroyed by the riots. The only 'settled population' consisted of the Punjabi refugees, an uprooted people who would take time to recreate their norms and social values. The Punjabi in his homeland was a person very different from his Delhi counterpart. They were a gracious, generous and very honourable people. The new dominant culture of India's capital was focused relentlessly on career building and short-term advantages, and nothing else. Uninhibited by the traditional values of Indian society, its motto was: 'Anything goes, so long as it serves your purpose.' In terms of public morality or good taste, you were not answerable to anybody, because there was no informal social authority to impose sanction. What I had to put up with was an extreme example of this value-free philosophy of life, of a total cultural and moral anomie. No one seemed to think that what was being done was particularly reprehensible.

It was around this time that the readership in South Asian history at Oxford fell vacant. Once earlier, when my teacher Colin Davis retired in 1961, Professor Basham had encouraged me to apply for the post. It then went to Dr Ballhatchet who was certainly the most suitable candidate for the post with its clearly stated emphasis on the teaching of eighteenth-century Indo-British history. When the university decided to take over the Indian Institute building constructed with money raised exclusively for the purpose of supporting Indian studies, he left in disgust and went to his chair in SOAS. The next incumbent was Dr S. Gopal. Later, he was an applicant for the chair in Commonwealth history and returned to India when that post went to Professor Robinson.

When the readership was advertised this time round, a large number of Indian historians applied for the post. I did not because I had come to believe that the post was for scholars specializing in British policy in India and that was very far from my areas of interest. Around this time Professor Eric Stokes came to India and I met him for the first time. It came to be known that he was on the electoral board for the post. He was entertained a great deal as all visiting scholars to India are. But whenever the host was known to be an applicant for the readership, a hearty guffaw went up in the senior common rooms of Indian universities. I am glad I did not ask him over to my place though no one in his senses would have believed that Eric could be influenced by such gestures.

On his return to the UK, Professor Stokes wrote to me asking if I would be interested in being considered for the post. I cabled back to say 'yes', but on certain conditions. I had by then served as a senior professor in a major Indian university for some six years. My decision to apply for a readership would be criticized in any case. But what I did not wish under any circumstance was to be known as a failed candidate at my age and in my situation. He could go ahead and propose my name only if he felt sure that it would be accepted. Some months later, I heard from Oxford that I had been elected. I felt an immense sense of relief. I was happy to go to Oxford. I was happier to be able to leave Delhi.

One final episode will explain why this was so. Not long before I left, a strange character joined my class. He was known to be an employee of the CID and had already appeared for the MA examination in one of the less reputable universities of northern India. (Note: This is a politically incorrect statement. In India, all universities are equal, only one is less equal than others.) When one of the college lecturerships fell vacant, this man applied on the strength of his first in MA at the other university. Shortly before the interview, he came to my house with a very large box of very expensive sweets. I did not accept these and told him that his efforts were pointless. I would not be the person at the interview. Who then, he asked. I was not going to tell him that.

Next day I received a phone call from my income tax officer. Was everything all right? Touched by this sudden concern for my welfare, I answered in the affirmative. His next question: 'Is there an interview for a college lectureship tomorrow?' 'Maybe,' I answered, 'but we are not supposed to discuss these matters with outsiders.' Now he broke into Hindi and said, 'You look after my problem, I shall look after yours.' I had no problems to the best of my knowledge and I told him so and put the phone down. My next move was to call the vigilance department. I had no choice. The poor fellow was cautioned and probably sacked in due course.

What the worthy from the Criminal Intelligence Department must have done was very simple. He found out who my IT officer was, discovered something fishy in his service record and threatened him with disclosure unless he could pressurize me to give him the job. The fellow's simple-hearted assumption was that everyone had something to hide and I could not be an exception. That, with the best of intentions, a university teacher had little opportunity to cheat on income tax would not occur to someone like him. His efforts did not work this time. It evidently did later. This worthy scholar who had had a lifelong private war with the Goddess of Learning and was almost illiterate eventually made it to a college lectureship in Delhi. He must have gone much further since then. With his other main job in the CID, besides occasional income from blackmail, he probably had a very comfortable life. How I wish I had accepted his sweets—they looked delicious. My refusal had no impact on reality. One of the sweets on offer was known as anmol rattan which means priceless jewel. What an apt description of the donor!

There was one final drama I had to witness before I left Delhi. The gentlemen who had organized the slanderous letter campaign now appeared in the role of patriotic defenders of national honour. I, a senior professor in a major Indian university, had accepted the lowly job of a reader in a foreign country and an imperialist country at that, merely out of a desire for a marginally more affluent lifestyle. For shame! Well, these very gentlemen had rejoiced when one of their numbers had committed a similar crime a few years earlier. But the ways of patriotism, like God's, are indeed mysterious.

Leaving home

I left Delhi for the UK on the evening of 20 January 1973. It was a dismal rainy day. Shortly before I left I received a call from Andre to tell me that his wife had just given birth to a girl, their first child. My mind was filled with a sudden sadness. I shall not see that child grow up, I thought. The people who worked for me, including the lady who had looked after my daughter, had gathered on the lawn of our house. She was crying, and at one point my daughter burst into tears. The children of the peon who lived in the quarters for Class IV staff behind our house had a surprised look on their face. They could not quite take in the fact that we were going away for good. I realized that leaving one's home in the full knowledge that this was for good was never easy. I had come to dislike Delhi. But there was so much here very dear to me—my friends, my garden, this house where I had lived for several years, the sheer beauty of the campus and the Ridge and the pleasures I had had in the varied eateries of the city.

There was something more, which went deeper. We had grown up in the forlorn hope that we would live to see India gain her independence. Delhi was the capital of that independent India, the independent India of our boyhood dreams. Despite the many frustrations I had suffered there—the death of our dreams of a healthy, altruistic, ethically correct state concerned for the welfare of the multitudes—the pulsation of power I felt in that city meant more to me than I realized. It was our capital, that power was ours and, despite myself, I had a certain pride in that corrupt, self-serving, heartless place. It was the metropolis of a great nation and that nation was us. How could I not feel a pang in leaving home and leaving this place which symbolized the hopes and aspirations of many millions.

16

Back at Oxford

Unhappy Beginnings

My sojourn in England as an employee of Oxford University started inauspiciously. The plane was late in reaching Heathrow. It was an evening in late January and already quite dark outside. To complicate matters, the immigration officer did not seem particularly pleased to see us. I had not expected to see any red carpets spread out to receive me but nor had I anticipated what actually happened.

There was one peculiar custom concerning the admission of people who came to the UK to work through legitimate channels. They had to have a medical examination in their country of origin by a doctor approved by the British embassy/high commission. A copy of the certificate was to be produced at the immigration. But no such prior health check was prescribed for the members of the family. They were to have a health check at the airport, at the discretion of the immigration officer. If the traveller happened to be British-born, this restriction did not apply to him/her even if he/she came from a place in the grip of a pandemic. He/she was evidently shielded from all risk of disease by the magic of his/her place of birth. To facilitate matters, we carried with us health certificates for my wife and daughter from the doctor recommended by the British high commission in Delhi. We produced all these documents. The immigration officer, a member of the British National Party judging by his behaviour, said quite bluntly, 'These papers mean nothing to me. I cannot do anything about your daughter because as a British-born person she has automatic right of entry. But your wife must have a health examination.' It was getting late and the man could not tell us when the doctor would come. My daughter began to cry. 'Stop her,' the immigration officer barked. 'You do that,' I told him in exasperation. Presently, the doctor came. He seemed highly embarrassed because he understood perfectly what was going on. He merely went through the gestures of an examination and declared my wife fit to enter the UK. The immigration officer grudgingly stamped our passports and we were at last allowed entry as holder of legitimate employment and family.

The people who had come to receive us had left by then. According to the restrictions on foreign exchange imposed by the Reserve Bank of India we had been allowed to buy only twenty-four pounds, at the rate of eight pounds per person. Since I would have 'a gainful employment' in the UK any amount beyond the permitted eight pounds was not available to us. With that very meagre sum in my pocket, I was forced to take a taxi hoping that the amount would be enough to pay for the fare. I had informed the university office that I should need some advance owing to the restrictions on foreign exchange in India and hoped that my problems would come to an end the next morning.

The accommodation the college had arranged for me came as another shock. It was a two-bedroom flat in an apartment block. The rooms were smaller than anything I had been used to and had not been cleaned properly. It was stone cold when we entered, because the heating had not been turned on. My heart sank when I saw this flat. Is this what I had come for leaving my very comfortable life in Delhi? The dons whose houses I had visited as a student at Oxford had a very different lifestyle, especially if they lived in college accommodation. Even as a student in Oxford I had never lived in such squalor. I had hoped to bring over my parents for a visit as soon as possible. There would be hardly any room here for them to stay. And then my fairly large collection of books was on its way. There was no possible way in which I could fit them in this diminutive accommodation. My first impulse was to send in a resignation letter the next morning and take the first available flight back to India. No, I had no intention of going back to Delhi, but finding a job in India would not be a problem. I murmured these very negative thoughts to myself. My wife overheard me and advised me not to act on an impulse.

I had indeed overreacted. My problem was not beyond solution. Next morning, I went and saw our bursar, a retired air vice marshal. He was very pleasant and accommodating. He assured me that a more spacious accommodation would be provided in a week or so in one of the houses owned by the college. The next port of call was the warden's office. I had read his book on Spain and had respect both for his very considerable scholarship and his elegant style. I found him easy-going and relaxed. He asked me a question I had not expected, 'What do you think would have happened if we (meaning the British) had not come to your country?' I told him what I honestly believed. He was posing a very large counterfactual: it was very difficult, if not impossible, to conjecture on that scale. One could think of at least a dozen alternative possibilities. But, I added, it seems fairly certain that there would be no unified Indian state. As a matter of fact there was not one in spite of the British intervention. Post-British India consisted of two states (which eventually became three).

Over the years I came to know Sir Raymond Carr (then a simple Mr) somewhat better. His rather eccentric and dishevelled exterior, it seemed to me, was the camouflage for a very shrewd and capable administrator. Ours was a body of very diverse and complex group of men and women and he managed us, without appearing to, very deftly. What amazed me about him was his apparently disorganized lifestyle which still provided the framework for profound scholarship. Once I asked him about this. He read very fast and started work very early in the morning, he said. By the time the offices were open, he had already put in several hours of scholarly work.

I had hoped that with the solution of the accommodation problem, I could now focus on my professional tasks. But I had to cope with an unexpected problem. My daughter Sukanya had been to school in three different cities in the USA and Australia. I had no reason to think that she would suffer from culture shock in Britain. But I was mistaken. I had put her in a public school which accepted day scholars. One morning she woke up very tearfully and said that she hated her school. The girls were very different from the fellow students she had known elsewhere. They laughed at her. One of them had asked if her father was a bus driver or the owner of a curry shop. The other girls did tell this young person off, but Sukanya found it hard to cope with this sort of behaviour. I suggested that she should give this school a try for a few more days. If she still felt unhappy there, I would try and move her to another school. If that too did not work, I would go back to India. After a few days she said that it was okay. But this was not quite true. She had a rather miserable time at this school, but never told us about it. Had I known the truth, her entry into adolescence would have been less fraught. After her O-level exams, she moved to the Oxford High School for Girls. There she found a very congenial environment.

My first few days at St Antony's reminded me of my first days in Balliol: nobody talked to me or took any notice of me whatsoever. This caused no culture shock because I had half anticipated something like this. Then one day, probably in the second week of my stay in Oxford, while we were queuing for lunch, one of our colleagues turned round and asked, 'Raychaudhuri?' I was relieved to find this first crack in the ice. Next, at the weekly governing body meeting, the warden with a vague gesture in my direction introduced me to the other members. This was all very reassuring. But from my American and London experiences I had half hoped that there would be a party to welcome newcomers, me included. No such luck. It dawned on me slowly that the high-table dinners and just the existence of the senior common room made such additional formalities unnecessary and I was quite content with that.

Only, I had formed a profound aversion for the governing body meetings from the very first occasion, a case of anything but love at first sight. I had had enough of academic administration in Delhi to last a lifetime and decided that I could make better use of my time at Oxford. The feeling that the governing body meetings were largely a waste of time was shared by others and over the years the number of meetings was reduced to a minimum. I spent my time at these meetings mainly in contemplating nature visible through the large floor-to-ceiling glass windows. The college had lovely gardens. I am aware that this passivity earned for me a very negative reputation as a man of limited intelligence ('keeps staring vacantly' is one comment I overheard) who also happened to be very awkward socially. But I was not going to give up the pleasures of marginalization in order to improve my image.

There was only one meeting of the governing body that I found rather amusing. Our college, for long a victim of old-fashioned patriarchy, used to have one ladies' night every term. The said evening had to be renamed when we elected a woman fellow. Spouses' night? What about any colleague whose sexual orientation was homoerotic? The term 'spouse' covered partners of the same sex. Not quite, since same-sex marriage was not yet legal in the UK. Who had talked of legality? The suggested new name was not 'legal spouses' night'. What about fellows and bedfellows? The bursar objected. The college could not afford that since some fellows were known to have more than one bedfellow. I do not remember how this terminological problem was solved.

My hope that at Oxford I would avoid administrative tasks was only half fulfilled. The emphasis on democratic consensus in all matters, which really provides only an outlet for the energies of those who care for that sort of thing, is a great bane of Oxford life. Before I knew where I was, I was a member of ten or more committees, which meant twenty to thirty wasted hours each term. I honestly believe that the Americans have tackled the relevant problem better, entrusting the varied administrative tasks to persons in an alternative stream of career within academe. It precludes amateurishness and saves time for those reluctant to get involved in administration. I am second to none in my love of democracy, but I enjoy it most when others are carrying out the relevant tasks. In India, the system in situ was oligarchic with democratic trappings. That underlying reality was not entirely absent in Oxford: there was a real establishment at the top, of course not designated as such, but they too were subject to checks and balances. Nobody could get away with being dictatorial.

There was however one great difference with Delhi. There the academic council meetings, an overly democratic institution, often assumed the form of a shouting match between the chair and the members, with no referee or umpire to settle the disputes. At Oxford, genuine and deep mutual dislike might lie just below the surface. But shouting? No, never. Only once on a very fraught occasion, I remember the warden saying at a GB meeting, 'Please, let us keep an even keel.' In an overpopulated country where simply to be heard one has to shout, shouting does not, in fact cannot, equal barbarism. Incidentally, in the British Parliament, a model to the rest of the world, shouting is tolerated so long as the language remains parliamentary. Probably, you can describe a person as 'born of unmarried parents' but never call him/her a bastard. Well, not quite. John Major made one exasperated reference to the Euro-bastards, but not inside the hall of Parliament. In the largest democracy on earth, fisticuffs are almost encouraged. In a hot country, when the debates become very dull, some entertainment and physical activity become necessary just to keep awake.

The Professional Life

As a don, I had three or four different identities at Oxford: a fellow of St Antony's College which provided me with food (free, for self and spouse, if we so wished), accommodation (for a modest payment) and membership of a community (free of charge though outsiders who came as associate members had to pay a fairly hefty fee); the reader in modern South Asian history (ever since the Partition of

India the words Indian history had been thus replaced even though India was a geographical, not a political, term; but the Pakistanis, many of whom would have preferred their country to be a part of Arabia, were allergic to the word 'India') earning my monthly salary from the university; and member of two faculties—modern history and Oriental studies, in which capacity I wasted a lot of time but gained nothing in return. Since the reader's room in the Indian Institute (to repeat, built with Indian money) had been taken away by the university, it had been replaced by one in the building where the faculty of Oriental studies was located. I was driven out of that one too in due course, but that is another story. Each of these three or four identities carried some administrative responsibilities which explained the ten committees and more than thirty meetings per term I was expected to attend. I confess, some of these I never attended. I was encouraged in this by an eminent colleague who in his many years as a don had never attended any meeting of one of these august committees, though he was very active in the governing body.

My physical presence in the Oriental Institute building where I usually had my eleven o'clock coffee, unless I was at the Indian Institute Library on top of the New Bodleian, led to a close acquaintance with colleagues in that faculty. I shared directly the interests of the Indologists who thereby became good friends. Among the people I got to know was Mr Hulin, who was very grateful for the kindness he and his family had received while touring India. He was not very popular with some of our colleagues. He told me that his children fell seriously ill on their return from India, even though for six weeks they had consumed nothing but tea and bananas. I pointed out that very probably their illness was not in spite but because of that dietary regime. He had a house on Boar's Hill with nameplates in English and cuneiform describing the building as Shalmanezar's Palace. The cuneiform tablet had been collected from the site of the excavation. The Palace contained an elaborate toy railway system which snaked through all the rooms. I was bemused to discover that at Oxford, Egypt was treated as a part of the Orient. This was the Egypt of the Pharaohs, mind you, not the country's modern, Arab version.

I wondered why the Greek islands to the east of Egypt were not considered a part of the Orient. I was later to discover that at the Australian National University, Indian studies were a part of the Pacific studies. Why not? After all, the waters of the world's oceans are not divided by boundary lines. In fact, at St Antony's where most of the teaching and research was entrusted to mutually exclusive 'centres', India was allocated to the Centre for Far Eastern Studies. The French described their possessions in Indo-China as extreme Orient. Including India in the Far East was merely a shade more extreme. When Richard Story, the very famous historian of Japan was about to retire, he suggested to the governing body that I should take over as director of the Far East Centre. A colleague who had forgotten the mysterious arrangements mentioned above asked how I, a reader in South Asian history, could take charge of Far Eastern studies. 'Karma,' I explained. Being unconvinced by Hindu cosmology, he was evidently not satisfied.

As a graduate student in the 1950s, I had found that modern Indian studies were totally isolated from everything else in the university. There were a number of research students, mostly Indian and Pakistani, working with Colin Davis and a few undergraduates who had opted for the special paper on Warren Hastings. These were the limits of modern Indian studies. The isolation remained unbroken in the next two decades. Dr Gopal, my predecessor, found the special paper on Warren Hastings somewhat obsolete, and got it removed from the syllabus. It was not replaced by anything else. This meant that when I came to Oxford, I had no undergraduate teaching to do. In fact, except for a couple of research students, I had no clearly assigned academic duties. I wondered whom I should deliver my statutory twelve lectures per term to and on what themes. Well, I sought to solve that problem in a ramshackle manner and set about the task of introducing a new special subject. I also decided to try and establish links between Indian studies and other cognate fields.

Professor Robinson, professor of Commonwealth history, proved to be a great help and advised that I should include in my list of prescribed documents a large quantity of state papers in order to secure the approval of the more conservative members of the board of studies. It might be relevant here to quote a memorable statement from one of the more influential members of that board. 'You underemployed professors and readers who teach specialized subjects like Russia, India, Africa or China have no idea as to what most students want. They wish to study general subjects, like the medieval English Parliament.' Quite. The Speaker's function in the said Parliament was absolutely central to any serious knowledge of history. It was in fact the centre point of all humanistic disciplines. Well, eventually I drew up a syllabus focused on a phase of the encounter between the Raj and Indian nationalism. It included some of Gandhi's activities. Some students had heard his name (usually spelt Ghandi) and that would help. The list of prescribed documents did contain a heavy dose of state papers. Since the Raj was popularly known in India as the Kaghazi Raj, a regime based on (and producing an unlimited quantity of) papers, this posed no problem. That satisfied the demands of serious scholarship. What more could one wish for? The syllabus was duly approved.

My second line of effort took the form of starting with the help of colleagues, seminars which would cover more than one region, including India, sorry, South Asia. Being a member of St Antony's, I was in an ideal position to do this. The Far East Centre, soon renamed the Asian Centre, was the ideal location for seminars dealing comparatively with several countries as also the subject of cultural encounters. I also became an active participant in the seminars on comparative economic history and Commonwealth history. Mark Elvin's work on Chinese economic history was theoretically and methodologically of great interest to me. I did borrow some of his theoretical formulations for my chapters in the *Cambridge Economic History of India*. Patrick O'Brien and Christopher Platt, both economic historians (the latter was professor of Latin American history), were also very supportive. But during my first year of employment at Oxford I had to live with the basic fact that I had no prescribed course to lecture on. To fill the gap, I offered to teach Bengali. This was taken up by Professor Gombrich, the

Boden professor of Sanskrit, and some of his students. Bengali being a 'daughter language' of Sanskrit, they picked up a fair amount of Bengali with ease in a short time. Later, when a Centre for Indian Studies was established at St Antony's for a few years with a grant from the Government of India, we could arrange for the teaching of a number of modern Indian languages on demand.

The said centre during its short life could bring over eminent Indian scholars in a wide range of subjects as also writers, great musicians, dancers and film-makers. My object was to stimulate an awareness of India and interest in research in various areas of enquiry concerning its past and present. I believe the effort did not fail entirely. At one point in time, the special subject on India attracted the largest number of undergraduates in the history faculty. When Professor Judith Brown took charge as professor of Commonwealth history and was later joined by my successor, Dr David Washbrook, the popularity of this special subject increased further.

From the second year of my employment, I began to lecture on the new special subject and the more general theme of imperialism and nationalism. This was a satisfying experience. Even more interesting for me was the class where students read their comments on the 'gobbets' or selected extracts from the documents. From the beginning, it was clear to me that even those who came to the subject without any previous knowledge had clearly articulated ideas on the subject, determined largely by their social background or the ideologies to which they had been exposed. Most of them had been brought up in the unquestioning belief that the Empire was a good thing and that the British in India had played a civilizing role. They were aware that India had a civilization of sorts, but it was encrusted with superstition, irrationality and barbarous practices besides incurable poverty, a part of the long-term state of things. The Raj had done its best to improve things, but still there was a long way to go. I never questioned these beliefs directly, but simply encouraged the students to read the documents and the secondary literature and come to their own conclusion. Later, when my very good friend, Professor Judith Brown was appointed professor of Commonwealth history, she kindly agreed to take this class on documents jointly with me. This proved interesting, because while my regard for her historical scholarship was genuine, our perceptions of modern Indian history were not identical. The students, I hoped, benefited from the insight that one can derive very different conclusions from the same set of documents. A small number of students had at some point acquired radical ideology. The infrequent debates between them and the believers in imperial beneficence added colour to these classes. I had always enjoyed teaching. The system in Oxford which allowed scope for exchange of ideas with the students was more satisfying than anything in my previous pedagogic experience.

I was soon invited by *The Historical Journal* published from Cambridge to write a review article on the growing literature which dealt with indigenous politics in India under the Raj. There was a background to this. A group of young scholars at Cambridge, led by their mentors, Professor Gallagher and Dr Anil Shil, had developed a highly interesting thesis regarding the structure and dynamics of Indian politics under colonial rule. A volume of essays and a number of monographs encapsulated these ideas. They did not speak with the same voice, but nevertheless they came to be described as 'the Cambridge School' ignoring the serious objection of the people involved. I found their central thesis insightful and rewarding. The Raj, they wrote, was based on the active cooperation or acquiescence of the majority of politicized Indians. The Cambridge historians explained how that cooperation worked. It was necessarily an interest-based explanation. The nationalist rejection of cooperation was also explained in similar terms. This caused great outrage among Indian historians who attacked the central thesis as a continuation of the old imperialist perception of Indian nationalism as the ideology or rather the strategy of a cynical few trying to lead the loyal masses into the path of sedition. In my review article I stated my reasons as to why I found the new thesis an ingenious and acceptable explanation of the political cooperation on which the Raj was based, but also why one could not accept the thesis that rejection of cooperation and militant nationalism were simply the other side of the same coin.

I soon heard that my essay had been taken as an attack on the Cambridge historians. To be frank, I was mortified. I liked and respected these colleagues. Gallagher was a good friend. The last thing I wanted to do was to attack them. I would have no hesitation in attacking someone like Niall Ferguson, whom I consider a propagandist for imperialism rather than a serious historian, but the Cambridge historians were a very different kettle of fish. They were neither propagandists for any empire nor blind critics of Indian nationalism, though quite cynical about it as about many other things in history. I had recorded my views in the honest belief that criticism of a historical argument would be taken as such and never thought that it would be interpreted as an attack on anybody, especially a personal one. I discovered that this essay, taken with my criticism of my good friend Morris, had earned me the reputation of being a person who attacked other scholars. This is the last thing I wished for but there it was. My one consolation was that Eric Stokes in his review essay on the literature on modern Indian history described me as a person holding moderate rather than extreme views.

I saw no reason to modify my central belief that all empires were built around a hard core of evil, the cynical self-interest of small groups in an alien society seeking to profit from the weakness of other people. I use the term 'evil' to indicate things which caused a great deal of misery to multitudes of human beings not counterbalanced by the limited welfare that followed from orderly government. The Belgian king's notorious comment that he had heard Japan was a wealthy country and would like to lay hands on that wealth is matched by Clive's equally atrocious statement pointing out how the revenues of Britain had been enhanced by his acquisition of territories in eastern India. This sums up the central motivation of imperialism. Incidentally, Clive never claimed that the conquest had conferred any benefit on the conquered and his successor, Warren Hastings, spoke very openly of the harm the British had done to the conquered races. But that does not mean that two hundred years of governance by a highly civilized country conferred no benefit at all on the subject people. Even in their own interest, the rulers had to fatten the calf they wished to slaughter for their table. Only on one point there should be clarity of perception. The empire was not about the welfare of the subject people, even though some benefit did accrue from it. And Gandhi's belief that ruling over other people was fundamentally degrading for the conqueror also reflects a true insight.

I discovered repeatedly at Oxford that with rare exceptions, most people in Britain believed that the Raj was of great benefit to Indians. A Labour supporter among our colleagues, a brilliant historian, told me of the comparative beneficence of the British Empire, that had it been any other nation, the transfer of power would have been a bloody process. I pointed out that it was indeed a very bloody process, though the British managed to save their skins. Some half a million people died in the Partition riots, largely because Mountbatten, contrary to his promise, virtually withdrew from the task of maintaining law and order, sending the war-worn army personnel back to the UK while India burned. No comparable concern was shown for the welfare of the armed forces in fighting a long war of attrition against the insurgents in Malay or when the British army was deployed to help the Dutch to regain their lost empire in South-east Asia. A bursar, who had risen from the shop floor to the post of manager of a nationalized industry, once asked me what we had gained by becoming independent. I saw little point in throwing statistics at him, but talked very briefly of the increased longevity as also rise in literacy and per capita income. I could see from his expression that he did not believe me. I added a question which was certainly not to his liking. I asked if he believed that the Japanese today were far more efficient in every way than the British and he answered 'Yes'. In answer to my next question as to how he would feel if the Japanese took over the administration of the UK, he had no answer.

I found that even my radical colleagues had not really heard about the Bengal famine of 1943 which took three million lives. When told about it, some of them did not see what the government of the day had to do with the calamity. One famous historian told me on his return from a first visit to India that he had never heard of Britain's exploitative role in India until then though he had studied the history of Britain and her empire at Oxford. The climax of this empire worship was a poster outside the room of a colleague in another college. It read something like 'It takes a great mind to appreciate a great empire.' I knew that such people existed but had not expected to encounter one of them in an Oxford faculty. As the possessor of a very small mind, I felt duly humbled. The possessor of a great mind, it appeared, had taken a dislike to me. When I presented a paper at the Commonwealth history seminar on race relations under the Raj, he came and stretched himself on the floor: one was expected to take this as a joke I suppose. I thought that to enhance the jocularity of the situation he would fart loudly at any moment. He did not, for reasons unknown. The series was on race relations in various parts of the empire. After the famous Africanist Terence Ranger presented his paper, someone in the audience remarked very audibly, 'Who was responsible for appointing such a person as a professor at Oxford?'

I came across an extreme example of conservative attitudes to empire during the debate on the question of conferring a degree, honoris causa, on Mrs Thatcher. One of the pillars of the establishment made a statement which I found quite incredible. Explaining the savage cuts in the education budget which had severely damaged science education in particular, the famous academic said, with a distinct tremor in his voice, 'Our glo-o-o-rious empire is no more.' There were two problems about this lament. First, a substantial section of the congregation, consisting of people with master's degrees of the university, did not have any share in the glo-o-o-rious empire, but were among its victims. Secondly, this was the first time I heard a conservative historian acknowledge that Britain had profited from the empire: the empire, we had been told all along by their likes, was a pure exercise in philanthropy whereby the benefits of a high civilization were conferred on the less enlightened people of the world. Material gain? Really! How could one even think of such a thing!

Over the years, I repeatedly met highly intelligent and very learned people who had a deep faith in the beneficence of the British Empire. With that went a somewhat simplistic view of the relations between the two people, the British and the Indian. After Attenborough's film on Gandhi was screened, I came across a spectrum of responses to it. The evening I went to see the film, I had the impression that the audience was stunned by what they saw and left the hall in pin-drop silence. One of my eminent colleagues said that he did not know about the brutal oppression shown in the film. I referred him to Lord Listowel's book, *India under the Lathi*, about the suppression of the Civil Disobedience movement in the 1930s, under a Labour government. Amazingly, no one, I repeat no one, I met at Oxford seemed to have read the book. Some ladies we met at a party asked us if the scenes like the massacre at Jallianwala Bagh were not imaginary, introduced to dramatize the story. One don commented that Dyer was justified in his action because the Sikhs at the meeting were carrying daggers and spears. But for Dyer's action there would have been a violent rising. Much later, I met a daughter of Sir Michael O'Dwyer, the governor of Punjab at the time of the troubles, at Nirad Chaudhuri's house. She was planning to write a book on her father's administration of the province. She had just received enlightening information from Nirad Babu and was delighted with it. 'I have just learnt that Gandhi was a bania by caste. That explains a lot. The British were in India to do good to the Indians. A bania used to wheeling and dealing could not possibly understand that.'

Another charming lady I met at a gathering of old India hands was the daughter of an ICS officer who had been the district magistrate of Midnapore for some time: three of his predecessors had been killed by the revolutionaries. 'Within a week of his arrival in the district headquarters my father had as guests at his table the local leaders of the Indian National Congress,' she proudly explained. This family legend on which she had evidently been brought up seemed an unlikely story to me, because in Bengal, especially in the 1930s, British district magistrates were not in the habit of socializing with Indians, particularly Congressmen. The situation in the provinces where the Congress formed governments in 1937 was somewhat different. When the lady asked me about my background, I mentioned my nationalist connections and the fact that we had participated in the Quit India movement. She was deeply embarrassed and apologized.

I saw in this response two unrealistic assumptions. First, most if not all Indians were loyal admirers of the Raj who would appreciate the attitude of a decent-minded English district magistrate. Second, if they happened to be connected with militant nationalism in any way, they must bear in their hearts an undying hatred of the British and their rule, the two being inextricably linked. I asked her if she, as a British citizen, bore any hatred towards the German people with whom Britain had fought two devastating wars. She saw what I had in mind. I went on to explain that Indian nationalism had never preached hostility towards the British people. The struggle was for bringing to an end a situation unacceptable to us. This had been achieved. A residue of hostility would be highly unlikely. That is not how the human mind worked. Besides, the educated Indian was deeply imbued with Western culture channelled through Britain, unfortunately not under the most congenial of circumstances. Rejecting Britain would mean rejecting a large part of oneself. That was not possible.

I have often wondered how highly intelligent and very decent people can see nothing but good in the domination of one nation over another. My long stay in Oxford, a major centre of empire worship, gave me some insight into this apparently unlikely phenomenon.

Our very good friend, Lady Penelope Betjeman, an amateur Indologist and in every sense a friend of India, knew Sir Michael O'Dwyer, a major figure in the nationalist demonology of the empire, when she was a child. She said that he was a kind but stern old man, an epitome of ideal Victorian fatherhood. To him, all Indians were children, only some of whom were incredibly naughty, had to be shut up in dark rooms and occasionally chastised with rods (read lathis, whips and, in extreme cases, guns). For the rest, a benign sternness, strong government in other words, was all that was required—a government stern but just, and at heart not unkind in their own eyes. I have no difficulty in believing that Sir Michael was a kind and good man, only unbelievably vain and obtuse. Many a Victorian father must have been just that. And unless one was a person of exceptional intelligence, like Penelope, one could not possibly see this man as a part and instrument of something innately evil. Catching totally innocent young men, tying them up on frames at crossroads and whipping them, being careful to choose only those who could take it, seemed to him a perfectly just dispensation. No, he did not order these things, but the military authorities who did had his full approval.

Incidentally, Penelope was the daughter of Lord Chetwode, commander-in-chief of the Indian army and a romantic hero of the First World War. She grew up in the house which later became Nehru's official residence as prime minister of India. She went back to India every year to roam around on horseback in the Kulu Hills, her favourite haunt. She died at the beginning of one such intended journey. She got off her horse, lay down on the hilly ground and her heart stopped. What an appropriate end to a wonderful life! She once showed me something which underlined the comic (as also the very dishonest) side of the Raj. She was wearing a gold bangle made of third-century Gupta coins. It was a gift from Sir John Marshal, the very famous director general of archaeology in India, associated with the excavation of the prehistoric ruins of Mohenjo-Daro and Harappa. Sir John was courting Penelope at the time. She jilted him, a just retribution it seems, for courting one's lady with stolen goods.

Many of the good people I met, who took a pride in the imperial record, were descended from persons who made and sustained the empire, successful members of the professional classes. They must have been brought up on stories of their ancestors' selfless service to the Raj, the purity of their idealism and their total personal rectitude. To such men and women, the empire could not be anything but a noble edifice. If their ancestors had been involved in anything particularly nasty, either they did not know anything about that or had heard only highly bowdlerized versions of the event. My very good friend, Richard Symonds, was in charge of rehabilitation during the Bengal famine of 1943. He told research students who interviewed him that the relief measures were inadequate but I doubt if he described to anyone in England the horrors he had seen, or talked about the incredibly stupid errors of which they were the result. An ancestor of another good friend, an aficionado of Indian literature, was the central figure in a nineteenth-century cause célèbre. He had kicked a Bengali gentleman and declared that one should first kick a Bengali and speak to him only after that. Indian journals had a field day publishing satirical poems on the episode. I do not think that my good friend had even heard of this grotesque event.

The art of brushing uncomfortable facts under the carpet is well developed in this country and the establishment is the ultimate past master in that art. I think you need such skills to continue to have any faith in your own human decency if you rule a worldwide empire for some two hundred years. Only the totally stupid can turn a blind eye to the many acts of cruelty and the coarsening of sensibilities which subsumes racial arrogance without some psychological device to help one live with these negative realities. To repeat, there is a strand of profound stupidity in the beliefs and attitudes that sustained the Raj but the British with their many achievements down the centuries were of course neither a stupid nor an insensitive people. Imperial idiocy was a necessary part of a very necessary psychological defence mechanism. Incidentally, the importance of sheer stupidity as a major force in history is an idea I got from Jack Gallagher. The great majority of the British people have no knowledge of the nastiness that was the empire and hence have no difficulty in taking pride in its record.

One more thing. I had a brief taste of what a record of domination, cultural or political, may mean to an individual. In Den Pasar airport, Bali, a Hindu territory, the immigration officer asked me if I was a Hindu. I answered 'yes' and he greeted me with the Sanskrit expression, *swastim astu*, peace (or well-being) be with you. This cultural indicator of influence spread over many centuries filled me with a sense of pleasure. What of people who see and hear their language used wherever they go? It would be inhuman not to feel proud. We Indians take great pride in the alleged fact that our cultural influence spread to remote corners of Asia without any act of conquest. Not true. The Cholas conquered large chunks of Southeast Asia. The Bengalis are very proud of the fact that Prince Vijaya Simha, a Bengali according to one view, conquered Simhala, Ceylon, in remote antiquity. The story of his conquest, one of ghastly betrayal and cruelty, has never been taught in any school in Bengal or India. People prefer to remember ancestral glory, not the monstrosities perpetrated by men whose genes are in your bloodstream. Empire worship comes naturally to the privileged classes in Britain. The underprivileged whose blood was shed to build that empire, the children of the sailors, the soldiers and the petty clerks who had a horrid time in remote and unbearably hot countries, living on a pittance and suffering from sexual deprivation and syphilis, gaining hardly anything in return has been brainwashed into believing that the Raj was a matter of pride and profit for them too.

Colleagues and Friends

Perhaps what really enhanced the quality of my life at Oxford was getting to know some of our colleagues fairly intimately. I cannot go into that experience without sounding sycophantic, but let me try. Professor Robinson, Robbie to his friends and colleagues, professor of Commonwealth history, was a much decorated bomber pilot in the Second World War. His war experiences had made him cynical and one got the impression that he had suffered as a young person because of his working-class background. His father was an unemployed worker during the Depression and this had meant serious hardship in his childhood. As an undergraduate at Cambridge, he had adopted an artificial accent, but nobody was fooled by it, he told me. He had an instinctive dislike of people with a 'fruity accent' as he put it. I found his cynical wisdom attractive—it equipped him to cope with the many problems of his life. During the war his plane was shot down in North Africa. Robbie survived, because his parachute got entangled in the branches of a tree. He was eighteen when this happened and still a virgin. He thought with good reason that he was going to die. His one wish in the face of death was that if he survived, he would like to 'know women', in the Biblical sense of the term. He spent his whole working life as an Oxbridge don, but his respect for these two institutions was strictly limited. He did not think much of academic activity either but took a certain pride in his own capacity for objectivity. His views on the economic motives behind free trade had undergone a 180-degree turn from the days he and Gallagher wrote their seminal essay, 'Imperialism of Free Trade', to the time when they published their equally seminal *Africa and the Victorians*. He took some pride in this because it proved his capacity to see straight, his pragmatism, which is one of the few things he considered worthwhile. I did not agree with his perceptions of empire (his understanding of 'economic motive' I found rather restricted) but benefited from his philosophy of life, the lesson that it was silly to take anything too seriously. Oddly enough, despite his genuinely radical sympathies he had some attachment to the idea of empire. He considered the Falklands War justified though he, like me and millions of others, did find Mrs Thatcher revolting. 'Do you think we could not have held on to India?' he once asked me. 'You surely could have for some more time, may be even a decade or two,' I answered, 'but at the cost of a great deal of bloodshed.'

One of the persons whose company I enjoyed most was Richard Story whose views on virtually everything were the polar opposite of all that I believed in. It was his bonhomie and love of life that I found very attractive. He was a great lover of Charleston, a vigorous dance from the days of his youth, and would perform it with gusto at the least provocation though his moderately bulky body was something of a hindrance. Besides, there were not many left who were adept in that challenging art form. I certainly never saw his wife, Dorothy join him in this terrifying entertainment.

Dick, with my friend Hugh Toye, worked for Military Intelligence during the war. He never talked about that experience. Hugh was in charge of debriefing the Indian National Army prisoners. This task induced in him a great admiration for the leader of that army (he was one of the very few British scholars who had an appreciation and understanding of Indian nationalism)—Netaji Subhash Chandra Bose and he wrote a remarkably fine biography of the man. Its title read *The Springing Tiger*, a description of the symbol on the INA flag. A book with such a title, written by Colonel Toye, was appropriately classified under 'Hunting' in the Indian Institute Library. Dick turned his scholarly attention to Japan and became one of the best historians of that country.

One evening, at dessert following the high-table dinner, after more than an advisable quantity of port had been consumed, Dick explained to me his philosophy of life: 'Whenever it is not necessary to change, it is necessary not to change.' There is a justly famous sketch of a dinosaur on the wall of an Oxford building with a gentle admonition in graffiti: 'Remember the dinosaur.' It refused to change, a very appropriate piece of advice to traditional Oxford. I drew Dick's attention to that admonition. Now he was really furious. 'Dinosaurs? Dinosaurs!' he almost spluttered. 'You think they fared badly? They ruled the planet for 160 million years by refusing to change one bit. It was only an unfortunate meteor that wiped them out or else they would still be here. And homo sapiens? Sapiens indeed. They are already on their way out after a few million years thanks to their monkeying with nature. Our sensible cousins, the chimps, did no such things. Have you ever heard of a chimp making a nuclear bomb? They are far too sensible. Come and see me in hundred and sixty million years, if your degenerate species is still around.' I share his pessimism regarding our degenerate species and look forward to our appointment in 160 million years. Only, Dick has left neither address nor any phone number. How I wish he had.

I was walking down Woodstock Road one morning when a colleague told me of Dick's death. I instinctively turned round and was about to set out for his home. My colleague was embarrassed and told me that in England only immediate family gathered together at times of bereavement. I had not learnt this despite my long sojourn in England. I recalled the preferred style of death in the middle ages when the dying person orchestrated the drama of final departure before a large audience. And I also recalled the Indian practice where it is expected that you call when a friend or relation died. Later, when Dorothy had come to terms with her grief to some extent, I told her that I was about to call on her when I heard of Dick's death. She kept quiet for a moment and said, 'I wish you had called.' 'How could I? It is not your custom,' I said. 'Who cares?' she responded, 'It would have pleased Dick, wherever he was, and comforted me. He was very fond of you.' Dorothy lived long enough to suffer a gratuitous tragedy. Her son, a skiing instructor, was killed in a climbing accident. She bore her pain with fortitude, but her heart was broken.

The list of colleagues whose friendship enhanced the quality of my life would be long. Looking back, what strikes me is the great variety in their personalities: Theodore Zeldin, the maverick historian, who was uncompromisingly original in his approach to historical enquiry, exploring phenomena like happiness and intimacy on a global scale; Mark Elvin with his intense and almost aggressive approach to the study of the Chinese past; Tony Kirk-Greene, who came from the colonial civil service and could have been a very decent and capable member of the Indian Civil Service; Christopher Platt, who had offered to start a journal in cooperation with me but withdrew, discouraged by my reputation as one who attacked people; the very gentle and civilized cousin of Edward Said, Albert Hourani, the world authority on the intellectual history of modern Arabs, with whom I had seriously planned to do a study of occidentalism, that is, the Asian perceptions of the West, a book which would have materialized but for his untimely death; and Richard Symonds, whom Gandhi had befriended.

The list could go on and on. I wonder if I could have met so many different types of personalities in one small place in any other country. The individualism, often of an eccentric variety, encouraged by Britain's social culture, perhaps explains this great variety. I remember with pleasure the long talks I had with Theodore on various dimensions of Indian culture, his many questions of which I could only answer a few. His curiosity encompassed the totality of man's past. I understand he was also well read in the sciences, but we never discussed that side of his intellectual interest, owing no doubt to my total ignorance of that area of knowledge. Richard Symonds wrote a fine book on Oxford and the Empire. He called me his 'godfather' because I sponsored him for an associate membership at St Antony's several times. A Quaker, he went to India with Alexander who later became Gandhi's adviser during the negotiations for transfer of power. Richard was a UN adviser in Kashmir and wrote a book on the Partition of India which is popular in Pakistan but not in India because it traced the origins of the Kashmir problem to some repressive actions of the Dogra maharaja. This is no part of the Indian canon on the subject. Richard was no imperialist but he did have an admiration for the Raj and all that it stood for. It was too soon to judge the British Empire in India, he used to tell me. Maybe he was right. I last saw him at an informal dinner on my eightieth birthday which the college had generously organized. He died a few days after that. Christopher Platt also died prematurely in consequence of an accident.

I have reasons to be grateful to my colleague, Professor Judith Brown who succeeded Robbie as professor of Commonwealth history. I understand that the two bits of good fortune which came my way in the last year of my tenure at Oxford, a DLitt degree and a chair ad hominem owed much to her support. Her three books on Gandhi will long remain the standard historical texts on the subject because while books on Gandhi are plentiful, these are the only ones, to my knowledge, which can claim to be based on detailed documentary research. Her political biography of Nehru also deserves to be read with respect. I do not agree with her approach and many of her conclusions, but cannot be blind to the great value of her scholarly achievement. Similarly, while as a non-believer, I have perspectives on life and death which are totally different from hers, I do admire the grace of her very Christian personality. While I fail to see any objective truth underlying religious belief, I have repeatedly come across men and women whose lives have been deeply enriched by faith.

I was privileged to meet the very famous Sir Ernst Gombrich through his son, my friend Richard, the Boden professor of Sanskrit. On that occasion I was accompanied by the famous Bengali writer Nabaneeta Dev Sen. The lady, who was a bit short on social inhibition, decided to indulge her childhood hobby, collecting autographs, tore out a page from an exercise book and requested Sir Ernst for an autograph. The great man obliged and asked her in genuine surprise how she had heard about him, because he knew nothing about India. Nabaneeta replied, 'Sir Ernst, perhaps you do not know that you are not entirely unknown in the wider world.' Sir Ernst looked genuinely surprised.

Oxford provided me with one of the most unlikely encounters of my life. My friend, Simon Digby, world authority on India under the sultanate, had organized a party for Mrs Mildred Archer who had been awarded a DLitt degree for her authoritative work on Company Paintings, that is, the pictures and prints on India produced during the days of the East India Company. Mildred's husband, Mr Archer of the ICS, had produced a vast amount of high quality research on the folk art and tribal life in India. Both husband and wife were very interesting individuals. Mr Archer introduced himself in the most unusual way: 'You must have heard of me. I am Archer the Butcher.' I had certainly heard of him, I replied, but not of his reputation as a butcher. He explained that in Bihar, where he was posted, that was his reputation. This was due to an incident in 1942. The Quit India movement there was gathering strength. The activists had surrounded the collectorate. A ten-year-old boy was climbing up the flag staff to tear down the Union Jack and replace it with the Congress tricolour, later to become, with slight modification, India's national flag. The English superintendent of police advised Archer, then the district magistrate, that if the boy succeeded, this would be the signal for a violent rising as far as the flag could be seen and it would be extremely difficult to control it. Archer felt constrained to authorize the firing. He said he remembers the frail body of the ten- year-old falling to the ground in a curve. He added that the scene kept coming back to him in nightmares almost every night. I have rarely felt more sorry for any man. This sensitive and compassionate human being was also a victim of the empire. Soon after his retirement, he committed suicide. Nobody knows why.

When Mrs Archer heard that I was from East Bengal she asked me which district I came from. Barisal, I replied. Her brother was for some time the district magistrate of Barisal, she said. Frank Bell was the name. I knew Mr Bell, I told her. How? Well, he sent me, my brother and my father to prison in 1942–43. Mildred looked embarrassed. No reason for embarrassment, I assured her. It was all in a day's work, what Frank Bell had done to us. In fact we had gone into the movement expecting much worse. About a month later, I received a letter from Frank Bell, asking if it was true that he had sent me to prison. I wrote back mentioning my father's name and our role in the Quit India movement. Yes, now he remembered, he wrote in reply.

I invited Bell to speak to our South Asian history seminar. He accepted my invitation with some alacrity. I did not know him personally, but had seen him on the streets of Barisal several times. An inexperienced young man, he was very anxious about the civil defence against the Japanese and wanted to make sure that everything necessary was being done. I saw him now after some forty years. He looked old and worn out. Life had not been very kind to him after he left India. I felt a little sorry for him. He was at some pain to explain how he had acted within the law in all he did to us. I assured him that as nationalist cadres, we had no grudge against him. We got what we expected, in fact less. I did not add that his action in reducing by 75 per cent our allowance from our estate, then in the hands of the court of wards, was not legal, strictly speaking, nor was the charade of a criminal case against the political prisoners on charges of rioting inside the jail. I got the impression that he really did not know what his underlings had done inside the prison. I saw no point in enlightening him. For some time, we exchanged letters. Then it stopped. I do not know if he is still alive.

When I mentioned this encounter to my mother, she kept quiet for a while and then said, 'The Mahatma asked us not to bear grudges, but that does not mean you have to make friends with Frank Bell. He did his best to starve us.' How could I tell her that I rather liked the man? Besides, he honestly believed that we were trying to overthrow a legitimate and noble regime. He was at least as much a victim of the empire as we were. Gandhi's famous reply to John Bull that the worst victims of imperialism were not the Indians, but the British, sums up for me a historical truth for reasons I have just cited—physical suffering and humiliation are less damaging than any loss of one's basic human values.

One of the most unusual personalities I got to know very well at Oxford was my famous countryman, Nirad C. Chaudhuri, who became both famous and notorious overnight with his *Autobiography of an Unknown Indian*, dedicated to the memory of the British Empire. I knew him slightly back in India. In fact, he was a resident of Delhi the greater part of the time I was working in that city, but after one encounter I had not felt very enthusiastic about getting to know him better. That was a serious mistake. His certainly was one of the most original minds I have encountered in my life. E.M. Forster once remarked about him that he was the one Indian he had met who could stand up to any Western person in his knowledge of Western civilization. He came to England in 1972 to receive the Duff Cooper Prize for his *Continent of Circe*, a study of contemporary Indian culture in a historical context, and stayed on to write a biography of Max Mueller at the request of the Mueller family. He wrote three more substantial books during his long sojourn in Oxford, being supported by the publishers and, when that source ran out, by an income support grant as also some funding from the Royal Society of Literature. He used to live in a house on Lathbury Road which belonged to the University College, the rent paid by the council. This very successful author was, unbelievably, a very poor man.

Nirad Babu, a highly talented and eccentric individual, had a bad reputation among a large section of Indians. He was accused of having sucked up to the British with a totally negative and grotesque representation of India. This perception was only a partial truth. His ill repute derived mainly from his famous/notorious dedication of his autobiography. Nirad Chaudhuri was not a person to 'suck up' to anyone and his accounts of the civilization in India were by no means consistently negative. His description of the British in India under the Raj as 'the Nazis of their time' with fairly heavy documentation to support that characterization, does not suggest that the writer was a mindless admirer of the British. The fact of the matter was that he did hate his own social class, who had disappointed him, largely because opportunities for men like him under the Raj were strictly limited (he refused to see the causal connection) and the Britain he admired so much was a country known to him only from books, an ideal world. His encounter with the real England of the twentieth century, especially its sexual mores, was less satisfactory. I imagine that, in this respect, any actual encounter with Victorian England would not have been more satisfying for him. As to his perception of India, in fact, he had a profound admiration for and a very original understanding of India's classical civilization, Mughal architecture and modern Bengali literature. He considered Tagore one of the truly great writers of all times and ten of his short stories a treasure of world literature comparable only to the very best produced in the course of the four millennia of human civilization. I often requested him to write up his ideas on ancient Indian civilization, but he was too busy being critical of contemporary Indians, rebarbarized, as he put it, to have time to write up his very creative perceptions of the country's past.

His hatred of his own social class was deep and abiding. One of his better known books in Bengali has the title *Atmaghati Bangali* (Suicidal Bengalis). Its thesis is that many Bengalis are highly talented but due to a fault in their social nature, they make no use of their talents. The thesis derives from his life experience. Many of his highly talented contemporaries did live wasted lives. This, however, was not by their choice. For many of his generation, the choice was between unemployment and a clerical job. Nirad Babu himself began his life as a clerk. It is not easy to nurse one's creativity when suffering from penury and daily humiliation, powerfully described in some of Tagore's most well-known poems. Nirad Babu had great plans for a twenty-volume history of India which he was certainly capable of producing. But all these plans came to nothing. In his fifties he produced his famous autobiography as a desperate antidote to his frustrations. This was not suicidal behaviour but a very common fate of highly talented individuals who had no choice but to let their talent wither. Once I had called on him soon after his wife's death. He was weeping bitterly and read out a passage from one of his Bengali works describing the miserable poverty of his early life which diminished their married happiness. He suddenly closed the book and said, 'I shall never forgive the Bengalis for this, never.' To him the cause of his misfortune was not foreign rule, indifferent to the fate of the subject population and a near-total absence of opportunities for vast numbers of gifted persons, but his countrymen who did bicker pathetically over the few crumbs from their master's table which was their share. I could never convince him otherwise. He was not a man to listen to anyone.

His one embarrassing weakness was a proneness to show off. It arose, to my understanding, from a sense of uncertainty regarding his family's social standing especially in the rural society of his childhood. The snobbery regarding caste status in Bengali society was further vitiated in the colonial era by a new snobbery about economic/professional status. Nirad Babu's family appears to have been a victim of this twofold snobbery and they fought back in odd ways. His village home had chandeliers hanging from its asbestos roof. The claim that they came from an old landed family, equivalent of at least the British squirearchy, if not something higher, was also part of the same response. I have explained my reasons for this conclusion in my Bengali autobiography and there would be no point in repeating them here. It would require a substantial essay on Bengali social hierarchy to explain my meaning to an audience unfamiliar with the relevant details. One expression of this defensive posture was the family's claim to a lifestyle superior to that of average Bengalis. My wife had nurtured a plant, red Pui, a favourite vegetable of all

Bengalis. Once she cooked it and I asked Mrs Chaudhuri if I could bring some of the dish for her. She was of course enthusiastic, but Mr Chaudhuri imposed a fatwa: such food, fit only for the hoi polloi, was not to enter his august home. He invented ever new criteria to underline his social superiority. Whisky is a favourite drink of the urban Bengali. It was hence proscribed in his house where only fine champagne, claret, Burgundy and cognac (VSOP) were admissible. Hugh Toye was very keen to meet him. I agreed to introduce him adding that I would not be responsible for the consequences. Well, the evening came and went and Nirad Babu expectedly dropped a wide variety of bricks. Next morning, I called Hugh to find out his reaction. 'Well, the evening went well,' Hugh said, 'but I preferred him as the Unknown Indian.'

At times his one-upmanship landed him in highly embarrassing situations. The Royal Society of Literature, that was considering a grant for him, sent two representatives to assess his requirements. Nirad Babu invited them to lunch and brought out his very expensive china and silver for the occasion. The champagne, which had been resting in his cellar for some twenty years, had a fabulous price tag by that time. One of the guests, a hereditary Lord, expressed his appreciation of the wine. 'I do not drink anything cheaper,' Nirad Babu commented. 'I could not afford that,' was His Lordship's response. Nirad Babu was embarrassed and said that he rarely drank and brought out his good wines only for his very special guests. On another occasion Jackie Onassis, who was working on a book on India invited him to the Ritz. He told her that when in the US, he called only on people whose names were in the social register. She used to do the same, Mrs Onassis responded, but could no longer afford it. Nirad Babu evidently was under no comparable constraint.

Nirad Chaudhuri honestly believed that he was an Englishman in dhoti. But the dhoti he never failed to wear at home under his trouser was the true indicator of his identity. Highly emotional, mercurial and extremely gregarious, a man who was ready to expound his esoteric ideas to his cleaning ladies if they had the time to listen and totally devoid of snobbery when it came to actual contact with

Back at Oxford

other human beings, Nirad Babu was probably the most Bengali person of my acquaintance. He was gratified when his image in India, especially Bengal, changed for the better. He declared that he had always wished to be accepted in Bengal. Not true—he did everything in his power to be disliked by Bengalis. Nor was he in any sense an 'unknown Indian'. When he published his autobiography, he was already very well known in Bengal as a scholar, a very learned journalist and a literary critic. He edited one of the best-known Bengali journals. That fame meant nothing to him, as the title of his autobiography indicates. What really mattered was acceptance and recognition in the West.

He was famous for his fantastic memory, especially in India where great value is attached to this faculty. After all, the four Vedas were handed down by word of mouth, probably for some two thousand years or more. Once I called on him after a holiday in Egypt. He asked me very detailed questions about the topography of the Valley of Kings. It seemed as if he had visited the place recently. Ancient Egypt was a part of the syllabus for the MA degree in history at Calcutta University and Nirad Babu had studied it with interest some sixty years ago. There was no book on Egypt in his collection at Oxford. But what he had read then had stuck to his memory. We had studied Breasted's standard history of ancient Egypt; he read the reports of the country's Archaeological Survey. Extensive reading and great memory are objects of aspiration to the Bengali literati. The Sadler Commission, appointed to enquire into the affairs of the Calcutta University, had noted this propensity. I have met people whose extensive knowledge was comparable to Nirad Babu's. There were several persons in the older generation who had the reputation of knowing all of Shakespeare by heart. One of my teachers in Calcutta University had memorized the entire Mahabharata.

But Nirad Babu's memory was no athletic feat. It arose from his varied and profound interest in life. His memory was rooted in his vibrant joy in the varied spectacle of his sensory and intellectual experience. There was something childlike about his intellectual curiosity.

His neighbour once told me how he first met him. One morning at 9 a.m. he responded to the doorbell and saw Nirad Babu standing at his door in his usual three piece suit, bow tie and bowler hat. He explained the purpose of his visit. He could see from his bedroom his neighbour's back garden and was attracted by a rare flower he had read about. He knew that the colour of its petals on their top side was different from that on the bottom side. He had come to see the bottom side of the said petals, not visible from his window. When he read a Bengali novel, he tried to trace the route of the protagonists' journeys. He asked me to bring from Berlin a picture of the famous unfinished bust of Nefertiti. He was pleased like a child to receive it and immediately set about improving the coloured photo. Next time I went, the picture had become three dimensional. He asked me to feel its three dimensionality. How exactly was I to do that? It was a bust endowed with a lovely bosom. Though the lady was more than three thousand years old, it would not be right to outrage her modesty.

I have written at some length about Nirad Chaudhuri because he was a very remarkable man and in some ways a central figure in modern Indian culture. As one critic remarked, his autobiography is the sort of book people will read two hundred years from now. I believe I was privileged to know him better than anyone else and could also see him clearly in the context of our history. I felt it was my duty to record my impressions for all it was worth. I owe him much. What I have written is a small tribute, but it would be a false one if it became only a panegyric.

Joys of Teaching and Occasional Sorrows

What I enjoyed most at Oxford were my teaching duties. One of the things I found particularly appealing was the opportunity the system provided for communication with one's students. This was not entirely in tune with the culture of zealously guarding one's privacy, but here if you wished to profit by getting to know your students you could. There was a certain pattern to the interest in Indian (sorry, South Asian) history among the students. The majority of my undergraduates were British and nearly all the graduate students were from South Asia—Indians, Pakistanis, Bangladeshis and Sri Lankans—only two or three from the UK, and a few from the USA. Incidentally, my British graduate students were among the best, but being less aggressive/ambitious than their South Asian counterparts, have not made a mark in quite the same way. One reason why the British students did not opt for research on India in larger numbers was the paucity of employment opportunities. One of them, probably the brightest of the lot, used his inherited property to fund his three years of research. But in his second year he got a very lucrative offer from a well-known company. His starting salary would be four times the amount of what I was earning. Reluctant to see his efforts wasted, he got his status as a research student downgraded and submitted his thesis for a BLitt degree and of course got it. He asked me for a 'character certificate' adding a curious request: 'Please do not mention that I have got a research degree.' Evidently, in the eyes of the private sector, spending a couple of years at Oxford, getting smart without anything to show for it was perfectly okay. But a research degree was unacceptable. It was proof of a scholarly temperament, something totally unsuitable for the ups and downs of the world of commerce and industry. I remembered that in pre-modern India, ambitious parents discouraged their sons from studying Sanskrit, because serious scholarship was the high road to poverty. Don't we know?

Many of my graduate students have achieved great success in life. Several of them are now famous professors in Indian universities, some in the USA. Two of them are among the leading lights of the subalern studies collective. Gyanendra Pandey's essays on the construction of communalism deftly probes the unreliability of 'eyewitness accounts' and government record, using techniques suggested by Foucault and Derrida, and developed in the Indian context by Ranajit Guha. Shahid Amin's brilliant study of the events at Chauri Chaura illuminates how the peasant masses interpreted the message of Gandhi. Mahesh Rangarajan, now a professor at Delhi (recently appointed director, Nehru Museum), has made significant contribution to ecological history. Very recently, Nandini Panda has published her monograph on Hindu law which proves quite decisively that the said law had very little to do with the Hindu smriti texts but simply reflected the shifting requirements of British policy in the late eighteenth century. The two monographs on Bengali Muslims by Tazeen Murshid and Rafi Ahmed have really changed our perspectives on the subject. Maureen Tayal, who sadly withdrew from academic life, wrote a penetrating study of Gandhi in South Africa. My student, Suranjan Das, is the vice chancellor of Calcutta University, Rudrangshu Mukherji one of the most influential journalists in India and Chitta Panda the curator of Victoria Memorial. I do take great pride in my students and their achievements. I like to believe that I have a small contribution to their academic development.

Every summer I had a party for my graduate students and other friends. The guests on these occasions numbered fifty to sixty. My wife who gave teaching lessons in cookery at the adult education centres had a justified reputation as a fine cook and she cooked an elaborate meal for these parties. Evidently, her reputation as a cook had reached India. Once I met a visitor from India at a friend's house. Yes, he told us, his friends had told him that he must meet my wife when he visited Oxford, because she was a great cook. No one had told him anything about me, he added politely. Perfectly understandable.

In my teaching duties perhaps what gave the greatest pleasure were the undergraduate tutorials of which I did six hours every week in term. Many of the students were teenagers and most of the time came with set ideas about the Raj. I was extremely careful not to upset them, because their beliefs were rooted not in their intellect but their emotions. If I could make them see that the same data could lead to differing conclusions, depending on the framework of reference, I felt I had done my duty as a teacher. Also, I tried to convey the idea that history is not about the perception or discovery of any given truth but about competing assessments of what an ever expanding body of evidence and ever new explanatory devices might imply.

My memory of the happy time I spent with my undergraduates discussing their essays is marred by two episodes, one of them particularly painful. Oxford colleges have been hosting summer programmes by American universities for some time now. The American universities allow specified number of credits for the time thus spent by their students at Oxford. I occasionally agreed to teach individual students who had signed up for such programmes. One young girl who came to me for tutorials in Indian history looked very young indeed. I doubt if she was more than sixteen. Her first essay was very childish. An assiduous student, she had read everything I had recommended, but having no background knowledge of the subject, had failed to understand anything at all. Probably, she was also rather dim. Without criticizing her essay, I discussed in detail what a different approach to the subject might produce. After a few minutes, she burst into tears. I felt like a murderer. I tried to reassure her that hers was not a bad essay. I had only been trying to point out possible alternative approaches to the topic. But she was not to be consoled. She knew she was a fool, she said. In her home university, they were only given grades for their term papers, never any criticism of what they had written. Now she would return home with a very bad grade, wasting her parents' money. They had paid for her stay in Oxford but were not that rich, she added. I felt truly mortified.

The second episode which casts a shadow on my experience of teaching is more grim. Incidentally, it concerns the very last tutee I had and the very last tutorial in my teaching career. The undergraduate, again, was a girl and very young. She was extremely conscientious and quite clever. In the last week of my teaching, I got a phone call from her college secretary to say that she was ill but could she come someday next week? I agreed. She came and told a horrendous story. She was not ill but had been raped by a fellow student in her college. The boy, who was about twenty, had invited her to his room for a cup of coffee at night. She stayed on longer than she should have. And that led to the rape. What happened to the boy, I asked. He had been sent down for a term, too mild a punishment in my judgement. At first sight, this looks like a cynical attempt on the part of the college to avoid scandal. They should have reported the matter to the police, as the law demanded. But could I have done that, I wondered. It meant ruining the life of a promising young person. But the boy had probably ruined the life of his fellow student and certainly deserved the severest punishment. But how easy is it to be instrumental in helping justice to prevail? I am glad that I have not worked for any judicial establishment.

As a person sensitive to political developments and with egalitarian sympathies, I could not but take an interest in British politics though I stopped short of becoming a Labour Party activist, something which I had seriously considered. When Mrs Thatcher became the prime minister of the country, a long dark period began in the history of Britain. I discovered, not entirely to my surprise, that a very large section of the public shared my total loathing of her. Her artificial voice, acquired probably with the help of teachers, summed up for me the repellent nature of her personality. Her social attitudes (the infamous statement that there was nothing called society), her promotion of an ideology of everyone for him/herself and let devil take the hindmost, her fondness for Pinochet combined to produce in me a feeling of physical sickness whenever she appeared on the television screen. I would change the channel as soon as I saw her. I was pleased to discover that I was not alone in this. It was so easy to dislike her intensely. Expectedly, I found she was the darling of people whom I happened to detest. With that B-movie hero, Reagan in the USA and this woman in the UK emerging as world leaders, I thought that the West was entering an age of extreme reaction. Worse, I thought, than that of the post-Vienna settlement years in Europe. Her popularity had sunk very low when the Falklands War happened to save her. Tom Dalyell's belief that the Belgrano was sunk at her order in order to ensure that the avoidable war should take place, to revive her sinking electoral fortunes, very probably has more than a grain of truth in it.

Two very exceptional incidents brought the distant world of

Back at Oxford 347

politics straight into the life of our sheltered community at Oxford. The city of dreaming spires got really agitated on these occasions. Not very long after the Bangladesh war, at the instance of some leaders of the establishment at Oxford, it was proposed that Zulfiqar Ali Bhutto, an old Oxford man and then the prime minister of Pakistan should be honoured with an honorary degree. It was well known that he had been one of the instigators behind the massacre in Bangladesh. Richard Gombrich decided to oppose the proposal in the Congregation. The vice chancellor, Sir John Habakkuk, tried to dissuade him but he would not budge. When the proposal was voted on, it was rejected by a paper-thin majority. There was some doubt about that result. The Pakistan embassy tried to dissuade the authorities from proceeding any further. But the more arrogant members of the establishment were very confident of their power and decided to hold a second meeting of the Congregation. This time the proposal was overwhelmingly defeated. The matter did not end there. One pillar of the establishment published his account of the episode in *The Listener* with very snide remarks about Professor Gombrich. He also gave an interview to a tabloid alleging that Richard's hostility to Bhutto had much to do with his own Jewish roots. I thought that this was beneath contempt. The fact that people had tried to dissuade the author of that essay and his friends from pushing the matter further after Bhutto appointed Tikka Khan, the butcher of Dhaka, commander-in-chief of the Pakistan army was not mentioned in this article.

The person who was most humiliated by this event was the vice chancellor. That all members of the establishment do not have similar personalities was proved by his subsequent conduct. As I have mentioned before, I knew Sir John Habakkuk from the days of his visit to Delhi. When the Spalding chair in Eastern religion and ethics fell vacant and I was nominated by the Oriental studies faculty to represent them on the electoral board, the vice chancellor asked me to come and see him. He told me confidentially that he knew that Gombrich would be a leading contestant for the post. But given his role in the decision to deny the honorary degree to Bhutto, some very powerful people were likely to oppose his election, on the ground that he was not a 'dependable person'. Sir John did not wish him to suffer unjustly. That is why he had called me to have an objective assessment of Gombrich's suitability for the post. I told him what I honestly believed—of Richard's great contribution to the study of religious belief and practice from an anthropological point of view. But at the meeting of the electoral board, it became clear that the majority was clearly determined not to elect him. One of them suggested the name of Professor Matilal, who was not a candidate for the post. He was the world authority on the sceptical tradition in Indian philosophy and also a very advanced student of mathematical philosophy. No doubt, it was a very worthy choice. But what I appreciated most in this whole business was the vice chancellor's anxiety to protect the interests of a man who had been the cause of his humiliation.

Some people never learn. It has long been customary for Oxford to confer an LLD degree, honoris causa, on any alumnus who becomes the prime minister of Britain. Why Mrs Thatcher's supporters and admirers in the university had not taken steps to do so in the early stages of her prime ministership is not clear. In the sixth year of her prime ministership, when her unpopularity was at its height, the proposal was suddenly mooted by the council. It is rumoured that Mrs Thatcher herself had demanded it and refused to listen when told that the time might be inappropriate for the move. Well, the negative response to the proposal was immediate and immense. On the day the vote was taken, the Sheldonian was filled to capacity. The serious scientists who spend most hours of the day in their laboratories and are rarely seen in public came to vote against the proposal in their white aprons, straight from their work. One of them explained to me that her policies had pushed British science backwards by some twenty years and it would never be able to catch up with world science again. This is the occasion when I heard the famous lament about the loss of 'our glo-o-orious empire'. Well, the proposal was defeated by an overwhelming majority, perhaps further diminishing imperial glory.

I have just referred to the election of Professor Matilal to the Spalding chair. His Oxford experience throws light on a deplorable side of life in this university, the fact that some members of this august institution lack elementary civility. Matilal was a formidable philosopher deeply admired by Oxford philosophers like Dummet and Strawson. But his life at All Souls was not a happy one. He was socially a very diffident person, partly because he had a sense of insecurity about his accent and spoken English generally. These were no worse than that of several non-English colleagues of my acquaintance, but what mattered was that Matilal was bothered by it. In Canada, where he had taught for many years, it had not mattered and he had achieved international fame despite any limitation, real or imagined. But at All Souls the supposed limitations did matter or so it seemed to him. He told me that nobody in that institution talked to him. This, of course, was not literally true. He had some very good friends in the college. He invited me several times to lunch or dinner at his college and I found that his complaint had some basis in truth. Possibly, one reason for this was his habit of letting his sentences trail away into near-silence, at times rendering them incomprehensible. To make matters worse, a prize fellow, one of the world's leading creeps, used to walk up to him at the college governing body meetings and tell him that these meetings were not for visiting fellows, pretending that he did not know who Matilal was.

I have still not got over my surprise that this creep was a member of a civilized community, not to mention an Oxford faculty member. Later, on two occasions he accosted two Indian students (one of them is now a fellow of an Oxford college) at the dinner for short-listed candidates for the prize fellowships and exclaimed, 'We have not done badly by you, have we?' Let me elucidate the meaning of this pregnant comment, in case you have not got it. The 'we' refers to the British people, of which, unfortunately for them, this being is a component. 'You' refers to Indians. His remark refers to the progress in civilization achieved by Indians, allegedly under British tutelage (until that happy development our ancestors were jumping from branch to branch), which enabled two of them to get as far as being shortlisted for the prize fellowships at All Souls, that is, only one step short of the gates of heaven. One often hears of the clash of civilizations these days and I feel very sorry for a civilization represented by George Bush and his like or, for that matter, by creatures like this one. It reminds me of one of Gandhi's famous comments on Western civilization—that it would be a good idea.

Sadly, the racism underlying his incredible boorishness was not his exclusive monopoly at Oxford. A school friend of my daughter once remarked that the blacks in South Africa should be grateful to the whites, presumably for the system of apartheid. The child must have acquired this gem of wisdom at home. She was the daughter of a famous academic with South African connections. The child who had asked my daughter about her Pakistani father's means of livelihood was also the daughter of a great savant. Once at a college dinner, I was sitting close enough to a famous chemist to overhear what he was saying. In all probability, the comment was meant for my benefit. The great man was expounding on the innate sycophancy of Indians, who never failed to smile ingratiatingly when they talked to him. That smiling comes more naturally in some cultures than in others did not occur to this learned man. In Oxford, I learnt one very important lesson—that true learning and a powerful intellect can coexist in an individual with obscene values like racism and a total bluntness of sensibilities. Nirad Chaudhuri quoted at length from an Oxford don's Indian diary who found that the Bengalis had the thin legs one associates with slaves. Really? I thought slaves developed very strong legs to cope with their horrendous tasks. This was written in the 1930s and the observer was a student of English literature. Evidently, this fellow of Pembroke had deep anthropomorphic interest. In recent years, when hatred of Muslims is spreading like a contagion among educated Hindus and I find it difficult to talk to people I have known for years, the lesson I learnt at Oxford helps me to tolerate this misfortune. Only, in the case of the UK what I encountered is a minority phenomenon and is the legacy of past distortions in social culture. In India, to the best of my understanding, the evil in our midst is a new disease and we are in serious danger of being overpowered by it. I hope I am mistaken, but we seem to be going the way the German people went under the Nazis. Some leaders of the neo-Hinduism are conscious imitators of the Nazi dogma and practice.

In case I have given the impression that the behaviour described above is typical of Oxford, let me mention an incident which, to me, is fortunately much more representative of social mores at this place. Once, at high-table dinner in our college I was amused to meet one of the new breed of Thatcherite MPs who had probably missed out on a proper upbringing in their childhood. He asked me about my area of specialization and, when I mentioned Indian social and economic history, launched into a fairly lengthy discourse meant to illuminate me on the economy of India under the Raj. It gave me much pleasure to discover that Mrs Thatcher's party had the kindness not to exclude the genuinely ignorant and stupid: for me it modified their reputation for ruthlessness. This particular MP could not have been more gormless or less literate if he tried. In all fairness, his intentions were very worthy. He was really trying hard to educate (civilize if you like) me. Some of my colleagues were listening to this harangue, petrified. When the young man moved away, they came and apologized to me profusely. Incidentally, those who apologized were supporters of the said MP's party. I mention this episode to underline the fact that Oxford is a very civilized place, but the university, being a human institution, inevitably has among its members and guests, its quota of fools and barbarians. The latter do not constitute the majority. May be there is a God after all; though creations like Bush and Thatcher enhance one's doubts.

Matilal became a good friend, though I could not keep pace with his concern for extreme abstraction, the characteristic feature of India's sceptical philosophy, less known in the West than her mystical tradition. This very gentle and highly civilized person met an untimely death. He was suffering from severe aches and pains for some time and once he asked me to accompany him to the hospital for some tests. His wife was away from Oxford at the time. When the tests were over, I was summoned by the doctors to join the patient and be told the result. There was a certain ruthlessness about their pronouncement. They first asked if he was adequately insured. On being told that he was, they informed us that Matilal had developed cancer of the bone marrows and was likely to live another three to eight years, most likely the former. He remained calm. We came back to his home. He lived exactly another three years, the last of them in very great pain. He used to say repeatedly that he had no wish to die then but accepted the fact that he would have to. Once he read out for me the account of Duryodhana's death from the Mahabharata. Duryodhana was the evil prince, but in his own judgement he had not strayed from the Kshatriya code of honour and died a hero's death through a violation by his enemies of that code on righteous war. Matilal smiled and explained that he too had done no wrong and yet had to suffer the injustice of a very painful death. There the simile stopped. Two days before he died, he dictated his last essay for an Indian magazine.

Since I have mentioned two very outstanding fellow Bengalis at Oxford in my time, I think I should also mention a third one, probably the most famous Indian of my generation, Amartya Sen. He had left Delhi to take up a chair at the London School of Economics. He moved from London to Oxford when he accepted the chair in economic development. I heard from one of the electors that the meeting of the board which elected him was perhaps the shortest in the history of the university. When the chairman asked for nominations, the first elector said 'Sen'. The rest agreed. The meeting was over in a few minutes. Later, when he was elected to the Adam Smith chair with which went a fellowship at All Souls, he was a member of the electoral board. The other members turned to him and requested him to accept the chair. That was the end of the matter. He went on to reach new heights as University Professor at Harvard, Master of Trinity at Cambridge and finally a Nobel laureate in Economics and Bharat Ratna, Jewel of India, the highest honour conferred on civilians by the Indian state. He has turned his attention in recent years to the cultural traditions of India. His interpretations of the

Back at Oxford

'Hindu' tradition combat the narrow and highly misleading views of the RSS/VHP (Vishwa Hindu Parishad) extremists who dominated Indian politics for some years and may do so again in the foreseeable future. Incidentally, Amartya, the grandson of one of the country's greatest Sanskrit scholars, was taught the language in his childhood and can speak it fluently.

My Research

I owe to Oxford one major benefit. Whatever limited creativity I had was nearly stifled in Delhi. I got it back in Oxford. The ink in my pen had dried up. Now it came back, as it were, in a very satisfying way. I am a minor academic with no earth-shaking achievements to my credit. But here I shall record my research output at Oxford because, after all, this book is about me and though obscure, I am, after all, a don, and research is supposed to be a central activity in a don's life. The readers, assuming that there will be some, may skip the next few paragraphs which deal with my academic work at Oxford over the years. Here I first got down to writing my chapters for the *Cambridge Economic History of India* and in a few years completed the work of editing the first volume in collaboration with Irfan Habib. The job was a shade more complicated than it sounds. We had some thirty contributors from many different parts of the world, including Japan and the Soviet Union. The standard of written English in the said two countries left something to be desired. And it is easier to write something oneself than to edit someone else's writing. It was, in fact, an uphill task. Then, one of my very learned contributors was my friend Simon Digby, who died very recently. He was to write the chapter on India under the sultanate. This great scholar was inclined to fight shy of producing written work. I hoped to circumvent that problem through a very special arrangement which he accepted: we would meet for lunch every day and he would bring a page of his chapter. This way the lunches became profoundly enjoyable (there is no other way I could hope to meet this wonderful man every day) and there was some hope that the chapter would be written. Half way through this process, he stopped coming for the lunches and I got a letter from him to say that he was going to Pakistan for an indefinite period, but he was leaving his notes in a steel trunk which I was welcome to use in any way (I mean the notes, not the trunk) I liked. Well, there were enough notes in the trunk to produce several volumes. I took from these what seemed most relevant and decided to complete the chapter with Irfan Habib's help.

Irfan, incidentally, was not the easiest of collaborators. He had a built-in psychological resistance to answering letters. I pointed out repeatedly that there is no injunction in either the Koran (the source of his ostensible faith) or *Das Kapital* (the source of his true belief) against answering letters. But to no effect. I wrote to his wife, Saira and got some action, but not nearly enough. In desperation, I went to Aligarh with Simon's notes and all, determined to settle in Irfan's house until the work was finished. The social mores at Aligarh reminded one of the Mughal court. It was all low bows and elaborate apologies. I had a distinct feeling, whenever I went there, that I was back in the eighteenth century with all its airs and graces. However, this time my strategy worked. What I believe really produced results was the prospect of having me as a permanent guest in the Habib home. There are well-defined limits to human endurance. Irfan was truly activated and did a brilliant job of editing the chapters which were within his area of expertise, that is, 90 per cent of the volume. The end product was very expensive by Indian standards. Not many institutions and hardly any academic in India can afford the prices charged for the publications of the Cambridge University Press (CUP). The CUP brought out an Indian edition in collaboration with an Indian publisher to be sold at a fraction of the book's sterling price. It sold out in a week. The book is recommended reading wherever medieval Indian history is taught and hence it continues to sell. The profits, alas, go to the CUP, but we are pleased to have contributed to the cause of learning. Apparently, our forced renunciation makes it possible for the Cambridge University Press to produce books like

Back at Oxford

the *Hittite Dictionary* which unfortunately is not a best-seller. So be it. Only, the task took several years of my life.

Here it may be relevant to mention my work for a volume which was for the publishers a potboiler. Only, if I had depended on work like this I would have to live on raw food because my pot could not have boiled on that quantity of fuel. *The Times* brought out *An Illustrated Atlas of World History*. It had hundred plates and the editor, Professor Barraclough, invited me to contribute the maps and notes on India for a very modest sum. We later learned that the book had sold a million copies and been translated into every major European language, as well as several Asian ones. When the publishers brought out a new edition, they invited us to revise our contributions—for fifty pounds per plate. I did not answer that letter. So far as I know, none of the other contributors did either. For those whose hearts bleed for 'the creators of wealth' this incident may have something to say. Of course, in this instance the publishers created the wealth and were hence entitled to consume it. We, the contributors, only produced the matter they printed and should be happy with one meal a day.

Looking for New Pastures

During the years I was working on the *Cambridge Economic History*, my interest shifted from economic history to a very different area of the human experience, the mental world of the Indian intelligentsia, the Bengali bhadralok in particular. In 1972, shortly before I was considered for the Oxford post, I went to a conference on the history of Bengal at the East-West Centre in Hawaii, where I presented a preliminary paper on Bengali family life and ethical values over a three-hundred-year period. This was included in the conference papers published as a self-contained volume. The project took shape in my head as a study of the mental world of the Bengali bhadralok in the nineteenth century and when I finished my work on the *Cambridge Economic History*, I took it up in all seriousness. That was more than thirty-five years ago. I do not know if I shall live long enough to complete it. But I have not abandoned all hope yet.

Meanwhile three very different books have come out of this project as chips from my workshop—a study of Bengali perceptions of the West in the nineteenth century, a collection of essays on various aspects of the Bengali sociocultural experience in the same period and the translation from Bengali of an unpublished autobiography of a child widow, jointly edited by Professor Geraldine Forbes and myself. And two years ago my memoirs were serialized in the Bengali literary magazine *Desh* and then published as a volume named *Bangal-nama* (that is, the memoirs of a yokel from East Bengal). It also subsumes the socio-political history of the period covered. I am tickled pink by the fact that the book has been at the top of the best-seller list in the two Bengals over a period of nearly two years. Talking of identities, one central concern of this volume, the self which has persisted through my shifting experiences and the habitation of many different social worlds, is structured round my identity as a yokel from East Bengal. I share the joy of life which allows people of that description to survive against near-impossible odds, their obstinacy in the face of multiple threats and their gawkiness which they carry without embarrassment. Nothing embarrasses a yokel from East Bengal and they get foul-mouthed when enraged as must be evident from some passages in the present volume. Maybe, that is what gave me the reputation of being a person who 'attacks people'. I have tried to feel ashamed of the last-mentioned propensity and failed.

More Personally

I have written very little about my personal life in this book, partly because what I would have the courage to write is not worth writing about. I am ashamed of many things I have done. An intimate autobiography minus those bits would be an experiment with lies and half-truths of very little value. A narrative, warts and all, might be of interest to psychologists and perhaps to the connoisseurs of

Back at Oxford

pornography, but it takes great courage to make money that way. Sadly, I lack that courage. But I have reached a point in my story where a few details of my personal life seem relevant.

I came to Oxford in January 1973. It was my fond wish to bring my parents to Oxford for a visit. I found that my father had sent my mother to a tutor to learn English in anticipation of this journey. She was very shy about this and kept it a secret. When she eventually did visit Oxford some years later, she had acquired a certain fluency in the language. Ours was supposed to be a reformed and forward-looking family, but my father had married my mother at his father's behest when she was a girl of ten. I still wonder how my grandfather, a very forward-looking person in every other way, could violate the law of the land in this manner. The age of consent had been set at twelve by an act of the Central legislature of which he was a member. My father was a strikingly handsome man and my parents' was a very happy and successful marriage. Yet one of my mother's great regrets in life was that she had missed out on school and college education, even though she had read a vast amount in the Bengali language. If in her late sixties she could pick up a foreign language in a few months, she surely had the ability to absorb formal education. She had been denied this for no good reason. Probably my grandfather could not accept the idea of sending a bride of his family to school with the children of 'common people'. But this was no excuse. My mother was quite bitter on this point. I believe that the Indian feminists actually understate, not overstate, the case against Indian patriarchy.

My father in his youth had made plans for going to the UK to qualify as a barrister. A passage had been booked on a P. & O. boat. Then the local civil surgeon, an Englishman, advised him that his father would have a heart attack and die if he left for England. Well, the plans were abandoned. My grandfather did die of a heart attack anyway soon afterwards. But my father's plans were abandoned for good. He could not face leaving his child bride without anyone to look after her for three years. We remember from our childhood the steel trunks with his name on them meant for his cabin luggage. In his mid-seventies, he was very excited at the prospect of his childhood dream coming true. But this was not to be. England remained for him a land unvisited. In the last year of his life, he developed cancer of the lungs and died very painfully. Our specialist advised that there would be no point in taking him to the UK. We would have to carry him from the plane in a stretcher and he would remain bedridden the rest of his stay. Instead of bringing my parents to England, I had to make a journey to Calcutta to be at his bedside when he was dying very painfully. He looked at me and said that he had wasted his life. I reminded him that he had spent it serving his country. Yes, he said, but what came of it? The Partition and misery for millions? I then talked about Gandhi. Yes, of course, he said, how could he forget that? His face brightened up. Once in a millennium such men came to the earth 'to destroy unrighteousness and save the virtuous' he said, quoting the Gita. He had followed one such man. That was a rare privilege. No, he was of the blessed. His life had not been wasted. That was the last conversation I had with him. I remember feeling an animal pain for which there was no antidote. We had drifted apart over the years but I had loved this man very dearly all my life.

The 1980s were a decade of tragedies for me. In 1986, my very good friend and brother-in-law, Sailen Sen, died. He was a very senior officer in the Department of Income Tax and was about to retire. A frustrated academic, he had given up plans to study at Oxford, hurt by some remark of his father. He went and sat for the exams for the civil service and was offered a job in the income tax department. He hated the job even though, being a conscientious worker and totally honest, he flourished in it and went very high. Honesty is a dangerous indulgence in that department and it nearly cost him his life. Some assessors working under him were actually killed. It was customary for most senior officers in the department to accept employment in the private sector on retirement. Sailen had decided not to do this but engage instead in research. He had collected a vast number of books with this project in view. Astrologers in India are in the habit of calling on highly placed officers uninvited, hoping to gain in unspecified ways from such access. A friend of Sailen brought one of them to his office one afternoon. He read Sailen's palm and said, very firmly, that he would work till the last day of his life. 'No chance,' Sailen said. He retired on 31 December 1985. Next day, he was on his way to clear his table and called on a friend midway. The friend's office was on the sixth floor. The lift was out of order and he had to climb the stairs. He asked for a glass of water and was gone before it came. His huge collection of books, several thousand in number, was presented to the National Library as had been that of his father, the historian S.N. Sen. The last time I went to the said library, these had not yet been accessioned, a comment on the work culture of the region. Incidentally, the disease is no longer confined to India. A friend went to a university library in this country to borrow my volume of essays, *Perceptions, Emotions, Sensibilities*. It was acquired five years ago, but has not been accessioned yet.

To return to the theme of death and desolation, most of my near relations and close friends of my generation are gone. At eighty-five, one expects this to happen. But the process started much earlier. In the 1980s, my very close friend, Amal Dutt, died in Dhaka while he was jogging. A member of the Indian Administrative Service, he has been described by Attenborough in his book on the making of his film on Gandhi as 'the redoubtable Mr Dutt' who helped him when there was unreasonable resistance from politicians and other bureaucrats. What Lord Attenborough does not mention is that this uprightness cost Amal dear. He could not be refused promotion to the highest level of bureaucracy, secretary to the government, but was denied access to real power. He really could not care less. His wife was very sick for the greater part of their married life. Theirs was a case of love at first sight: Aruna was the girl he met on his first day at the postgraduate class. But she went into a decline when their first child, a very beautiful little boy, died of brain cancer at the age of six. Amal looked after her with devotion for more than twenty years. He never lost his joy of life. Somehow happiness was not his lot. He married a second time when Aruna died, but this did not bring him much happiness either. He belonged to the first generation of post-independence bureaucrats who were scrupulously honest and quietly idealistic, refusing to yield to political pressure. In many parts of India now, a man like him would not survive very long as a government official.

Within my family circle death came in quick succession. My mother died in 1989. I had reached Delhi and delayed my departure to Calcutta for two days for no particular reason. The night before I was to leave for Calcutta, I received a call from my elder brother to tell me that my mother was dead. Hers had been a sad life. Her eldest son was born handicapped, thanks to a medical error and died in childhood. She had never quite overcome the heart-rending sorrow caused by that death. She was very proud of her husband and the family she had married into. She also cherished the fact that she had met all the 'greats' of Indian nationalism—the Mahatma, Nehru, the Ali brothers, Bose (who came and stayed in our house in Barisal) Azad et al. But our poverty hurt her and she regretted most the denial of formal education. And it struck me that we, her children, had neglected her in the sense that we had taken her for granted and did not look into her needs, both material and psychological, as we should have. She was not the easiest of persons but had never complained about her privations or of the loss of status she had suffered when we moved to Calcutta as penniless evacuees. She was a very proud lady and despite her great strength never got reconciled to her status as a refugee.

A year after my mother's death, my elder brother, Arun died too. I had been very close to him in my childhood and early youth, but over the years we had drifted apart. He was a highly intelligent and talented person. He could have succeeded in any of half a dozen professions. He was an excellent actor and had acted for some time in the company set up by the doyen of the Bengali stage, Sisir Bhaduri. He was an accomplished speaker and could have been a very successful lawyer. He tried his hand in starting a journal just before independence. Many of the great figures of post-independence India contributed to it, including Radhakrishnan and Nehru. He published a volume of short stories in Bengali, which was very well received. But he opted for the one profession which did not suit him—business. He lacked the required tenacity. He tried his hand at export and did very well initially, exporting asbestos. Then he invested in an asbestos mine, after a leading scientist had examined the site. The local farmers, incidentally, had advised him against buying it. They, not the scientist, proved to be right. There was no mineral a few inches below the surface. My brother failed to pay back the loans he had taken from the banks. A senior manager of the State Bank of India who had approved of the loan was demoted and my brother was blacklisted, which meant he could no longer have a bank account. In short, he was totally ruined. His marriage collapsed and he died not long afterwards. He was still in his early sixties. I have never been able to take much pleasure in such limited success as I have had in my life. The bleakness in the lives of two persons so close and dear to me, my father and brother, somehow made me feel guilty. I could never get rid of an irrational feeling that what had come my way should have gone to others who better deserved them. I have known many persons in different stages of my life who were much more talented than I was. But the race has not been with them.

My younger brother, Apu, younger to me by seventeen years, was born in 1943 shortly after my father was taken to prison. I am very fond of children and he was almost like a son to me. He grew up to be a smart and capable fellow, just the type meant for the modern corporate sector. And he did well, except that he lacked any discipline in his personal life. His heavy drinking proved to be a serious handicap in his career. He died of liver failure before he reached sixty.

Now in our family, only my sister, Sujata, and I are the survivors. Of the friends from my generation, there are only a few left. One lives in north England, a second in New York and a third in Calcutta. As I see them very rarely, life has become somewhat lonely despite the fact that I have many friends in the younger generations. These include my students. But they have their own lives of which, necessarily, we are no part. There is an element of toleration and kindness in the friendship of people much younger to oneself. I appreciate and enjoy that, but, to repeat, I am no part of their lives.

Glimpses of Moksha

I should like to record here two experiences which I have found profoundly enriching in two very different ways. Once I saw a little plaque outside a colleague's house which seemed rather funny to me at the time. It read 'Happiness is having grandchildren' or something to that effect. In March 1994, my daughter got married. The first of September 1998 is the most important day of my life. On that day, the gods of the Hindu pantheon, all 330 million of them, scattered flowers on our earth, as they usually do on such occasions. A celestial light flooded the world. The angels picked up their harps and played appropriate melodies. Leela Lakshmi Wignaraja, my granddaughter and the most beautiful girl in the entire world, was born that day. I cannot express in writing the sheer intensity of my joy in receiving her and then seeing her grow up into a lovely human being. I now understood the truth behind the words on that plaque which had seemed rather banal when I read it. I have never known deeper or greater happiness. Fatherhood is joyous, but the happiness it gives is clouded by one's other concerns, the responsibility of rearing a child, one's material aspirations, the hundred and one things that distract a man of the world from focusing on what is really worthwhile in one's life. This was undiluted happiness, the intensity of one's emotions enhanced by the affection which only a child can give. The relative calmness one feels in the knowledge that the end cannot be far off, the soothing glow of a summer evening which helps things fall into their appropriate places in our scheme of things, allows one to enjoy to the full the wonderful gifts of life. Leela now lives several thousand miles away from us. I see her twice a year. And as she puts it, she is only a phone call away. She has, at thirteen, decided that she wants to be a defence lawyer, inspired by characters like Ironside in their heroic roles on the big and small screens. But she has been advised recently that there is little money in that line of practice. Being a realist, she is aware that both candies and electronic toys cost money and hence may consider corporate law instead.

If the advent of Leela Lakshmi was a supreme gift of life, the other illuminating experience has more to do with death. My cardiac consultant had advised me that my aortic stenosis was catching up with me and that 'something would have to be done'.

'Something' meant an open heart surgery and the replacement of the affected valve with animal tissue or a metallic valve. Chance of survival? Ninety per cent, said the doctor. In other words, there was a ten per cent risk. I did not feel wildly enthusiastic about such an operation, preferring to die in my own bed rather than on the operation table. But eventually, I agreed because everybody else was very keen that I should. Well, if the heart happens to belong to someone else, perhaps such keenness comes relatively easily.

I went into the operation theatre half expecting to die. When next morning my wife, sitting by my hospital bed, informed me that it was all over and I had come out of the operation alive, though not exactly kicking, I first thought that I was dreaming. And then I felt the soft smooth touch of the bedclothes on my skin and could see through my window at the John Radcliffe Hospital, the fields of rape seed flowers on Shotover Hill bursting with colour in bright sunshine. I felt a gust of deep physical pleasure spreading through my body, a sense of bliss at being alive. This, I thought, was moksha, the much vaunted liberation from sorrow and the negativities of life. All one needs is to be alive and let the intense physical happiness at being so suffuse one's mind and body. What matters that our time on earth is so short! The brevity itself sharpens the pleasure of being alive. The wisdom so lauded in our mystical philosophy was simply an unencumbered awareness of reality, the physical fact of existence. Nearness to death, I felt, had made a gift of that wisdom to me. I had been blessed.

A State Honour

The Indian state has obliged me with an honour, Padma Bhushan. I am so glad it came during the rule of a coalition headed by a former colleague. Even though it is a state honour rather than a gift from a particular government, to accept it when the Hindu extremists ruled would have been very painful. Successive governments have been a source of disappointment. One cannot rejoice at the wonders of globalization and high rates of growth when some three hundred million are in a perpetual state of semi-starvation. But in boyhood and youth, we had dreamt of this state hardly ever hoping to see that dream come true. It is at last a reality, however different that reality may be from our hopes and aspirations. It was deeply gratifying and humbling to receive an honour from that state of our youthful dreams, from the hands of a President I respected in our hall of honour in what is now our presidential palace. I could see from where I sat among the honorands, our prime minister, a former colleague and a Sikh in his resplendent turban. Next to him sat our Speaker of the Parliament, a Bengali and a communist in snow-white dhoti and kurta. Around me were the honorands in varied regional dresses, among the visitors their families (including mine, and, most important, Leela Lakshmi) in beautiful sarees and shalwar-kameez. Here was the India dreamt of by poets, thinkers and patriots. There was one absence. The very poor who could not afford to dress decently, or for that matter afford to have two square meals a day, were not there. But can one live in the not entirely unrealistic hope that they too would sit in our hall of honour before many years have gone by? Meanwhile, I cannot reject the fulfilment of our old dreams, despite all its blemishes and many perversions.